Math for Financial Literacy

Instructor's Annotated Edition

by

Todd Knowlton
Smooth Fusion, Inc.
Lubbock, TX

Paul Gray Jr.
Cosenza & Associates LLC
Houston, TX

Publisher
The Goodheart-Willcox Company, Inc.
Tinley Park, Illinois
www.g-w.com

Library of Congress Cataloging-in-Publication Data

Knowlton, Todd
 Math for financial literacy / by Todd Knowlton, Paul Gray Jr.
   p. cm.
 Includes index.
 ISBN 978-1-60525-786-0
 1. Financial literacy--Study and teaching (Secondary) 2. Finance, Personal--Mathematics. 3. Teenagers--Finance, Personal. I. Gray, Paul Douglas. II. Title.
 HG179.K5793 2013
 332.02400835--dc23
                                                    2012008678

Attributions for unreferenced images:
Cover: Shutterstock (John T Takai)
Chapter, unit, and section openers: Shutterstock (rook76)
Financial $marts: Shutterstock (Bruce Rolff)
Teamwork: Shutterstock (gorandrenkov)
Unit 1: Shutterstock (Tyler Olson)
Unit 2: Shutterstock (Monkey Business Images)
Unit 3: Shutterstock (David Kelly)
Unit 4: Shutterstock (Civdis)

Introduction

Math for Financial Literacy is written to help students form connections between mathematical concepts and real-world financial situations. It is important for students to become financially capable and understand topics such as making money, spending money, and saving money. The connections students form as they move through the text will help them become aware of the importance of math in becoming financially capable. *Math for Financial Literacy* prepares students to be competent consumers and positive contributors to the economy.

The text is presented in four units. Unit 1 focuses on how people earn money and the manner in which they are paid. Unit 2 delves into topics including banking, payment methods, and budgeting. Unit 3 explores obtaining and responsibly using credit, avoiding the pitfalls of debt, and using informed decision making when buying. Unit 4 provides insight into building and protecting wealth. The text culminates with a capstone Stages of Life Project. The project provides an opportunity for students to apply what they have learned in the text to their own day-to-day-activities. This experience will help them focus on how their needs and wants will change over the course of their lives. Throughout the text, students are asked to apply strategies and formulas to real-world problems. This will help them develop the financial literacy and analytical skills required in today's economy.

About the Authors

Todd Knowlton is the cofounder and president of Smooth Fusion, Inc., a digital marketing technology firm. Todd's career has been a journey in technology and education. He pioneered early successes in online education, worked as an educational technology consultant, and served on Microsoft's Academic Advisory Council. Since 1994, Todd has authored or coauthored over 20 books that teach computer programming. He has presented technology education workshops and seminars, including presentations for the Texas Computer Education Association and the International Society for Technology in Education. Currently, Todd serves on the Texas Tech University College of Engineering Dean's Council. He holds a bachelor's degree in computer science from Texas Tech University.

Paul Gray Jr., EdD, is the chief curriculum officer for Cosenza & Associates, a consulting firm specializing in mathematics and science. During his teaching career, Paul taught mathematics and science to junior and senior high school students in Chickasha, Oklahoma. Recently, he held the position of director of mathematics and science for Pearland ISD. Paul serves on the boards of directors for several statewide organizations, including the Texas Council of Teachers of Mathematics (TCTM), Texas Association of Supervisors of Mathematics (TASM), and Conference for the Advancement of Mathematics Teaching (CAMT). He is also the author of the textbook *Modeling with Mathematics: A Bridge to Algebra 2*. Paul received his bachelor's degree in meteorology from the University of Oklahoma and holds his master's degree and doctorate in curriculum and instruction from the University of Houston.

Reviewers

The author and publisher would like to thank the following industry and teaching professionals, who provided valuable input to the development of this text.

Immanda M. Bellm
Math Teacher
Clearwater Middle School
Waconia, Minnesota

Timothy Bufford
Marketing Teacher
Cross Creek High School
Augusta, Georgia

Tammy D. Bullock
Business and Information Technology Teacher/CTE
    Department Chair
Loudoun County High School
Leesburg, Virginia

Robert Carson
Business Teacher/Co-Op Coordinator/FBLA Advisor
Burlington Township High School
Burlington, New Jersey

Frances G. Daniels
Marketing Teacher
Florence Career Center
Florence School District One
Florence, South Carolina

Janice Findley
Career & Technical Education Department Chair
Chantilly High School
Chantilly, Virginia

Nancy Hanlon
Member Services Director
Washington DECA
Seattle, Washington

Kyle Imhof
Associate
Clintsman Financial Planning
Southlake, Texas

Holly B. Laird, MBA
Business and Finance Teacher
Leesville Road High School
Raleigh, North Carolina

Candy Nowlin
Career and Technology Teacher
Shallowater High School
Shallowater, Texas

Barba Aldis Patton
Associate Professor of Curriculum and Instruction
University of Houston–Victoria
Victoria, Texas

Debbie Plato
Teacher/CTE Department Chair
The Colony High School
The Colony, Texas

Robyn Sleight
Career & Technical Education Coordinator
Alta High School
Caynons School District
Sandy, Utah

Jodie C. Wachowski
Applied Arts & Technology Department Chair
Maine East High School
Park Ridge, Illinois

Mark Williams
Financial Literacy Teacher
Independence High School
Provo, Utah

Melissa Zeevi
Technology Teacher
Saddle Brook High School
Saddle Brook, New Jersey

Brief Contents

Table of Contents

Chapter 13
Financial Planning 422

Unit 4
Summative Assessment . . . 448

Financial Literacy Simulation: Stages of Life Project 452

Selected Answers 486

Glossary 493

Index 501

Organization

The text begins with Skills Workshops that provide a foundation for learning.

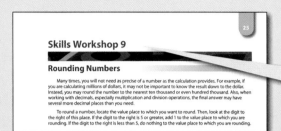

Skills Workshops provide guided practices for 15 essential math skills.

Each chapter and section opener begins with a consistent plan for success.

Chapters are divided into manageable **sections** for better comprehension of the content that is being presented.

Each chapter opens with a **Reading Prep** activity, which aligns to specific Common Core State Standards. These activities set the stage for student engagement with the content.

Real student quotes help students connect to the content on a personal level seen through the eyes of a peer.

Objectives define the goals for learning the section content and align to the main headings in the section.

A list of important business and academic **terms** creates a framework for students to build a personal finance glossary.

Money Matters opens each chapter with interesting facts about money, our economy, and other important financial literacy topics.

Build Your Math Skills provide a warm-up for math skills needed in the lesson.

Content

Content is presented in a step-by-step, systematic manner that promotes mathematical thinking.

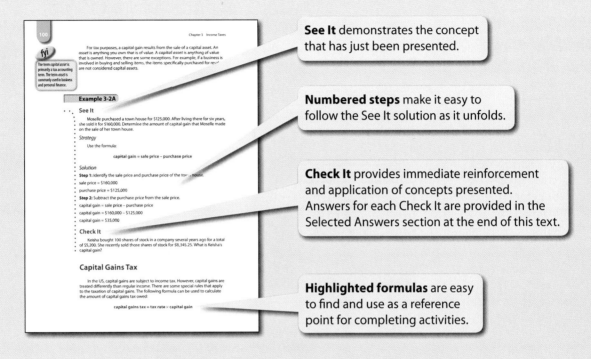

See It demonstrates the concept that has just been presented.

Numbered steps make it easy to follow the See It solution as it unfolds.

Check It provides immediate reinforcement and application of concepts presented. Answers for each Check It are provided in the Selected Answers section at the end of this text.

Highlighted formulas are easy to find and use as a reference point for completing activities.

Special features bring relevancy to math and financial literacy topics enabling students to make real-life connections.

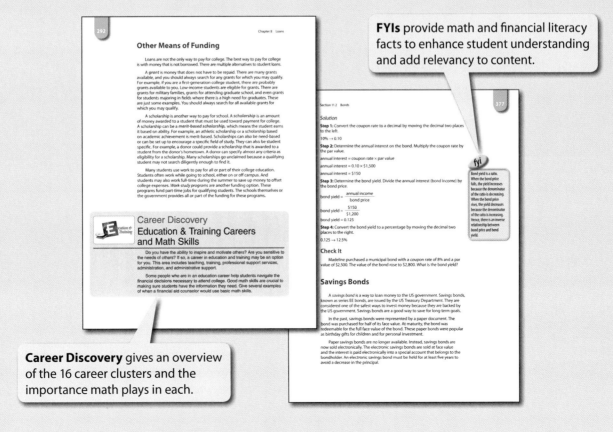

FYIs provide math and financial literacy facts to enhance student understanding and add relevancy to content.

Career Discovery gives an overview of the 16 career clusters and the importance math plays in each.

Assessment

Opportunities are provided for formative assessment within the chapter to confirm learning as the content is explored.

Through point-of-coverage assessment at the end of each section, each **Checkpoint** activity confirms understanding of content before progressing to the next topic.

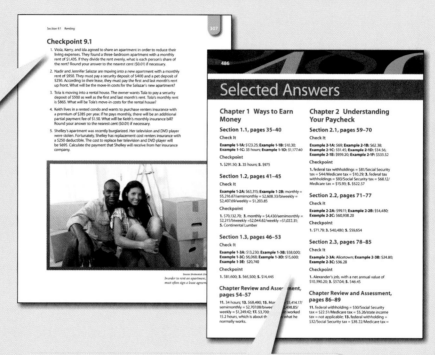

Solutions to odd-numbered Checkpoint activities appear in the Selected Answers section at the end of this text. These solutions are also located on the G-W Learning companion website at www.g-wlearning.com.

End-of-chapter activities provide additional opportunities for review and assessment of content presented in the chapter.

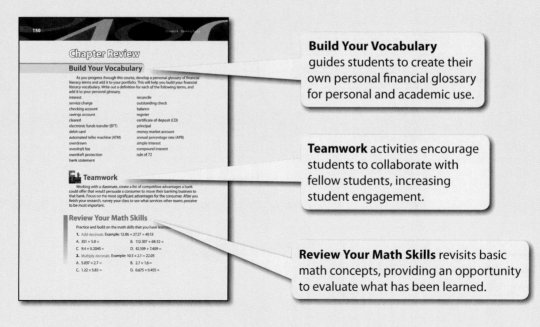

Build Your Vocabulary guides students to create their own personal financial glossary for personal and academic use.

Teamwork activities encourage students to collaborate with fellow students, increasing student engagement.

Review Your Math Skills revisits basic math concepts, providing an opportunity to evaluate what has been learned.

Assessment

Self-assessment activities are organized by sections, making it easy to refer to presentation of concepts in the chapter.

Multiple formative assessment opportunities are provided for each section in the chapter in the form of computational practice as well as word problems.

Reinforce Your Understanding enables students to demonstrate understanding of concepts learned in the chapter.

Apply Your Technology Skills offer meaningful exercises that authentically incorporate technology. Data files are provided at www.g-wlearning.com.

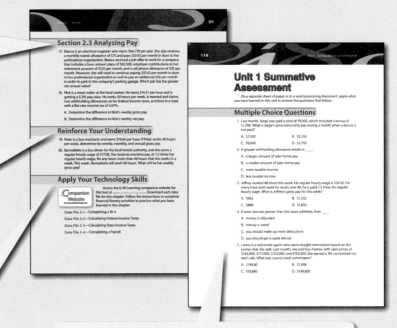

Summative Assessment enables students to self assess what they have learned at the end of each unit.

A financial literacy simulation concludes the text, guiding students through a project-based learning activity.

The **Stages of Life Project** follows the four stages of life and the impact of short- and long-term financial planning.

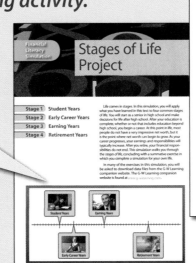

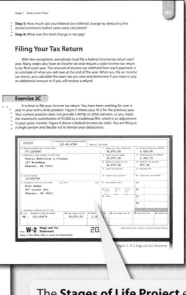

The **Stages of Life Project** encourages students to apply what they have learned to real-world decision-making.

jumpstartclearinghouse.org

This product also aligns with the National Standards in K–12 Personal Finance Education published by the Jump$tart Coalition for Personal Financial Literacy®.

Introduction to Skills Workshops

In this text, you will learn how to apply basic math concepts to the tasks you will use in the real world, including earning a paycheck, managing a bank account, using credit cards, and creating a budget. These and other practical topics will help you become financially capable and responsible. However, in order to successfully complete this text, you will need to develop proficiency with some basic mathematical skills. The skills workshops are designed to provide one way to review basic mathematical skills.

You are encouraged to use a calculator to complete the problems in this text. It is important that you learn how to *apply* formulas in this text, rather than perfecting computational skills. Select a calculator with advanced-math functions. There are many different types of calculators that can be used, from handheld or desktop calculators to software applications on a computer. The first skills workshop discusses how to use a calculator for math problems.

The skills workshops are set up using the See It, Check It method used throughout this text. The See It section shows how to complete the task being explained. The Check It section provides you the opportunity to complete the task on your own.

See It
Illustrates the task

Teaching Tip:
Best practices show that an effective use of the skills workshops would be as a teaching tool for students who, as they move through the text, require additional practice with basic mathematical skills. It is important to focus on application of formulas and financial mathematics.

Check It
You do the task

Skills Workshops Contents

1 Using a Calculator for Math Problems
2 Solving Word Problems
3 Order of Operations
4 Understanding Place Value
5 Understanding Integers
6 Adding and Subtracting Whole Numbers and Decimals
7 Adding and Subtracting Negative Numbers
8 Multiplying and Dividing Whole Numbers and Decimals
9 Rounding Numbers
10 Multiplying and Dividing Fractions
11 Adding Fractions
12 Subtracting Fractions
13 Calculating a Percentage
14 Representing Percentages as Fractions and Decimals
15 Interpreting Graphs

Skills Workshop 1

Using a Calculator for Math Problems

The purpose of this text is to teach you how to *apply* formulas as you learn financial responsibility. You will not be perfecting computational skills. Therefore, you are encouraged to use a calculator to complete the problems in this text.

Shown below is the calculator that comes standard with the Windows 7 operating system. This version is called the scientific calculator. To display this version, select the **View** pull-down menu and click **Scientific** in the menu.

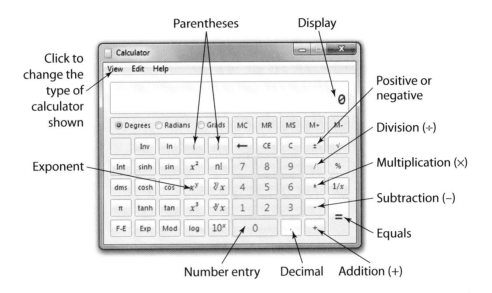

Parentheses   Display

Click to change the type of calculator shown

Exponent

Positive or negative

Division (÷)

Multiplication (×)

Subtraction (–)

Equals

Number entry   Decimal   Addition (+)

See It

You have a list of expenses for the month: $15.47, $10.50, $675, $35.51, $75.84, $112.05. Calculate your total expenses for the month.

Step 1: Using the calculator keypad, enter 15.47 and press the addition (+) key.

Step 2: Enter 10.50 and press the addition key. Continuing in this manner, enter 675, 35.51, and 75.84, pressing the addition key after each number is entered.

Step 3: Enter 112.05 and press the equal (=) key. The total is displayed: 924.37

Step 4: Write down the total and add the dollar sign: $924.37. Note: some calculators can be set to automatically display the dollar sign.

Check It

Use a calculator to perform the following operations.

1. $12 + 0.6 =$

2. $5 - 0.2 =$

3. $16 \times 4.2 =$

4. $8 \div 6.2 =$

5. $12 - 0.6 =$

6. $5 + 0.2 =$

7. $16 \div 4.2 =$

8. $8 - 6.2 =$

9. $12 \div 0.6 =$

10. $5 \times 0.2 =$

Answer:
1. 12.6
2. 4.8
3. 67.2
4. 1.29
5. 11.4
6. 5.2
7. 3.81
8. 1.8
9. 20
10. 1

Skills Workshop 2

Solving Word Problems

Word problems are exercises in which the problem is set up in text, rather than presented in mathematical notation. You must identify the elements of the math problem and solve it. There are many strategies for solving word problems. Some of the common strategies include making a list or table; working backward; guessing, checking, and revising; and substituting simpler numbers to solve the problem.

Strategy	How to Apply
List or table	Identify information in the problem and organize it into a table to identify patterns.
Work backward	When an end result is provided, work backward from that to find the requested information.
Guess, check, revise	Start with a reasonable guess at the answer, check to see if it is correct, and revise the guess as needed until the solution is found.
Substitute simpler information	Use different numbers to simplify the problem and solve it, then solve the problem using the provided numbers.

See It

Joi had minor service done on her car. The bill was $341.48 for parts and labor. She was charged for 2.5 hours of labor, and the labor rate was $121 per hour. How much were the parts? Since the end result is provided, work backward from there to find the requested information.

Step 1: Determine what is added to get the total bill.

parts + labor = $341.48

Step 2: Insert what is known.

parts + (2.5 hours × $121 per hour) = $341.48

parts + $302.50 = $341.48

Step 3: Subtract the labor charge from the total bill to find the cost of the parts.

parts = $341.48 − $302.50 = $38.98

Check It

1. Jamal bought a dozen fruit cups for $8.46. Half of the fruit cups were premium and cost twice as much as the others. How much does one premium fruit cup cost?

2. Lauren received $0.83 in change from a purchase. If she received three quarters and pennies, how many pennies did she receive?

Answer:
1. $0.94
2. eight

Skills Workshop 3

Order of Operations

The order of operations is a set of rules stating which operations in an equation are performed first. The order of operations is often stated using the acronym *PEMDAS*. PEMDAS stands for parentheses, exponents, multiplication and division, and addition and subtraction. This means anything inside parentheses is computed first. Exponents are computed next. Then, any multiplication and division operations are computed. Finally, any addition and subtraction operations are computed to find the answer to the problem. The equation is solved from left to right by applying PEMDAS.

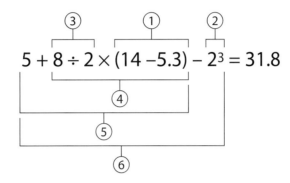

$$5 + 8 \div 2 \times (14 - 5.3) - 2^3 = 31.8$$

See It

Working from left to right, use PEMDAS to solve the equation:
$8.2 \times (10 - 7)^2 + 9 \div 3 =$

Step 1: Solve the part of the equation inside parentheses $(10 - 7 = 3)$.

Step 2: Solve the exponent $(3^2 = 9)$.

Step 3: Solve the multiplication and division $(8.2 \times 9 = 73.8; 9 \div 3 = 3)$.

Step 4: Solve the addition and subtraction outside of parentheses $(73.8 + 3 = 76.8)$.

Check It

1. $(3.2 + 1.8)^3 - 25 \div 5 =$

2. $8 - (4 \times 3) + 2^3 \div 2 =$

3. $3 + 4.5 - 27 \div 9 =$

4. $11^2 + (45 \times 2) =$

5. $(2 \times 4)^2 - (21 - 18)^2 =$

6. $9 + 2 - 3 \times 6 =$

7. $48 \div 6 + 9^2 - (3^2)^2 =$

8. $2.5 + (9 \div 3)^3 - 14 =$

9. $88 \times 2 - (9 + 1.85)^2 =$

10. $10.5 + 3.2 \div (18.97 - 19.65 + 2.68) =$

Answer:
1. 120
2. 0
3. 4.5
4. 211
5. 55
6. −7
7. 8
8. 15.5
9. 58.2775
10. 12.1

Skills Workshop 4

Understanding Place Value

Place value is a basic element of a number system. A digit's position, or place, in a number determines the value of the digit. Each place represents ten times the place to its right. This is a *base ten* system. The number shown below is seven trillion, eight hundred sixty-three billion, one hundred fifty-nine million, two hundred thirty-seven thousand, five hundred eighty-four and one thousand eight hundred seventy-five ten thousandths.

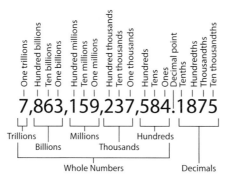

See It

Write this number using digits: ten billion, five hundred eighty-three million, two hundred nineteen thousand, four hundred and sixty-three.

Step 1: The largest value in this number is billions (10).

Step 2: The next largest value is millions (583).

Step 3: The next largest value is thousands (219).

Step 4: The smallest value is hundreds (463).

Step 5: Compose the number separating the values with commas (10,583,219,463).

Check It

Write the following numbers in words.

1. 489,815

2. 1,347

3. 25,185,492,235.05

4. 13,034,765,192,486

5. 2.9375

Write the following numbers in digits.

6. ten thousand, four hundred and fifty-eight

7. thirty-seven and one hundred eighty-five thousandths

8. fourteen billion, one hundred fifty-six million, two hundred five thousand, eight hundred eleven

9. four hundred nineteen thousandths

10. nine million, six hundred eighteen thousand, seven hundred twenty-one and ninety-eight hundredths

Answer:

1. four hundred eighty-nine thousand, eight hundred and fifteen

2. one thousand, three hundred and forty-seven

3. twenty-five billion, one hundred eighty-five million, four hundred ninety-two thousand, two hundred thirty-five and five hundredths

4. thirteen trillion, thirty-four billion, seven hundred sixty-five million, one hundred ninety-two thousand, four hundred and eighty-six.

5. two and nine thousand, three hundred seventy-five ten thousandths

6. 10,458

7. 37.185

8. 14,156,205,811

9. 0.419

10. 9,618,721.98

Skills Workshop 5

Understanding Integers

Integers are positive and negative whole numbers and zero. In other words, they are not decimals or fractions. A given integer is greater than another integer if it has a higher value. An integer has a higher value than all integers to its left on the number line. The integer 5 is greater than the integer 4 (5 > 4). An integer has a lower value than all integers to its right on the number line. The integer 4 is less than the integer 5 (4 < 5).

Integers

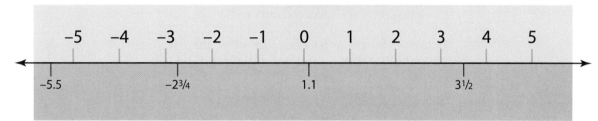

Not Integers

See It

Identify the integers in this series of numbers: $5, -2.6, 0, 3\frac{3}{4}, -9\frac{1}{8}, 10, 14\frac{2}{6}$.

Step 1: Eliminate from the list all fractions, both positive and negative ($3\frac{3}{4}$, $-9\frac{1}{8}$, $14\frac{2}{6}$).

Step 2: Eliminate from the list all decimals, both positive and negative (–2.6).

Step 3: The remaining list includes only integers (5, 0, 10).

Check It

Identify the integers in each series of numbers.

1. $128, 99.05, 105\frac{1}{3}, -115, 98, 103$

2. $\frac{3}{4}, -5, 0.4, \frac{1}{4}, 3, 0, 6$

3. $1, -35, 56.7, 0.001, \frac{15}{16}, 10, 756$

4. $45\frac{1}{4}, 978, -359, 0, 15.6, 37, 4\frac{5}{7}$

5. $8, -4\frac{2}{3}, -7, 9.01, 4, 2, \frac{7}{8}, -6.3$

6. $529, 749, -876, 697.4, 589.9, 567, 502$

7. $62.8, 76, 54\frac{1}{8}, 73.9, 58, 63\frac{6}{7}$

8. $4\frac{7}{8}, -3, 5\frac{1}{8}, -2\frac{4}{5}, 0, 5$

9. $242.2, 189, 252, 197\frac{1}{4}, 237$

10. $365, 180, 90, 30, 7$

Answer:
1. 128, –115, 98, 103
2. –5, 3, 0, 6
3. 1, –35, 10, 756
4. 978, –359, 0, 37
5. 8, –7, 4, 2
6. 529, 749, –876, 567, 502
7. 76, 58
8. –3, 0, 5
9. 189, 252, 237
10. 365, 180, 90, 30, 7

Skills Workshop 6

Adding and Subtracting Whole Numbers and Decimals

Whole numbers are numbers with no fractional or decimal portion. Decimals are numbers with digits to the right of the decimal point. To add a positive number, move to the right on the number line. To subtract a positive number, move to the left on the number line.

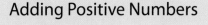

Adding Positive Numbers

```
0      5      10     15     20
├┼┼┼┼┼┼┼┼┼┼┼┼┼┼┼┼┼┼┼┼┤
```

Adding Negative Numbers

When adding or subtracting whole numbers and decimals, place each number in a vertical list, aligning the decimal points. Then, complete the operation starting with the place farthest to the right and working to the left. In an addition operation, carry the remainder to the top of the next column to the left. The result of *addition* is called the sum. In a subtraction operation, borrow from the next column to the left when needed. The result of subtraction is called the *difference*.

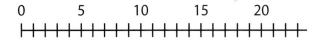

$$
\begin{array}{r}
{\scriptstyle 1\,1\,1} \\
685 \\
71.5 \\
+\,18.65 \\
\hline
775.15
\end{array}
\qquad
\begin{array}{r}
{\scriptstyle 2} \\
29 \\
56 \\
+\,17 \\
\hline
102
\end{array}
\qquad
\begin{array}{r}
{\scriptstyle 7} \\
9\!\!\not{8}\;{\scriptstyle 10} \\
23.3 \\
-\,54 \\
\hline
20.7
\end{array}
$$

See It

Find the sum of these numbers: 65.9, 88.7, and 12.

Step 1: Place the three numbers in a vertical list, aligning the decimal points.

Step 2: Add the tenths column (16) and carry the remainder (1).

Step 3: Add the ones column (16) and carry the remainder (1).

Step 4: Add the tens column (16). The sum is 166.6.

Check It

Answer:
1. 16.837
2. 13,090
3. 207.395
4. −35,391.59

1. $5.87 + 4.956 + 2.011 + 4 =$

2. $112,058 − 98,968 =$

3. $112.058 + 2.1 + 93.237 =$

4. $67,058.45 − 102,450.04 =$

Skills Workshop 7

Adding and Subtracting Negative Numbers

To add a negative number, move to the *left* on the number line. To subtract a negative number, move to the *right* on the number line.

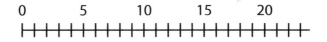

When subtracting negative numbers, the negative sign is cancelled by the operation. Subtracting a negative number is the same as adding a positive number of the same value: 2 – (–5) = 2 + 5 = 7. Identify the sign of each number, compare the sign to the operation, and determine which direction to move on the number line.

See It

Solve the equation: 10 – 5 – (–2) =

Step 1: The integers 10 and 5 are positive, but the integer 2 is negative.

Step 2: Positive 5 is subtracted from 10. Negative 2 is subtracted from the previous result, so change the operation to addition and remove the negative sign.

Step 3: Starting at 10 on the number line, move 5 places to the left to end at 5.

Step 4: Starting at 5 on the number line, move 2 places to the right to end at the answer of 7.

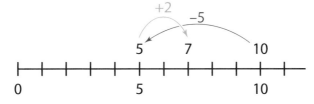

Check It

1. 5 – 7 =

2. 3 + 4 – 1 =

3. –8 + –3 =

4. 4 – (–7) + 3 =

5. 347 + 15 – 187 =

6. –38 + 19 – (–205) =

7. 1,108 – 386 + (–117) =

8. 94 – 18 + (–52) + 42 =

9. –61 + 39 + 9 – (–3) =

10. 2,039 – 761 – 78 + 15 =

Answer:
1. –2
2. 6
3. –11
4. 14
5. 175
6. 186
7. 605
8. 66
9. –10
10. 1,215

Skills Workshop 8

Multiplying and Dividing Whole Numbers and Decimals

To multiply whole numbers and decimals, place the numbers, called the *factors*, in pairs in a vertical list. Starting with the right-hand number on the bottom, find the partial products and add them. To find the number of decimal places needed in the final product, add the number of places in each number (two decimal places plus three decimal places means the product must have five decimal places).

$$437.05 \times 2.5 =$$

437.05	Two decimal places
$\times$ 2.5	One decimal place
218525	Product of 43705 times 5
874100	Product of 43705 times 20
1092625	Sum of the partial products
1,092.625	Count off three decimal places to find the final product

$$128.48 \div 5.5 =$$

23.36	Move the decimal point one place to the right in both the divisor and the dividend to make the divisor a whole number
55)1284.80	
110	Product of 2 times 55
184	Bring 4 down
165	Product of 3 times 55
198	Bring 8 down
165	Product of 3 times 55
330	Add a 0 to the dividend and bring it down
330	Product of 6 times 55
0	No remainder

To divide whole numbers and decimals, place the dividend under the division symbol and the divisor to the left of the division symbol. The answer, called the *quotient,* is placed above the division symbol. To solve the equation, work from the left of the dividend and estimate how many times the divisor goes into the first number or group of numbers. Carry the remainder down along with the next number and repeat the process. Do this until the final quotient is found. When dividing decimals, move the decimal point in the divisor until it is a whole number. Then, move the decimal point in the dividend the same number of places. The decimal point in the quotient should be above this moved decimal point.

See It

Find the product of 81.6 times 3.5.

Step 1: Place 81.6 over 3.5 in a vertical list and count the total number of decimal places (2).

Step 2: Multiply 816 by 5 ($816 \times 5 = 4,080$).

Step 3: Multiply 816 by 30 ($816 \times 30 = 24,480$).

Step 4: Add the partial products and count off two decimal places (285.60 or 285.6).

Check It

1. $1,024 \times 4.5 =$

2. $86.7 \div 3 =$

3. $4,327 \times 209 =$

4. $945.35 \div 36.5 =$

Answer:
1. 4,608
2. 28.9
3. 904,343
4. 25.9

Skills Workshop 9

Rounding Numbers

Many times, you will not need as precise of a number as the calculation provides. For example, if you are calculating millions of dollars, it may not be important to know the result down to the dollar. Instead, you may round the number to the nearest ten thousand or even hundred thousand. Also, when working with decimals, especially multiplication and division operations, the final answer may have several more decimal places than you need.

To round a number, locate the value place to which you want to round. Then, look at the digit to the right of this place. If the digit to the right is 5 or greater, add 1 to the value place to which you are rounding. If the digit to the right is less than 5, do nothing to the value place to which you are rounding.

See It

Round the number 23.987293 to four decimal places.

Step 1: Locate the fourth decimal place (23.987<u>2</u>93).

Step 2: Identify the value of the digit to the right of 2. This digit is 9, which is greater than 5 (23.9872<u>9</u>3).

Step 3: Add 1 to 2 and eliminate all digits to the right of the result (23.9873).

Check It

Round the following numbers to two decimal places.

1. 12.86905746

2. 152.19574

3. 76.559539

4. 4.129834

5. 98.9936756

6. Round to the nearest one dollar: $1,386,345.56.

7. Round to the nearest one hundred dollars: $1,386,345.56.

8. Round to the nearest one thousand dollars: $1,386,345.56.

9. Round to the nearest one hundred thousand dollars: $1,386,345.56.

10. Round to the nearest one million dollars: $1,386,345.56.

Answer:
1. 12.87
2. 152.2
3. 76.56
4. 4.13
5. 98.99
6. $1,386,346
7. $1,386,300
8. $1,386,000
9. $1,400,000
10. $1,000,000

Skills Workshop 10

Multiplying and Dividing Fractions

To multiply fractions, multiply all of the numerators. Also, multiply all of the denominators. Finally, simplify the fraction.

To divide fractions, invert the fraction that is the divisor. Then, multiply the two fractions. Finally, simplify the fraction.

See It

Find the product of these fractions: $\dfrac{2}{5}$, $\dfrac{3}{8}$, and $\dfrac{9}{10}$.

Solution

Step 1: Multiply the numerators ($2 \times 3 \times 9 = 54$).

Step 2: Multiply the denominators ($5 \times 8 \times 10 = 400$).

Step 3: Simplify the fraction ($\dfrac{54}{400} = \dfrac{27}{200}$).

Check It

1. $\dfrac{2}{3} \times \dfrac{4}{5} \times \dfrac{6}{7} =$

2. $\dfrac{41}{54} \times \dfrac{67}{100} =$

3. $\dfrac{21}{36} \times \dfrac{78}{90} \times \dfrac{1}{5} =$

4. $\dfrac{2}{7} \times \dfrac{4}{9} \times \dfrac{5}{8} =$

5. $\dfrac{14}{19} \div \dfrac{3}{8} =$

6. $\dfrac{2}{7} \div \dfrac{8}{21} =$

7. $\dfrac{41}{54} \div \dfrac{99}{100} =$

8. $\dfrac{31}{32} \div \dfrac{67}{72} =$

Answer:

1. $\dfrac{16}{35}$

2. $\dfrac{2747}{5400}$

3. $\dfrac{819}{8100}$

4. $\dfrac{5}{63}$

5. $1\dfrac{55}{57}$

6. $\dfrac{3}{4}$

7. $\dfrac{2050}{2673}$

8. $1\dfrac{65}{268}$

Skills Workshop 11

Adding Fractions

To add fractions, each fraction must have the same denominator. In some cases, this means calculating the *least common denominator*.

To find the least common denominator, list multiples of each denominator and then identify the smallest common value. Once you have the least common denominator, for each fraction determine what number is multiplied by the denominator to achieve the least common denominator and multiply the numerator by the same number.

Once all fractions have the same denominator, add the numerators. Finally, simplify the fraction.

See It

Find the sum of these fractions: $\frac{3}{8}$, $\frac{5}{16}$, and $\frac{11}{32}$. Calculate the least common denominator if needed, then add the numerators.

Step 1: Determine the least common denominator. In this case, 32 is the least common denominator because it is divisible by both 8 and 16.

Step 2: Multiply $\frac{3}{8}$ by $\frac{4}{4}$ ($\frac{3}{8} \times \frac{4}{4} = \frac{12}{32}$).

Step 3: Multiply $\frac{5}{16}$ by $\frac{2}{2}$ ($\frac{5}{16} \times \frac{2}{2} = \frac{10}{16}$).

Step 4: Add the fractions $\frac{12}{32}$, $\frac{10}{16}$, and $\frac{11}{32}$ ($\frac{12}{32} + \frac{10}{16} + \frac{11}{32} = \frac{11}{32}$) and simplify the result ($\frac{33}{32} = 1\frac{1}{32}$).

Check It

1. $\frac{4}{5} + \frac{3}{20} + \frac{1}{5} =$

2. $\frac{3}{16} + \frac{1}{2} + \frac{5}{8} =$

3. $\frac{1}{18} + \frac{2}{9} + \frac{1}{2} =$

4. $\frac{2}{3} + \frac{20}{21} + \frac{1}{7} =$

Answer:

1. $1\frac{3}{20}$

2. $1\frac{5}{16}$

3. $\frac{7}{9}$

4. $1\frac{16}{21}$

Skills Workshop 12

Subtracting Fractions

To subtract fractions, each fraction must have the same denominator. In some cases, this means calculating the *least common denominator.*

To find the least common denominator, list multiples of each denominator and then identify the smallest common value. Once you have the least common denominator, for each fraction determine what number is multiplied by the denominator to achieve the least common denominator and multiply the numerator by the same number.

Once all fractions have the same denominator, subtract the numerators. Finally, simplify the fraction.

See It

Find the difference between these fractions: $\frac{5}{18}$, $\frac{2}{9}$, and $\frac{1}{3}$. Calculate a least common denominator if needed, then subtract the numerators.

Step 1: Determine the least common denominator. In this case, 18 is the least common denominator because it is divisible by both 9 and 3.

Step 2: Multiply $\frac{2}{9}$ by $\frac{2}{2}$ ($\frac{2}{9} \times \frac{2}{2} = \frac{4}{18}$).

Step 3: Multiply $\frac{1}{3}$ by $\frac{6}{6}$ ($\frac{1}{3} \times \frac{6}{6} = \frac{6}{18}$).

Step 4: Subtract the numerators ($5 - 4 - 6 = -5$).

Step 5: Simplify the fraction $-\frac{5}{18}$. In this case, the fraction cannot be simplified.

Check It

1. $\dfrac{2}{5} - \dfrac{1}{20} - \dfrac{1}{5} =$

2. $\dfrac{5}{8} - \dfrac{3}{16} - \dfrac{1}{2} =$

3. $\dfrac{7}{9} - \dfrac{1}{18} - \dfrac{1}{3} =$

4. $\dfrac{20}{21} - \dfrac{1}{7} - \dfrac{2}{3} =$

Answer:

1. $\dfrac{3}{20}$

2. $-\dfrac{1}{16}$

3. $\dfrac{7}{18}$

4. $\dfrac{1}{7}$

Skills Workshop 13

Calculating a Percentage

You can find the percentage of a number or what percentage one number is of another number. To find the percentage of a number, change the percentage into a decimal by moving the decimal point two places to the left. Then, multiply the decimal by the number.

To find what percentage one number is of another, divide the first number by the second number. Then, convert the quotient into a percentage by moving the decimal point two places to the right.

See It

Calculate 14% of 1,248.

Step 1: Change 14% into a decimal by moving the decimal point two places to the left (14 → 0.14).

Step 2: Multiply 1,248 by 0.14 to find the answer (1,248 × 0.14 = 174.72).

Check It

1. What is 2.5% of $578?

2. What is 0.05% of 10.65?

3. What is 1.87% of 54.3?

4. What is 102.3% of 5.75?

Answer:
1. $14.45
2. 0.005325
3. 1.01541
4. 5.88225

See It

Calculate what percentage 27 is of 429.

Step 1: The divisor is 429. The dividend is 27.

Step 2: Divide 27 by 429 (27 ÷ 429 ≈ 0.63).

Step 3: Convert 0.63 to a percentage by moving the decimal point two places to the right (0.63 → 63%).

Check It

1. What percentage of 35 is 42?

2. What percentage of 117.5 is 9.8?

3. What percentage of 1,034 is 58.2?

4. What percentage of $184,352.90 is $105.98?

5. What percentage of $58.92 is $11.78?

Answer:
1. 120%
2. 8.3%
3. 5.6%
4. 0.06%
5. 20%

Skills Workshop 14

Representing Percentages as Fractions and Decimals

It is easy to convert between percentages, fractions, and decimals. A percentage is simply the numerator of a fraction with a denominator of 100. The word *percent* means *for every one hundred*, or per one cent. For example, 15% is equal to the fraction $\frac{15}{100}$, which can be simplified to $\frac{3}{20}$.

To change a percentage to a decimal, move the decimal point two places to the left. For example, 25.7% is equal to the decimal 0.257. To change a decimal to a percentage, move the decimal point two places to the right. For example, the decimal 0.072 is equal to 7.2%.

To change a fraction to a percentage, first convert it to a decimal by dividing the numerator by the denominator. Then, convert the decimal to a percentage by moving the decimal point two places to the right.

See It

Convert $\frac{42}{37}$ to a percentage.

Step 1: Convert the fraction to a decimal by dividing the numerator by the denominator ($42 \div 37 \approx 1.135$).

Step 2: Convert the decimal to a percentage by moving the decimal point two places to the right ($1.135 \to 113.5\%$).

Check It

1. Convert $\frac{5}{7}$ to a percentage.

2. Convert 2.6% to a decimal.

3. Convert 0.0385 to a percentage.

4. Convert 3% to a fraction.

5. Convert $\frac{9}{32}$ to a percentage.

6. Convert 98.72% to a decimal.

7. Convert 1.456 to a percentage.

8. Convert 45% to a fraction.

9. Convert $\frac{10}{15}$ to a percentage.

10. Convert 1.009 to a percentage.

Answer:
1. 71.4%
2. 0.026
3. 3.85%
4. $\frac{3}{100}$
5. 28.1%
6. 0.9872
7. 145.6%
8. $\frac{9}{20}$
9. 66.7%
10. 100.9%

Skills Workshop 15

Interpreting Graphs

Graphs are used to illustrate data in a picture-like format. Many times, it is easier to understand the data if they are shown in a graphical form instead of a numerical form in a table. For example, a line graph can be used to show the trend of financial markets over time. Three common types of graphs are bar graphs, line graphs, and circle graphs.

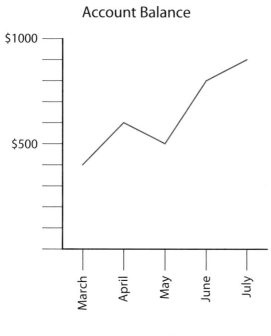

Line Graph

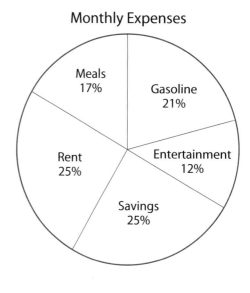

Circle Graph

See It

Using the line graph above, what was the highest account balance over the five months shown? Identify the highest point on the line graph and determine the dollar amount to which the point corresponds.

Step 1: Locate the highest point on the line graph, which occurred in July.

Step 2: From the highest point, draw a line to the vertical axis to determine the corresponding dollar amount ($900).

Check It

Use the line graph above to answer the questions.

1. In which month did the account have the lowest balance?

2. In which month was the account balance lower than the previous month?

3. What was the account balance in April?

4. In which month was the account balance $800?

Answer:
1. March
2. May
3. $600
4. June

Unit 1
Earning Money and Getting Paid

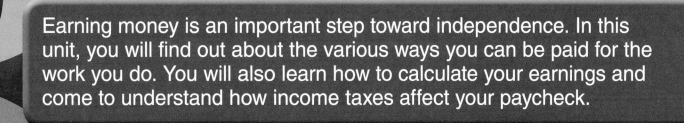

Earning money is an important step toward independence. In this unit, you will find out about the various ways you can be paid for the work you do. You will also learn how to calculate your earnings and come to understand how income taxes affect your paycheck.

1 Ways to Earn Money

Materials:
Instructor's Resource CD
Student Workbook
G-W Learning companion website
EXAMVIEW® Assessment Suite
Microsoft Excel®–compatible software
Calculator with advanced-math functions

Personal finance is all about money. By now, you have been spending money for years and, hopefully, have some experience with earning it. There may be more ways to earn money than you think. Chances are you may not have given much thought to what money is exactly. In this chapter, you will look at why money exists and some common ways to earn it.

Section 1.1	**Earning by the Hour**
Section 1.2	**Earning a Salary**
Section 1.3	**Other Ways to Earn**

College and Career Readiness

Reading Prep. Before reading, observe the objectives for each section in this chapter. Keep these in mind as you read, and focus on the structure of the author's writing—is the information presented in a way that is clear and engaging?

"Work doesn't just get you money. It builds character, strengthens confidence, and produces reputations." ~ Drew D.

Money Matters
Money Facts

- The first paper money in America was issued by the Massachusetts Bay Colony in 1690.

- When the Confederate States of America issued paper money in 1861, each note was signed by hand.

- In 1865, more than a third of all paper money in the United States was counterfeit.

- An image of Independence Hall appears on the back of the $100 bill. The clock is set at approximately 4:10. It is not known why that time was chosen.

- The clock on the $100 bill shows the Roman numeral IV on the clock face. On the actual Independence Hall clock, however, the clock face shows IIII, rather than IV.

- The $100 bill features Benjamin Franklin, who was never a president of the United States.

- Martha Washington is the only woman whose image has appeared on a US currency note. Susan B. Anthony was featured on a one-dollar coin.

- A $1 bill is only in circulation for about 18 months.

- It is a federal law that no living person may appear on US money.

Section 1.1 Earning by the Hour

Objectives
- **Describe the importance of money.**
- **Explain how to calculate hourly wages.**

Terms
- *bartering*
- *money*
- *hourly wage*
- *employer*
- *minimum wage*
- *overtime pay*

Teaching Tip:
Tell students that the *approximately equal to* sign is used here because the answer is not exact and rounding must be used.

Answer:
1. A. 13
   B. 12.5
   C. 67.1
   D. 20
2. A. 42.99
   B. 1223.08
   C. 2.36
   D. 102
3. A. $39.14
   B. $7.43
   C. $66.28
   D. $19
4. A. $1,458.33
   B. $4,000
   C. $1,384.62
   D. $9,230.08

Build Your Math Skills

Review these math skills to prepare for the lesson that follows.

1. Add decimals. Example: $5.4 + 3.6 + 2.4 = 11.4$

A. $7.6 + 3.6 + 1.8 =$

B. $3.4 + 3.7 + 5.4 =$

C. $51.4 + 14 + 1.7 =$

D. $5 + 3.6 + 11.4 =$

2. Round decimals to the nearest hundredth (0.01). Example: $22.875 \approx 22.88$

A. $42.988 \approx$

B. $1223.075 \approx$

C. $2.364 \approx$

D. $101.9977 \approx$

3. Multiply decimals. Round your answers to the nearest cent ($0.01).
Example: $\$15.25 \times 1.5 = \$22.875 \approx \$22.88$

A. $\$25.25 \times 1.55 =$

B. $\$5.50 \times 1.35 =$

C. $\$12.05 \times 5.5 =$

D. $\$7.60 \times 2.5 =$

4. Divide dollar amounts. Round your answers to the nearest cent ($0.01).
Example: $\$24,000 \div 12 = \$2,000$

A. $\$35,000 \div 24 =$

B. $\$24,000 \div 6 =$

C. $\$36,000 \div 26 =$

D. $\$48,000 \div 52 =$

What Is Money?

Ultimately, money is just a tool to make life more convenient. Before there was money, people traded one thing of value for another. For example, you might trade your services for a chicken and then trade that chicken for a bag of flour. **Bartering** is trading items other than money. Even in a society with money, bartering still exists. The problem with this system is that you have to find someone with something that you want who is also interested in something you have. **Money** is a tool that makes it easier to trade one thing of value for another; it is that simple. Rather than trading your work for a chicken, you can trade your work for money. You can then trade that money for whatever you need or want.

There are other advantages to using money. You cannot conveniently fold up a chicken and put it in your pocket. However, you can fold up money and put it in your pocket. Also, you cannot save a chicken to use as payment at a later date. But, you can save the money you have now to buy something in the future.

The symbol $=$ means *equal to* and is used to represent an exact relationship. The symbol $\approx$ means *approximately equal to* and is used when rounding or other estimation procedures are used.

Money works the way it does because the government regulates the money system. Society has agreed that money is a reliable way to manage earnings, purchases, and wealth. People have invented all kinds of ways to complicate the ways we earn, spend, and manage money. Being a smart user of the tool we call money is a critical part of creating a successful future.

Hourly Wages

Accepting a job that pays by the hour is one of the most common ways to earn money. The money most likely comes in the form of a paycheck. You may have had a job that paid by the hour. An ***hourly wage*** is the amount of money paid for each hour worked. Typically, the time worked is tracked on a *time sheet* or recorded by a *time clock* on a time card. To calculate how much you would get paid after working a certain number of hours, use this formula:

regular earnings = regular hourly wage × regular hours

When you accept a job, you become an *employee*. The ***employer*** is the person or company that hires you. By law, most employers are required to pay employees no less than an hourly wage known as the ***minimum wage.*** The minimum wage is adjusted from time to time by lawmakers.

Example 1-1A

See It

Rajaa has a part-time job at a local supermarket where he earns $7.50 per hour. The following table contains the number of hours he worked last week as seen on his time sheet. What were Rajaa's regular earnings last week?

Sunday	Monday	Tuesday	Wednesday	Thursday	Friday	Saturday
0	4	0	3.5	3	4	0

Strategy

Use the formula:

regular earnings = regular hourly wage × regular hours

Solution

Step 1: Find the number of regular hours Rajaa worked each day last week from the table.

Step 2: Add together the number of regular hours Rajaa worked each day to determine the total number of regular hours that he worked last week.

0 + 4 + 0 + 3.5 + 3 + 4 + 0 = 14.5 hours

Step 3: Multiply Rajaa's regular hourly wage by the total number of regular hours. Round to the nearest cent ($0.01) if necessary.

regular earnings = regular hourly wage × regular hours

regular earnings = $7.50 per hour × 14.5 hours

regular earnings = $108.75

Check It

Deborah has a part-time job at a local restaurant where she earns $7.25 per hour. The following table contains the number of hours she worked last week as seen on her time sheet. What were Deborah's regular earnings last week?

Sunday	Monday	Tuesday	Wednesday	Thursday	Friday	Saturday
0	0	5	4.5	3	4.5	0

Teaching Tip:
The complete solutions to the Check It problems can be found on the Instructor's Resource CD.

Answer:
$123.25

Example 1-1B

See It

Juanita has a full-time job as a receptionist in a physician's office. She works 40 hours a week and earns $450 per week. What is Juanita's regular hourly wage?

Strategy

Use the formula:

regular earnings = regular hourly wage × regular hours

Solution

Step 1: Record the number of regular hours Juanita works in one week and her regular weekly earnings.

number of regular hours = 40

regular weekly earnings = $450

Step 2: Divide Juanita's regular weekly earnings by the number of regular hours she works in one week.

$$\text{regular hourly wage} = \frac{\text{regular earnings}}{\text{regular hours}}$$

$$\text{regular hourly wage} = \frac{\$450}{40 \text{ hours}}$$

regular hourly wage = $11.25 per hour

Check It

Jamal has a full-time job as a veterinary technician. He works 40 hours a week and earns $412 per week. What is Jamal's regular hourly wage?

There is an *inverse relationship* between multiplication and division. An inverse relationship means that one operation is the reverse of the other. To find the regular earnings, multiply regular hourly wage by regular hours. To find the regular hourly wage, divide regular earnings by regular hours. The variables are the same, but the operation changes depending on the value for which you are solving.

Answer:
$10.30

Example 1-1C

See It

Ahmed works as a home health aide earning $10.40 per hour. One week, his regular earnings were $384.80. How many regular hours did Ahmed work that week?

Strategy

Modify the following formula, with the inverse relationship between multiplication and division in mind:

regular earnings = regular hourly wage × regular hours

Use the following:

$$\text{regular hours} = \frac{\text{regular earnings}}{\text{regular hourly wage}}$$

Solution

Step 1: Record Ahmed's regular hourly wage and his regular weekly earnings.

regular hourly wage = $10.40

regular weekly earnings = $384.80

Step 2: Divide the weekly earnings by the hourly wage.

regular earnings = regular hourly wage × regular hours

$$\text{regular hours} = \frac{\text{regular earnings}}{\text{regular hourly wage}}$$

$$\text{regular hours} = \frac{\$384.80}{\$10.40 \text{ per hour}}$$

regular hours = 37 hours

Check It

Courtney works as a court reporter in the municipal court system. Her regular hourly wage is $19.50 per hour. She usually earns $682.50 in a week. How many regular hours does Courtney usually work?

Answer:
35 hours

In 1938, the Fair Labor Standards Act (FLSA) became law. It set the first federal minimum wage and required employers to pay employees overtime for any time over 40 hours worked in a week.

Federal law protects employees from being required to work more than 40 hours in a week without extra pay. This extra pay is known as **overtime pay,** or simply *overtime*. For hours worked in excess of 40 hours in a workweek, the employee must be paid at least 1.5 times the regular hourly wage. Overtime pay of 1.5 times the regular hourly wage is often called *time-and-a-half*. Sometimes overtime pay is twice the regular hourly wage, which is often called *double time*.

time-and-a-half hourly earnings = regular hourly wage × 1.5

double time hourly earnings = regular hourly wage × 2

Example 1-1D

See It

Irene works as an aerobics instructor at a local fitness center. Her regular hourly wage is $14.75 per hour. She earns overtime pay of 1.5 times her regular hourly wage. Last week she worked 46 hours. What will Irene's total earnings, including overtime pay, be for the week?

Strategy

Use the formulas:

regular earnings = regular hourly wage × regular hours

time-and-a-half hourly earnings = regular hourly wage × 1.5

Solution

Step 1: Determine Irene's regular earnings for working 40 hours. Multiply her regular hourly wage by the number of regular hours that Irene worked.

regular earnings = regular hourly wage × regular hours

regular earnings = $14.75 per hour × 40 hours

regular earnings = $590

Step 2: Calculate the number of overtime hours that Irene worked. Subtract her number of regular hours worked from the total number of hours she worked.

number of overtime hours = total number of hours – number of regular hours

number of overtime hours = 46 hours – 40 hours

number of overtime hours = 6 hours

Step 3: Solve for Irene's overtime hourly wage. Multiply her regular hourly wage by 1.5. Round to the nearest cent ($0.01) if necessary.

overtime hourly wage = regular hourly wage × 1.5

overtime hourly wage = $14.75 per hour × 1.5

overtime hourly wage = $22.13 per hour

Step 4: Determine Irene's overtime earnings. Multiply Irene's overtime hourly wage by her number of overtime hours.

overtime earnings = overtime hourly wage × number of overtime hours

overtime earnings = $22.13 per hour × 6 hours

overtime earnings = $132.78

Step 5: Determine Irene's total earnings. Add Irene's regular earnings to her overtime earnings.

total earnings = regular earnings + overtime earnings

total earnings = $590 + $132.78

total earnings = $722.78

Teaching Tip:
Point out that in order to work out the formula for time-and-a-half hourly earnings, the regular earnings must be calculated first.

Check It

Sema works as an agricultural inspector. His regular hourly wage is $20.30. He receives overtime pay of time-and-a-half for any hours he works over 40 in one week. Because there is a busy growing season, Sema worked 52 hours one week. What were Sema's total earnings for this week?

Checkpoint 1.1

1. Michael has a part-time job as a telephone sales agent for an airline. He earns $13.25 per hour. The following table contains the number of hours he worked last week. How much money did Michael earn last week?

Sunday	Monday	Tuesday	Wednesday	Thursday	Friday	Saturday
0	0	4	5	3.5	5	4.5

2. Roberta works in a hospital lab as a medical technician. She works 40 hours per week and earns $700 per week. What is Roberta's hourly wage?

3. Rodrigo works as a billing clerk at the local school district. He earns $13.75 per hour. His earnings for one week are $481.25. How many hours a week does Rodrigo work?

4. Isabella works as a cargo inspector for the local port. She earns $22.50 per hour. Last week she worked 50 hours. For any hours over 40 hours per week she works, Isabella earns overtime pay. That pay is 1.5 times her regular hourly wage. What were Isabella's total weekly earnings, including overtime pay, for last week?

5. Thao works as a manager in a local grocery store. He earns $18.75 per hour, and last week he worked 46 hours. Because the six extra hours he worked were on a holiday, he received double time for those overtime hours. What were Thao's total weekly earnings, including overtime pay, for last week?

Section 1.2 Earning a Salary

Objectives

- **Explain how to calculate total salaries.**
- **Describe how to calculate salaries for each type of pay period.**

Build Your Math Skills

Review these math skills to prepare for the lesson that follows.

1. Divide a whole number by a decimal. Round your answers to the nearest hundredth (0.01). Example: $9 \div 3.2 = 2.81$

A. $12 \div 0.6 =$

B. $5 \div 0.2 =$

C. $16 \div 4.2 =$

D. $8 \div 6.2 =$

2. Divide a decimal by a whole number. Round your answers to the nearest hundredth (0.01). Example: $5.4 \div 6 = 0.90$

A. $6.5 \div 3 =$

B. $3.1 \div 7 =$

C. $2.32 \div 4 =$

D. $6.5 \div 1 =$

3. Add whole numbers and decimals. Round your answers to the nearest hundredth (0.01) Example: $7.4 + 2 = 9.4$

A. $13 + 4.12 =$

B. $16 + 7.68 =$

C. $8 + 12.25 =$

D. $10 + 6.86 =$

Answer:
1. A. 20
   B. 25
   C. 3.81
   D. 1.29
2. A. 2.17
   B. 0.44
   C. 0.58
   D. 6.5
3. A. 17.12
   B. 23.68
   C. 20.25
   D. 16.86

Salaried Employment

Many jobs pay a salary rather than an hourly wage. A *salary* is a fixed payment for a person's work, usually paid monthly or twice per month. For example, an employee might be paid an annual salary of $48,000. He or she might receive the salary in monthly payments of $4,000 or two payments per month of $2,000.

When employees earn a salary, they are paid to do a job. There may be less emphasis on the time required to do the job and more emphasis on getting the job done. Professional work or office work tends to be salary-based. Assembly-based or manual work is hourly because the work is connected to a timed and measured result.

Earning a salary is not always straightforward. A salary consists of a base pay plus other potential compensation. *Base pay* is the pay the employee receives for the work performed. Often other compensation is added to base pay. For example, a salaried employee might also earn a bonus. *Gross pay* is the total pay with bonus and before deductions:

gross pay = annual salary + bonus

fyi

If you have ever had a job, you probably have some experience with the fact that when you actually receive a paycheck, it is reduced by taxes and other deductions which are discussed later in this chapter.

Example 1-2A

See It

Lee is a paralegal in a local law firm. She earns an annual salary of $35,450. Her law firm offers bonuses based on the firm's total annual income. This year, Lee's firm is offering a bonus of 10% of her annual salary. This amounts to $3,545. What will be Lee's gross pay for this year?

Strategy

Use the formula:

$$\text{gross pay} = \text{annual salary} + \text{bonus}$$

Solution

Step 1: Identify Lee's annual salary and bonuses.

annual salary = $35,450

bonuses = $3,545

Step 2: Determine the sum of Lee's base salary and her annual bonus. Add her base salary to her bonus.

gross pay = annual salary + bonus

gross pay = $35,450 + $3,545

gross pay = $38,995

Check It

Raj is an architect for a local architecture firm. He earns an annual base salary of $60,300 and an annual bonus based on the firm's total income. This year, he will earn a bonus of 5% of his annual base salary, which is $3,015. What will be Raj's gross pay for this year?

Pay Periods

One of the decisions a company makes when preparing to pay employees is to select a pay period. A **pay period** is a repeating time frame that an employer uses to calculate and pay salaries and wages. The most common pay periods are *monthly, semimonthly, biweekly, and weekly.* For example, an employer might pay employees monthly on the last day of each month.

For a **monthly pay period,** salaried employees receive 1/12 of their annual salary on the last day of each month. With a monthly pay period, any day of the month can be selected as payday. Whichever day is chosen will be the payday each month.

The semimonthly pay period is common in companies that have a lot of salaried employees. A **semimonthly pay period** divides the month into two pay periods. Payday is often at the middle and the end of the month.

The **biweekly pay period** involves paying employees every two weeks. The payday is often on a Friday. The difference between a semimonthly and biweekly pay period is subtle, but important. Because a year consists of 52 weeks, there are 26 biweekly pay periods and only 24 semimonthly pay periods. This means that two months out of the year there will be three paydays in the same month. Some employees might occasionally like having three paydays in a month. However, it is important to remember that the pay period does not affect the overall amount of salary paid. Pay period just dictates when you receive the pay. The occasional three paychecks in a month are only making up for the fact that each biweekly paycheck is smaller than the same salary paid semimonthly. It is all just a matter of whether the annual salary is divided by 24 or 26.

The amount an employee is paid per period is represented by the following formula:

$$\text{amount per paycheck} = \frac{\text{gross annual pay}}{\text{number of pay periods per year}}$$

With a **weekly pay period,** employees are paid each week. Payday can be any day of the week. Weekly pay periods are often used for employees being paid by the hour, but salaried employees can be paid weekly as well.

For employees who are paid by the hour, there is usually a delay of a few days or more between the end of the pay period and the actual payday. The delay is to allow time for all employee time to be recorded and payroll to be processed. For example, if an hourly employee is paid each Friday, he or she may actually be getting paid for the pay period that ended the previous Friday.

You might consider using direct deposit for your paycheck. **Direct deposit** is the automatic deposit of your paycheck into your checking account. You would receive a document similar to a paycheck as a record of your pay.

You may have seen or heard the word *payroll*. The word *payroll* is actually used in many ways. The **payroll** is the list of employees a company pays. The total amount of money it takes to pay the employees is also sometimes referred to as the payroll. You also might hear someone say, "I need to process payroll," which is the act of paying the employees.

Financial $marts

Many employers now require employees to receive their paycheck through direct deposit. Direct deposit electronically transfers your paycheck directly to your checking account. Your employer still provides a record of your paycheck, but you do not receive an actual check. Direct deposit gets your money in your checking account more quickly than if you had to go to the bank to cash your paycheck.

Example 1-2B

See It

Jameson received a job offer with an annual gross pay of $50,000. Calculate the amount of gross pay Jameson would receive in each paycheck for each of the following pay periods: monthly, semimonthly, biweekly, and weekly.

Strategy

Use the formula:

$$\text{amount per paycheck} = \frac{\text{gross annual pay}}{\text{number of pay periods per year}}$$

Solution

Step 1: Determine Jameson's monthly pay. Divide his annual salary by 12. Round to the nearest cent ($0.01) if necessary.

$$\text{monthly pay} = \frac{\text{gross annual pay}}{12 \text{ pay periods}}$$

$$\text{monthly pay} = \frac{\$50{,}000}{12 \text{ pay periods}}$$

monthly pay = $4,166.67

Step 2: Determine Jameson's semimonthly pay. Divide his annual salary by 24. Round to the nearest cent ($0.01) if necessary.

$$\text{semimonthly pay} = \frac{\text{gross annual pay}}{24 \text{ pay periods}}$$

$$\text{semimonthly pay} = \frac{\$50{,}000}{24 \text{ pay periods}}$$

semimonthly pay = $2,083.33

Step 3: Determine Jameson's biweekly pay. Divide his annual salary by 26. Round to the nearest cent ($0.01) if necessary.

$$\text{biweekly pay} = \frac{\text{gross annual pay}}{26 \text{ pay periods}}$$

$$\text{biweekly pay} = \frac{\$50{,}000}{26 \text{ pay periods}}$$

biweekly pay = $1,923.08

Step 4: Determine Jameson's weekly pay. Divide his annual salary by 52. Round to the nearest cent ($0.01) if necessary.

$$\text{weekly pay} = \frac{\text{gross annual pay}}{52 \text{ pay periods}}$$

Teaching Tip:
Walk students through the process of division, explaining that when an equation includes a fraction, it signals that the top number (the numerator) is to be divided by the bottom number (the denominator).

$$\text{weekly pay} = \frac{\$50{,}000}{52 \text{ pay periods}}$$

$$\text{weekly pay} = \$961.54$$

Check It

Tameka recently graduated with a bachelor degree in soil and plant sciences. She received a job offer with an annual salary of $62,600. Calculate the amount of gross pay Tameka would earn in each paycheck for each of the following pay periods: monthly, semimonthly, biweekly, and weekly.

Answer:
monthly = $5,216.67
semimonthly = $2,608.33
biweekly = $2,407.69
weekly = $1,203.85

Checkpoint 1.2

1. Eduardo works as an accountant for a consulting firm. He earns an annual salary of $68,090 and an annual bonus based on the firm's performance. This year, Eduardo will earn a bonus of 3% of his annual salary, which is $2,042.70. What is Eduardo's annual gross pay?

2. Taj works as a hydrologist for the federal government. He earns an annual salary of $82,900. In addition, he earns a bonus equal to 6% of his annual salary, which is $4,974. What is Taj's annual gross pay?

3. Lucy is a curator at the local art museum. She earns an annual salary of $53,160. Calculate the amount of her paycheck if she is paid monthly, semimonthly, biweekly, or weekly.

4. Judith works as a court reporter for a county district court. She earns an annual salary of $57,270. Currently, she is paid semimonthly. Her employer is considering paying all employees biweekly. Calculate the amount of money in Judith's semimonthly paycheck. Then, calculate the amount of money that would be in Judith's paycheck if she were paid biweekly.

5. Michael has received two job offers. One offer, from Forestry Unlimited, has an annual salary of $48,000. The second offer, from Continental Lumber, has a semimonthly pay of $2,050. Which of the two job offers will provide Michael the most pay per month? Explain your answer.

Teaching Tip:
Checkpoint questions offer opportunities for formative assessment.

Answer:
1. $70,132.70
2. $87,874
3. monthly = $4,430
   semimonthly = $2,215
   biweekly = $2,044.62
   weekly = $1,022.31
4. semimonthly = $2,386.25
   biweekly = $2,202.69
5. Continental Lumber

Section 1.3 Other Ways to Earn

Terms

- *commission*
- *straight commission*
- *independent contractor*
- *contract*
- *oral contract*
- *entrepreneur*
- *income*
- *earned income*
- *unearned income*

Objectives

- **Explain how to calculate commission.**
- **Describe how to calculate earnings for an independent contractor.**
- **Explain how to calculate earned and unearned income.**

Build Your Math Skills

Review these math skills to prepare for the lesson that follows.

1. Convert percentages to decimals by moving the decimal two places to the left. Example: 74% → 0.74

A. 56% →

B. 9% →

C. 33% →

D. 98% →

2. Multiply whole numbers by decimals. Example: $25 \times 0.15 = 3.75$

A. $114 \times 0.25 =$

B. $0.18 \times 40 =$

C. $7 \times 0.05 =$

D. $0.50 \times 862 =$

3. Add decimals. Example: $8.52 + 4.5 = 13.02$

A. $53.6 + 4.12 =$

B. $16.92 + 7.68 =$

C. $8 + 12.25 =$

D. $10.85 + 6.86 =$

Commission

Another way people earn money is through commission. A **commission** is a fee that is usually a percentage of the amount of a business transaction. A *sales representative,* whose job it is to sell a service or product, often earns commission. For example, a sales representative might earn a commission of 10% of sales. With a 10% commission, a sales representative would earn $100 for every $1,000 of product or service sold:

commission = item price × number of items × commission rate

Example 1-3A

See It

Veronica is a salesclerk for a sporting goods store. She earns 12% of her sales as a commission. The following table shows Veronica's sales for a particular day.

What is Veronica's commission for this day?

Item	Item Price	Number of Items Sold
Football	$14.50	12
Swim goggles	$17.00	10
Socks	$12.00	8
Soccer cleats	$34.50	5

Strategy

Use the formula:

commission = item price × number of items × commission rate

Solution

Step 1: Change the commission rate from a percentage to a decimal. To do so, move the decimal point two places to the left. Fill in zeros as placeholders as necessary.

12% → 0.12

Step 2: Determine the commission for footballs. Multiply the item price, the number of items sold, and the commission rate.

commission = item price × number of items × commission rate

commission = $14.50 × 12 × 0.12

commission = $20.88

Step 3: Determine the commission for swim goggles. Multiply the item price, the number of items sold, and the commission rate.

commission = item price × number of items × commission rate

commission = $17 × 10 × 0.12

commission = $20.40

Step 4: Determine the commission for socks. Multiply the item price, the number of items sold, and the commission rate.

commission = item price × number of items × commission rate

commission = $12 × 8 × 0.12

commission = $11.52

Step 5: Determine the commission for soccer cleats. Multiply the item price, the number of items sold, and the commission rate.

commission = item price × number of items × commission rate

commission = $34.50 × 5 × 0.12

commission = $20.70

Teaching Tip: Remind students that 0.12 is really $\frac{12}{100}$.

Financial $marts

Making money is an important way to become self-sufficient. However, giving to others is also important. *Philanthropy* is the act of giving to others to help them or to provide for the goodwill of the community. It does not have to involve money. When you volunteer at a food bank, clean a public park, or tutor other students, you are being philanthropic.

Companies are often philanthropic. For example, an automobile dealer may provide a van to a Ronald McDonald House or make a monetary donation to the United Way. The employees of a company may also work as a group on a Habitat for Humanity home.

Find a way that you can be philanthropic and make a difference in the lives of others.

Step 6: Determine the total commission. Add the commission for each item together.

total commission = football + swim goggles + socks + cleats

total commission = $20.88 + $20.40 + $11.52 + $20.70

total commission = $73.50

Check It

Lakota is a real estate agent. He earns a 3% commission on each house that he sells. The commission is based on the sales price of each house. One month, Lakota sold three houses for $110,000, $177,000, and $154,000 respectively. What is Lakota's commission for that month?

Is commission a good way to be paid? That depends. For some jobs, the only compensation the employee earns is commission. ***Straight commission*** is when the only compensation received by an employee is commission. If the employee is a productive salesperson, the employee has the opportunity to increase earnings by increasing sales. Employees on commission should be motivated to increase their sales to increase their pay. But, there is a lot of risk for the employee if pay is based on straight commission.

Some employees receive a blend of salary and commission. For example, an employee might receive a salary that provides enough to cover basic expenses. To reward productivity, a commission may be added:

annual gross pay = annual salary + commission

Example 1-3B

See It

Jonathan is a sales representative for a book company. He earns a base annual salary of $35,000 plus a 3% commission of all sales that he makes. This year, Jonathan is on target to make about $375,000 in sales. Calculate Jonathan's projected annual gross pay.

Strategy

Use the formula:

annual gross pay = annual salary + commission

Solution

Step 1: Convert the commission rate from a percentage to a decimal. To do so, move the decimal point two places to the left. Fill in zeros as placeholders as necessary.

3% → 0.03

Step 2: Determine Jonathan's commission. Multiply his total annual sales by the commission rate (as a decimal).

commission = total annual sales × commission rate

commission = $375,000 × 0.03

commission = $11,250

Step 3: Determine Jonathan's annual gross pay. Add his annual salary and his commission together.

annual gross pay = annual salary + commission

annual gross pay = $35,000 + $11,250

annual gross pay = $46,250

Check It

Marianna is a manager at a retail electronics store. She earns a base annual salary of $25,000 plus a 2% commission on the store's sales. This year, the store's total annual sales will be about $1,650,000. Calculate Marianna's annual gross pay.

Answer:
$58,000

Working as an Independent Contractor

You do not have to be an employee to earn money and get paid. Another common way to perform work and earn a paycheck is as an independent contractor. An ***independent contractor*** is a person who provides a service to the public or to a company for money. For example, an individual who knows how to develop software could go to work for a company as an employee developing software. Or, the individual could become an independent contractor performing software development for any company or person that provides the opportunity. An independent contractor is sometimes referred to as a *freelancer* or *consultant*.

As an independent contractor, you enter into a contract with another person or company. A ***contract*** defines an agreement between two entities. In this case, the contract would outline the work to be done and the sum to be paid to the contractor. Many contracts are written and signed. However, even when you agree during a conversation to babysit a child for $20, you are entering into a form of contract called an oral contract. An ***oral contract*** is an agreement that has been acknowledged only through spoken words.

An independent contractor might be paid by the hour, by the project, or some other agreed-on way. How and when the contractor gets paid is defined by the contract. Pay periods do not apply because an independent contractor is not an employee. He or she is not paid as part of payroll. For example, a contractor might charge $60 per hour for the time it takes to complete the work. The contract might specify that the contractor be paid weekly for the hours completed. On the other hand, a contractor might charge $1,000 to complete a project. The contract might state that $500 be paid at the beginning of the project and $500 at the end. For the most part, whatever is agreed on by the parties to the contract is allowable.

An independent contractor is a type of entrepreneur. An ***entrepreneur*** is a person who starts a business venture and assumes the risk of its success or failure.

fyi

If you have ever mowed yards for individuals for pay or performed babysitting for pay, you were working as an independent contractor.

Teaching Tip:
Ask students to brainstorm types of jobs where people work as independent contractors.

To calculate contract earnings, multiply the agreed-on hourly rate by the number of hours worked:

contract earnings = hourly rate × number of hours

Example 1-3C

See It

Fatima is an independent contractor who performs tutoring services for high school students. She is hired at a rate of $35 an hour. Fatima worked 73.5 hours over a two-week period. Calculate Fatima's total contract earnings during this period of time.

Strategy

Use the formula:

contract earnings = hourly rate × number of hours

Solution

Step 1: Identify Fatima's hourly rate and the number of hours she worked.

hourly rate = $35 per hour

number of hours = 73.5 hours

Step 2: Determine Fatima's contract earnings. Multiply her hourly rate by the total number of hours worked.

contract earnings = hourly rate × number of hours

contract earnings = $35 × 73.5

contract earnings = $2,572.50

Check It

Brian is an independent contractor who develops software. He has a contract with a software company to work at a rate of $37 per hour. Brian worked 164 hours during May. Calculate his contract earnings for that month.

Answer:
$6,068

Income

Income is the money received by a person or company. For an individual, income could come from employment, contract work, or any other kind of activity that generates cash or the equivalent.

Earned income is pay that comes from your work. Examples of earned income are wages, commissions, and contract earnings. Tips, also known as *gratuities*, are also a source of earned income. Many employees who earn tips are paid less than minimum wage.

Shutterstock (wavebreakmedia ltd)

People earn money through hourly wages, a salary, or commission.

Unearned income is income that is not derived from your work. Examples of unearned income include earnings from investments, gifts, and renting property to others:

total income = earned income + unearned income

fyi

Tips are calculated by the customer based on a percentage of the bill. It is customary to tip 15% to 20% based on the quality of service.

Example 1-3D

See It

Mohamed has a job as a forensic science technician where he earns $55,040 per year. He also has investments that generate annual income. Mohamed's total income from last year was $62,190. What was Mohamed's unearned income?

Strategy

Use the formula:

unearned income = total income – earned income

Teaching Tip:
Discuss the difference between earned income and unearned income.

Solution

Step 1: Identify Mohamed's earned income and total income. His earned income is what he receives from his job. His unearned income is what he receives from his investments.

earned income = $55,040

total income = $62,190

Step 2: Determine Mohamed's unearned income. Subtract his earned income from his total income.

unearned income = total income − earned income

unearned income = $62,190 − $55,040

unearned income = $7,150

Check It

Rosie is a graphic designer whose annual salary is $48,140. She also owns rental properties that generate income annually. Rosie's total income last year was $63,740. What was Rosie's unearned income for the year?

Example 1-3E

See It

Jada is a public relations specialist. She earns $59,150 from her job and $11,000 as an independent contractor. Additionally, she receives $1,850 annually in dividends from stock that she owns. What is Jada's total annual income?

Strategy

Use the formula:

total income = earned income + unearned income

Solution

Step 1: Calculate Jada's earned income, which is what she receives from her job *and* her contract work. Add Jada's income from her job to the income she earned as an independent contractor.

earned income = income from job + income from contract

earned income = $59,150 + $11,000

earned income = $70,150

Step 2: Determine Jada's total income. Add her earned income and unearned income (stock dividends) together.

total income = earned income + unearned income

total income = $70,150 + $1,850

total income = $72,000

Career Discovery
Architecture & Construction Careers and Math Skills

People with careers in architecture and construction are involved in the design, preconstruction planning, construction, and maintenance of structures. They may design, build, restore, or maintain homes, bridges, industrial plants, dams, hospitals, highways, and shopping malls. Some careers may involve landscape architecture, urban planning, and interior design.

Careers in these professions require strong math skills, as exact measurements, calculations, and spatial relations are important components of the job. People in these professions must be able to create plans with precise specifications. Give a scenario in which a person with underdeveloped math skills could cause major problems for someone in this profession.

Check It

Mikhail works as a waiter in a restaurant while attending college. Last year, his annual salary was $6,708. He also earned an additional $11,532 in tips. Mikhail also received a scholarship of $2,500 to cover room and board. What was Mikhail's total income for last year?

Answer:
$20,740

Checkpoint 1.3

Teaching Tip:
Checkpoint questions offer opportunities for formative assessment.

1. Margaret is a regional sales representative for a cable television company. She earns a straight commission of 15% of all sales in her region. Last year, there were $544,000 in sales for the region. What was Margaret's total commission last year?

2. Brooke is a sales representative for a company that sells medical devices. She earns a base annual salary of $50,000 along with a commission of 4% of her total sales. Last year, Brooke sold $750,000 worth of medical devices. What was Brooke's annual gross pay last year?

3. Niko works for an online media relations company. He earns a base annual salary of $40,000 plus a commission of 5% of the sales that he makes to each of his clients. This year, Niko is on target to sell about $510,000 worth of services to his clients. What will Niko's annual gross pay be?

4. Janet is an independent contractor for a consulting firm that provides corporate training services. She bills $1,200 per day for delivering a corporate training workshop. She recently negotiated a contract with the firm to provide 12 days of corporate training workshops for the month of August. What will Janet's income from this contract be?

Answer:
1. $81,600
2. $80,000
3. $65,500
4. $14,400
5. $14,445

5. David works as a firefighter, receiving an annual salary of $47,730. He also owns stocks that pay a dividend. Last year, David earned $62,175 in total income. What was David's unearned income?

Chapter Review

Build Your Vocabulary

As you progress through this course, develop a personal glossary of financial literacy terms and add it to your portfolio. This will help you build your financial literacy vocabulary. Write out a definition for each of the following terms, and add it to your personal glossary.

bartering	weekly pay period
money	direct deposit
hourly wage	payroll
employer	commission
minimum wage	straight commission
overtime pay	independent contractor
salary	contract
base pay	oral contract
gross pay	entrepreneur
pay period	income
monthly pay period	earned income
semimonthly pay period	unearned income
biweekly pay period	

 ## Teamwork

Working with your team, prepare a *pro and con* chart for each of the following types of employment: hourly-wage-based, commission-based, salary-based, tip-based, and independent contractor. Prepare a separate page for each method of earned income. For each method of pay, list the pros and cons of each type of earned income. Also, give examples of jobs that are in each category. Share your opinions with the class.

Review Your Math Skills

Practice and build on the math skills that you have learned.

1. Add whole numbers and decimals. Round your answers to the nearest hundredth (0.01). Example: 7.4 + 2 = 9.4

A. 17 + 6.81 =   B. 2.45 + 12 =

C. 11.23 + 5 =   D. 6 + 9.38 =

2. Add decimals. Example: 5.4 + 3.6 + 2.4 = 11.4

A. 6.5 + 9.1 + 1.2 =   B. 12.3 + 2.2 + 5.4 =

C. 40.2 + 17 + 6.9 =   D. 72.3 + 2 + 13.33 =

Answer:
1. A. 23.81
   B. 14.45
   C. 16.23
   D. 15.38
2. A. 16.8
   B. 19.9
   C. 64.1
   D. 87.63

3. Add decimals. Example: 5.79 + 1.6 = 7.39

A. 42.3 + 9.22 =

B. 51.99 + 3.46 =

C. 7 + 15.48 =

D. 27.7 + 0.97 =

4. Divide a decimal by a whole number. Round your answers to the nearest hundredth (0.01). Example: 0.01 ÷ 12 = 8.33

A. 7.3 ÷ 2 =

B. 9.48 ÷ 8 =

C. 4.71 ÷ 6 =

D. 11.67 ÷ 4 =

5. Divide a whole number by a decimal. Round your answers to the nearest hundredth (0.01). Example: 12 ÷ 0.01 = 1200

A. 10 ÷ 0.71 =

B. 7 ÷ 6.41 =

C. 19 ÷ 0.423 =

D. 8 ÷ 12.52 =

6. Divide dollar amounts. Round answers to the nearest cent ($0.01). Example: $120 ÷ 8 = 15

A. $68,000 ÷ 24 =

B. $25,000 ÷ 12 =

C. $33,000 ÷ 12 =

D. $57,000 ÷ 24 =

7. Multiply decimals. Round your answers to the nearest cent ($0.01). Example: $13.25 × 1.25 = $16.5625 ≈ $16.56

A. $35.25 × 2.75 =

B. $6.45 × 1.65 =

C. $15.10 × 7.5=

D. $7.05 × 1.5 =

8. Multiply whole numbers by decimals. Example: 41 × 0.25 = 10.25

A. 263 × 0.05 =

B. 0.231 × 20 =

C. 8 × 0.75 =

D. 0.5 × 23 =

9. Convert percentages to decimals by moving the decimal two places to the left. Example: 74% → 0.74

A. 42% →

B. 6% →

C. 53% →

D. 76% →

10. Round decimals to the nearest hundredth (0.01). Example: 22.875 ≈ 22.88

A. 58.568 ≈

B. 4,179.3809 ≈

C. 8.876 ≈

D. 321.9817 ≈

3. A. 51.52
    B. 55.45
    C. 22.48
    D. 28.67
4. A. 3.65
    B. 1.19
    C. 0.79
    D. 2.92
5. A. 14.08
    B. 1.09
    C. 44.92
    D. 0.64
6. A. $2,833.33
    B. $2,083.33
    C. $2,750
    D. $2,375
7. A. $96.94
    B. $10.64
    C. $113.25
    D. $10.58
8. A. 13.15
    B. 4.62
    C. 6
    D. 11.5
9. A. 0.42
    B. 0.06
    C. 0.53
    D. 0.76
10. A. 58.57
    B. 4,179.38
    C. 8.88
    D. 321.98

Section 1.1   Earning by the Hour

11. Brenda works at a local dairy, where she earns $10.80 per hour. Last week, she earned $367.20. How many hours did Brenda work?

12. Jayden works as a nurse in a local hospital, where he earns $18.40 per hour. He normally works 40 hours in a week. He was offered overtime this week at 1.5 times his normal hourly wage. If Jayden works 48 hours this week, what will be his weekly earnings, including overtime pay?

Answer:
11. 34 hours
12. $956.80

Section 1.2   Earning a Salary

13. Rico works as a film and video editor for a production company. He earns an annual salary of $61,890 and an annual bonus based on the company's profits. This year, he will earn a bonus of $6,600. Determine Rico's annual gross pay for this year.

14. Keoma has received a job offer to work as a mathematics teacher at a local high school. Her annual gross pay will be $37,500 per year. Calculate the amount of Keoma's paycheck if she were paid monthly, semimonthly, biweekly, or weekly. Round your answer to the nearest cent ($0.01) if necessary.

15. Noah works as an audiologist. He earns an annual salary of $64,970. Calculate the amount of his paycheck if he were paid monthly, semimonthly, biweekly, or weekly. Round your answer to the nearest cent ($0.01) if necessary.

Answer:
13. $68,490
14. monthly = $3,125
    semimonthly = $1,562.50
    biweekly = $1,442.31
    weekly = $721.15
15. monthly = $5,414.17
    semimonthly = $2,707.08
    biweekly = $2,498.85
    weekly = $1,249.42

Section 1.3   Other Ways to Earn

16. Eva is a salesclerk at an appliance store. She earns an 8% commission of her sales. The following chart shows her sales for one week. Determine Eva's commission for the week.

Item	Item Price	Number of Items Sold
Refrigerator	$1,200	4
Washing machine	$650	7
Clothes dryer	$600	7
Dishwasher	$450	6

17. Ricardo works as a manager in a department store. He earns a base annual salary of $30,000 plus a 3% commission of his department's sales. If his department's sales for the month average $40,000, what will Ricardo earn each month?

18. Kelly is a landscape architect who works as an independent contractor. She earns $55 per hour designing commercial landscape features. Kelly recently negotiated a contract for a new office building that she estimates will require 78 hours of work. What will Kelly's contract earnings be?

Answer:
16. $1,300
17. $3,700
18. $4,290

Reinforce Your Understanding

19. Kelvin works at a sandwich shop after school and on weekends. The chart that follows shows the days and hours per day he worked last week. He normally works 15 to 20 hours per week. Did he work more hours than usual, fewer hours than usual, or about the same number of hours as usual?

Sunday	Monday	Tuesday	Wednesday	Thursday	Friday	Saturday
0	3.25	4.15	0	4.2	3.6	0

20. Using the answers to the calculations you made above, if Kelvin is paid $10.20 per hour, what are his wages for last week?

Apply Your Technology Skills

Companion Website
www.g-wlearning.com

Access the G-W Learning companion website for this text at www.g-wlearning.com. Download each data file for this chapter. Follow the instructions to complete financial literacy activities to practice what you have learned in this chapter.

Data File 1-1— Researching Wages

Data File 1-2— Completing a Timecard

Data File 1-3—Calculating Wages

Data File 1-4—Calculating Commissions

Answer:
19. Kelvin worked 15.2 hours, which is about the same as what he normally works.
20. $155.04

Teaching Tip:
The Apply Your Technology Skills activities offer project-based authentic assessment opportunities.

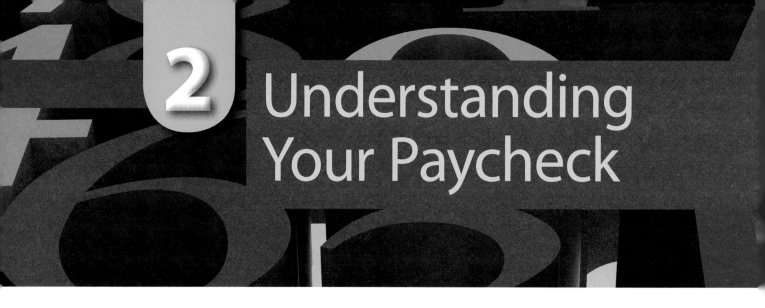

2 Understanding Your Paycheck

Materials:
Instructor's Resource CD
Student Workbook
G-W Learning companion website
EXAMVIEW® Assessment Suite
Microsoft Excel®–compatible software
Calculator with advanced-math functions

In the last chapter, you learned about earning money and the most common ways people are paid for their work. If you have ever had a job and received a paycheck, you probably noticed that some of the money you earned did not make it into your check. This chapter is about understanding your paycheck and what happens to that money. The skills you will learn in this chapter will be very valuable in your future.

College and Career Readiness

Reading Prep. Review the table of contents for this text. Trace the development of the content that is being presented from simple to complex ideas.

> *"It is very rewarding to have a job and make your own money."*
> ~ Micah B.

Money Matters
Checks

- The use of checks originated from bills of exchange, which were used as early as the 8th century to buy and sell products.

- The first widespread use of checks was documented in Holland in the early 1500s.

- In the late 17th century, the Bank of England began issuing handwritten notes in exchange for deposits to attract customers. Any note presented to the Bank of England was exchanged for its value in gold or coins.

- The term *check* can be traced back to 18th century England, when serial numbers were placed on these notes to keep track of, or *check* on them.

- The Commercial Bank of Scotland was the first bank to personalize checks. In 1811, it started printing checks with the customer's name.

- The use of checks in the United States peaked in the mid-1990s at more than 30 billion checks per year.

- Shortly after the peak in use of physical checks, their use quickly declined. Today, electronic checks used to conduct online transactions are more common than physical checks.

Section 2.1 Calculating Taxes

Objectives

- **Determine federal withholding using a tax table.**
- **Define and calculate FICA taxes.**
- **Calculate state income taxes.**
- **Determine net pay.**

Build Your Math Skills

Review these math skills to prepare for the lesson that follows.

1. Change percentages to decimals by moving the decimal two places to the left. Example: 12% → 0.12

A. 15% →

B. 5% →

C. 6.2% →

D. 7.5% →

2. Multiply decimals. Round your answers to the nearest cent ($0.01).
Example: $15.25 × 1.5 = $22.875 ≈ $22.88

A. $125 × 0.15 =

B. $48,000 × 0.062 =

C. $150 × 0.075 =

D. $245 × 0.04 =

3. Add and subtract decimals. Example: $175.85 + $85.55 = $261.40

A. $495.63 + $70.05 =

B. $960 + $63.42 =

C. $547.58 − $32.10 =

D. $940.67 − $67.85 − $53.25 =

Answer:
1. A. 0.15
   B. 0.05
   C. 0.062
   D. 0.075
2. A. $18.75
   B. $2,976
   C. $11.75
   D. $9.80
3. A. $565.68
   B. $1,023.42
   C. $515.48
   D. $819.57

Federal Withholding

Anyone who has ever received a paycheck knows that the amount of the actual check is less than the total earnings, or *gross pay*. A **deduction** is any amount that is subtracted from gross pay. When money is taken out of your check, it is said to be *withheld* from your pay. The most common deduction from your check is for taxes. First look at withholding for federal taxes, which is known as *federal withholding*.

In the US, employers are required to withhold money from employee pay and send that money to the government. Money withheld from employees for federal taxes is not actually the tax the employee owes. The withholding is an *estimate* of the taxes that the employee will owe for the year.

The amount of money that is withheld from your pay is based on a variety of factors, including:

- the amount of money you earn;

- your marital status; and

- the number of dependents.

When you file your federal tax return, you determine if the estimated taxes withheld from your pay cover the taxes you owe. You might be required to pay more, or, if you overpaid, may receive a refund.

Sometimes employees think that their net pay is the only money they have earned. As a financially aware person, you should know that even though some of your money is withheld for FICA and income taxes, it is still yours. You just don't have any control over where it goes. The money deducted for FICA taxes is set aside for when you retire. The federal and state income taxes are the fees you pay for services like defense, law enforcement, and the construction and maintenance of highways. You should consider your net pay as the earnings over which you have direct control.

The amount of money you earn affects the amount withheld from your paycheck because federal income tax is a progressive tax. A *progressive tax* means the more a person makes, the higher the rate of taxation. Marital status is another factor used when calculating withholding. A tax table is used to look up the amount of tax to be withheld. Withholding taxes for single employees is different from withholding taxes for married employees who file taxes together with their spouses. There is a tax table for single employees and a separate tax table for married employees who file jointly.

Withholding allowances are the number of dependents you have. The number of dependents you have changes the amount of taxes withheld. A *dependent* is a child or other person who you are supporting financially. In other words, they are dependent on your support. The more dependents you have, the less tax will be withheld. When you file your tax return, your taxable income will be reduced to account for the fact that you are supporting other people. *Taxable income* is the portion of your earnings that is taxed when you file your tax return.

When you begin working for an employer, you will complete a W-4 withholding allowance certificate as shown in Figure 2-1. This form has a worksheet to help you determine your withholding allowances. The fewer allowances you claim, the more taxes will be deducted from your paycheck.

Cut here and give Form W-4 to your employer. Keep the top part for your records.

Form W-4
Department of the Treasury
Internal Revenue Service

Employee's Withholding Allowance Certificate

▶ Whether you are entitled to claim a certain number of allowances or exemption from withholding is subject to review by the IRS. Your employer may be required to send a copy of this form to the IRS.

OMB No. 1545-0074

20--

1 Type or print your first name and middle initial.	Last name	2 Your social security number

Home address (number and street or rural route)

3 ☐ Single   ☐ Married   ☐ Married, but withhold at higher Single rate.

Note. If married, but legally separated, or spouse is a nonresident alien, check the "Single" box.

City or town, state, and ZIP code

4   If your last name differs from that shown on your social security card, check here. You must call 1-800-772-1213 for a replacement card. ▶ ☐

5   Total number of allowances you are claiming (from line **H** above **or** from the applicable worksheet on page 2)   **5**

6   Additional amount, if any, you want withheld from each paycheck   .   .   .   .   **6** $

7   I claim exemption from withholding for 20--, and I certify that I meet **both** of the following conditions for exemption.
   • Last year I had a right to a refund of **all** federal income tax withheld because I had **no** tax liability **and**
   • This year I expect a refund of **all** federal income tax withheld because I expect to have **no** tax liability.
   If you meet both conditions, write "Exempt" here .   .   .   .   ▶   **7**

Under penalties of perjury, I declare that I have examined this certificate and to the best of my knowledge and belief, it is true, correct, and complete.

Employee's signature
(This form is not valid unless you sign it.) ▶

Date ▶

8 Employer's name and address (Employer: Complete lines 8 and 10 only if sending to the IRS.)	9 Office code (optional)	10 Employer identification number (EIN)

For Privacy Act and Paperwork Reduction Act Notice, see page 2.

Cat. No. 10220Q

Form **W-4** (20--)

Source: Department of the Treasury, Internal Revenue Service

Figure 2-1.
Form W-4

Figure 2-2 shows a portion of a tax table. This tax table is for single people who are paid weekly. To use this tax table, look for the weekly earnings. The earnings should fall into one of the ranges defined in the columns on the left side of the table. Then, move across the row to the number of allowances the employee has claimed. The number where row and column meet is the amount of federal withholding for that pay period.

This is only a portion of a tax table. The complete tax table is more than 100 lines long and applies to earnings up to $2,140 per pay period. If earnings are greater than $2,140, a different table must be used. The tables are updated each year, so the two shown here may not be for the current year. Figure 2-3 shows the tax table used for married persons who are paid weekly.

Columns on a tax table are read top to bottom. Rows are read left to right.

Teaching Tip:
You may want to project or otherwise show Figure 2-2 and guide students from finding the wage values in the left across to the row containing the appropriate number of deductions. You may want to model this more than once for different values.

SINGLE Persons—WEEKLY Payroll Period
(For Wages Paid through December 20--)

And the wages are—		And the number of withholding allowances claimed is—										
At least	But less than	0	1	2	3	4	5	6	7	8	9	10
		The amount of income tax to be withheld is—										
$300	$310	$32	$21	$12	$5	$0	$0	$0	$0	$0	$0	$0
310	320	33	22	13	6	0	0	0	0	0	0	0
320	330	35	24	14	7	0	0	0	0	0	0	0
330	340	36	25	15	8	1	0	0	0	0	0	0
340	350	38	27	16	9	2	0	0	0	0	0	0
350	360	39	28	18	10	3	0	0	0	0	0	0
360	370	41	30	19	11	4	0	0	0	0	0	0
370	380	42	31	21	12	5	0	0	0	0	0	0
380	390	44	33	22	13	6	0	0	0	0	0	0
390	400	45	34	24	14	7	0	0	0	0	0	0
600	610	77	66	55	45	34	23	14	7	0	0	0
610	620	78	67	57	46	35	25	15	8	1	0	0
620	630	80	69	58	48	37	26	16	9	2	0	0
630	640	81	70	60	49	38	28	17	10	3	0	0
640	650	83	72	61	51	40	29	18	11	4	0	0
650	660	84	73	63	52	41	31	20	12	5	0	0
660	670	86	75	64	54	43	32	21	13	6	0	0
670	680	87	76	66	55	44	34	23	14	7	0	0
680	690	89	78	67	57	46	35	24	15	8	0	0
690	700	90	79	69	58	47	37	26	16	9	1	0
700	710	92	81	70	60	49	38	27	17	10	2	0
710	720	94	82	72	61	50	40	29	18	11	3	0
720	730	97	84	73	63	52	41	30	20	12	4	0
730	740	99	85	75	64	53	43	32	21	13	5	0
740	750	102	87	76	66	55	44	33	23	14	6	0
900	910	142	124	106	90	79	68	57	47	36	25	15
910	920	144	126	109	91	80	70	59	48	38	27	16
920	930	147	129	111	93	82	71	60	50	39	28	18
930	940	149	131	114	96	83	73	62	51	41	30	19
940	950	152	134	116	98	85	74	63	53	42	31	21
1,050	1,060	179	161	144	126	108	91	80	69	59	48	37
1,060	1,070	182	164	146	128	110	93	81	71	60	49	39
1,070	1,080	184	166	149	131	113	95	83	72	62	51	40
1,080	1,090	187	169	151	133	115	98	84	74	63	52	42
1,090	1,100	189	171	154	136	118	100	86	75	65	54	43

Source: Department of the Treasury, Internal Revenue Service

Figure 2-2. Single Persons Federal Withholding Table

MARRIED Persons—WEEKLY Payroll Period
(For Wages Paid through December 20--)

And the wages are—		And the number of withholding allowances claimed is—										
At least	But less than	0	1	2	3	4	5	6	7	8	9	10
		The amount of income tax to be withheld is—										
$550	$560	$44	$33	$26	$9	$2	$5	$0	$0	$0	$0	$0
560	570	46	35	27	20	13	6	0	0	0	0	0
570	580	47	36	28	21	14	7	0	0	0	0	0
580	590	49	38	29	22	15	8	1	0	0	0	0
590	600	50	39	30	23	16	9	2	0	0	0	0
600	610	52	41	31	24	17	10	3	0	0	0	0
610	620	53	42	32	25	18	11	4	0	0	0	0
620	630	55	44	33	26	19	12	5	0	0	0	0
630	640	56	45	35	27	20	13	6	0	0	0	0
640	650	58	47	36	28	21	14	7	0	0	0	0
1,050	1,060	119	108	98	87	76	66	55	44	34	26	19
1,060	1,070	121	110	99	89	78	67	57	46	35	27	20
1,070	1,080	122	111	101	90	79	69	58	47	37	28	21
1,080	1,090	124	113	102	92	81	70	60	49	38	29	22
1,090	1,100	125	114	104	93	82	72	61	50	40	30	23
1,100	1,110	127	116	105	95	84	73	63	52	41	31	24
1,110	1,120	128	117	107	96	85	75	64	53	43	32	25
1,120	1,130	130	119	108	98	87	76	66	55	44	34	26
1,130	1,140	131	120	110	99	88	78	67	56	46	35	27
1,140	1,150	133	122	111	101	90	79	69	58	47	37	28
1,250	1,260	149	138	128	117	106	96	85	74	64	53	42
1,260	1,270	151	140	129	119	108	97	87	76	65	55	44
1,270	1,280	152	141	131	120	109	99	88	77	67	56	45
1,280	1,290	154	143	132	122	111	100	90	79	68	58	47
1,290	1,300	155	144	134	123	112	102	91	80	70	59	48
1,300	1,310	157	146	135	125	114	103	93	82	71	61	50
1,310	1,320	158	147	137	126	115	105	94	83	73	62	51
1,320	1,330	160	149	138	128	117	106	96	85	74	64	53
1,330	1,340	161	150	140	129	118	108	97	86	76	65	54
1,340	1,350	163	152	141	131	120	109	99	88	77	67	56
1,350	1,360	164	153	143	132	121	111	100	89	79	68	57
1,360	1,370	166	155	144	134	123	112	102	91	80	70	59
1,370	1,380	167	156	146	135	124	114	103	92	82	71	60
1,380	1,390	169	158	147	137	126	115	105	94	83	73	62
1,390	1,400	170	159	149	138	127	117	106	95	85	74	63

Source: Department of the Treasury, Internal Revenue Service

Figure 2-3. Married Persons Federal Withholding Table

Example 2-1A

See It

Chloe works as a medical transcriptionist. She earns $644.80 per week. Chloe is single and claims two withholding allowances—one for her and one for her child. Determine the amount of federal income tax that will be withheld from Chloe's weekly paycheck.

Strategy

Use the appropriate tax table in Figure 2-2 or 2-3.

Solution

Step 1: Determine the row that shows Chloe's weekly wages. Read down the columns on the left until you find the row that includes Chloe's weekly wages of $644.80. The amount, $644.80, is between $640 and $650.

Step 2: Determine the column containing the number of Chloe's withholding allowances, which is two.

Step 3: The cell where the row and column intersect shows the amount of money that will be withheld from Chloe's weekly paycheck.

$61 will be withheld each week from Chloe's paycheck for federal income taxes

Check It

Brandon works as an animal trainer, training service dogs for people with disabilities. He earns $625.27 per week. Brandon is single and claims one withholding allowance. What is the amount of federal income tax that will be withheld from Brandon's weekly paycheck?

Social Security and Medicare Deductions

Employers are required to deduct a percentage of employee income for Social Security and Medicare. **Social Security taxes** pay for retirement and disability benefits. **Medicare** provides health insurance for people over 65 years of age. This program also covers individuals with certain disabilities. Together, these taxes are known as FICA taxes. FICA stands for the *Federal Insurance Contributions Act*.

FICA taxes are a percentage of the employee's gross pay that is withheld from each paycheck. The employer withholds 6.2% from each paycheck for Social Security tax. The amount earned over $106,800 is not subject to Social Security tax. This is often called the *Social Security cap*. For example, if someone earns $183,085 per year, Social Security tax is deducted for the first seven months of the year. What that person earns for the remainder of the year does not have Social Security tax deducted from it.

Social Security tax = gross pay × tax rate

The Social Security tax is shared by the employee and the employer. The employer pays a matching amount of Social Security taxes for each employee. Therefore, the employer will also pay 6.2% of the employee's gross pay.

Career Discovery
Government & Public Administration
Careers and Math Skills

Government and public administrations career areas involve working in a governmental position or on issues related to government matters. Seven pathways make up this cluster. These pathways include government, national security, foreign service, planning, revenue and taxation, regulation, and public management and administration. Places of work range from nonprofit organizations to overseas locations or local, state, or federal governments.

Budgets are a big part of many public administration positions. How would having a strong understanding of finance help those seeking a career in government or public administration?

Example 2-1B

See It

Determine the amount of Social Security tax that will be withheld from Chloe's weekly paycheck. Recall she earns $644.80 per week.

Strategy

Use the formula:

Social Security tax = gross pay × tax rate

Solution

Step 1: Identify Chloe's gross pay and the Social Security tax rate.

gross pay = $644.80 per week

Social Security tax rate = 6.2%

Step 2: Convert the tax rate from a percentage to a decimal by moving the decimal two places to the left.

6.2% → 0.062

Step 3: Multiply Chloe's gross pay by the Social Security tax rate. Round to the nearest cent ($0.01) if necessary.

Social Security tax = gross pay × tax rate

Social Security tax = $644.80 × 0.062

Social Security tax = $39.98

Check It

Maria is a teller at a bank. She is paid biweekly, and her gross pay for each paycheck is $1,006.15. Determine the amount of Social Security tax that will be withheld from Maria's paycheck.

Answer:
$62.38

Medicare taxes are withheld in addition to Social Security taxes. The employee pays 1.45% of total earnings in Medicare taxes. However, unlike Social Security taxes, there is no cap on earnings subject to Medicare taxes. All of an employee's earnings, regardless of the amount, are subject to Medicare taxes.

Medicare tax = gross pay × tax rate

Like Social Security taxes, the employer pays a matching amount in Medicare tax on the employee's earnings.

Example 2-1C

See It

For Chloe's weekly earnings of $644.80, determine the amount of Medicare tax that will be withheld from her weekly paycheck.

Strategy

Use the formula:

Medicare tax = gross pay × tax rate

Solution

Step 1: Identify Chloe's gross pay and the Medicare tax rate.

gross pay = $644.80 per week

Medicare tax rate = 1.45%

Step 2: Convert the tax rate from a percentage to a decimal by moving the decimal two places to the left.

1.45% → 0.0145

Step 3: Multiply Chloe's gross pay by the Medicare tax rate. Round to the nearest cent ($0.01) if necessary.

Medicare tax = gross pay × tax rate

Medicare tax = $644.80 × 0.0145

Medicare tax = $9.35

Check It

Daniel is an aviation technician earning $2,168.75 semimonthly. Determine the amount of Medicare tax that will be withheld from each of his paychecks.

> Teaching Tip:
> Review with students how to use their calculators for multi-step calculations.

> Answer:
> $31.45

State and City Income Taxes

Most states, and even some cities, impose their own income taxes. Of the states that have an income tax, most use a progressive tax. Recall that a progressive tax means the rate rises as income level increases.

Currently, seven states have a ***flat-rate tax,*** or *flat tax,* meaning all employees pay the same percentage regardless of income level. Seven other states have no personal state income tax.

Calculating a flat tax is very straightforward. The taxable income is simply multiplied by the flat tax rate to get the amount of tax due. Remember from earlier in this chapter that taxable income is the portion of your income that is

Employees who commute to a state or city that has established income taxes typically must pay the taxes on the money earned in that state or city, regardless of where the employee lives.

Teaching Tip:
Explain to students how the state income tax works in your state. What is the current rate?

subject to taxation. States usually base their income taxes on the taxable income calculated for federal taxes. States with a flat income tax generally tax income at rates between 3% and 5%.

$$\text{state income tax} = \text{gross pay} \times \text{tax rate}$$

Example 2-1D

See It

Chloe lives in a state that has a 4% flat-rate tax. Based on her weekly earnings of $644.80, determine the amount of state income tax that will be withheld from her weekly paycheck.

Strategy

Use the formula:

$$\text{state income tax} = \text{gross pay} \times \text{tax rate}$$

Solution

Step 1: Identify Chloe's gross pay and the state income tax rate.

gross pay = $644.80 per week

state income tax rate = 4%

Step 2: Convert the tax rate from a percentage to a decimal by moving the decimal two places to the left.

4% → 0.04

Step 3: Multiply Chloe's gross pay by the state income tax rate. Round to the nearest cent ($0.01) if necessary.

state income tax = gross pay × tax rate

state income tax = $644.80 × 0.04

state income tax = $25.79

Check It

Desmond lives in a state that has a flat-rate state income tax of 4.35%. He works as a train engineer, earning $794.40 per week. What is the amount of state income tax that will be withheld from his paycheck?

Answer:
$34.56

A progressive state income tax is often based on a table similar to the one shown in Figure 2-4. As each income range increases, the percentage of tax also increases.

Taxable income is over...	But not over...	Tax is...
$0	$6,000	1% of taxable income
$6,000	$18,000	$60 plus 2% of taxable income over $6,000
$18,000	$24,000	$300 plus 3% of taxable income over $18,000
$24,000	$36,000	$480 plus 4% of taxable income over $24,000
$36,000	$48,000	$960 plus 6% of taxable income over $36,000
$48,000	No limit	$1,680 plus 8% of taxable income over $48,000

Figure 2-4. Progressive Tax Table

Example 2-1E

See It

Cassandra lives in a state that has a state income tax and uses a progressive tax rate as shown in the table. She works as a crane operator and her annual taxable income is $43,350.52. Use the table to determine Cassandra's state income tax.

Strategy

Use the tax table shown in Figure 2-4.

Solution

Step 1: Use the table to determine which row contains the range in which Cassandra's income falls.

$43,350.52 falls between $36,000 and $48,000.

In other words, $36,000 < $43,350.52 < $48,000.

Step 2: Use the formula given in the table for Cassandra's income range.

$960 plus 6% of taxable income over $36,000

Step 3: Determine the amount of taxable income over $36,000 by subtracting $36,000 from Cassandra's total annual income.

taxable income over $36,000 = annual taxable income − $36,000

taxable income over $36,000 = $43,350.52 − $36,000

taxable income over $36,000 = $7,350.52

Step 4: Convert the tax rate from a percentage to a decimal by moving the decimal two places to the left.

6% → 0.06

Teaching Tip:
Remind students of the meaning of the greater than (>) and less than (<) signs.

Step 5: Determine the amount of tax due on the taxable income over $36,000.

partial tax due = 0.06 × taxable income over $36,000

partial tax due = 0.06 × $7,350.52

partial tax due = $441.03

Step 6: Determine the total state income tax by adding the tax due to the base rate in the formula.

total state income tax = $960 + partial tax due

total state income tax = $960 + $441.03

total state income tax = $1,401.03

Check It

Answer:
$959.20

Cassandra's neighbor, Fernando, is a photographer who earns an annual gross pay of $35,980. What is Fernando's total flat-rate state income tax?

Net Pay

Teaching Tip:
Project or otherwise display Figure 2-5, pointing out the area on the stub that indicates net pay.

Net pay is the final calculated amount of a paycheck after federal taxes, FICA taxes, and state taxes are withheld. Net pay is sometimes called *take-home pay,* because it is the portion of your earnings that you can take home. Figure 2-5 is an example of a paycheck stub, which is also known as an *earnings statement.*

Use the following formula to calculate net pay:

net pay = gross pay – (federal tax withholdings + Social Security tax + Medicare tax + state income tax withholdings)

Employee:	Joe Park 225 West Second Street Frankfort, KY 40601-0225		**Date:** 6/24/--	Jake's Skateboards 82 Hudson Hollow Road Frankfort, KY 40601-0082	
Gross Pay $345.00	**Fed. Income Tax Withheld** $18.06	**State Income Tax Withheld** $13.80	**FICA Tax Withheld** $21.39	**Medicare Tax Withheld** $5.00	**Net Pay** $286.75
Gross Pay Year-to-Date $8,484.50	**Federal Year-to-Date** $444.16	**State Year-to-Date** $339.38	**FICA Year-to-Date** $526.04	**Medicare Year-to-Date** $123.03	**Net Pay Year-to-Date** $7,051.89

Figure 2-5. Paycheck Stub

Example 2-1F

See It

You remember that Chloe earns $644.80 per week. She is single and claims two withholding allowances. Chloe also lives in a state with a 4% flat-rate state income tax. Use this information, along with the Social Security tax rate of 6.2% and Medicare tax rate of 1.45%, to calculate Chloe's net pay in one paycheck.

Strategy

Use the formula:

net pay = gross pay − (federal tax withholdings + Social Security tax + Medicare tax + state income tax withholdings)

Solution

Step 1: Identify Chloe's gross pay and her taxes and withholdings. Use your previous work to save time.

gross pay = $644.80 per week

federal tax withholdings = $61

Social Security tax = $39.98

Medicare tax = $9.35

state income tax = $25.79

Step 2: Determine the total amount of Chloe's taxes and withholdings.

total withholdings = federal tax withholdings + Social Security tax + Medicare tax + state income tax withholdings

total withholdings = $61 + $39.98 + $9.35 + $25.79

total withholdings = $136.12

Step 3: Determine Chloe's net pay by subtracting her total withholdings from her gross pay.

net pay = gross pay − total withholdings

net pay = $644.80 − $136.12

net pay = $508.68

Check It

Brandon works as an animal trainer who trains service dogs for people with disabilities. Recall that Brandon earns $625.27 per week. He is single and claims one withholding allowance. His state has a flat-rate state income tax of 4.63%. Calculate Brandon's net pay. Use your previous work to save time.

Teaching Tip:
To help students better understand the arithmetic involved, show them the sums to be added in Step 2 vertically.

Answer:
$533.52

Answer:
1. federal tax withholdings = $81
   Social Security tax = $44
   Medicare tax = $10.29
2. federal tax withholdings = $90
   Social Security tax = $56.16
   Medicare tax = $13.13
3. federal tax withholdings = $93
   Social Security tax = $68.12
   Medicare tax = $15.93
4. $235.74
5. $522.57

Checkpoint 2.1

Use the tax tables shown in Figures 2-2 and 2-3 for the following exercises. Use 6.2% as the Social Security tax rate and 1.45% as the Medicare tax rate.

1. Thomas is a police dispatcher who earns $709.62 per week. He is single and claims one withholding allowance. Determine his federal tax withholdings, Social Security tax, and Medicare tax.

2. Britney is a private detective who earns $905.77 per week. She is single and claims three withholding allowances. Determine her federal tax withholdings, Social Security tax, and Medicare tax.

3. Jesus is an anthropologist who earns $1,098.75 per week. He is married and claims three withholding allowances. Determine his federal tax withholdings, Social Security tax, and Medicare tax.

4. Annika works as an optometrist. She earns $4,447.92 semimonthly. She lives in a state with a flat-rate state income tax of 5.3%. Determine the amount of state income tax that is withheld from each of Annika's paychecks.

5. Aziz works as a bookkeeper and earns $685 weekly. He is single, claims zero withholdings, and lives in a state with a flat-rate state income tax of 3.07%. Determine Aziz's net pay.

Section 2.2 Benefits

Objectives

- **Identify typical employee benefits.**
- **Describe how to calculate other important employee benefits.**
- **Determine the value of a job offer by calculating employee benefits.**

Terms

- *employee benefits*
- *fringe benefits*
- *pre-tax deduction*
- *stipend*
- *job expense*

Build Your Math Skills

Review these math skills to prepare for the lesson that follows.

1. Change percentages to decimals by moving the decimal two places to the left. Example: 8% → 0.08

A. 12% →

B. 4% →

C. 5.3% →

D. 4.35% →

2. Multiply decimals. Round your answers to the nearest cent ($0.01). Example: $13.25 \times 1.25 = \$16.5625 \approx \$16.56$

A. $125 \times 0.12 =$

B. $36,000 \times 0.04 =$

C. $235.55 \times 0.075 =$

D. $512.50 \times 0.11 =$

3. Add and subtract decimals. Example: $180.05 + \$75.65 - \$55.30 = \$255.70 - \$55.30 = \$200.40$

A. $247.84 + \$72.48 =$

B. $780 - \$122.78 =$

C. $78.66 + \$45.62 - \$18.44 =$

D. $193.48 + \$50 - \$29.95 =$

Answer:
1. A. 0.12
   B. 0.04
   C. 0.053
   D. 0.0435
2. A. $15
   B. $1,440
   C. $17.67
   D. $56.38
3. A. $320.32
   B. $657.22
   C. $105.84
   D. $213.53

Employee Benefits

Many employers offer insurance, retirement plans, paid time off, and other employee benefits. *Employee benefits* are anything of value that is offered or provided to employees in addition to wages. Common employee benefits include health insurance, sick leave, and vacation time. Benefits may also include things like a company-owned automobile, a health club membership, and continuing education. Employers can offer practically anything as an employee benefit. Another term used to describe these benefits is *fringe benefits.*

Not all employers offer their employees the same benefits. However, many benefits are generally accepted as standard for full-time employees:

- health insurance
- vision insurance
- dental insurance
- life insurance
- disability insurance

fyi

Insurance is a product that provides financial protection against a specific loss. In exchange for protection, the insurance company is paid a *premium*. A premium is the customer's cost for this protection.

- unemployment insurance
- paid time off/ vacation time
- retirement plan

Benefits offered by employers can vary widely. Small companies may offer little or no employee benefits. Larger companies may offer standard benefits, or they may offer many less common benefits. For example, in addition to insurance and time off, some companies offer employees dining facilities, gyms, on-site doctors, dry cleaning, and more.

Pre-Tax Deductions

Some benefits are paid for by the employer. Other benefits are offered as an option by the employer but must be paid for by the employee. These are pre-tax deductions. *Pre-tax deductions* are payments employees make for the cost of benefits. For example, an employer may negotiate a dental insurance plan for its employees. However, should the employee wish to have dental insurance, the employee authorizes that money be withheld from his or her check to pay for that insurance. Other employers may choose to pay for employee dental insurance, in which case no money would be withheld for dental coverage. Sometimes, the employer and employee share the cost of insurance.

Often, an employee has the option to add dependents, such as a spouse or children, to certain benefit plans. For example, it is common for an employee to add dependents to a health, vision, or dental insurance plan. With most employers, the cost of adding dependents is at least partially paid by the employee. The cost of adding those dependents is withheld from the employee's paycheck and used to pay the insurance premiums for the dependents.

As you learned earlier in this chapter, taxes are withheld from earnings when you receive your paycheck. Some deductions from pay occur before taxes are calculated and others are deducted after taxes are calculated. So what difference does that make? Well, if the money is withheld before taxes are calculated, then that money is not taxed. In other words, an employee's taxable income is reduced by the amount withheld before taxes. For example, assume an employee is paying $400 per month to add his or her children to an employer's health insurance plan. That adds up to $4,800 annually. If that money is deducted before taxes, the employee is likely to have to pay less in taxes. To calculate the tax savings, use the following formula:

$$\textbf{tax savings} = \textbf{premium} \times \textbf{tax rate}$$

Example 2-2A

See It

Nita works as an economics professor at a university. She earns $7,740 every month. She carries health insurance for herself and her two children. The total premium for each month is $535.25. At this income level, Nita's federal tax rate is 25%. Calculate the amount of tax savings Nita will have if she has her health insurance premiums withheld from her paycheck before her taxes are calculated.

Strategy

Use the formula:

$$\textbf{tax savings} = \textbf{premium} \times \textbf{tax rate}$$

Solution

Step 1: Determine Nita's monthly premium and the tax rate.

premium: $535.25

tax rate: 25%

Step 2: Convert the tax rate from a percentage to a decimal by moving the decimal two places to the left.

25% → 0.25

Step 3: Multiply the premium by the tax rate.

tax savings = premium × tax rate

tax savings = $535.25 × 0.25

tax savings = $133.81

Check It

Omar is a loan officer at a local bank. He carries health insurance for himself, his wife, and their three children. The monthly premium for health insurance that is deducted from his paycheck is $660.72. Omar's salary places him in the 15% federal income tax rate. Calculate the amount of tax savings Omar will have if his health insurance premiums are withheld from his paycheck before his taxes are calculated.

Answer:
$99.11

Other Benefits

Most benefits have a measurable value. For example, if your employer provides health insurance for you, the value of that benefit could be measured by finding out what such a plan would cost if you purchased it on your own. Other benefits are easier to value. For example, your employer provides a $40 monthly cell phone allowance. That is the equivalent of receiving an additional $480 per year. Sometimes, employees receive extra pay in the form of a stipend. A *stipend* is usually paid for taking on additional work duties or for completing work-related classes.

Source: Shutterstock (iofoto)

You will see deductions from your paycheck, such as federal income tax.

If the job is hourly, or has overtime or commission as a component, you may have to estimate the gross pay. You could also use monthly values and monthly gross pay to arrive at a total monthly value of the job.

When assessing a job offer, you should consider the value of the benefits. Add that to the gross pay to determine the total value of the job. First, add up the total value of all benefits:

total annual employee benefits = benefit one + benefit two + benefit three

Then, add the total benefits to the gross pay to get the total job value:

total annual value of job = annual gross pay + total annual employee benefits

Example 2-2B

See It

Jazmin has a job as a hostess at a local restaurant. She earns $8.78 per hour and usually works about 80 hours per month. Jazmin also receives a monthly allowance of $35 for her work uniform. She is responsible for cleaning her uniform and ordering new uniforms as necessary. What is the total annual value of Jazmin's job?

Strategy

Use the formula:

total annual value of job = annual gross pay + total annual employee benefits

Solution

Step 1: Determine Jazmin's approximate monthly gross pay. Multiply her hourly wage by the number of hours she works in a month.

monthly gross pay = hourly wage × number of hours per month

monthly gross pay = $8.78 per hour × 80 hours

monthly gross pay = $702.40

Step 2: Determine Jazmin's approximate annual gross pay. Multiply her monthly gross pay by 12 (the number of months in a year).

annual gross pay = monthly gross pay × 12

annual gross pay = $702.40 × 12

annual gross pay = $8,428.80

Step 3: Determine the annual value of Jazmin's uniform allowance. Multiply the monthly allowance by 12 (the number of months in a year).

annual uniform allowance = monthly uniform allowance × 12

annual uniform allowance = $35 × 12

annual uniform allowance = $420

Step 4: Determine the total annual value of Jazmin's job. Add her annual gross pay and her annual uniform allowance.

total annual value of job = annual gross pay + annual uniform allowance

total annual value of job = $8,428.80 + $420

total annual value of job = $8,848.80

Check It

Arturo is a curator at a local historical museum. He earns an annual salary of $53,160. Each month, he also receives $35 for a cell phone and $75 for travel. Determine the total annual value of Arturo's job.

Job expenses must also be considered when valuing a job offer. ***Job expenses*** are any costs an employee has to pay because of the job he or she was hired to do. For example, you may be required to purchase a uniform. Or you may be required to provide your own tools. You may have union dues. You may have parking expenses. Even the cost of commuting to and from work is a job expense.

You should subtract job expenses to get the true value of the job offer:

annual value of job = annual gross pay + total annual employee benefits – job expenses

Answer:
$54,480

A stipend is another way someone can be paid. A *stipend* is an allowance to defray costs.

Example 2-2C

See It

Melissa is an auditor for a bank. She earns an annual salary of $68,960. Because her job requires her to travel to the different branches of the bank, she also receives a $90 monthly travel allowance. In addition, she receives a $45 monthly allowance for a cell phone. Melissa also belongs to her professional labor union and pays monthly dues of $23.50. Determine the annual value of Melissa's job.

Strategy

Use the formula:

annual value of job = annual gross pay + total annual employee benefits – job expenses

Solution

Step 1: Determine Melissa's total monthly benefits. Add together her monthly travel allowance and her monthly cell phone allowance.

total monthly benefits = monthly travel allowance + monthly cell phone allowance

total monthly benefits = $90 + $45

total monthly benefits = $135

Step 2: Determine Melissa's total annual benefits. Multiply her total monthly benefits by 12 (the number of months in a year).

total annual benefits = total monthly benefits $\times$ 12

total annual benefits = $135 $\times$ 12

total annual benefits = $1,620

Step 3: Determine Melissa's total annual job expenses. Multiply her total monthly expenses by 12 (the number of months in a year).

job expenses = total monthly expenses $\times$ 12

job expenses = $23.50 $\times$ 12

job expenses = $282

Step 4: Determine Melissa's annual job value. Add her annual gross pay and total annual benefits. Then, subtract her total annual job expenses.

annual value of job = annual gross pay + total annual benefits – job expenses

annual value of job = $68,960 + $1,620 – $282

annual value of job = $70,298

Check It

Benjamin is a plumber who earns $28.92 per hour. His annual gross pay is typically $60,160. Because he must travel for his job, his company gives him a monthly travel allowance of $110. He also receives a $15 monthly cell phone allowance. Benjamin also pays union dues in the amount of $32.15 a month. In addition, he also must pay $28 per month for shop tools and supplies. Determine the annual value of Benjamin's job.

Checkpoint 2.2

1. Carmen is a diver for the local police department. She purchases health insurance and dental insurance for herself and her husband. Her total monthly premiums are $478.63. Carmen's federal income tax rate is 15%. Determine Carmen's monthly tax savings by having her insurance premiums withheld before taxes are calculated.

2. Joaquin is a materials engineer. He purchases health, dental, and vision insurance through his employer. His monthly premiums are: $78.55 for health insurance, $24.17 for dental insurance, and $18.85 for vision insurance. Joaquin's federal income tax rate is 28%. Determine his monthly tax savings by having his insurance premiums withheld before taxes are calculated.

3. Johanna is a watchmaker with a base annual salary of $38,960. She receives a monthly travel allowance of $85 because she travels between different stores that her employer owns. She also receives an annual stipend of $500 because she recently completed an advanced certification course. Calculate the total annual value of Johanna's job.

4. Bernice is a meeting planner who earns an annual base salary of $53,300. She receives a cell phone allowance of $17.50 per month. Bernice also has her professional organization membership dues of $8.35 per month deducted from her paycheck. What is the annual value of Bernice's job?

5. Tommy is an insurance claims adjuster who earns an annual base salary of $60,200. He also receives a cell phone allowance of $23 per month. Tommy must pay for parking at his office building, which costs $68.50 per month. What is the annual value of Tommy's job?

Section 2.3 Analyzing Pay

Terms
- *monetary value*
- *raise*

Objectives
- **Analyze the value of a job based on monetary value.**
- **Describe the value of receiving a raise in pay.**

Build Your Math Skills

Review these math skills to prepare for the lesson that follows.

1. Change percentages to decimals by moving the decimal two places to the left. Example: 7.5% → 0.075

A. 6% →

B. 28% →

C. 2.9% →

D. 16.2% →

2. Calculate percentages of numbers. Round your answers to the nearest cent ($0.01). Example: 6% of $1,200 = 0.06 × $1,200 = $72

A. 3% of $28,500 =

B. 6.5% of $17,000 =

C. 8% of $52,300 =

D. 15% of $22,715 =

Answer:
1. A. 0.06
   B. 0.28
   C. 0.029
   D. 0.162
2. A. $855
   B. $1,105
   C. $4,184
   D. $3,407.25

Comparing Jobs

In the previous section, you calculated the value of a job. However, these calculations only considered the monetary value of the job. *Monetary value* describes what something is worth in money alone. For example, the monetary value of a house is the amount of money for which you can sell the house. The monetary value of a job is an important consideration when comparing jobs. To compare the monetary value of two different jobs, first determine the annual value of each using the following formula:

annual value of job = annual gross pay + total annual employee benefits – job expenses

Example 2-3A

See It

Esther recently graduated with a degree in hotel and restaurant management. She has received two job offers. Job offer number one provides a base salary of $52,220 with a monthly cell phone allowance of $15 and monthly parking charges of $45. Job offer number two provides a base salary of $48,660 with a monthly cell phone allowance of $25, a monthly travel allowance of $40, and monthly parking charges of $25. Which of the two jobs has the higher monetary value?

Strategy

Use the formula:

annual value of job = annual gross pay + total annual employee benefits – job expenses

Solution

Step 1: For job offer number one, determine the total annual employee benefits. Multiply the monthly cell phone allowance by 12 (the number of months in one year).

total annual employee benefits = monthly cell phone allowance × 12

total annual employee benefits = $15 × 12

total annual employee benefits = $180

Step 2: For job offer number one, determine the total annual job expenses. Multiply the monthly parking charges by 12 (the number of months in one year).

total annual job expenses = monthly parking charges × 12

total annual job expenses = $45 × 12

total annual job expenses = $540

Step 3: For job offer number one, determine the annual job value. Add the annual gross pay to the total annual employee benefits. Then, subtract the total annual job expenses.

annual value of job = annual gross pay + total annual employee benefits – job expenses

annual value of job = ($52,220 + $180) – $540

annual value of job = $51,860

Step 4: For job offer number two, determine the total monthly employee benefits. Add the monthly cell phone allowance and the monthly travel allowance.

total monthly employee benefits = monthly cell phone allowance + monthly travel allowance

total monthly employee benefits = $25 + $40

total monthly employee benefits = $65

Step 5: For job offer number two, determine the total annual employee benefits. Multiply the total monthly employee benefits by 12 (the number of months in one year).

total annual employee benefits = total monthly employee benefits × 12

total annual employee benefits = $65 × 12

total annual employee benefits = $780

Step 6: For job offer number two, determine the total annual job expenses. Multiply the monthly parking charges by 12 (the number of months in one year).

total annual job expenses = monthly parking charges × 12

total annual job expenses = $25 × 12

total annual job expenses = $300

Step 7: For job offer number two, determine the net annual job value. Add the annual gross pay to the total annual employee benefits. Then, subtract the total annual job expenses.

net annual value of job = annual gross pay + total annual employee benefits – job expenses

net annual value of job = $48,660 + $780 – $300

net annual value of job = $49,140

Step 8: Compare the annual value of job number one to the annual value of job number two to determine which is greater.

annual value of job number one = $51,860

annual value of job number two = $49,140

$51,860 > $49,140

annual value of job number one > annual value of job number two

Job number one has a higher annual value than job number two.

Check It

Samir currently has a job as an emergency management director in Beeville. He earns an annual base salary of $62,180 along with a monthly cell phone allowance of $22 and a monthly travel allowance of $65. He has been offered a job as the emergency management director in Alicetown. It has an annual base salary of $63,700, a monthly cell phone allowance of $20, a monthly travel allowance of $60, and monthly parking charges of $35. Which job has the higher annual value?

Answer:
Alicetown

A job may have value beyond its monetary value. If the job allows you to work in an industry that you love, that adds value. If you would be working with great people, that could add value to a job. Other things that could add value are opportunity for advancement or job security.

Teaching Tip:
Ask students to make a list of nonmonetary benefits of a job.

On the other hand, a job might have negatives that lower the value of the job. For example, your supervisor could be difficult to work with. A company having financial problems could also affect the value of your job.

Some employees choose to work for less pay or fewer benefits. They choose jobs that offer values that outweigh money. For example, the job may require fewer hours of work or provide for a flexible schedule.

Getting a Raise

A *raise* is an increase in pay. For hourly employees, a raise is usually an increase in the amount earned per hour. For salaried employees, a raise is an increase in annual salary.

Raises are provided to reward employees for:

- serving with the same company for a certain length of time;

- taking on additional responsibilities; or

- doing a particularly good job.

Financial $marts

Your salary or rate of pay is a private matter. Privacy is an important topic these days. With the ease of electronic transmission of information, it is important that an individual's privacy be protected. Personal information that was previously only on paper is now in computer databases. If those records are accidentally made public or purposely transmitted by an employee entrusted with that data, there could be many negative consequences.

Reputable companies strive to protect your personal information. Always ask for privacy statements from companies with which you do business. These privacy statements put in writing the company's policy for sharing your personal information with others.

Example 2-3B

See It

Rubie works as a clerk earning $16.60 per hour. She just learned that she will receive a 3.5% raise. If Rubie works 40 hours per week, how much more will she earn per week after her raise?

Strategy

Use the formula:

amount of raise = weekly gross pay × rate of raise

Solution

Step 1: Determine Rubie's current weekly gross pay. Multiply her hourly wage by the number of hours she works per week.

weekly gross pay = hourly wage × number of hours

weekly gross pay = $16.60 per hour × 40 hours

weekly gross pay = $664

Step 2: Convert the percentage of the raise to a decimal by moving the decimal two places to the left.

3.5% → 0.035

Step 3: Determine the amount of the raise. Multiply Rubie's weekly gross pay by the decimal equivalent of the rate of the raise.

amount of raise = weekly gross pay × rate of raise

amount of raise = $664 × 0.035

amount of raise = $23.24

Check It

Jackson works as a ticket clerk for a passenger rail company. He earns $16.67 per hour. After his annual performance review, Jackson will receive a 4.25% raise. If Jackson works 35 hours per week, how much more will he earn per week after the raise?

Answer:
$24.80

Based on what you have learned in this chapter, it is probably no surprise that a raise will affect your paycheck deductions. Therefore, you cannot assume that a $1,000 annual raise in salary puts an extra $1,000 in your pocket. It is important to be able to analyze the actual effect of a raise.

Most benefits are not affected by a raise. But federal withholding, FICA, and state income taxes *are* affected by a raise.

Example 2-3C

See It

Ted works as a travel guide for a mountain resort, earning $15.72 per hour. He is single and claims one withholding allowance. He works in a state with a flat-rate income tax of 4.63%. He will receive a raise of 5% of his hourly rate. Ted is paid weekly, and works 40 hours in one week. Determine the actual amount of Ted's new weekly pay rate, after taxes and withholdings.

Teaching Tip:
Project or otherwise display Figures 2-2 and 2-3 as you demonstrate the **See It** portion of Example 2-3C.

Strategy

Use the withholding tables shown in Figures 2-2 and 2-3, along with the formula:

net pay = gross pay − (federal tax withholdings + Social Security tax + Medicare tax + state income tax withholdings)

Solution

Step 1: Convert the percentage of a raise to a decimal by moving the decimal two spaces to the left.

$5\% \rightarrow 0.05$

Step 2: Determine Ted's new hourly wage after his raise. Multiply his current hourly wage by the rate of raise. Then add the raise to his current hourly wage.

new hourly wage = hourly wage × rate of raise + hourly wage

new hourly wage = $15.72 × 0.05 + $15.72

new hourly wage = $0.79 + $15.72

new hourly wage = $16.51

Step 3: Determine Ted's weekly gross pay, both before and after the raise. Multiply the hourly wage by the number of hours.

before raise:

gross pay = hourly wage × number of hours

gross pay = $15.72 per hour × 40 hours

gross pay = $628.80

after raise:

gross pay = new hourly wage × number of hours

gross pay = $16.51 per hour × 40 hours

gross pay = $660.40

Step 4: Determine the amount of federal income tax withholdings from Ted's weekly paycheck. Use the tax tables found in Figures 2-2 and 2-3. Ted is single and claims one withholding allowance.

before raise:

$628.80 is between $620 and $630

federal withholdings = $69

after raise:

$660.40 is between $660 and $670

federal withholdings = $75

Step 5: Determine the amount of Social Security tax that Ted will have withheld from his paycheck.

Multiply his gross pay by the Social Security tax rate of 6.2%, or 0.062. Round to the nearest cent ($0.01).

before raise:

Social Security tax = gross pay × tax rate

Social Security tax = $628.80 × 0.062

Social Security tax = $38.99

after raise:

Social Security tax = gross pay × tax rate

Social Security tax = $660.40 × 0.062

Social Security tax = $40.94

Step 6: Determine the amount of Medicare tax that Ted will have withheld from his paycheck. Multiply his gross pay by the Medicare tax rate of 1.45%. Round to the nearest cent ($0.01).

before raise:

Medicare tax = gross pay × tax rate

Medicare tax = $628.80 × 0.0145

Medicare tax = $9.12

after raise:

Medicare tax = gross pay × tax rate

Medicare tax = $660.40 × 0.0145

Medicare tax = $9.58

Step 7: Determine the amount of state income tax that Ted will have withheld from his paycheck. Multiply his gross pay by the state income tax rate of 4.63%. Round to the nearest cent ($0.01).

before raise:

state income tax = gross pay × tax rate

state income tax = $628.80 × 0.0463

state income tax = $29.11

after raise:

state income tax = gross pay × tax rate

state income tax = $660.40 × 0.0463

state income tax = $30.58

Step 8: Determine Ted's net pay before his raise.

net pay = gross pay − (federal tax withholdings + Social Security tax + Medicare tax + state income tax withholdings)

net pay = $628.80 − ($69 + $38.99 + $9.12 + $29.11)

net pay = $628.80 − $146.22

net pay = $482.58

Step 9: Determine Ted's net pay after his raise.

net pay = gross pay − (federal tax withholdings + Social Security tax + Medicare tax + state income tax withholdings)

net pay = $660.40 − ($75 + $40.94 + $9.58 + $30.58)

net pay = $660.40 − $156.10

net pay = $504.30

Step 10: Determine the difference in Ted's net pay. Subtract Ted's net pay before his raise from Ted's net pay after his raise.

difference in net pay = net pay after raise − net pay before raise

difference in net pay = $504.30 − $482.58

difference in net pay = $21.72

Check It

Lorraine is a historian for the history museum. She earns $26.55 per hour, is paid weekly, and works 40 hours per week. She is married and claims two withholding allowances. Lorraine lives in a state with a flat-rate income tax of 3.5%. After her annual job performance review, she learned that she will receive a 4.5% raise. Determine the change in Lorraine's net pay per paycheck.

fyi

To determine the percentage of a raise, divide the difference in net pay by the original amount of net pay prior to the raise. In Ted's case:

$$\frac{\$21.72}{\$482.58} \approx 4.5\%$$

This is the actual percentage increase in Ted's net pay, as opposed to the 5% increase in his gross pay, once withholdings and taxes are taken into account.

Answer:
$36.28

Checkpoint 2.3

1. Javier is a short-order cook in a diner. He earns $10.11 per hour. He works 80 hours per month and receives a monthly allowance of $25 for his uniforms. His friend, Alexander, is also a short-order cook in a different diner. Alexander earns $10.85 per hour and also works 80 hours per month. Alexander receives a monthly allowance of $15 for his uniforms, but has to pay labor union dues of $17.15 per month. Whose job has a higher annual value?

2. Olivia is a land surveyor who earns $56,700 annually. She receives a monthly cell phone allowance of $22.50. She spends about $55 per month out of her own pocket for fuel to drive to different work sites. She has received a job offer for an office-based position as a survey analyst. It pays an annual base salary of $62,370. However, she will need to join the municipal workers labor union with dues of $11.55 per month. She will also have to pay $45 per month to park in the city garage. Which job has the higher annual value?

3. Amir is a coal miner who earns $21.94 per hour and works 40 hours per week. His recently negotiated labor contract will give him a 6.5% raise. How much more gross pay per week will Amir have after this raise?

4. Belinda works as a pharmacy technician in a nursing home. She earns $14.10 per hour and works 40 hours per week. She just received a 4.75% raise. How much higher will Belinda's gross pay per week be because of this raise?

5. Nathaniel is an insurance underwriter. He earns $31.45 per hour, is paid weekly, and works 40 hours per week. He is married and claims four withholding allowances. Nathaniel lives in a state with a flat-rate income tax of 5.3%. He will receive a 5.25% raise. Determine the change in Nathaniel's net pay per paycheck. Use the tax tables in Figures 2-2 and 2-3 to find the federal withholding.

Answer:
1. Alexander's job, with a net annual value of $10,390.20
2. Survey analyst, with a net annual value of $61,691.40
3. $57.04
4. $26.79
5. $46.45

Chapter Review

Build Your Vocabulary

As you progress through this course, develop a personal glossary of financial literacy terms and add it to your portfolio. This will help you build your financial literacy vocabulary. Write out a definition for each of the following terms, and add it to your personal glossary.

deduction

progressive tax

withholding allowance

dependent

taxable income

Social Security tax

Medicare

FICA

flat-rate tax

net pay

employee benefits

fringe benefits

pre-tax deduction

stipend

job expense

monetary value

raise

Teamwork

Ask a parent or grandparent what they remember about the first time they were ever paid for a job. What did they do for the money? How much were they paid? Was it in cash or a paycheck? Did they save the money or spend it? Compare what you learned in your interview with a partner. Which answers were similar? Which were different? What conclusions can you draw from the two interviews about how different people and different generations deal with money? Explain what you have learned to the class.

Teaching Tip:
Help students to recall that ≈ means *approximately equal to.* This symbol is used in these instances because students are asked to round to the nearest hundredth.

Review Your Math Skills

Practice and build on the math skills that you have learned.

1. Divide money amounts. Round answers to the nearest cent ($0.01).
Example: $32,000 ÷ 8 = $4,000

A. $16,500 ÷ 44 =

B. $46,000 ÷ 16 =

C. $52,600 ÷ 26 =

D. $34,500 ÷ 52 =

2. Round decimals to the nearest hundredth (0.01). Example: 22.875 ≈ 22.88

A. 13.698 ≈

B. 35,954.439 ≈

C. 163.966 ≈

D. 1,429.7799 ≈

Answer:
1. A. $375
   B. $2,875
   C. $2,023.08
   D. $663.46
2. A. 13.70
   B. 35,954.44
   C. 163.97
   D. 1,429.78

3. Calculate percentages of numbers. **Round your answers to the nearest hundredth (.01). Example:** 6% of $1,200 = 0.06 × $1,200 = $72

A. 2% of $8,500 =   B. 7.5% of $16,000 =

C. 8% of $22,300 =   D. 14% of $22,715 =

4. Change percentages to decimals by moving the decimal two places to the left. **Example:** 12% → .12

A. 17% →   B. 3% →

C. 9.3% →   D. 8.5% →

5. Add decimals. **Example:** 36.5 + 7.35 + 72.4 = 116.25

A. 4.6 + 2.3 + 12.5 =   B. 7.3 + 8.4 + 4.6 =

C. 45.9 + 21 + 4.6 =   D. 12 + 5.3 + 1.9 =

6. Multiply decimals. **Round your answers to the nearest cent ($0.01). Example:** $34.15 × 2.5 = $85.375 ≈ $85.38

A. $86.25 × 3.25 =   B. $42.91 × 2.15 =

C. $21.45 × 1.55 =   D. $6.73 × 4.5 =

7. Add decimals. **Example:** $75.15 + $54.96 = $130.11

A. $773.49 + $27.85 =   B. $6,980 + $14.63 =

C. $68.16 + $25.90 =   D. $409.75 + $72.58 + $25.35 =

8. Add and subtract decimals. **Example:** $84.52 + $53.56 − $35.33 = $102.75

A. $457.34 + $24.87 =   B. $889 − $372.22 =

C. $37.85 + $59.60 − $31.84 =   D. $134.98 + $150 − $9.57 =

9. Change percentages to decimals by moving the decimal two places to the left. **Example:** 7.5% → .075

A. 7% →   B. 38% →

C. 66.9% →   D. 16.3% →

10. Multiply decimals. **Round your answers to the nearest cent ($0.01). Example:** $15.25 × 1.5 = $22.875 ≈ $22.88

A. $125 × 0.15 =   B. $36,000 × 0.04 =

C. $235.55 × 0.075 =   D. $245 × 0.04 =

3. A. $170
    B. $1,200
    C. $1,784
    D. $3,180.10
4. A. 0.17
    B. 0.03
    C. 0.093
    D. 0.085
5. A. 19.4
    B. 20.3
    C. 71.5
    D. 19.2
6. A. $280.31
    B. $92.26
    C. $33.25
    D. $30.29
7. A. $801.34
    B. $6,994.63
    C. $94.06
    D. $507.68
8. A. $482.21
    B. $516.78
    C. $65.61
    D. $275.41
9. A. 0.07
    B. 0.38
    C. 0.669
    D. 0.163
10. A. $18.75
    B. $1,440
    C. $17.67
    D. $9.80

Section 2.1 Calculating Taxes

Determine the federal withholding, Social Security tax, Medicare tax, and state income tax, if applicable, for each of the following individuals. Use the tax tables shown in Figures 2-2 and 2-3 for the problems in this section.

11. Lucretia, who works part-time as a substance abuse counselor, earns $18.15 per hour and works 20 hours per week. She is single and claims one withholding allowance. She lives in a state with no state income tax.

12. Luis, who works part-time as a nurse's aide in a nursing home, earns $11.90 per hour and works 28 hours per week. He is single and claims zero withholding allowances. He lives in a state with a flat-rate income tax of 3.5%.

13. Betty, who works as an animal control worker, earns $15.41 per hour and works 40 hours per week. She is married and claims two withholding allowances. She lives in a state with a flat-rate income tax of 4.35%.

Section 2.2 Benefits

14. Angela is a veterinarian who earns $7,714 per month. She pays $435 per month for health insurance for herself and her children. Her federal tax rate is 25%. How much money will Angela save by having insurance premiums withheld before taxes are calculated?

15. Sam is an agricultural inspector who earns $3,528 per month. He pays $258 per month for health insurance and $56.23 per month for vision insurance for himself and his wife. His federal tax rate is 15%. How much money will Sam save by having insurance premiums withheld before taxes are calculated?

16. Lynn works on an aircraft assembly line, earning $45,230 per year. Her employer contributes an additional $65 per month to her retirement plan, and she pays $22.78 per month in labor union dues. Determine the net annual value of Lynn's job.

Section 2.3 Analyzing Pay

17. Bianca is an electrical engineer who earns $84,770 per year. She also receives a monthly transit allowance of $75 and pays $37.43 per month in dues to her professional organization. Bianca received a job offer to work for a company that includes a base annual salary of $83,500, employer contributions to her retirement account of $125 per month, and a cell phone allowance of $35 per month. However, she will need to continue paying $37.43 per month in dues to her professional organization as well as pay an additional $55 per month in order to park in the company's parking garage. Which job has the greater net annual value?

18. Nick is a meat cutter at the local market. He earns $14.51 per hour and is getting a 5.3% pay raise. He works 40 hours per week, is married and claims two withholding allowances on his federal income taxes, and lives in a state with a flat-rate income tax of 3.07%.

    A. Determine the difference in Nick's weekly gross pay.

    B. Determine the difference in Nick's weekly net pay.

Answer:
17. Bianca's current job has a greater net annual value of $85,220.84.
18. A. $30.76
    B. $24.52

Reinforce Your Understanding

19. Peter is a bus mechanic and earns $19.64 per hour. If Peter works 40 hours per week, determine his weekly, monthly, and annual gross pay.

20. Bernadette is a bus driver for the local transit authority, and she earns a regular hourly wage of $17.08. She receives overtime pay, at 1.5 times her regular hourly wage, for any hours more than 40 hours that she works in a week. This week, Bernadette will work 48 hours. What will be her weekly gross pay?

Answer:
19. weekly gross pay = $785.60
    monthly gross pay = $3,404.27
    annual gross pay = $40,851.20
20. $888.16

Apply Your Technology Skills

Access the G-W Learning companion website for this text at www.g-wlearning.com. Download each data file for this chapter. Follow the instructions to complete financial literacy activities to practice what you have learned in this chapter.

Teaching Tip:
The Apply Your Technology Skills activities offer project-based authentic assessment opportunities.

Data File 2-1—Completing a W-4

Data File 2-2—Calculating Federal Income Taxes

Data File 2-3—Calculating State Income Taxes

Data File 2-4—Completing a Payroll

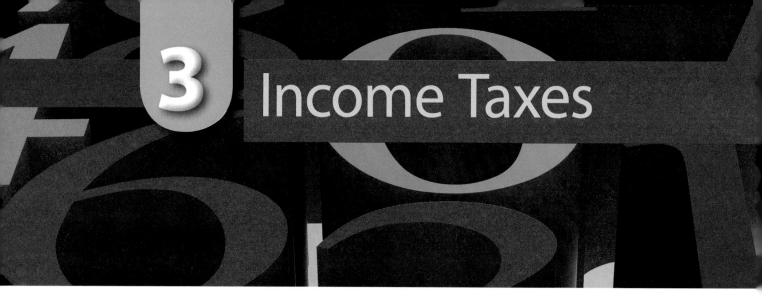

3 Income Taxes

Materials:
Instructor's Resource CD
Student Workbook
G-W Learning companion website
EXAMVIEW® Assessment Suite
Microsoft Excel®–compatible software
Calculator with advanced-math functions

In the previous chapter, you learned how taxes and other benefits affect the amount of money you take home. However, the taxes withheld from your paycheck are only an *estimate* of income tax due. In this chapter, you will learn more about income taxes and how *actual* taxes due are calculated and reported.

Section 3.1 **Federal Taxes**

Section 3.2 **Capital Gains Taxes**

Section 3.3 **Other Income Taxes**

College and Career Readiness

Reading Prep. In preparation for reading the chapter, read the 16th Amendment to the Constitution, which established the federal income tax.

"Taxes are necessary, but still frowned upon." ~ Orby M.

Money Matters
Taxes

- In ancient Greece, the tax professional was considered the noblest man in society.

- During the Civil War, the tax on a gold watch was $1.50.

- The 16th Amendment to the US Constitution established the income tax. It was ratified, or approved by all of the states, in 1913.

- Of the 160 million individual income tax returns filed in 2010, over 109 million resulted in refunds. The average refund amount was $3,003.

- In 1938, a wallet manufacturer included a sample Social Security card in their wallets to show that the card would fit. More than 5,000 purchasers of the wallet confused the sample card for their own and filed their tax returns using the Social Security number on the sample card.

- During World War I, the income tax rate in the US rose as high as 77%.

- More than 160 million individual income tax returns were filed in 2010. Over 71 million of those were filed electronically rather than on paper.

Section 3.1 Federal Taxes

Objectives

- **Explain the process of filing a tax return.**
- **Describe taxable income and calculate federal income tax.**
- **Calculate tax due and refunds.**

Terms

- *federal income tax return*
- *tax return preparer*
- *W-2 form*
- *gross income*
- *adjusted gross income*
- *IRA*
- *deduction*
- *tax deductible*
- *standard deduction*
- *exemption*

Build Your Math Skills

Review these math skills to prepare for the lesson that follows.

1. Subtract decimals. Example: $5,610 − $471.98 = $5,138.02

A. $100 − $34.15 =

B. $417.32 − $58.95 =

C. $315.78 − $93.53 =

D. $804.05 − $315.83 =

2. Add decimals. Example: $210.30 + $558.09 = $768.39

A. $571.18 + $384.57 =

B. $315.04 + $79.63 =

C. $79.16 + $217.74 =

D. $801.06 + $56.79 =

3. Use the order of operations rules to simplify these expressions. Example: $4 + 5 \times 6 \div 2 = 19$

A. $3 + 4 \times 2.5 =$

B. $45 − 3 \times 7 + 4 =$

C. $\$4,500 + 2 \times \$3,700 =$

D. $\$43,325 − 3 \times \$2,250 =$

Answer:
1. A. $65.85
   B. $358.37
   C. $222.25
   D. $488.22
2. A. $955.75
   B. $394.67
   C. $296.90
   D. $857.85
3. A. 13
   B. 28
   C. $11,900
   D. $36,575

Filing a Tax Return

Each year, individuals are required to file a report that states their income and other financial information. With this information, they can calculate the taxes that they owe to the federal government. A **federal income tax return,** often simply called a *tax return,* is a form used to file income tax with the Internal Revenue Service. The tax return is due by April 15 each year. The return reports the income received from the previous calendar year, January 1 through December 31. The government agency that manages this process is the *Internal Revenue Service (IRS).*

A *tax return* is a form that helps a person or company calculate the amount of federal income tax owed. A tax return must be submitted if income was received from any source during the year. This includes earned income and unearned income. Individuals who do not work, but receive unearned income from other places, such as child support or investments, are also required to file a tax return. In this text, assume that the taxpayer is receiving income from an employer.

Federal withholding is an estimate of taxes due. An employer withholds money from employee paychecks and sends this money to the government. When a tax return is completed, the amount of money that has already been withheld by the employer is included on the tax return. If the amount of tax

fyi

April 15 is often referred to as *tax day*.

due is greater than the federal withholding for the year, the employee owes additional tax to make up the difference. However, if the amount of federal withholding is greater than the tax due, the employee gets a refund of the amount that has been overpaid.

Tax returns can be very complicated or fairly simple. There are a number of forms for filing tax returns, as shown in Figure 3-1. Each form is for a specific type of taxpayer. If you do not have any dependents or complicated taxable income, you may be able to complete and file your own tax return.

For many individuals, however, assistance from a tax return preparer is necessary. A **tax return preparer,** or simply *tax preparer*, is any person who completes tax returns for others. Tax preparers use the information provided to them to prepare the tax return. It is important to select a qualified tax preparer, such as a CPA. A *CPA* is a certified public accountant.

However, no matter who completes the form, the taxpayer is legally responsible for what is reported on the form. The taxpayer must supply accurate, truthful information.

Taxable Income

The purpose of completing a tax return is to calculate the tax owed on income. Once the tax owed is calculated, the next step is to see if any additional tax needs to be paid. If not, the taxpayer must determine whether a refund of overpaid taxes is due.

To arrive at that conclusion, there are several steps and pieces of information required. For many taxpayers, much of this information is on a W-2 form that comes from their employer. A **W-2 form** summarizes an employee's earnings and the amounts withheld from the employee's paychecks for the year. Figure 3-2 shows a sample W-2.

A tax form requires that all income for the calendar year be reported on separate lines. These income amounts are then added to get the gross income. **Gross income** is the total earned and unearned income within a specific period of time. All wages, salaries, and commissions are included in this amount. If you have a job where you receive tips or bonuses, those are included in gross income. If you have a savings or a bank account that pays interest, the interest is also included in gross income. Profits from a business are yet another source of income.

Form	When to Use
Form 1040	Use if you cannot use the 1040A or 1040EZ. This form is for people who have high incomes and large deductions.
Form 1040A	Taxable income must be $100,000 or less with no itemized deductions.
Form 1040EZ	Used for single people with no deductions and no unearned income.

Figure 3-1.
Tax Forms

22222	a Employee's social security number 123–45–6789	OMB No. 1545-0008		
b Employer identification number (EIN) 75-1234567			**1** Wages, tips, other compensation 20,304.22	**2** Federal income tax withheld 2,137.65
c Employer's name, address, and ZIP code Main Street General Store 123 Main Street Juneau, AK 99801			**3** Social security wages 20,304.22	**4** Social security tax withheld 1,238.86
			5 Medicare wages and tips 20,304.22	**6** Medicare tax withheld 294.41
			7 Social security tips	**8** Allocated tips
d Control number 123456789			**9** Advance EIC payment	**10** Dependent care benefits
e Employee's first name and initial Last name Suff. Scott T. Ross 3456 Marine Way Juneau, AK 99803			**11** Nonqualified plans	**12a**
			13 Statutory employee Retirement plan Third-party sick pay	**12b**
			14 Other	**12c**
				12d
f Employee's address and ZIP code				
15 State Employer's state ID number	**16** State wages, tips, etc.	**17** State income tax	**18** Local wages, tips, etc.	**19** Local income tax **20** Locality name

Form **W-2** Wage and Tax Statement   20XX   Department of the Treasury—Internal Revenue Service
Copy 1—For State, City, or Local Tax Department

Figure 3-2.
W-2 Form

There are some adjustments to gross income that are allowable. ***Adjusted gross income (AGI)*** is gross income minus selected government-approved deductions. The government allows for specific deductions from gross income, such as contributions to health savings accounts and/or an IRA. An ***IRA*** is an individual retirement arrangement. To calculate adjusted gross income, use the following formula:

adjusted gross income = gross income – adjustments to gross income

Example 3-1A

See It

Sandra is a cartographer. Her gross income last year was $60,970. She also had adjustments to her income that included $4,145.50 for moving expenses, $5,000 for her IRA contribution, and $675 for her health savings account deduction. What is Sandra's adjusted gross income?

Strategy

Use the formula:

adjusted gross income = gross income – adjustments to gross income

Solution

Step 1: Determine Sandra's adjustments to gross income. Add her moving expenses, retirement savings, and her health savings account contributions.

adjustments to gross income = moving expenses + IRA contributions + health savings account contributions

adjustments to gross income = $4,145.50 + $5,000 + $675

adjustments to gross income = $9,820.50

Step 2: Subtract the adjustments to gross income from Sandra's annual gross income.

adjusted gross income = gross income – adjustments to gross income

adjusted gross income = $60,970 – $9,820.50

adjusted gross income = $51,149.50

Check It

Carlos is a landscape architect. His gross income last year was $66,880. Adjustments to Carlos' gross income include alimony expenses of $8,025.60, moving expenses of $1,183.74, and contributions to a health savings account of $1,600. What is Carlos' adjusted gross income?

Teaching Tip:
The complete solutions to the Check It problems can be found on the Instructor's Resource CD.

Answer:
$56,070.66

Next, there are deductions and exemptions to AGI. A *deduction* is an adjustment to income that comes *after* the adjusted gross income is determined. Certain expenses qualify as deductions. They reduce the amount of taxable income. For example, contributions to charity are common deductions. You have probably seen or heard a nonprofit organization point out that donations are *tax deductible*. An expense that is *tax deductible* qualifies as a deduction from AGI. Other tax-deductible expenses include:

- some medical and dental expenses,

- some types of other taxes, and

- interest paid on a mortgage loan.

These deductions are added together and are called *itemized deductions*. Deductions are listed on a separate tax form and totaled. A tax form used to show itemized deductions is called a *schedule*. The total of these deductions is subtracted from the AGI.

If you prefer not to itemize your deductions, or if you do not have many deductions, you can choose to take the standard deduction. The *standard deduction* is a fixed amount that can be claimed instead of listing individual deductions. For many people, the standard deduction is larger than the total of their itemized deductions. In that case, the standard deduction should be claimed. The standard deduction changes every year. In this text, the standard deduction for a person filing as single is $5,800 and for a married couple filing jointly is $11,600.

An *exemption* is an amount that you can claim for each person who depends on your income. Employees claim withholding allowances for their dependents. This is where those allowances come into play. For each dependent that can be claimed, a certain amount of income is exempt from tax. You can claim one exemption for yourself as long as no one else claims you as a dependent. Married couples filing jointly can claim two exemptions plus one for each child they may have. Like the standard deduction, the exemption amount can change each year. In this text, the personal exemption is $3,700.

Once the amount of deductions and number of exemptions are determined, taxable income can be calculated:

taxable income = adjusted gross income – deductions – exemptions

Example 3-1B

See It

Malcolm and Rhonda are married and have three children. They are filing a joint income tax return. Their combined adjusted gross income is $135,742.87. They plan to claim the standard deduction. What is Malcolm and Rhonda's taxable income?

Strategy

Use the formula:

taxable income = adjusted gross income – deductions – exemptions

Solution

Step 1: Determine Malcolm and Rhonda's deduction amount.

Since they are married and filing jointly, their standard deduction is $11,600.

Step 2: Determine the number of exemptions claimed by Malcolm and Rhonda.

Malcolm and Rhonda can claim two exemptions for themselves and one exemption for each of their three children.

They may claim a total of 2 + 1 + 1 + 1, or 5 exemptions.

Step 3: Determine the exemption amount. Multiply the personal exemption by the number of exemptions claimed.

exemption amount = personal exemption × number of exemptions

exemption amount = $3,700 × 5

exemption amount = $18,500

Step 4: Subtract the deductions and exemption amount from the adjusted gross income.

taxable income = adjusted gross income – deductions – exemptions

taxable income = $135,742.87 – $11,600 – $18,500

taxable income = $105,642.87

Teaching Tip:
Whenever students are asked to find the sum of more than two numbers, have them set the equation vertically, especially when decimals are involved.

Check It

Hasan is a college student with a part-time job in a restaurant. His parents do not claim him as a dependent. He is single and has no children. Last year, Hasan's adjusted gross income was $9,980.78. He will claim the standard deduction rather than itemize his deductions. What is Hasan's taxable income?

Each person who files a tax return must also determine his or her *filing status*. A person's filing status affects the amount of tax paid on taxable income. The options for filing status are listed in Figure 3-3.

Employers who hire teens must follow US Department of Labor laws. The Fair Labor Standards Act states that teens who are 14 or 15 years old are permitted to work three hours a day and 18 hours a week when school is in session. During weeks when school is not in session, teens can work a full eight-hour day and 40 hours a week. There are no limits for teens who are 16 and older.

Each status may carry a different standard deduction and different tax rates. For example, a single parent may qualify for head of household status. Filing as head of household will reduce the tax due, as compared to filing as single. For married people, the advantage of filing separately or jointly varies based on individual circumstances.

Tax Due and Refunds

Once taxable income is determined, the tax due can be calculated. If taxable income is less than $100,000, a tax table is used to look up the tax due. Figure 3-4 is a partial tax table with only a few select income ranges represented. For income over $100,000, the income is multiplied by a particular percentage to calculate tax due. An actual tax table is many pages long and is updated each year. Compare the tax due to the amount withheld from your pay using the following formula:

amount of taxes owed or refund = tax due – total withholdings

This will tell if you owe additional tax or whether you have paid in more than what is due. If the total withholding for federal income tax exceeds the tax due, a refund of the difference is paid to the taxpayer.

Filing Status	Description
Single	For unmarried people who do not qualify for head of household filing status.
Married Filing Separately	For married people who intend to file separate tax returns.
Married Filing Jointly	For married people who intend to file one tax return including the income and deductions of both individuals.
Head of Household	For unmarried people who can claim a dependent and have cared for a dependent for more than half a year.

Figure 3-3.
Filing Status

If taxable income is...		And you are...			
at least:	but less than:	single:	married filing jointly:	married filing separately:	head of household:
$5,000	$5,050	$503	$503	$503	$503
5,050	5,100	508	508	508	508
17,400	17,450	2,189	1,764	2,189	2,006
17,450	17,500	2,196	1,771	2,196	2,014
17,500	17,550	2,204	1,779	2,204	2,021
24,300	24,350	3,224	2,799	3,224	3,041
24,350	24,400	3,231	2,806	3,231	3,049
24,400	24,450	3,239	2,814	3,239	3,056
36,800	36,850	5,331	4,674	5,331	4,916
36,850	36,900	5,344	4,681	5,344	4,924
36,900	36,950	5,356	4,689	5,356	4,931
42,200	42,250	6,681	5,484	6,681	5,726
42,250	42,300	6,694	5,491	6,694	5,734
42,300	42,350	6,706	5,499	6,706	5,741
79,600	79,650	16,031	12,156	16,330	14,674
79,650	79,700	16,044	12,169	16,344	14,686
79,700	79,750	16,056	12,181	16,358	14,699
99,800	99,850	21,568	17,206	21,986	19,724
99,850	99,900	21,582	17,219	22,000	19,736
99,900	99,950	21,596	17,231	22,014	19,749
99,950	100,000	21,610	17,244	22,028	19,761

Figure 3-4.
Tax Table

Example 3-1C

See It

Jeremiah is an animal scientist. Last year his taxable income was $36,866. He is single, and his total federal tax withholdings for the year were $5,913. Determine whether Jeremiah owes additional taxes or will receive a tax refund. Calculate the amount that he owes or will be refunded.

Strategy

Use the tax table shown in Figure 3-4 and the formula:

amount of taxes owed or refund = tax due – total withholdings

Solution

Step 1: Use the tax table to determine Jeremiah's tax due. Find the row containing his taxable income. Read across to the *single* column.

Jeremiah's tax due is $5,344.

fyi

Some people confuse the term return and refund because they sound similar. Remember, the *return* is the report you send to the government. The *refund* is the money you get back if you have overpaid in federal withholding.

Step 2: Determine whether Jeremiah owes additional taxes or will receive a tax refund. Compare Jeremiah's tax due with his total withholdings.

tax due = $5,344   total withholdings = $5,913

$5,344 < $5,913

Since the tax due is less than the total withholdings, Jeremiah will receive a tax refund.

Step 3: Determine the amount of Jeremiah's tax refund. Subtract the tax due from the total withholdings.

amount of refund = total withholdings – tax due

amount of refund = $5,913 – $5,344

amount of refund = $569

Jeremiah will receive a tax refund of $569.

Check It

Tonya and Nicholas are married and filing jointly. Their combined taxable income is $79,649. Tonya had $5,873 in federal taxes withheld from her paycheck. Nicholas had $5,913 withheld from his paycheck. Determine whether Tonya and Nicholas owe additional taxes or will receive a tax refund. Calculate the amount that they owe or will be refunded.

Checkpoint 3.1

1. Eva is an agronomist for the local farm bureau. Last year, her gross income was $62,600. Adjustments to her income include an IRA contribution of $4,115, a student loan interest deduction of $556.72, and moving expenses of $3,323.65. What was Eva's adjusted gross income?

2. Jackie is a museum curator. Last year, her gross income was $53,160. Adjustments to her income include moving expenses of $5,847.60, student loan interest of $1,008.72, and a contribution to a health savings account of $750. What was Jackie's adjusted gross income?

3. Trish and Miguel are married and have two children. Their combined adjusted gross income for last year was $61,593. They will claim the standard deduction. Determine their taxable income.

4. Ming is single and had a taxable income last year of $17,548. Her total withholdings were $2,665. Determine whether Ming owes additional taxes or will receive a tax refund. Calculate the amount that she owes or will be refunded.

5. Ethan and Isadora are married, filing jointly, and their combined taxable income is $99,861. Ethan had $9,047 withheld from his paycheck. Isadora had $7,116 withheld from her paycheck. Determine whether Ethan and Isadora owe additional taxes or will receive a tax refund. Calculate the amount that they owe or will be refunded.

Section 3.2 Capital Gains Taxes

Objectives

- **Explain the concept of the capital gains tax.**
- **Describe how to calculate simple capital gains taxes.**
- **Explain how to calculate capital losses.**

Terms

- *capital gain*
- *asset*
- *capital asset*
- *long-term capital gain*
- *ordinary income*
- *short-term capital gain*
- *capital loss*
- *investment*

Build Your Math Skills

Review these math skills to prepare for the lesson that follows.

1. Add and subtract decimals. Example: $5,610 – ($471.98 + $71.04) = $5,066.98

A. $1,017 – $412.43 =

B. $58.76 + $104.45 =

C. $44,215 – ($5,019 + $3,229) =

D. $27,019 – ($454.13 + $798.10) =

2. Change percentages to decimals by moving the decimal two places to the left. Example: 15% → .15

A. 28% →

B. 6.75% →

C. 5.9% →

D. 12% →

3. Multiply decimals. Round your answers to the nearest cent ($0.01). Example: $13.10 × 0.15 = $1.965 ≈ $1.97

A. $1,513.40 × 0.15 =

B. $3,781.19 × 2.5 =

C. $79.16 × 4 =

D. $1,507 × 0.062 =

4. Subtract whole numbers, where the answer may be a negative integer. Example: $524 – $830 = –$306

A. $55,603 – $37,019 =

B. $6,412 – $8,017 =

C. $308 – $591 =

D. $17,806 – $5,376 =

Answer:
1. A. $604.57
   B. $163.21
   C. $35,967
   D. $25,766.77
2. A. 0.28
   B. 0.0675
   C. 0.059
   D. 0.12
3. A. $227.01
   B. $9,452.98
   C. $316.64
   D. $93.43
4. A. $18,584
   B. –$1,605
   C. –$283
   D. $12,430

What Is a Capital Gain?

Taxes can be complicated. It does not help when even the *names* of taxes sound complicated. The capital gains tax is one of those taxes that sounds complex. However, the concept is not that difficult to grasp.

Suppose you bought a rental property for $150,000. After owning it for a few years, you sold the property for $170,000. Because you sold the property for more than you paid for it, you actually made money when you sold it. The money you made is a capital gain. A **capital gain** is a profit that results from selling something for more than you paid for it. A capital gain can be calculated using the following formula:

capital gain = sale price – purchase price

For tax purposes, a capital gain results from the sale of a capital asset. An *asset* is anything you own that is of value. A *capital asset* is anything of value that is owned. However, there are some exceptions. For example, if a business is involved in buying and selling items, the items specifically purchased for resale are not considered capital assets.

Example 3-2A

See It

Moselle purchased a town house for $125,000. After living there for six years, she sold it for $160,000. Determine the amount of capital gain that Moselle made on the sale of her town house.

Teaching Tip:
Ask students to list assets that they own. Are any of the assets valuable enough that they could be sold for more than students paid for them?

Strategy

Use the formula:

$$\text{capital gain} = \text{sale price} - \text{purchase price}$$

Solution

Step 1: Identify the sale price and purchase price of the town house.

sale price = $160,000

purchase price = $125,000

Step 2: Subtract the purchase price from the sale price.

capital gain = sale price – purchase price

capital gain = $160,000 – $125,000

capital gain = $35,000

Check It

Keisha bought 100 shares of stock in a company several years ago for a total of $5,200. She recently sold those shares of stock for $8,345.25. What is Keisha's capital gain?

Answer:
$3,145.25

Capital Gains Tax

In the US, capital gains are subject to income tax. However, capital gains are treated differently than regular income. There are some special rules that apply to the taxation of capital gains. The following formula can be used to calculate the amount of capital gains tax owed:

$$\text{capital gains tax} = \text{tax rate} \times \text{capital gain}$$

Career Discovery
Finance Careers
and Math Skills

Finance careers involve the management and use of money. The career pathways in this cluster include financial and investment planning, business financial management, banking, and insurance. Careers in finance exist in all parts of the economy.

Strong calculation skills and attention to detail are key qualities for these workers. Professionals who work in finance present data to clients and colleagues on a regular basis. Describe a situation in which someone in finance would have a need to use basic math skills on the job.

For tax purposes, the length of time the asset was held affects the tax rate. A *long-term capital gain* is any profit from the sale of an asset that was held more than a year. The tax rate an individual pays on long-term capital gains is lower than the tax rate that an individual pays on ordinary income. *Ordinary income* is income earned from sources other than capital gains, such as wages.

A *short-term capital gain* is any profit from the sale of an asset that was held less than a year. Short-term capital gains are taxed at the same rate as ordinary income. This is a higher rate than tax on long-term capital gains.

The actual tax rates for capital gains are changed occasionally by the US Congress. Historically, rates have ranged from 7% to 33%. You can easily find the current capital gains tax rates by visiting the IRS website.

It is assumed that those who hold assets for a short time are buying and selling assets as a primary source of income. This is why short-term capital gains are taxable like ordinary income.

Example 3-2B

See It

Several years ago, Sean purchased $4,500 worth of stock in the company for which he works. Last year, he sold that stock for $5,314.83. If the capital gains tax rate is 15%, calculate the amount of capital gains tax that Sean will pay.

Strategy

Use the formulas:

capital gain = sale price – purchase price

capital gains tax = tax rate $\times$ capital gain

Solution

Step 1: Determine Sean's capital gain. Subtract the purchase price from the sale price.

capital gain = sale price – purchase price

capital gain = $5,314.83 – $4,500

capital gain = $814.83

Step 2: Convert the tax rate from a percentage to a decimal by moving the decimal two places to the left.

15% → 0.15

Step 3: Determine the capital gains tax. Multiply the capital gain by the tax rate. Round to the nearest cent ($0.01) if necessary

capital gains tax = tax rate × capital gain

capital gains tax = 0.15 × $814.83

capital gains tax = $122.23

Check It

Alexi and Martina purchased a lakefront lot several years ago for $75,000. They sold it this year for $96,500. If the capital gains tax rate is 15%, calculate the amount of capital gains tax that Alexi and Martina will pay.

Answer:
$3,225

---

fyi

If you have more capital losses than capital gains, you can deduct a portion of your net capital losses from your ordinary income.

Teaching Tip:
Engage students in a discussion regarding the difference between saving and investing.

Capital Losses

As you may be able to guess, when you sell a capital asset for less than you paid for it, the result is a *capital loss.* Investments are another source of capital gains and losses. An *investment* is any purchase you make in hopes of making money. For instance, you may invest money in a business. Or, you may purchase real estate as an investment rather than as your personal home. Investments often lose value. A capital loss results when an investment is sold at a price lower than the purchase price. The formula for calculating a capital loss is the same as the capital gain formula:

capital loss = sale price – purchase price

Example 3-2C

See It

Cheng purchased shares of a mutual fund for $9,500. Over a year later, he sold the shares for $7,875.34. What is Cheng's capital loss?

Strategy

Use the formula:

capital loss = sale price – purchase price

Solution

Step 1: Identify the sale price and purchase price of the shares.

sale price = $7,875.34

purchase price = $9,500

Step 2: Subtract the purchase price from the sale price.

capital loss = sale price − purchase price

capital loss = $7,875.34 − $9,500

capital loss = −$1,624.66

Check It

Roland purchased a house as an investment property for $185,000 three years ago. This year, he sold the house for $150,775. What is Roland's capital loss?

> **fyi**
>
> In financial math, a negative number indicates a loss. In accounting, negative numbers are also used to indicate the direction of cash flow.

Answer:
$34,225

For tax purposes, only capital losses on investments are tax deductible. So, for example, if you have a capital loss on real estate you purchased strictly as an investment, the loss is tax deductible. But, a capital loss incurred selling your own personal home would not be tax deductible.

For the most part, however, capital losses are used to offset capital gains. For example, suppose you made a $1,000 profit on one investment but lost $600 on another investment. The capital loss of $600 would offset your $1,000 capital gain to give you a net capital gain of $400.

Example 3-2D

See It

Marinella invested $5,000 in each of two different municipal bond funds. Three years later, she sold her shares in both bond funds. Her shares in one bond fund sold for $5,718.19. Her shares in the other bond fund sold for $3,997.68. What is Marinella's net capital gain or loss?

Strategy

Use the formula:

capital gain or loss = sale price − purchase price

Solution

Step 1: Determine Marinella's capital gain or loss from the first bond fund.

capital gain or loss = sale price − purchase price

capital gain or loss = $5,718.19 − $5,000

capital gain or loss = $718.19

Since this is a positive number, Marinella has a capital gain from the sale of shares in this bond fund.

Step 2: Determine Marinella's capital gain or loss from the second bond fund.

capital gain or loss = sale price – purchase price

capital gain or loss = $3,997.68 – $5,000

capital gain or loss = –$1,002.32

Since this is a negative number, Marinella has a capital loss from the sale of shares in this bond fund.

Step 3: Add the capital gain and loss together.

net capital gain or loss = capital gain + capital loss

net capital gain or loss = $718.19 + (–$1,002.32)

net capital gain or loss = $718.19 – $1,002.32

net capital gain or loss = –$284.13

Since this is a negative number, Marinella has a net capital loss of $284.13.

Check It

Malik purchased a condominium for $250,225 to use as an investment. He also purchased stock in a lumber company for $6,000. Two years later, he sold the condominium for $240,095. He sold the stock for $7,119. What is Malik's net capital gain or capital loss?

Teaching Tip:
Checkpoint questions offer opportunities for formative assessment.

Adding a negative number is the same as subtracting a positive number.

Answer:
1. $2,000
2. –$1821.88
3. $3,217.50
4. $727.50
5. –$653

Checkpoint 3.2

1. Wendy purchased an empty lot in her neighborhood for $45,000. Two years later, she sold the lot for $47,000. What is Wendy's capital gain on this investment?

2. Barret purchased shares of stock in an airline for a total of $7,812.71. Two years later, he sold the shares of stock for a total of $5,990.83. What is Barret's capital loss on this investment?

3. Milton and Janessa purchased a house for $85,900 to use as rental property. They sold the house three years later for $107,350. If the capital gains tax rate is 15%, what is the capital gains tax on the sale of Milton and Janessa's investment?

4. Frederick purchased a boat for $40,150. He sold the boat three years later for $45,000. If the capital gains tax rate is 15%, what is the capital gains tax on the sale of the boat?

5. Diya purchased shares of stock in a beverage company for $6,100. She also purchased shares in a communications company for $3,650. A few years later, she sold the stock in the beverage company for $5,078 and sold the stock in the communications company for $4,019. What is Diya's net capital gain or loss?

Section 3.3 Other Income Taxes

Objectives
- **Identify and describe components of self-employment tax.**
- **Describe estate and inheritance taxes.**
- **Explain the concept of the gift tax.**

Build Your Math Skills

Review these math skills to prepare for the lesson that follows.

1. Change percentages to decimals by moving the decimal two places to the left. Example: 12.4% → .124

A. 6.2% →　　　　　B. 2.9% →

C. 15.1% →　　　　D. 4.5% →

2. Find the percentage of a whole number. Round your answers to the nearest cent ($0.01). Example: 13% of $450.30 = 0.13 × $450.30 = $58.539 ≈ $58.54

A. 6.5% of $1,100 =　　　B. 15% of $832 =

C. 11.5% of $568 =　　　D. 2.9% of $1,500 =

Answer
1. A. 0.062
　 B. 0.029
　 C. 0.151
　 D. 0.045
2. A. $71.50
　 B. $124.80
　 C. $65.32
　 D. $43.50

Self-Employment Tax

There are many ways to earn money that do not involve working for an employer. If you create your own job and work for yourself, you are considered to be **self-employed.** Most self-employed people have a particular skill that they utilize or business that they operate. For example, a self-employed person might maintain lawns and landscapes, make and sell items over the Internet, offer tennis lessons, photograph weddings, or provide services as an interior decorator. Any marketable product or service can be a foundation for self-employment. Independent contractors and entrepreneurs are self-employed.

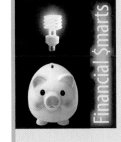

Financial Smarts

You may not think you need to file an income tax return if you don't make a lot of money. However, if you had any earned income in a given year, you should file a tax return. Certain low-income earners may claim the earned income tax credit (EITC), which can increase the amount of a refund beyond the level of taxes withheld. The EITC was established in 1975. It was intended to be an incentive to work as well as a way to provide qualifying individual and families with additional income.

Self-employed people have no employer to pay a share of the FICA tax. So they pay the equivalent of both the employee and employer contributions of FICA. FICA is the combination of Social Security taxes and Medicare taxes. Together they are called the **self-employment tax.** The employee pays 6.2% for Social Security tax and the employer pays 6.2%. Therefore, a self-employed person must pay a total of 12.4% on earnings for Social Security taxes. The formula for calculating self-employment tax follows:

self-employment tax = tax rate × contract earnings

fyi

The employee also pays Medicare tax. The employer makes a matching payment. Self-employed individuals must pay both the employee share and the employer share. The Medicare rate is 1.45%, so the self-employed person must pay a total of 2.9% on earnings for Medicare taxes.

Because self-employed people do not have regular paychecks for withholding FICA and federal income tax, the self-employed must be much more diligent with recordkeeping and savings for taxes. Depending on the amount of taxes a self-employed person owes, he or she may have to pay estimated taxes every three months.

Self-employed people are also subject to income tax like everyone else. However, self-employed people are able to deduct business expenses from their taxes that regular employees are not able to deduct. Examples of deductible expenses could be uniforms, equipment, or a cell phone that is used to conduct business.

Example 3-3A

See It

Alexis is a photographer who works as an independent contractor. Three of her recent jobs included photographing a wedding for $1,750, an anniversary celebration for $750, and a political fund-raiser for $1,800. Determine Alexis's self-employment taxes for these three contracts. Use the self-employment tax rate of 15.3%.

Strategy

Use the formula:

self-employment tax = tax rate × contract earnings

Solution

Step 1: Determine Alexis's total earnings for the three jobs. Add the contract amounts together.

contract earnings = wedding + anniversary + political fund-raiser

contract earnings = $1,750 + $750 + $1,800

contract earnings = $4,300

Step 2: Convert the self-employment tax rate from a percentage to a decimal by moving the decimal two places to the left.

15.3% → 0.153

Step 3: Determine Alexis's self-employment tax. Multiply her total contract earnings by the self-employment tax rate.

self-employment tax = tax rate × contract earnings

self-employment tax = 0.153 × $4,300

self-employment tax = $657.90

Check It

Kai teaches music lessons as an independent contractor. Last month, he taught 41 music lessons at $65 each. Determine the amount of Kai's self-employment taxes for last month, using the tax rate of 15.3%.

Answer:
$407.75

Estate and Inheritance Taxes

A person's *estate* is the total of his or her possessions, including assets and debts. The term *estate* is used mostly when referring to a person's possessions at the time of their death. However, because the person is deceased, the ownership of their estate must be transferred to another person or group of people.

When an estate is transferred to another person, for example from a parent to a child, it may be subject to estate tax. **Estate taxes** are taxes paid out of the value of the estate before the estate is transferred to the heirs. An **heir** is a person receiving an inheritance. An **inheritance** is an individual's portion of an estate.

A legal document called a *will* states the wishes of the deceased person, including who receives his or her estate.

Source: Shutterstock (Paul Matthew Photography)
Calculating income tax can be very simple, or very complicated.

Many estates never pay estate taxes because the government allows a certain amount of an estate's value to pass to heirs without tax. The amount varies from year to year, but has been more than $1,000,000 for some time. In other words, if an estate is worth less than $1,000,000, there would be no estate tax.

Inheritance taxes are imposed by some states on the person receiving an inheritance. Because in the US inheritance tax is a state tax, the rules vary from state to state. Many states have no inheritance tax at all. Others vary the rate of inheritance tax based on how closely the heir is related to the deceased. If inheriting from a parent, the rate would be lower than if inheriting from some unrelated person. The following formula is used to calculate inheritance tax:

inheritance tax = tax rate × value of inheritance

Example 3-3B

See It

Maya lives in Pennsylvania where there is a flat rate inheritance tax of 4.5% for lineal descendants (children or grandchildren), 12% for siblings, and 15% for all other people. After a favorite aunt passed away, Maya inherited stocks worth $75,000. What is Maya's inheritance tax?

Strategy

Use the formula:

inheritance tax = tax rate × value of inheritance

Solution

Step 1: Convert the inheritance tax rate from a percentage to a decimal by moving the decimal two places to the left.

15% → 0.15

Step 2: Determine Maya's inheritance tax. Multiply the value of her inheritance by the inheritance tax rate.

Inheritance tax = tax rate × value of inheritance

inheritance tax = 0.15 × $75,000

inheritance tax = $11,250

Check It

Davi lives in a state with an inheritance tax of 10% for shares of an inheritance up to $50,000. Davi's uncle left him a vehicle worth $22,500. Determine the amount of inheritance tax that Davi must pay.

Gift Tax

Teaching Tip:
Make the point that the gift tax is on the person who gives the gift, not the receiver.

The gift tax may surprise you. The name implies that if you receive a gift you may have to pay tax on that gift. The truth is, however, that money or anything else of value that someone gifts to you is not taxable, as long as it is truly a gift. That means you cannot give any service or exchange anything of value for the gift. Any taxes that may be associated with a gift are the responsibility of the giver.

The gift tax is actually not a tax. The *gift tax* is a law that limits the amount of money a person can give away as a gift without potentially costing their estate additional taxes. The reason this tax exists is to prevent a person from avoiding estate taxes by giving their money away before they die.

If your Aunt Josephine decided to give you $5,000, you will pay no tax on that $5,000 as income. If she gave you $100,000, you would still pay no tax on that money. But, if Aunt Josephine gave you more than the limited amount, *she* would have to pay the gift tax for the amount that was over the limit.

For example, suppose Diego has an estate valued at $2 million. And suppose the amount of money exempted from estate tax is currently $1.5 million. If, before his death, Diego gave $1 million as a gift to his son, then Diego's estate would be below the estate tax exemption and, therefore, no estate tax would be due. To prevent that scenario, the gift tax rule allows only a certain amount to be gifted before the gift begins to lower the estate tax exemption. In other words, the gift tax prevents a person from avoiding estate taxes by giving their money away quickly. It does, however, allow for a certain amount to be given as a gift annually with no tax consequence.

Checkpoint 3.3

Teaching Tip:
Checkpoint questions offer opportunities for formative assessment.

1. Yosef works as an independent contractor providing corporate leadership training. He earns $1,250 per day. Last month he delivered eight days of training. How much self-employment tax will Yosef pay for last month's work? Use the self-employment tax rate of 15.3%.

2. Ali works part-time as an independent contractor who bakes wedding cakes. Last month, he made seven cakes at $450 each. How much self-employment tax will Ali pay for last month's work? Use the self-employment tax rate of 15.3%.

3. Angelica is a computer programmer who works as an independent contractor. She just completed a contract for $3,500. What is the self-employment tax that Angelica will pay for her income on this contract? Use the self-employment tax rate of 15.3%.

4. Bernard lives in a state with a flat rate inheritance tax of 4.5%. He recently inherited a condominium worth $110,075. What is the amount of inheritance tax that Bernard will have to pay?

5. Andrea lives in a state with a flat rate inheritance tax of 6.34%. She was named as a beneficiary on her cousin's life insurance policy, and recently inherited $50,000 from that insurance policy. How much inheritance tax will Andrea have to pay?

Answer:
1. $1,530
2. $481.95
3. $535.50
4. $4,953.38
5. $3,170

Chapter Review

Build Your Vocabulary

As you progress through this course, develop a personal glossary of financial literacy terms and add it to your portfolio. This will help you build your financial literacy vocabulary. Write out a definition for each of the following terms, and add it to your personal glossary.

federal income tax return	long-term capital gain
tax return preparer	ordinary income
W-2 form	short-term capital gain
gross income	capital loss
adjusted gross income	investment
IRA	self-employed
deduction	self-employment tax
tax deductible	estate
standard deduction	estate tax
exemption	heir
capital gain	inheritance
asset	inheritance tax
capital asset	gift tax

 ## Teamwork

Working with a classmate, conduct research on how the federal government and your state use tax revenues. Create a circle chart that shows the proportion of revenue spent on different areas for the federal government and for your state. What conclusions can you draw from the data you found? Share your charts and conclusions with the class.

Review Your Math Skills

Practice and build on the math skills that you have learned.

1. Subtract decimals. Example: $5,610 − $471.98 = $5,138.02

A. $200 − $34.15 =   B. $417.32 − $68.95 =

C. $1,315.78 − $93.53 =   D. $2,804.05 − $315.83 =

2. Add decimals. Example: $412.63 + $136.55 = $549.18

A. $751.84 + $2,834.75 =   B. $5,429.21 + $227.92 =

C. $47.62 + $176.47 =   D. $618.16 + $2,256.49 =

3. Add and subtract decimals. **Example:** $5,610 − ($471.98 + $71.04) = $5,066.98

A. $1,017 − $12.43 =

B. $358.76 + $104.45 =

C. $44,215 − ($5,019 + $4,228) =

D. $27,019 − ($1,454.13 + $798.10) =

4. Use the order of operations rules to simplify these expressions. **Example:** $4 + 5 \times 6 \div 2 = 19$

A. $2 + 4 \times 9 \div 3 =$

B. $10 + 14 \times 5 \div 7 =$

C. $1 + 6 \times 5 \div 2 =$

D. $15 + 20 \times 8 \div 16 =$

5. Subtract whole numbers, where the answer may be a negative whole number. **Example:** $24 − $120 = −$96

A. $15,503 − $88,955 =

B. $367 − $543 =

C. $1,118 − $1,504 =

D. $9,533 − $9,532 =

6. Find the percentage of a whole number. **Round your answers to the nearest cent ($0.01).** Example: 12% of $150.30 = 0.12 × $150.30 = $18.036 ≈ $18.04

A. 5.22% of $1,900 =

B. 25.2% of $82 =

C. 1.33% of $119 =

D. 8.79% of $1,200 =

7. Multiply decimals. **Round your answers to the nearest cent ($0.01).** Example: $13.10 × 0.15 = $1.965 ≈ $1.97

A. $3,359.54 × 0.25 =

B. $8,359.97 × 4.75 =

C. $49.16 × 0.22 =

D. $200.05 × 0.032 =

8. Change percentages to decimals by moving the decimal two places to the left. **Example:** 12.4% → 0.124

A. 13.2% →

B. 12.9% →

C. 25.1% →

D. 5.5% →

9. Find the percentage of a whole number. **Round your answers to the nearest cent ($0.01).** Example: 13% of $450.30 = 0.13 × $450.30 = $58.539 ≈ $58.54

A. 33.5% of $1,400 =

B. 15% of $632 =

C. 12.75% of $568 =

D. 5.9% of $1,500 =

10. Change percentages to decimals by moving the decimal two places to the left. **Example:** 15% → 0.15

A. 37% →

B. 5.85% →

C. 9.9% →

D. 13% →

3. A. $1,004.57
   B. $463.21
   C. $34,968
   D. $24,766.77
4. A. 14
   B. 20
   C. 16
   D. 25
5. A. −$73,452
   B. −$176
   C. −$386
   D. $1
6. A. $99.18
   B. $20.66
   C. $1.58
   D. $105.48
7. A. $839.89
   B. $39,709.86
   C. $10.82
   D. $6.40
8. A. 0.132
   B. 0.129
   C. 0.251
   D. 0.055
9. A. $469
   B. $94.80
   C. $72.42
   D. $88.50
10. A. 0.37
    B. 0.0585
    C. 0.099
    D. 0.13

Section 3.1 Federal Taxes

11. Janelle teaches adult literacy classes at the local community college. Last year, her gross income was $51,080. Adjustments to her income include an IRA contribution of $4,086.40 and moving expenses of $178.93. What was Janelle's adjusted gross income?

12. Louie is single and had a taxable income last year of $36,918. His total withholdings were $6,014. Determine whether Louie owes additional taxes or will receive a tax refund. Calculate the amount that he owes or will be refunded.

13. Ren and Yolanda are married and filing jointly and have two children. Last year, their combined taxable income was $79,738. Ren had $13,589 in taxes withheld from his paycheck. Yolanda is not employed outside the home. Determine whether Ren and Yolanda owe additional taxes or will receive a tax refund. Calculate the amount that is owed or will be refunded.

Answer:
11. $48,814.67
12. Louie will receive a refund of $658.
13. They will receive a refund of $1,408.

Section 3.2 Capital Gains Taxes

14. Joseph purchased stock in a utility company for $2,390. A year later, he sold the stock for $3,072.54. What is the capital gain on the sale of Joseph's stock?

15. Ten years ago, Meredith purchased a vacation home for $154,075. She recently sold the vacation home for $200,115. If the capital gains tax rate is 15%, how much will Meredith owe in capital gains taxes from this sale?

16. Cleo invested money in municipal bonds. She purchased $2,175 in San Lorenzo bonds and $3,484 in Mesa Heights bonds. A few years later, she sold the San Lorenzo bonds for $2,418.73 and the Mesa Heights bonds for $3,072.16. What is Cleo's net capital gain or net capital loss?

Answer:
14. $682.54
15. $6,906
16. –$168.11

Section 3.3 Other Income Taxes

17. Elias lives in a state with a flat rate inheritance tax of 4.65%. He recently inherited furniture from his aunt that is valued at $13,660. Calculate the amount of inheritance tax that Elias will owe.

18. Randall works as an independent contractor providing information technology services. He recently completed a contract for $6,425. Calculate Randall's self-employment taxes that he will pay on his earnings from this contract. Use the self-employment tax rate of 15.3%.

Answer:
17. $635.19
18. $854.53

Reinforce Your Understanding

19. Ariel works as a graphic designer earning an annual salary of $48,140. Calculate her gross pay per paycheck if she is paid weekly, biweekly, semimonthly, or monthly.

20. Farah is a fire investigator. She earns an annual salary of $56,170 and is paid weekly. Farah lives in a state with a flat rate income tax of 4.35%. She will receive a raise of 3% of her base salary. Her federal withholdings are $92 before the raise and $96 after the raise. Determine the change in Farah's net pay per paycheck.

Apply Your Technology Skills

Access the G-W Learning companion website for this text at www.g-wlearning.com. Download each data file for this chapter. Follow the instructions to complete financial literacy activities to practice what you have learned in this chapter.

Data File 3-1—Comparing Tax Return Options

Data File 3-2—Comparing Tax Return Software

Data File 3-3—Completing a 1040EZ

Data File 3-4—Completing a 1040A

Answer:
19. weekly pay = $925.77
    biweekly pay =
       $1,851.54
    semimonthly pay =
       $2,005.83
    monthly pay =
       $4,011.67
20. $48.04

Teaching Tip:
The Apply Your Technology Skills activities offer project-based authentic assessment opportunities.

Unit 1 Summative Assessment

On a separate sheet of paper or in a word processing document, apply what you have learned in this unit to answer the questions that follow.

Multiple Choice Questions

1. Last month, Jorge was paid a total of $9,000, which included a bonus of $1,500. What is Jorge's gross bimonthly pay during a month when a bonus is not paid?

   A. $7,500

   B. $5,250

   C. $9,000

   D. $3,750

2. A greater withholding allowance results in ____.

   A. a larger amount of take-home pay

   B. a smaller amount of take-home pay

   C. more taxable income

   D. less taxable income

3. Jeffrey worked 48 hours this week. His regular hourly wage is $18.50. For every hour each week he works over 40, he is paid 1.5 times his regular hourly wage. What is Jeffrey's gross pay for this week?

   A. $962

   B. $1,332

   C. $888

   D. $1,850

4. If taxes due are greater than the taxes withheld, then ____.

   A. money is refunded

   B. money is owed

   C. you should make up more deductions

   D. you should get a rapid refund

5. Leona is a real estate agent who earns straight commission based on the homes that she sells. Last month, she sold four homes with sales prices of $144,000; $177,000; $152,000; and $193,000. She earned a 3% commission on each sale. What was Leona's total commission?

   A. $199.80

   B. $1,998

   C. $19,980

   D. $199,800

Answer:
1. D
2. A
3. A
4. B
5. C

Matching

Match the letter beside each equation to the situation to which it applies.

A. amount per paycheck = $\dfrac{\text{gross annual pay}}{\text{number of pay periods per year}}$

B. amount of raise = weekly gross pay × rate of raise

C. amount of taxes owed/refund = tax due − total withholdings

D. commission = item price × number of items × commission rate

E. double time hourly earnings = regular hourly wage × 2

F. net pay = gross pay − (federal tax withholdings + Social Security tax + Medicare tax + state income tax withholdings)

G. regular earnings = regular hourly wage × regular hours

H. tax savings = premium × tax rate

I. total annual value of job = annual gross pay + total annual employee benefits

J. total income = earned income + unearned income

6. Bella wants to know how many memberships she needs to sell to reach $500 in commission.

7. Jean wants to see how her new pay rate will affect her gross earnings.

8. Jonah wants to know how much he can save by having the cost of his train ticket deducted from his paycheck before taxes are taken out.

9. Kyle wants to compare weekly and biweekly paycheck amounts.

10. Marianne wants to weigh two job offers.

11. Yuki and June want to find out how much income they received from wages and investment returns.

12. Oscar wants to calculate the amount of his paycheck after FICA taxes are taken out.

13. Gwen wants to see if she will owe taxes or receive a refund.

14. Tomas wants to see how much more he would earn working a national holiday than he would working a regularly scheduled workday.

15. Drew wants to find out how much he will get paid this week if he works a total of 15 hours.

Answer:
6. D
7. B
8. H
9. A
10. I
11. J
12. F
13. C
14. E
15. G

True/False Questions

16. *True or False?* Bartering is trading one thing of value for another.

17. *True or False?* Workers who are paid a salary are paid by the hour.

18. *True or False?* Social Security taxes pay for retirement and disability benefits.

19. *True or False?* A federal income tax return is used to calculate taxes owed to the federal government.

20. *True or False?* Unearned income is the money a person gets from doing a job.

Answer:
16. True
17. False
18. True
19. True
20. False

Mastery Questions

21. Mercedes received two competing job offers as an insurance claims adjuster. Great Plains Insurance Co. offered her an annual salary of $50,660. Liberty of South Plains Insurance Co. offered her a monthly salary of $4,000 with an additional annual bonus of up to 5% of her annual salary based on company performance. Based on pay alone, which of the two offers should Mercedes take? Assume that she would receive the full 5% bonus.

22. Teresa works as a chemistry professor at a local university. She purchases health insurance, with a monthly premium of $332.37, and dental insurance, with a monthly premium of $52.48, for herself and her children. Her income level places her at the 28% federal income tax rate. Teresa decided to have her health insurance and dental insurance premiums deducted before taxes were calculated. What are Teresa's annual tax savings?

23. Brianna is a salaried employee of a lumber company, and her annual salary is $32,130. Brianna will receive a raise of $1,000 of her annual salary. She lives in a state with a flat rate income tax of 3.5%. Her federal withholdings after the raise are $27. Determine Brianna's new weekly paycheck, including: gross pay; Social Security tax, Medicare tax, and state income tax deductions; and net pay.

Answer:
21. Great Plains Insurance Co.
22. $1,293.12
23. weekly gross pay = $637.12
    Social Security tax = $39.50
    Medicare tax = $9.24
    state income tax = $22.30
    weekly net pay = $539.08

24. Patricia works as a geologist. Last year her adjusted gross income was $73,380. She is single and has no children. However, she uses itemized deductions instead of the standard deduction. Her itemized deductions for last year appear in the table shown. What is Patricia's taxable income?

Mortgage	Property taxes	State income tax	Business expenses	Charitable contributions
$4,035	$3,819	$3,268	$500	$9,338

25. Herman has a full-time job as a technical writer with an annual gross pay of $63,640. Adjustments to his income include $3,312 to an IRA and $1,700 to a health savings account. His withholdings for the year total $6,021. Herman had $14,280 in itemized deductions. He is single and has one child, whom he claims as a dependant. Determine Herman's adjusted gross income and taxable income. Then, use the tax table found in Figure 3-4 to determine whether Herman owes additional taxes or will receive a refund. Calculate the amount of the additional taxes or the tax refund.

24. $48,720
25. adjusted gross income = $58,628 taxable income = $36,948 Herman will receive a refund of $665.

Unit 2
Banking, Purchasing, and Budgeting

It is one thing to make money. It is another to make your money work for you. Putting your money in the bank is usually the first step. In this unit, you will learn about how to open and manage a bank account. You will also explore the many ways that you can purchase and pay for things you want and need. To make sure that you will have the money for the things you need, you will also learn to create a budget.

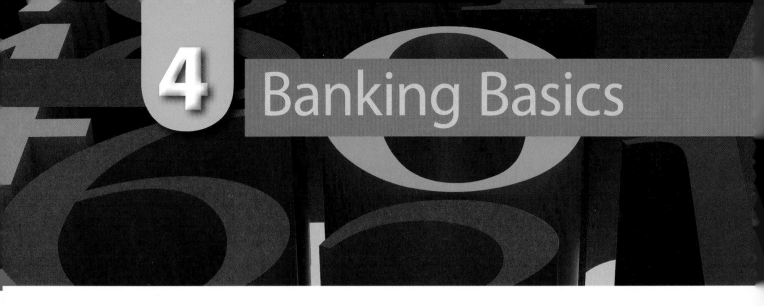

4 Banking Basics

Materials:
Instructor's Resource CD
Student Workbook
G-W Learning companion website
EXAMVIEW® Assessment Suite
Microsoft Excel®–compatible software
Calculator with advanced-math functions

Banks play an important role in helping you keep and manage your finances. By putting your money in a bank or other financial institution, you have more options for making payments and for using the money you have on deposit. Establishing a bank account and managing it wisely are important skills.

Section 4.1 **Opening an Account**

Section 4.2 **Checking Accounts**

Section 4.3 **Savings Accounts**

College and Career Readiness

Reading Prep. As you read this chapter, determine the point of view or purpose of the author. What aspects of the text help to establish this purpose or point of view?

"I have a bank account. It's a safe place for the money I earn from working and depositing my checks each month." ~ Cody B.

Money Matters
Federal Deposit Insurance Corporation (FDIC)

- Can a bank go out of business? Yes, banks are businesses and they can fail. In 1929, when the stock market crashed and the United States plunged into the Great Depression, depositors lost their money. Banks had no reserves to cover losses.

- The FDIC insures customer accounts in the event that the bank fails. The FDIC insures a customer's checking, savings, certificates of deposits, IRA, and money market accounts. It does not insure safe deposit boxes.

- In 1933, to avoid such losses in the future, the US government created the Federal Deposit Insurance Corporation, known as the FDIC.

- The most recent bank failures happened in the financial crisis of 2008. Several well-known retail banks and investment banks faced closure.

- When the FDIC was established in 1935, it insured customer accounts up to $5,000. Today, a customer account is insured up to $250,000.

- The FDIC is guaranteed by the US government. A bank should display the FDIC sign showing that it is a member.

- Since the creation of the FDIC, bank customers have not lost any of their money deposited in an institution insured by the FDIC.

Section 4.1 Opening an Account

Objectives

- **Explain the purpose of a checking and savings account.**
- **Describe the process of opening an account.**
- **Calculate a bank deposit.**

Terms

- *interest*
- *service charge*
- *checking account*
- *savings account*
- *service charge*

Build Your Math Skills

Review these math skills to prepare for the lesson that follows.

1. Add decimals. Example: $75.15 + $141.78 = $216.93

A. $278.05 + $39.94 =

B. $90.19 + $15.85 =

C. $1,013.59 + $509 =

D. $403.75 + $393.76 =

2. Subtract decimals. Example: $7,019.05 − $5,489.47 = $1,529.58

A. $105.19 − $73.84 =

B. $90.18 − $56.11 =

C. $835.64 − $76.53 =

D. $1,738 − $516.83 =

Answer:
1. A. $317.99
   B. $106.04
   C. $1,522.59
   D. $797.51
2. A. $31.35
   B. $34.07
   C. $759.11
   D. $1,221.17

Banking Overview

A *bank* is a business that provides tools for managing money. Banks make it easy to keep track of money and also keep it safe. Banks allow a customer to deposit money into an account for safekeeping and withdraw the money when needed. *Deposit* is a term used to describe the act of putting money into a bank.

The most common way to use the services of a bank is to deposit money. Rather than stuffing cash under a mattress, most people choose to deposit money in a bank. The customer deposits funds that may be taken out at a later date. The bank agrees to keep the funds safe while in the account. When you deposit money into a savings account, the bank pays you interest on your money. *Interest* is the fee banks pay depositors for the use of their money.

A bank puts your money to work. The bank pools depositors' money and lends it to others. The bank functions as a broker between the people with money to deposit and the people who need money to borrow. When the bank lends money to customers, they charge those customers interest. Charging interest is one of the ways the bank makes money to stay in business.

fyi

Banks are a type of *depository institution*. Credit unions and savings and loan associations are also depository institutions.

Teaching Tip: Discuss savings accounts with students. Ask how many of them have an account. Do they know how much interest they are making?

Opening an Account

Before you can deposit money into the bank, you must first open an account. Because you may occasionally need to physically visit the bank, location is often a major factor when deciding where to do business. Another factor may be the types of accounts a bank offers. For example, many banks offer *free*

Career Discovery
Business Management & Administration Careers and Math Skills

Careers in this cluster involve skills that businesses need to keep productive and running smoothly. Management, business financial management, accounting, and human resources are some career options. Business analysis, marketing, administration, and information are also supported in this cluster. Business people also need good computer skills, common sense, decision-making skills, and problem-solving abilities.

Broad skills in planning, organizing, and evaluating business operations are essential in the business world. Describe how good math skills are interwoven with these broad skills.

Many banks offer student accounts that do not have a service charge. When you open an account, ask if the bank offers no-fee student accounts.

Teaching Tip:
Data File 4-1, which can be found at the G-W Learning Companion website for this text, contains an application for opening a bank account. Walk students through the process of completing an application.

checking. This means that as long as you meet certain requirements, you will pay no service charge for your checking account. A *service charge* is a fee a bank charges for having an account.

When opening an account, you will be asked to complete an application. It will ask you to provide personal information, such as your name, address, and Social Security number. You will also be required to show identification to prove that you are who you say you are. When your account is opened, you will be given an account number for the account. The *account number* is a number unique to your account at that bank. When you conduct business with the bank, the account number is how you identify your account.

Banks offer a variety of accounts. In general, there are two main accounts that most people use: a checking account and a savings account. A *checking account* is an account that allows a customer to deposit money and write checks from the account. A *check* is a document that authorizes a bank to transfer money to another person or entity. A checking account is an important tool for financial management. It allows you to manage your money in forms other than cash. A customer can deposit money into his or her checking account and withdraw money in various ways. He or she can even withdraw cash.

A *savings account* is an account that pays interest to the account holder but limits the number of withdrawals per month. You will learn more about checking accounts and savings accounts later in this chapter.

Making a Deposit

After you open an account, you are ready to start making deposits. A deposit can be presented to a bank in cash or as a check. Increasingly, deposits are made as online transfers or direct deposits from employers. Depending on the bank and the type of account, there may be a minimum amount of money required to open an account. It is not unusual to see a bank require an initial minimum deposit of $100.

A *deposit slip* is used to document the funds you deposit. Figure 4-1 is an example of a deposit slip.

On the deposit slip, you will list each item that you are depositing. List the dollar amount of all paper cash, the dollar amount of coins, and the dollar amount of each check. When you make a deposit, you also have the option of receiving a portion of the deposit back as cash. This portion is indicated on the deposit slip as *less cash received*. The remaining amount of money that you deposit into your account is called the *net deposit*. The following formula is used to calculate a net deposit:

net deposit = currency + coins + check amount – less cash received

Example 4-1A

See It

Chandra has two checks that she needs to deposit into her checking account. One check is for $516.73. The other check is for $175.96. She also wants to receive $50 in cash back from her deposit. What is Chandra's net deposit?

Strategy

Use the formula:

net deposit = currency + coins + check amount – less cash received

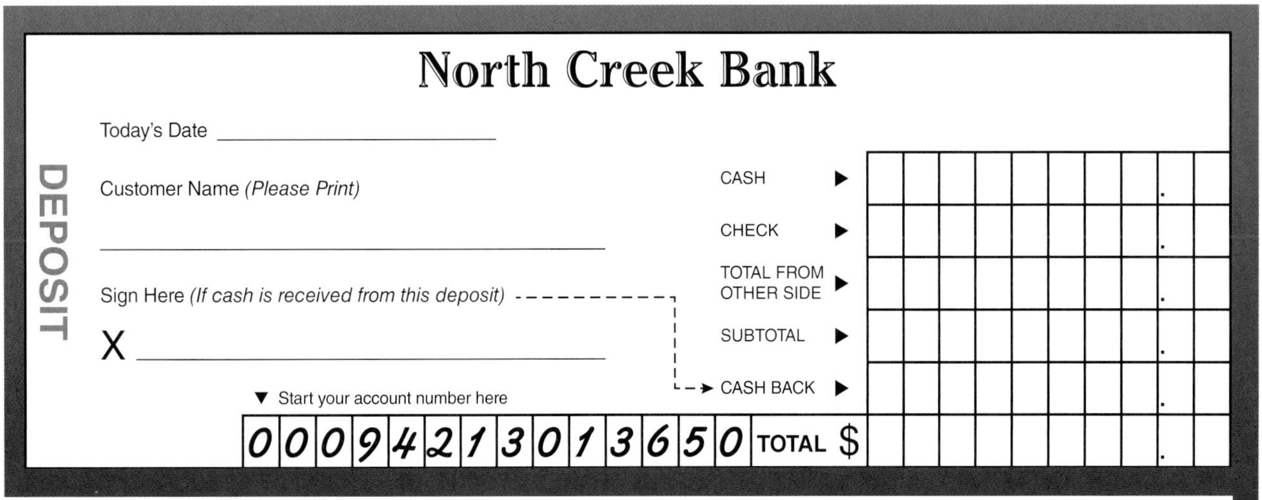
North Creek Bank

DEPOSIT

Today's Date

Customer Name *(Please Print)*

Sign Here *(If cash is received from this deposit)*

X

▼ Start your account number here

0009421301365 0

CASH ▶

CHECK ▶

TOTAL FROM OTHER SIDE ▶

SUBTOTAL ▶

CASH BACK ▶

TOTAL $

Figure 4-1. Deposit Slip

Solution

Step 1: Identify each part of the deposit as indicated on the deposit form.

currency = $0

coins = $0

check amount = $516.73 and $175.96

less cash received = $50

Step 2: Determine the total check amount of Chandra's deposit. Add the amount of each check.

check amount = check one + check two

check amount = $516.73 + $175.96

check amount = $692.69

Step 3: Determine the net deposit. Subtract the less cash received from the check amount.

net deposit = check amount – less cash received

net deposit = $692.69 – $50

net deposit = $642.69

Check It

Rodolfo has two checks that he needs to deposit into his checking account. One check is for $108.93, and the second check is for $372.47. He wants to receive $75 cash back from his deposit. What is Rodolfo's net deposit?

Teaching Tip:
The complete solutions to the Check It problems can be found on the Instructor's Resource CD.

Answer:
$406.40

Teaching Tip:
Checkpoint questions offer opportunities for formative assessment.

Checkpoint 4.1

1. Sabrina has $125 in cash left over from her recent vacation. She also has a reimbursement check for $117.92. She wants to deposit both into her checking account. What is her net deposit?

2. Amos is making a deposit from his business. He has $728 in cash, $65.23 in coins, and $1,316.78 in checks. What is Amos' net deposit?

3. Nikki is an independent contractor and has two checks that she needs to deposit. The checks are in the amounts of $1,712.34 and $1,904.77. She also needs to receive $200 in cash back from her deposit. What is Nikki's net deposit?

4. Tyrell owns a small business selling furniture. He received three checks from customers in the amounts of $908.74, $332.17, and $415.96, which he wants to deposit in his business' checking account. How much is Tyrell's net deposit?

5. Gayle is a geologist. She received a paycheck for $2,585.91 and a travel reimbursement check for $718.43. She wants to receive $150 cash back from her deposit. What is Gayle's net deposit?

Answer:
1. $242.92
2. $2,110.01
3. $3,417.11
4. $1,656.87
5. $3,154.34

Section 4.2 Checking Accounts

Objectives

- **Identify the information on a check.**
- **Describe the way checks work.**
- **Manage and reconcile a checking account.**
- **Explain how to use and update a check register.**

Terms

- *cleared*
- *electronic funds transfer (EFT)*
- *debit card*
- *automated teller machine (ATM)*
- *overdrawn*
- *overdraft fee*
- *overdraft protection*
- *bank statement*
- *reconcile*
- *outstanding check*
- *balance*
- *register*

Build Your Math Skills

Review these math skills to prepare for the lesson that follows.

1. Add decimals. Example: $68.74 + $90.14 = $158.88

A. $25.14 + $84.08 =   B. $475.03 + $58.79 =

C. $64.13 + $36 =   D. $85.13 + $113.87 =

2. Subtract decimals. Example: $847.08 − $113.85 = $733.23

A. $604.75 − $132.53 =   B. $454.39 − $75 =

C. $395.43 − $182.19 =   D. $596 − $185.79 =

Answer:
1. A. $109.22
   B. $533.82
   C. $100.13
   D. $199
2. A. $472.22
   B. $379.39
   C. $213.24
   D. $410.21

Writing a Check

The traditional way to spend money from a checking account is to write a paper check. A paper check, like the sample shown in Figure 4-2, includes some important pieces of information:

- check number
- date
- person or entity to be paid
- amount—in numbers and in words
- memo line
- signature line
- routing number
- account number

Check Number

The *check number* identifies the check. The numbers increase with each check. Most new checking accounts begin with check 1001 or another common starting point. A check number is essential for recordkeeping.

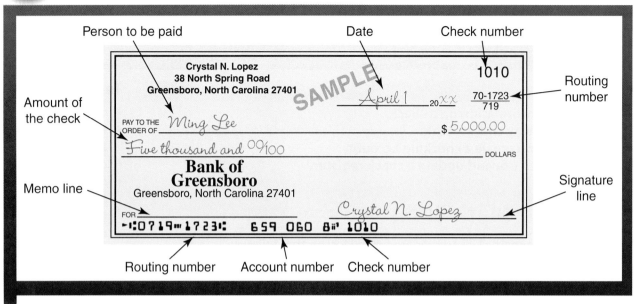

Figure 4-2. Elements of a Check

Date

The *date* is when the check is written. This date becomes important for recordkeeping. Never postdate a check. To *postdate* a check means to write a check with a date in the future.

Person or Entity to Be Paid

The phrase *pay to the order of* is a fancy way of indicating who gets the money. This should be the legal name of the person or entity receiving the check. You may call the guy receiving the check *Dad*. His bank knows him by his first and last name.

Amount

In order to be official, the *amount* of the check should be written in both words and numbers. The words and numbers must match. Officially, the words spell out the legal amount of the check. The place where you write the numbers is called the *courtesy box*. It is there to make it easier to read than reading the words.

Memo Line

The *memo line* is optional. You can use this line to write a reminder or other information about why you wrote the check. Or, if you are paying a bill, you might write your account number on the memo line. This way the company knows to apply it to the correct account. It is also a good way to track how you are spending your money.

Teaching Tip:
Explain to students that while use of the paper check is on the decline, electronic payment forms, such as peer-to-peer (P2P) payments, electronic bill payment, and the use of debit cards are on the rise.

Signature Line

The *signature line* is your authorization to pay the holder of the check. Once you write a check, the recipient is holding a legal document authorizing the transfer of money. Your signature is giving permission to your bank to transfer the money to the person in the *pay to the order of* line.

Routing and Account Numbers

All banks are assigned a specific identification number called a *routing number*. This number is used to find the correct bank after the check is deposited or cashed. Suppose you mail a check across the country to a friend. Your friend deposits the check in her checking account. Your friend's bank will then use that routing number to find the bank that holds your money so that the money can be withdrawn from your account.

Your *account number* is also on each check you write. This number is necessary so that when the check comes to your bank for payment, the bank knows from which account to take the money.

Source: Shutterstock (Goodluz)

Online banking allows you to manage your money 24 hours a day.

How Checks Work

When you write a check, the money does not leave your account until the check is presented to the bank. When the check is processed and the money is transferred out of your account, the check has *cleared* the bank. When you write a check and put it in the mail, the money may not leave your account for several days. It may take that long for the check to travel through the mail. It may then take several more days for the recipient to deposit or cash the check.

People write fewer checks than they did five or ten years ago. One reason for this is the availability of computers. This has resulted in more convenient ways to transfer money using online banking. Common tasks, like paying a monthly bill, are often done by electronic funds transfer. An *electronic funds transfer (EFT)* is the transfer of money from one person or entity to another without any cash or checks involved. Online banking allows you to do your banking seven days a week, 24 hours a day. Most banks provide this service at no additional cost.

Increasingly, when a buyer presents a paper check for payment, the seller scans the check, which captures the buyer's checking account information and the amount of the check. The paper check is given back to the buyer. Funds are electronically taken from the buyer's bank account and deposited into the seller's bank account. No further processing of the check is required.

Another way to access money in your checking account is by using a debit card. A *debit card* carries information linked to your account. With a debit card, you can authorize the bank to transfer money from your account to someone else. For example, if you use a debit card at a restaurant, the cost of your purchase is taken from your checking account. That amount is then transferred to the restaurant as payment for your meal.

Studies have proven that when people spend with a debit card rather than actual cash, they spend more. When you use cash, you are more aware of the amount of money you are spending because you have to physically hand it to someone. When you use a debit card, you are more likely to say, "make that a large," or "sure, an apple pie sounds great," without thinking about the extra money you are spending. When using a debit card, be sure to keep track of what you are spending.

Using an ATM is still another way to take money out of your account. An *automated teller machine (ATM)* is a computerized machine that allows you to do a few basic banking functions without going to a bank. The primary use of an ATM is to retrieve cash from your account. It can also be used to make deposits and check an account balance. In some locations, ATMs can be used to perform other functions, such as buying postage stamps and paying bills. ATMs charge fees for their services. If the ATM belongs to your bank, you may be able to withdraw money with no fee. If you use an ATM not associated with your bank, you may pay $1 or more per transaction. Sometimes, you may be required to pay two additional fees. The ATM may charge you a fee and your bank may also charge you a fee for using an ATM other than one that belongs to your bank.

fyi

ATMs are sometimes called *cash machines* because they are primarily used to withdraw cash.

Whether you use a paper check, debit card, or the ATM, the new balance in your checking account can be determined by subtracting the amount of the payment from the existing balance of the account:

new balance = existing balance – amount of payment

It is your responsibility to know your account balance and to spend within the limits of your balance. Your account will become *overdrawn* if you spend more than you have in your account. When an account is overdrawn, the bank will charge an *overdraft fee* as a penalty. When an account is overdrawn, the bank will generally refuse to honor the transactions that your balance cannot pay. In the case of checks, the check may be returned to the person or entity that originally received it. Many businesses will charge the customer a fee for writing a check that does not clear. Therefore, the cost of writing a check that will not clear can be substantial. Those who regularly and intentionally write bad checks can even be arrested.

Some banks offer *overdraft protection* that will cover checks that go over your balance within certain limits. There are generally fees for using overdraft protection.

People sometimes postdate checks because there is not enough money in their account to cover the check. The hope is that the person will not cash the check until the future date written on the check. However, if someone cashes the check before the date, and your account cannot cover the check, you will have to pay an overdraft fee.

Example 4-2A

See It

Ignacio has a checking account balance of $942.43. He used his debit card to purchase lunch for himself and his mother. The lunch bill total, including tax and tip, was $32.17. What is the new balance in Ignacio's checking account?

Strategy

Use the formula:

new balance = existing balance – amount of payment

Solution

Step 1: Determine the existing balance and amount of the debit card payment.

existing balance = $942.43

amount of payment = $32.17

Step 2: Determine the new balance. Subtract the amount of the payment from the old balance.

new balance = existing balance – amount of payment

new balance = $942.43 – $32.17

new balance = $910.26

Check It

Mary Helen has a checking account balance of $458.03. She wrote a check to the Cleveland County Community College bookstore for $76.12. What is Mary Helen's new checking account balance?

Answer:
$381.91

Reconciling a Bank Statement

Banks offer multiple ways to access information about your account. Online banking is the most popular. Most banks also offer a way to access basic information through a telephone call or through text messaging. Banks also summarize account activity on a regular basis, usually monthly, in a report called a statement. A **bank statement,** also called a *statement,* lists all account activity for the reporting period. This includes all deposits, withdrawals, and fees. Fees may include a service charge for services the bank provides. The statement also shows the balance at the beginning and end of a reporting period. Images of the checks that have cleared your account are generally part of the statement to help you identify which checks have cleared.

Bank statements are sometimes printed and delivered by mail. Most banks prefer that you receive your statement electronically. By going to the online banking website and logging into your account, you can download your bank statements and view your recent transactions.

When you receive your statement, you should reconcile your account. To *reconcile* a bank account:

- confirm each transaction on the statement against your own records;

- mark your records to show which items have cleared the bank; and

- verify that you and the bank agree on your balance.

The balance shown by the bank may not automatically match the balance in your records. This happens when transactions have not yet cleared the bank. An *outstanding check* is a check that has not yet been presented to the bank for payment or deducted from your account. For example, if you have written an $800 check to pay your rent, you have reduced your available funds by $800. Until your bank receives that outstanding check, your balance at the bank will not reflect the reduction. That is why it is important to keep your own records and not rely only on the bank's balance. Many people make the mistake of relying on their current bank balance to determine whether they have money to spend, and, as a result, their account ends up overdrawn.

To reconcile your records with the statement, take the information from the statement and adjust the balance to compare to your records. The following equation can be used:

adjusted balance = statement balance + outstanding deposits – outstanding payments

fyi

Most people underestimate their account balance to make sure they do not bounce a check. To do so, round down to the nearest dollar or ten dollars.

Teaching Tip:
Explain to students that reconciling a bank account can be a very time-consuming task. If the balance amount is incorrect, it may be necessary to recalculate back to before the point of the last correct reconciliation. Attention to detail is critical when recording transactions in a check register.

Example 4-2B

See It

Damien received his bank statement and reconciled it with his check register. The statement balance is $1,093.17. However, there is an outstanding deposit of $215.19. There are also outstanding payments of $118.18 and $35.41 that did not clear the bank before the statement was printed. What is Damien's adjusted balance?

Strategy

Use the formula:

**adjusted balance = statement balance + outstanding deposits –
outstanding payments**

Solution

Step 1: Determine the total outstanding payments. Add the two outstanding payments together.

outstanding payments = payment one + payment two

outstanding payments = $118.18 + $35.41

outstanding payments = $153.59

Step 2: Identify the statement balance, outstanding deposits, and outstanding payments.

statement balance: $1,093.17

outstanding deposits: $215.19

outstanding payments: $153.59

Step 3: Add the statement balance and outstanding deposits.

statement balance + outstanding deposits = $1,093.17 + $215.19

statement balance + outstanding deposits = $1,308.36

Step 4: Subtract the outstanding payments from the sum in the previous step.

adjusted balance = statement balance + outstanding deposits – outstanding
                            payments

adjusted balance = $1,308.36 – $153.59

adjusted balance = $1,154.77

Check It

Muriel received her bank statement showing a balance of $516.83. Not shown on the statement are deposits of $75.12 and $228.90 and payments of $129.15 and $217.47. What is Muriel's adjusted balance?

Teaching Tip:
Remind students that it is important to record any electronic transactions or payments they make in their check registers.

Answer:
$474.23

Keeping Track of Your Money

fyi

Many banks allow customers to see images of checks and deposits when viewing account information online.

The current amount of money in your account is called your **balance.** It is important to know your balance at all times. To spend money from your account, there must be enough money in the account. The way you keep track of your balance is by keeping a register. A **register** is a list of transactions and a running total of the balance after each transaction. Figure 4-3 shows a sample check register. You can see how this person's paycheck deposit raised the account balance and how paying bills and other spending lowered the balance.

Number	Date	Description	Payments		✓	Deposit		Balance	
	1/1	Initial deposit			✓	1,125	00	1,125	00
	1/10	Check deposit			✓	1,234	67	2,359	67
	1/12	Transfer to savings	150	00	✓			2,209	67
501	1/13	Void						2,209	67
502	1/13	Ace Realty, rent	410	00	✓			1,799	67
503	1/14	CTS for cable	29	95	✓			1,769	72
504	1/14	Access One, Internet service	35	40	✓			1,734	32
505	1/14	Dells Dept. Store for clothes	56	39	✓			1,677	93
506	1/14	Drugs, Inc. for medicine	12	54	✓			1,665	39
507	1/14	Elm Valley Electric for bill	55	84	✓			1,609	55
508	1/14	Municipal Utilities, water bill	29	18	✓			1,508	37
509	1/14	Reed's Garage, auto repair	165	32				1,415	05
510	1/14	Elm Valley Telephone, bill	54	28	✓			1,360	77
511	1/14	Sofa Hut, furniture	295	00	✓			1,065	77
512	1/14	Mobile Inc., cell phone bill	20	00	✓			1,045	77
513	1/14	Safe Storage, storage rental	43	29				1,002	48
514	1/15	EV College, tuition	145	00	✓			857	48
515	1/15	Food Basket for groceries	98	54	✓			758	94
ATM	1/18	Cash withdrawal	60	00	✓			698	94
	1/19	Check deposit			✓	84	10	783	04
ATM	1/27	Cash withdrawal	60	00				723	04
	1/28	Check deposit				75	00	798	04
	1/28	Service fee	3	00				795	04

Person or entity to be paid

Checks and withdrawals

Checkmark indicates that item appears on bank statement

Credits

Balance column

Figure 4-3.
Check Register

Example 4-2C

See It

Joanna received her monthly bank statement in the mail. Her check register for the same period is shown. Reconcile Joanna's checking account using the information shown.

My National Bank
1234 Commerce Street
Jonesboro, AR 72401

Statement July 20--

Checking Account

Account Number	12345678
Previous Balance	$1189.20
Deposits/Credits	965.34
Checks/Debits	881.89
Service Fee	$0.00
Current Balance	$1272.65

Deposits and Other Credits

Date	Number	Description	Amount
7/1		Deposit	$482.67
7/15		Deposit	482.67

Checks and Other Debits

Date	Number	Description	Amount
7/4	361	Check	$425.00
7/8		Debit–Lemmon's Grocery	34.44
7/12	362	Check	106.39
7/13		Debit–Hannah's Drive-In	4.77
7/15	363	Check	68.12
7/19		Debit–Lemmon's Grocery	78.20
7/19	364	Check	100.00
7/28		Debit–ZoomMart	36.00
7/29		Debit–MegaMoviePlex	16.00
7/29		Debit–MegaMoviePlex	12.97

Teaching Tip:
Point out that paying careful attention to a bank statement is more than just keeping track of spending. Doing this also makes it easier to spot potential unauthorized use of an account, which may signal that identity theft has occurred.

Number	Date	Description	Payment	✓	Deposit	Balance
						$1227 20
	6/30	Debit—ZoomMart	38 00	✓		1189 20
	7/1	Paycheck		✓	482 67	1671 87
361	7/1	Rent	425 00	✓		1246 87
	7/8	Debit—groceries	34 44	✓		1212 43
362	7/8	Utilities	106 39	✓		1106 04
	7/13	Debit—lunch	4 77	✓		1101 27
363	7/13	Cell phone bill	68 12	✓		1033 15
	7/15	Paycheck		✓	482 67	1515 82
	7/19	Debit—groceries	78 20	✓		1437 62
364	7/19	Transfer to savings	100 00	✓		1337 62
	7/28	Debit—ZoomMart	36 00	✓		1301 62
365	7/28	Car insurance	289 00			1012 62
	7/29	Debit—movie tickets	16 00	✓		996 62
	7/29	Debit—movie concessions	12 97	✓		983 65

Strategy

Compare the bank statement and the check register. To confirm the balance on the check register, use the formula:

adjusted balance = statement balance + outstanding deposits – outstanding payments

Solution

Step 1: Use the check mark column in the check register to indicate which items from the check register also appear on the bank statement. Also verify that the amounts on the bank statement match the check register.

Step 2: For any item without a check mark, decide whether it is a deposit or a payment. These are the outstanding items.

Check 365, for $289, is an outstanding payment.

Step 3: Determine the adjusted balance.

adjusted balance = statement balance + outstanding deposits – outstanding payments

adjusted balance = $1,272.65 – $289.00

adjusted balance = $983.65

Step 4: Compare the adjusted balance to the balance in the check register. If the account reconciles, these values will be equal. If not, then there are additional issues with either the bank statement or the check register.

adjusted balance = check register balance

$983.65 = $983.65

The account is reconciled.

Check It

Clayton received his bank statement for the month of December. His check register for December is shown along with the bank statement. Reconcile Clayton's account using the information shown.

First National Bank
1004 Chickasha Avenue
Chickasha, OK 73019

Statement December 20--

Checking Account

Account Number	87654321
Previous Balance	$940.00
Deposits/Credits	971.42
Checks/Debits	1396.55
Service Charge	$4.95
Current Balance	$509.92

Deposits and Other Credits

Date	Number	Description	Amount
12/7		Deposit	$485.71
12/21		Deposit	485.71

Checks and Other Debits

Date	Number	Description	Amount
12/2	257	Check	$350.00
12/3	258	Check	103.45
12/3		Debit–Lee's Pharmacy	17.15
12/4		Debit–Mike's Music	9.95
12/11	260	Check	115.49
12/12	259	Check	511.12
12/13	261	Check	161.74
12/15		Debit–Wills' Department Store	127.65

Number	Date	Description	Payment		✓	Deposit		Balance	
								$940	00
257	12/1	Rent	350	00				590	00
258	12/2	Groceries	103	45				486	50
	12/3	Debit–drugstore	17	15				469	40
	12/4	Debit–Online music store	9	95				459	45
	12/7	Paycheck				485	71	945	16
259	12/8	Credit card bill	511	12				434	04
260	12/8	Phone bill	115	49				318	55
261	12/12	Groceries	161	74				156	81
	12/14	Debit–clothing	127	65				29	16
	12/21	Paycheck				485	71	514	87
	12/28	Debit–electric bill	104	66				410	21
	12/30	Bank service charge	4	95				405	26

Example 4-2D

See It

A portion of Mischa's check register for her checking account is shown as follows. The next check Mischa writes is check number 228 on August 29 to Park Central High School for $41.53. List the steps that are required to record the check in the register. What is the new balance?

Number	Date	Description	Payment		✓	Deposit		Balance	
								$754	92
224	8/21	Four Corner's Grocery	32	11				722	81
225	8/24	Electric bill	235	67				487	14
226	8/27	Cable company	105	32				381	82
	8/28	Paycheck				2382	17	2763	99
227	8/23	Mortgage payment	1565	78				1198	21

Strategy

Follow the pattern in the check register.

Solution

Step 1: Record the check number in the check register.

Step 2: Record the date in the check register.

Step 3: Record the transaction description, typically the person to be paid, in the check register.

Step 4: Record the amount of the payment in the check register. Place the dollars in the dollars column, and the cents in the cents column.

Step 5: Calculate the new balance. Subtract the payment from the balance in the previous line of the register.

new balance = old balance – payment

new balance = $1,198.21 – $41.53

new balance = $1,156.68

Step 6: Record the new balance in the check register. Place the dollars in the dollars column, and the cents in the cents column.

Check It

Using the same check register, Mischa writes check number 229 on September 3 to the phone company for her cell phone bill. The check is written for $212.48. Identify the steps to record this transaction in the check register. Then determine the new balance.

Answer:
$944.20

Checkpoint 4.2

1. Shantel has a checking account balance of $318.59. She wrote a check to United Farmers Market for $52.17. What is Shantel's new checking account balance?

2. William has a checking account balance of $783.47. He wrote a check to his credit card company for $442.65. What is William's new checking account balance?

3. On February 28, Katherine wrote check number 1021 to Hooper's Market for $189.43. Her beginning balance was $584.77. Calculate the new balance.

4. Last month, Katherine received her January bank statement in the mail, showing a balance of $1,518.78. The following were not shown on the statement: a deposit of $125.78 and debit charges that she made for $49.44 and $113.93. What is Katherine's adjusted balance?

5. Katherine's bank statement for February also showed that three checks had not cleared in the following amounts: $221.07, $119.98, and $189.43. What is Katharine's new adjusted balance?

Teaching Tip:
Checkpoint questions offer opportunities for formative assessment.

Answer:
1. $266.42
2. $340.82
3. $395.34
4. $1,481.19
5. $950.71

Section 4.3 Savings Accounts

Terms

- *certificate of deposit (CD)*
- *principal*
- *money market account*
- *annual percentage rate (APR)*
- *simple interest*
- *compound interest*
- *rule of 72*

Objectives

- **Describe how a savings account works.**
- **Explain the restrictions on a certificate of deposit.**
- **Describe how a money market account differs from other savings accounts.**
- **Calculate simple and compound interest.**

Build Your Math Skills

Review these math skills to prepare for the lesson that follows.

1. Convert percentages to decimals by moving the decimal two places to the left. Example: 15% → 0.15

A. 18% →

B. 2.5% →

C. 6% →

D. 1.95% →

2. Multiply decimals. Round your answer to the nearest cent ($0.01) Example: $158.97 × 0.05 = $7.9485 ≈ $7.95

A. $550 × 0.12 =

B. $225.78 × 0.25 =

C. $110.79 × .05 =

D. $1,945 × 0.07 =

3. Use exponents. Example: $5^3 = 5 \times 5 \times 5 = 125$

A. $3^4 =$

B. $4^3 =$

C. $1.5^2 =$

D. $$15^2 =$

Ways to Save Money

As you learned earlier, a *savings account* is an account that pays interest to the account holder and limits the number of withdrawals per month. Many banks limit withdrawals to six per month. Because of the withdrawal restriction, a savings account generally does not allow checks or debit card transactions on the account. A savings account is useful for accumulating cash that you may need to access easily. A savings account does not take the place of a checking account.

An example of a good use for a savings account is for an emergency fund. Many people set aside money each month in a savings account to cover emergency expenses that may arise. An unexpected car repair is an example of an emergency expense.

Young people who do not need a checking account often use a savings account as their only bank account. As they receive money, they can put it in a savings account for safekeeping and also earn some interest on the money in the account.

fyi

A savings account earns interest at some of the lowest rates. Therefore, the primary purpose of the savings account is to hold money safely rather than to earn interest.

With online banking, it is possible to view both your checking and savings accounts and transfer money between them. This is helpful if you like to transfer money into your savings each month. It is also helpful if you need to write a check for an emergency expense. You can go online and transfer money from savings into checking to cover the check. Be sure to record the transactions. You can use the following formulas:

new savings account balance = beginning savings account balance – amount of transfer

new checking account balance = beginning checking account balance + amount of transfer

Example 4-3A

See It

Mei had an unexpected car repair and needed to transfer money from her savings account to her checking account. Before the transfer, her checking account balance was $450.13, and her savings account balance was $1,819.45. Mei transferred $450 from her savings account to her checking account. What is the new balance in each of Mei's accounts?

Strategy

Use the formulas:

new savings account balance = beginning savings account balance – amount of transfer

new checking account balance = beginning checking account balance + amount of transfer

Solution

Step 1: Subtract the amount of the transfer from the initial savings account balance.

new savings account balance = beginning savings account balance – amount of transfer

new savings balance = $1,819.45 – $450

new savings balance = $1,369.45

Step 2: Add the amount of the transfer to the initial checking account balance.

new checking account balance = beginning checking account balance + amount of transfer

new checking balance = $450.13 + $450

new checking balance = $900.13

⋮ Check It

Mateo had an unexpected kitchen appliance repair and needed to transfer money from his savings account to his checking account. Before the transfer, his checking account balance was $389.14. His savings account balance was $2,042.86. Mateo transferred $375.15 from his savings account to his checking account. What is the new balance in each of Mateo's accounts?

Certificates of Deposit

Another way to save money at a bank is by purchasing a certificate of deposit. A **certificate of deposit (CD)** is an account that earns a higher interest rate than a regular savings account. A CD is a special bank account that requires the investor to pledge the money to the bank for a specified period of time. In exchange, the bank pays a higher interest rate to the investor than what is available in a standard interest-bearing savings account.

Typically, a minimum amount is deposited for a set period of time. You agree to leave the money in the CD and not withdraw or add any money to the amount. At the end of the time period, the bank will pay you the principal plus the interest. **Principal** is the beginning amount of your deposit. Buying a CD is a way to keep a good interest rate. Interest rates can change at any time on a savings account. Once you buy a CD, the rate stays the same the entire time of the agreement period.

For example, a bank may offer a six-month CD at an interest rate that is higher than the rate of a regular savings account. The CD may also have a minimum balance. As long as you leave the money undisturbed in the bank for the full six-month term, you will receive the promised interest rate.

CD interest rates vary depending on conditions in the current economy. If interest rates are historically low, then the bank may offer a higher interest rate for a longer commitment. For example, a five-year CD may pay a significantly higher interest rate than a one-year CD. During times when rates are historically high, the bank may actually offer lower rates on longer-term CDs.

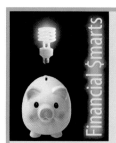

Financial $marts

The ability to save money is a good trait to have. Too many people have little or no savings. When people don't have an emergency fund, they can feel stress. When you have money saved, however, you can relax because you are prepared. Not only can savings help you cover an emergency expense, savings can also make it possible to enjoy a trip with friends or make a large purchase. Being a person who earns interest rather than one who pays interest to others is one way to be financially smart.

Money Market Accounts

A **money market account** is similar to an interest-bearing bank account. However, a money market account often requires a minimum balance, and the number of monthly transactions is limited. Unlike a CD, you can add and withdraw money at any time. The interest rate paid can also change at any time with market conditions.

Earning Interest

When you put money in a savings account, certificate of deposit, or money market account, you are actually renting out your money to another customer of the bank. The bank does not just put your money in the vault. The bank uses your money, along with the money of the other depositors, to loan to others. So when you put your money in a savings account, you are renting out your money to the bank. When the bank loans the money to others, they will charge interest. As an incentive to put your money in the bank, the bank will pay you a small amount of interest. The bank makes money by charging more interest to others than they pay you.

Simple Interest

The rate of interest charged or interest earned is usually expressed as a percentage. When people say they are earning 2.5% interest, they are most likely referring to the annual percentage rate of the account. The *annual percentage rate (APR)* is the rate of return on an investment for a one-year period. For example, you have $1,000 in a savings account that is earning 2.5% interest. By leaving the money in that account for one year, the account would grow by 2.5% due to accumulating interest. Therefore, instead of $1,000, you would have $1,025.00. Earning $25 by putting that $1,000 in the bank may not sound like much of an accomplishment. However, all you had to do to earn that money was not spend your $1,000.

This interest calculation is what is known as simple interest. *Simple interest* is interest paid only on an original sum of money, or principal. Think of the principal as the money being loaned or borrowed.

The formula for calculating simple interest is:

interest = principal × interest rate × time

This formula is commonly expressed as:

I = Prt

Example 4-3B

See It

Chun deposited $1,500 into a 12-month CD with an annual interest rate of 2.45% that is compounded quarterly. What is the amount of interest that Chun earned in the first quarter?

Strategy

Use the formula:

interest = principal × interest rate × time

fyi

Multiplication is represented in many ways. Usually, in a formula containing constants (numbers) and variables (letters), no symbol is used. Instead, the numbers and letters are written together in one or more terms. The simple interest formula will often appear simply as *I = Prt*.

Solution

Step 1: Determine the quarterly interest rate. Divide the annual interest rate by 4.

quarterly interest rate = annual interest rate ÷ 4

quarterly interest rate = 2.45% ÷ 4

quarterly interest rate = 0.6125%

Step 2: Convert the quarterly interest rate to a decimal by moving the decimal two places to the left.

0.6125% → 0.006125

Step 3: Calculate the amount of quarterly interest paid. Multiply the principal, quarterly interest rate, and number of quarters. Round to the nearest cent ($0.01).

interest = principal × interest rate × time

interest = $1,500 × 0.006125 per quarter × 1 quarter

interest = $9.19

Check It

Rashad deposited $1,200 into a 24-month CD. The annual interest rate is 3.5% and is compounded quarterly. What is the amount of interest that Rashad will earn in the first quarter?

Answer:
$10.50

Example 4-3C

See It

Lisa Marie deposited $575 into an account that earns simple interest at a rate of 1.25% per year. At the end of two years, what is the balance of Lisa Marie's account, assuming that she makes no additional deposits?

Strategy

Use the formula:

$$I = Prt$$

Solution

Step 1: Determine the principal, interest rate, and amount of time of the investment.

principal = $575

interest rate = 1.25% per year

time = 2 years

Step 2: Convert the interest rate from a percentage to a decimal by moving the decimal two places to the left.

1.25% → 0.0125

Step 3: Multiply the principal, interest rate (as a decimal), and time.

interest = principal × interest rate × time

interest = $575 × 0.0125 per year × 2 years

interest = $14.38

Step 4: Determine the new account balance with interest. Add the interest and the principal.

new account balance = initial account balance + interest

interest = $575 + $14.38

interest = $589.38

Check It

Gerald deposited $750 into an account that earns simple interest at a rate of 2.29% per year. If Gerald leaves this money in the account for three years, what will be the account balance at the end of the three years? Assume that he makes no additional deposits into the account during this time.

Answer:
$801.53

Compound Interest

On most savings accounts, you are paid interest each month on the average balance for the previous month. Once you are paid that interest, the balance is increased. In other words, your principal has increased. The next month you will be earning interest on your original principal plus the interest earned in previous months. ***Compound interest*** is interest calculated on the principal and accumulated interest.

Compounding can happen annually, monthly, or even daily. The more frequent the compounding period, the sooner you start earning interest on previously earned interest. In most cases, the difference is minor over a year. For example, if you deposited $1,000 into a savings account at 2.5% interest, compounding monthly results in approximately 25 cents more interest in a year than if compounded annually.

However, compound interest is very powerful over long periods of time. By putting $1,000 in an investment that returns 5% interest for 40 years, that $1,000 would grow to more than $7,000 without adding any money to the account other than the interest being earned.

Compound interest is related to simple interest in that it is calculated by multiplying the principal, interest rate, and amount of time. Compound interest differs from simple interest in that the interest rate is applied repeatedly, instead of once. Because this requires the multiplication of the same number, the interest rate, the formula for compound interest contains an exponent.

fyi

Exponents are used in mathematics to indicate repeated multiplication.

The formula for compound interest is:

$$\text{final amount} = \text{principal} \times (1 + \text{interest rate})^{\text{number of years invested}}$$

This formula is commonly expressed as:

$$M = P(1 + i)^n$$

Example 4-3D

See It

Aaliyah inherited $5,000 from her grandmother. She deposited the money into a savings account that earns 3% compound interest annually. If Aaliyah leaves the money in this account for 20 years and makes no additional deposits, what will the account balance be?

Strategy

Use the formula:

$$\text{final amount} = \text{principal} \times (1 + \text{interest rate})^{\text{number of years invested}}$$

Solution

Step 1: Identify the principal, annual interest rate, and number of years that the principal will be invested.

principal = $5,000

interest rate = 3%

number of years invested = 20 years

Step 2: Convert the interest rate to a decimal by moving the decimal two places to the left.

3% → 0.03

Step 3: Substitute the values into the formula.

final amount = principal × (1 + interest rate)$^{\text{number of years invested}}$

final amount = $5,000 × (1 + 0.03)^{20}

Step 4: Follow the order of operations. First, simplify the quantity inside the parentheses by adding 1 and 0.03.

final amount = $5,000 × (1 + 0.03)^{20}

final amount = $5,000 × (1.03)^{20}

Step 4: Follow the order of operations. Next, simplify the exponent by raising 1.03 to the 20th power. Use a calculator and round to the nearest ten-thousandth (0.0001) if necessary.

final amount = $5,000 × (1.03)^{20}

final amount = $5,000 × 1.8061

Step 5: Follow the order of operations. Multiply $5,000 by 1.8061.

final amount = $5,000 × 1.8061

final amount = $9,030.50

Check It

Garrett received a bonus check from work for $3,760. He decided to invest the money in an account that yields 4% compound interest annually. If Garrett leaves the money in the account and makes no additional deposits, what will be the balance of the account in 15 years?

Answer:
$6,771.38

In most cases, interest is compounded quarterly, monthly, or even daily. Even so, the compounding period is based on the annual interest rate, divided by the number of compounding periods. The more frequently interest is compounded, the higher investment return you receive. This is because you are receiving interest on the interest from previous compounding periods. If interest is compounded at a more frequent rate than annually, the formula used to calculate compound interest is adjusted to account for the additional compounding periods:

$$M = P\left(1 + \frac{i}{n}\right)^{nt}$$

In this formula, M represents the balance at the end of the investment period, P represents the principal, i represents the annual interest rate, n represents the number of compounding periods per year, and t represents the time in years of the investment period.

The order of operations can be remembered by using the acronym PEMDAS:
- **P**arentheses
- **E**xponents
- **M**ultiplication/**D**ivision
- **A**ddition/**S**ubtraction

Example 4-3E

See It

Suppose that in the previous example, in which Aaliyah inherited $5,000 from her grandmother, she deposited the money into a savings account that earns 3% interest, compounded quarterly instead of annually. If Aaliyah leaves the money in this account for 20 years and makes no additional deposits, what will be the account balance?

Strategy

Use the formula:

$$M = P\left(1 + \frac{i}{n}\right)^{nt}$$

Solution

Step 1: Identify the principal (*P*), annual interest rate (*i*), number of compounding periods per year (*n*), and amount of time of the investment (*t*).

principal: $P = \$5,000$

annual interest rate: $i = 3\%$

number of compounding periods per year: $n = 4$

amount of time of the investment: $t = 30$ years

Step 2: Determine the interest rate for each compounding period. Divide the annual interest rate by the number of compounding periods per year.

$$\text{quarterly interest rate} = \frac{i}{n}$$

Teaching Tip:
Remind students that the equation $\frac{i}{n}$ requires that the annual interest rate be divided by the number of compounding periods per year.

$$\text{quarterly interest rate} = \frac{3\%}{4}$$

quarterly interest rate = 0.75%

Step 3: Determine the total number of compounding periods. Multiply the number of compounding periods per year by the number of years of the investment.

total number of compounding periods = nt

total number of compounding periods = 4×30

total number of compounding periods = 120

Step 4: Convert the quarterly interest rate to a decimal by moving the decimal two places to the left.

$0.75\% \rightarrow 0.0075$

Step 5: Add one to the quarterly interest rate to account for the initial investment.

$1 + 0.0075 = 1.0075$

Step 6: Follow the order of operations. Raise 1.0075 to the 120th power. Round to the nearest ten-thousandth (0.0001) if necessary.

$1.0075^{120} \approx 2.4514$

Step 7: Multiply by the principal. Round to the nearest cent ($0.01) if necessary.

balance = principal $\times 2.4514$

balance = $\$5,000 \times 2.4514$

balance = $\$12,257$

Check It

Consider the previous example in which Garrett received a bonus check from work for $3,760. He decided to invest the money in an account that yields 4% interest anually that is compounded quarterly. If Garrett leaves the money in the account and makes no additional deposits, what will be the balance of the account in 15 years?

Answer:
$6,830.78

Source: Shutterstock (Diego Cervo)

Many people use smartphone apps to make and transfer payments even when they are on the go.

Rule of 72

How long will it take to double your savings or investments? There is a simple way to estimate that number. It is called the rule of 72. The ***rule of 72*** states that you simply divide the number 72 by the interest rate you are receiving. The answer is the number of years it takes to double your investment. The formula for the rule of 72 is:

number of years to double an investment = 72 ÷ interest rate

For example, if you are earning 6% interest, divide 72 by 6. The answer is 12. This means it will take you 12 years to double your money. So, in 12 years, if you leave that $1,000 in savings, you will have $2,000.

This may not sound like much money. Remember, the more you save, the larger the end result will be. All you have to do to double your money is not spend it.

Teaching Tip:
Reinforce the idea that the rule of 72 is only an estimate of how long it will take to double money invested.

Example 4-3F

See It

Susan and John are saving to pay for a college education for their son Jake. Jake is two years old. They have deposited $5,000 in an account that is paying 5.5%. How many years will it take for their investment to double?

Strategy

Use the formula:

number of years to double an investment = 72 ÷ interest rate

Step 1: Determine the interest rate.

interest rate = 5.5%

Step 2: Determine the number of years required for the investment to double. Divide 72 by the interest rate (in percentage form).

number of years = 72 ÷ interest rate

number of years = 72 ÷ 5.5

number of years ≈ 13

Check It

Aban deposited $4,000 into an account that earns 3.25% interest. How many years will it take for his investment to double?

Answer:
22 years

Checkpoint 4.3

1. Stella had an emergency plumbing repair and transferred $612.48 from her savings account to her checking account. Before the transfer, her checking account balance was $350.18. Her savings account balance was $2,225.69. What are Stella's new savings and checking account balances?

2. Ting deposited $2,125 into a savings account that earns 5% simple interest annually for four years. What will Ting's account balance be at the end of the four years? Assume that she makes no additional deposits during that time period.

3. Corey deposited $2,000 into a 36-month CD. The annual interest rate is 5.4% and is compounded quarterly. What is the amount of interest that Corey will earn in one quarter?

4. Sulema received a bonus check from work for $5,187.75. She decided to invest the money in an account with an annual interest rate of 3.75% that is compounded annually. If Sulema leaves the money in the account and makes no additional deposits, what will be the balance of the account in 16 years?

5. Latisha deposited $1,000 into an account that earns 4.25% interest. How many years will it take for her investment to double?

Chapter Review

Build Your Vocabulary

As you progress through this course, develop a personal glossary of financial literacy terms and add it to your portfolio. This will help you build your financial literacy vocabulary. Write out a definition for each of the following terms, and add it to your personal glossary.

interest

service charge

checking account

savings account

cleared

electronic funds transfer (EFT)

debit card

automated teller machine (ATM)

overdrawn

overdraft fee

overdraft protection

bank statement

reconcile

outstanding check

balance

register

certificate of deposit (CD)

principal

money market account

annual percentage rate (APR)

simple interest

compound interest

rule of 72

 ## Teamwork

Working with a classmate, create a list of competitive advantages a bank could offer that would persuade a consumer to move their banking business to that bank. Focus on the most significant advantages for the consumer. After you finish your research, survey your class to see what services other teams perceive to be most important.

Review Your Math Skills

Practice and build on the math skills that you have learned.

1. Add decimals. Example: 12.86 + 27.27 = 40.13

A. 351 + 5.8 =

B. 112.307 + 68.52 =

C. 9.4 + 0.2045 =

D. 42.109 + 7.409 =

2. Multiply decimals. Example: 10.5 × 2.1 = 22.05

A. 5.037 × 2.7 =

B. 2.7 × 1.6 =

C. 1.22 × 5.83 =

D. 0.675 × 0.455 =

Answer:
1. A. 356.8
   B. 180.827
   C. 9.6045
   D. 49.518
2. A. 13.5999
   B. 4.32
   C. 7.1126
   D. 0.307125

3. Convert percentages to decimals by moving the decimal two places to the left. **Example:** 22.5% → 0.225

A. 2.75% →

B. 0.05% →

C. 107.25% →

D. 3.75% →

4. Subtract decimals. **Example:** 12.5 − 3.4 = 9.1

A. 0.75 − 0.12 =

B. 72.105 − 43.9 =

C. 92.62 − 258.21 =

D. 0.587 − 2.4 =

5. Use exponents. **Example:** $5^2 = 5 \times 5 = 25$

A. $11^2 =$

B. $2^3 =$

C. $0.01^5 =$

D. $4^4 =$

6. Multiply decimals. **Example:** 4.7 × 22.01 = 103.447

A. 76.19 × 2.07 =

B. 1.003 × −7.9 =

C. 0.4576 × 0.03 =

D. 62.005 × 2.30924 =

7. Add decimals. **Example:** −21.0057 + 10.38 = −10.6257

A. 14.7 + 28.45 =

B. −107.4 + 12.87 =

C. −10.004 + −4.237 =

D. 114.027 + −5.173 =

8. Use exponents. **Example:** $0.1^2 = 0.1 \times 0.1 = 0.01$

A. $0.2^4 =$

B. $2.5^3 =$

C. $1.9^4 =$

D. $1.15^3 =$

9. Convert percentages to decimals by moving the decimal two places to the left. **Example:** 0.05% → 0.0005

A. 1.004% →

B. 138.48% →

C. −22.875% →

D. 0.01035% →

10. Subtract decimals. **Example:** −2.875 − 1.057 = −3.932

A. 34.017 − 0.248 =

B. 2.039 − (−1.309) =

C. 79.047 − 79.12 =

D. −3.455 − 104.2 =

3. A. 0.0275
   B. 0.0005
   C. 1.0725
   D. 0.0375
4. A. 0.63
   B. 28.205
   C. −165.59
   D. −1.813
5. A. 121
   B. 8
   C. 0.0000000001
   D. 256
6. A. 157.7133
   B. −7.9237
   C. 0.013728
   D. 143.1844262
7. A. 43.15
   B. −94.53
   C. −14.241
   D. 108.854
8. A. 0.0016
   B. 15.625
   C. 13.0321
   D. 1.520875
9. A. 0.01004
   B. 1.3848
   C. −0.22875
   D. 0.0001035
10. A. 33.769
    B. 3.348
    C. −0.073
    D. −107.655

Section 4.1 Opening an Account

11. Murphy is a travel agent and is making a bank deposit for her business at the end of the day. She has $495 in currency, $11.45 in coins, and $2,307.42 in checks. What is the net deposit that Murphy will be making?

12. Alonzo is depositing his birthday money into his savings account. He received three checks in the amounts of $25, $35, and $50. He is also depositing a refund check for $114.25. He wants to get $45 cash back. What is Alonzo's net deposit?

Answer:
11. $2,813.87
12. $179.25

Section 4.2 Checking Accounts

13. Sana has a checking account balance of $549.95. She wrote a check to Foley Brothers Department Store for $128.14. What is Sana's new checking account balance?

14. Enrique received his bank statement showing a checking account balance of $317.07. Not shown on the statement was a deposit of $354.38. Also, two checks he wrote for $78.04 and $412.95 were not shown. What is Enrique's adjusted balance?

15. Catalina received her bank statement showing a savings account balance of $1,056.33. Not shown on the statement were a deposit of $75 and two withdrawals of $320.50 and $86.10. What is Catalina's adjusted balance?

Answer:
13. $421.81
14. $180.46
15. $724.73

Section 4.3 Savings Accounts

16. Khadijah had an emergency car repair bill and transferred $715.98 from her savings account to her checking account. Before the transfer, her checking account balance was $478.61. Her savings account balance was $3,097.45. What are Khadijah's new savings and checking account balances?

17. Quentin deposited $1,264 into a savings account that earns 2.75% simple interest annually. What will Quentin's account balance be at the end of 2.5 years? Assume he makes no additional deposits during that time period.

18. Rina deposited $3,000 into a 12-month CD. The annual interest rate is 3.75% and is compounded quarterly. What is the amount of interest that Rina will earn in one quarter?

Answer:
16. new savings balance = $2,381.47 new checking balance = $1,194.59
17. $1,350.90
18. $28.13

Reinforce Your Understanding

Answer:
19. Plan A. In 10 years, Viola will have $2,501.73. If she invested in Plan B, she would only have $2,484.57.

19. Viola received a bonus check from her employer for $1,650. Her financial advisor found two different investment plans for her to consider. Plan A is an account that pays compound interest at a rate of 4.25% annually for ten years. Plan B is an account that pays compound interest at a rate of 5.25% annually for eight years. Which plan should Viola choose? Explain your answer.

20. Angelo is comparing bank account plans. First Community Bank offers a checking account that pays 1.1% interest on the final monthly balance, but charges $2.50 per ATM transaction. Central National Bank offers a checking account that charges a flat monthly fee of $5.95 for unlimited ATM transactions, but pays no interest. Angelo's check register for last month is as follows. Which bank should Angelo choose based on the data in the check register?

Number	Date	Description	Payment		✓	Deposit		Balance	
								1481	19
1015	2/2	Mortgage payment	761	18				720	01
	2/2	ATM withdrawal	100	00				620	01
	2/5	Paycheck				495	70	1115	71
1016	2/6	Credit card payment	322	74				792	97
D	2/7	Debit—groceries	144	57				648	40
	2/8	ATM withdrawal	100	00				548	40
D	2/10	Debit—drugstore	18	92				529	48
1017	2/14	Post office	17	95				511	53
	2/19	Paycheck				495	70	1007	23
D	2/20	Debit—movie theater	34	27				972	96
	2/21	ATM withdrawal	125	00				847	96
1018	2/21	Car insurance	221	07				626	89
D	2/25	Debit—Car Tronics	119	98				506	91

20. First Community Bank, since the bank charges after interest payment would only be $1.92, whereas at Central National Bank, the bank charges would be $5.95.

Apply Your Technology Skills

Companion Website
www.g-wlearning.com

Access the G-W Learning companion website for this text at www.g-wlearning.com. Download each data file for this chapter. Follow the instructions to complete a financial literacy activity to practice what you have learned in this chapter.

Teaching Tip:
The Apply Your Technology Skills activities offer project-based authentic assessment opportunities.

Data File 4-1—Completing an Application for a Bank Account

Data File 4-2—Filling out a Deposit Slip

Data File 4-3—Completing a Check Register

Data File 4-4—Investigating Bank Accounts

5 Making Purchases

Materials:
Instructor's Resource CD
Student Workbook
G-W Learning companion website
EXAMVIEW® Assessment Suite
Microsoft Excel®–compatible software
Calculator with advanced-math functions

You have probably been making purchases since you were a small child. However, there are some aspects of purchasing that require further study to be fully understood. In this chapter, you will learn the basics of purchasing, like making change and calculating sales tax. You will also learn about the various ways to pay for products and services and how to make the right decisions when making purchases.

Section 5.1	**Basics of Purchasing**
Section 5.2	**Payment Options**
Section 5.3	**Influences on Purchasing Decisions**

College and Career Readiness

Reading Prep. In preparation for reading the chapter, consider the many ways that you can purchase products. As you read, how does your knowledge of purchasing compare with the information provided in the chapter?

> *"I usually make purchases with a debit card, and I always look at the cost before going to pay for my purchases." ~ Keagan C.*

Money Matters
Online Shopping

- More online purchases are made on the first Monday following Thanksgiving than on any other day of the year.

- Approximately 75% of consumers make at least one Internet purchase per month.

- The World Wide Web browser was created in 1990 by Tim Berners-Lee.

- The Internet was opened for use by business and individuals in 1991.

- In 1994, Pizza Hut was the first restaurant to offer online ordering, to customers in Santa Cruz, California.

- The online retailer, Amazon, and online auction service, eBay, were introduced to the world in 1995.

- In 1998, the US Post Office began selling electronic postage stamps online.

- In 2011, online retail sales were approximately $200 billion per year in the United States.

- By 2016, it is predicted that online sales will increase to 62% of total retail sales.

Section 5.1 Basics of Purchasing

Objectives

- **Describe various types of markets.**
- **Calculate sales tax.**
- **Calculate discounts from coupons.**
- **Calculate tips.**

Terms

- *market*
- *good*
- *service*
- *market size*
- *sales tax*
- *coupon*
- *rebate*
- *tip*
- *comparison shopping*

Build Your Math Skills

Review these math skills to prepare for the lesson that follows.

1. Convert percentages to decimals by moving the decimal two places to the left. Example: 8.25% → 0.0825

A. 6.5% →

B. 15% →

C. 4.25% →

D. 7.875% →

2. Multiply decimals. Round to the nearest cent ($0.01) if necessary. Example: $45 × 0.08 = $3.60

A. $99 × 0.06 =

B. $15.25 × 0.10 =

C. $159.65 × 0.07 =

D. $20.50 × 1.08 =

3. Add decimals. Example: $78.13 + $2.19 = $80.32

A. $506.78 + $50.68 =

B. $98.17 + $7.15 =

C. $397.60 + $30.79 =

D. $119.17 + $105.67 =

Answer:
1. A. 0.065
   B. 0.15
   C. 0.0425
   D. 0.07875
2. A. $5.94
   B. $1.53
   C. $11.18
   D. $22.14
3. A. $557.46
   B. $105.32
   C. $428.39
   D. $224.84

Types of Markets

At a young age, you might have heard of little piggies going to market. Now, you go to supermarkets. You might go to flea markets or farmers' markets. You hear about the stock market. Companies do market*ing* to encourage you to go to a market. While you may think of a market as a place, a *market* is actually any arrangement that allows buyers and sellers to meet with the purpose of exchanging goods, services, or even information.

In accounting and economics, a *good* is a physical product, such as jewelry or a mobile phone. A good is *tangible,* meaning you can touch, smell, or taste it. A *service* is an activity of value, like a car wash, a cab ride, or website development. A service is *intangible,* even if the results of the service are tangible.

A market can be a traditional store, like a department store. A concession stand at a sporting event or concert is also a market. Classified ads, whether in a newspaper or online, are markets. Online auction sites, like eBay, are also markets. A garage sale is a type of market. Even a little kid with a lemonade stand is creating a market. There are many types of markets because there are many goods and services of value to trade.

fyi

The Grand Bazaar in Istanbul, Turkey, is one of the oldest and largest markets in the world. The Grand Bazaar opened in 1461 and attracts hundreds of thousands of visitors per day.

The market size for a particular good or service can change over time. For example, as the mobile phone market increased, the market size for wired phones, or *land lines,* decreased significantly.

The word *market* can also refer to the demand for an item. You might have heard the question raised, "Is there a market for that?" This question is whether there are buyers for the particular good or service. The answer is almost always *yes.* The real question is how many buyers there are. *Market size* refers to the number of buyers for a product or service. For example, in the US alone, billions of dollars are spent each year on bicycles and related parts and accessories. Therefore, you could safely say that the market size for bicycles in the US is large.

Increasingly, consumers are using the Internet as a market. Buying, selling, and trading through the Internet is called *e-commerce.* Through e-commerce, buyers and sellers can transact business without ever meeting face-to-face. Credit and debit cards are now used as often to make e-commerce transactions as they are to make purchases at actual stores.

Calculating Sales Tax

Teaching Tip:
Inform students that some goods incur an additional tax over and above the sales tax. These items are usually goods that are in high demand, such as gasoline. Have students discuss their experiences with sales tax and other taxes. Ask students why these items are taxed differently.

In most states, the majority of purchases are subject to sales tax. *Sales tax* is a tax collected on the sales price of a good or service. The tax is calculated using a flat rate. Sales tax is collected by the store or business making the taxable sale. The store or business keeps records of the sales and taxes collected. Then, the stores pass on the tax they have collected to the appropriate government agency. Sales tax rates and laws vary from state to state and city to city.

Sales tax is usually expressed as a percentage. Certain items are exempt from sales tax. For example, bread, eggs, fruits, and vegetables are often exempt. But prepared foods, such as restaurant food, or food sold ready to eat might be subject to sales tax. Sales tax is calculated using the following formula:

$$\textbf{sales tax} = \textbf{item price} \times \textbf{sales tax rate}$$

To calculate the total bill, with tax included, use the formula that follows:

$$\textbf{total bill} = \textbf{(total purchase price of taxable items} \times \textbf{sales tax rate)} + \textbf{sum of nontaxable items' purchase price}$$

Example 5-1A

See It

Micah purchased a new shirt for $39.95. The sales tax in his city is 8.25%. What is the amount of sales tax that Micah will pay for the shirt?

Strategy

Use the formula:

$$\textbf{sales tax} = \textbf{item price} \times \textbf{sales tax rate}$$

Solution

Step 1: Convert the sales tax rate from a percentage to a decimal by moving the decimal two places to the left.

$8.25\% \rightarrow 0.0825$

Step 2: Multiply the item price by the sales tax rate.

sales tax = item price $\times$ sales tax rate

sales tax = 39.95×0.0825

sales tax = $3.30

Check It

Belinda purchased a new barbecue grill for her family to use this summer. She paid $479.99 for the grill. The sales tax in her city is 6.75%. What is the amount of sales tax that Belinda will pay for the barbecue grill?

Answer:
$32.40

Example 5-1B

See It

Omar purchased items for a party. His list of items, along with their purchase price, is shown on the portion of his receipt. If a *T* appears next to the item price, the item was subject to sales tax. Omar lives in a city that has a 7.5% sales tax rate. Calculate Omar's total bill.

```
            PARTY CENTRAL
         1313 BLACKBIRD LANE
          LITTLE AXE, TX 76538

STREAMERS              $2.19  T
JUICE                  $3.79
PAPER PLATES           $0.99  T
CRACKERS               $3.15
CHEESE                 $7.98
SAUSAGES               $5.95
NAPKINS                $1.49  T
DELI CHICKEN (COOKED)  $4.49  T
```

Teaching Tip:
The complete solutions to the Check It problems can be found on the Instructor's Resource CD.

Strategy

Use the formula:

total bill = (total purchase price of taxable items × sales tax rate) + sum of taxable items' purchase price + sum of nontaxable items' purchase price

Solution

Step 1: Determine which items are subject to sales tax.

Read the receipt, and identify the items with a *T* next to the item price. The taxable items are streamers, paper plates, napkins, and deli chicken (cooked).

Step 2: Determine the total purchase price of the taxable items. Add the four numbers together.

total price of taxable items = $2.19 + $0.99 + $1.49 + $4.49

total price of taxable items = $9.16

Step 3: Convert the sales tax rate from a percentage to a decimal by moving the decimal two places to the left.

$7.5\% \rightarrow 0.075$

Step 4: Determine the sales tax. Multiply the total price of the taxable items by the sales tax rate.

sales tax = total purchase price of taxable items × sales tax rate

sales tax = $9.16 × 0.075

sales tax = $0.69

Step 5: Determine the sum of all nontaxable items. Add the prices of each nontaxable item.

total of all nontaxable items = sum of nontaxable item prices

subtotal = $3.79 + $3.15 + $7.98 + $5.95

subtotal = $20.87

Step 6: Determine the total. Add the total of all taxable items, the amount of sales tax, and the total of all nontaxable items.

total bill = sum of taxable items' purchase price + amount of sales tax rate + sum of nontaxable items' purchase price

total bill = $9.16 + $0.69 + $20.87

total bill = $30.72

Check It

Ivana went to the grocery store and purchased a few items. Her list of items, along with their purchase price, is shown on the receipt. If a *T* appears next to the item price, the item was subject to sales tax. Ivana lives in a city that has a 9.25% sales tax rate. Calculate Ivana's total bill.

Answer:
$28.30

```
CENTRAL GROCERY
    FOOD FOR LIFE

APPLES             $2.35
EGGS               $3.33
TOOTHPASTE         $2.99  T
LUNCHEON MEAT      $3.29
PAPER TOWELS       $5.99  T
BREAD              $1.49
GROUND BEEF        $4.98
FRUIT JUICE BLEND  $2.79  T
```

Saving Money on Purchases

Consumers can reduce the cost of purchases by using coupons, rebates, and comparison-shopping. A *coupon* is a certificate that grants a discount or even a free good or service to its holder. Coupons are generally distributed through the mail, online, in magazines, or in newspapers. The purpose of a coupon is to encourage a person to choose a particular product.

For example, say you need to buy some flour. If you received a coupon for a discount on a specific brand, you may be more likely to try that brand. The manufacturer of the flour is hoping that you like the product and that you will choose their brand in the future.

A coupon can offer a reduction in price by a percentage or may offer a specific discount. Coupons may have limits. For example, a coupon may specify that the buyer is limited to three items at the discounted price. To find the final purchase price of an item after using a coupon, use the following formula:

final purchase price = regular price – amount of the coupon

Example 5-1C

See It

Barbara used a coupon to save $1.25 on a bag of cat litter that was regularly priced at $5.49. What was the final purchase price of the cat litter after the coupon?

Strategy

Use the formula:

final purchase price = regular price – amount of the coupon

Solution

Step 1: Identify the amount of the coupon and the regular price of the item.

amount of coupon = $1.25

regular price of item = $5.49

Step 2: Subtract the amount of the coupon from the regular price of the item.

final purchase price = regular price of item – amount of coupon

final purchase price = $5.49 – $1.25

final purchase price = $4.24

Check It

Eduardo took his friend to lunch. He used a coupon to save $5.95 off the total bill. If the cost of lunch was $25.35, what is the price Eduardo paid?

Answer:
$19.40

Example 5-1D

See It

Melanie used a coupon for 25% off the item of her choice at her favorite department store. She purchased a coffeemaker that was regularly priced at $89.95. What is the final purchase price, before sales tax, of the coffeemaker?

Strategy

Use the formula:

final purchase price = regular price – amount of discount

Solution

Step 1: Convert the discount percentage to a decimal by moving the decimal two places to the left.

25% → 0.25

Instead of subtracting the discount percentage from the regular price, you can also determine the discounted price of an item by subtracting the percentage of the discount from 100% and multiplying that difference by the original price. In other words, receiving a 25% discount on an item is the same as paying 75% of the original price.

Step 2: Determine the amount of discount. Multiply the regular price by the discount rate (as a decimal). Round to the nearest cent ($0.01) if necessary.

amount of discount = regular price × discount rate

amount of discount = $89.95 × 0.25

amount of discount = $22.49

Step 3: Determine the final purchase price. Subtract the amount of discount from the regular price.

final purchase price = regular price – amount of discount

final purchase price = $89.95 – $22.49

final purchase price = $67.46

Check It

Jamal used a coupon for 35% off to purchase a necklace for his niece. If the original price of the necklace was $74.95, what was the final purchase price that Jamal paid, excluding sales tax, for the necklace?

Answer:
$48.72

A *rebate* is an offer to pay back a portion of the money a customer spent on an item. A rebate is often a larger discount than a coupon. Rebates can be $50, $100, or more and are usually offered at the place of purchase.

Financial Smarts

When you are making any kind of purchase, it pays to do your research. Whether you are buying a mobile phone, an appliance, an automobile, or even a meal, you have many options. An easy way to do research is to go online. Learn how to evaluate the product or service. If it is a product, learn to understand and compare its specifications. Search for reviews of products and services. Ask friends and family about their experiences.

However, there is generally added effort involved in redeeming a rebate. The customer pays the full price up front and then mails in the rebate or applies for the rebate online. This usually requires the customer to complete a form and submit proof of purchase. The proof of purchase can be a receipt or a portion of the package.

Be aware of the difference between a coupon and a rebate. A coupon is deducted from the regular price before tax is applied. Note that a coupon is more valuable than a rebate of the same value, since the item is taxed on a smaller amount of money. A rebate is a discount that is given after an item is purchased. Rebates often take many weeks to process. To determine the amount of the final cost of a purchase after a rebate is applied, use the following formula:

final cost = purchase price – rebate amount

Example 5-1E

See It

Preston purchased a DVD player and received a rebate of $45. The original purchase price, including sales tax, of the DVD player was $289.47. After Preston receives the rebate, what will be the final cost of the DVD player?

Strategy

Use the formula:

final cost = purchase price – rebate amount

Solution

Step 1: Identify the rebate amount and purchase price.

rebate amount = $45

purchase price = $289.47

Step 2: Determine the final cost. Subtract the rebate amount from the purchase price.

final cost = purchase price – rebate amount

final cost = $289.47 – $45

final cost = $244.47

Check It

Shari purchased backyard playground equipment for her two daughters. The purchase price of the equipment was $624.78. She also used a mail-in rebate of $75. What was the final cost of the backyard playground equipment?

Answer:
$549.78

Tips

With some purchases, a tip is expected. A **tip,** also called a *gratuity,* is an extra payment voluntarily made to a worker. For example, at a restaurant where food is served to you at a table, it is customary to tip the server 15–20% of the subtotal of the bill. Most agree that a server in a restaurant should be tipped 15% for adequate service and up to 20% for very good service. Even for poor service, at least 10% is usually left as a tip.

To determine the total amount of the bill with tax and tip, use the following formula:

total bill = amount of tip + sales tax + pretax subtotal

fyi

Sales tax is usually not included when calculating tips.

Teaching Tip:
Ask students to discuss their experiences with giving or receiving tips.

Example 5-1F

See It

Cheryl went to lunch with her sister. The bill before sales tax was $31.45. Because the service was excellent, she decided to leave a 20% tip. If the sales tax rate was 8%, what was the final amount of the final bill, including tip?

Strategy

Use the formula:

total bill = amount of tip + sales tax + pretax subtotal

Solution

Step 1: Convert the tip rate and the sales tax rate to decimals by moving the decimal two places to the left.

20% → 0.20

8% → 0.08

Step 2: Determine the amount of the tip. Multiply the subtotal by the tip rate (as a decimal). Round to the nearest cent ($0.01) if necessary.

amount of tip = subtotal × tip rate

amount of tip = $31.45 × 0.20

amount of tip = $6.29

Step 3: Determine the amount of sales tax. Multiply the subtotal by the sales tax rate (as a decimal). Tips are not included in the sales tax calculation. Round to the nearest cent ($0.01) if necessary.

sales tax = subtotal × sales tax rate

sales tax = $31.45 × 0.08

sales tax = $2.52

Step 4: Determine the amount of the final bill. Add the subtotal, amount of tip, and sales tax.

final bill = subtotal + amount of tip + sales tax

final bill = $31.45 + $6.29 + $2.52

final bill = $40.26

Check It

Lee took his girlfriend out to dinner. The pretax subtotal was $42.75. Lee decided to leave an 18% tip. The sales tax rate is 7.5%. What was the amount of the final bill?

Answer:
$53.66

The Internet is a good tool for comparison shopping. It can save you time and money if you don't have to make a physical trip to the store.

Another important way to save money on things you purchase is through comparison shopping. *Comparison shopping* is finding the price of an item at two or more stores. For example, the price of a certain pair of shoes is $30 at one store and $35 at another. With all other things being equal, you should buy the shoes from the first store. This would save you $5.

Checkpoint 5.1

Teaching Tip:
Checkpoint questions offer opportunities for formative assessment.

1. Darius purchased a new suit for $295.95. The sales tax rate on clothing is 6.25%. What is the final purchase price of the suit, including sales tax?

2. Fatima purchased new plants for her yard. She used a coupon for 20% off her entire purchase, which was $195.50 before sales tax. What is the pretax purchase price of the plants, after the coupon discount is deducted?

3. Keenan purchased a bag of dog food for $48.23. He received a mail-in rebate for $7.50. What will be the final cost of the bag of dog food if Keenan uses the mail-in rebate?

4. Natsumi went on a business lunch. The pretax bill was $55.60. She decided to leave a 15% tip. The sales tax rate is 8.25%. What was the final amount of the bill?

Answer:
1. $314.45
2. $156.40
3. $40.73
4. $68.53
5. $69.62

5. Makalo took his grandmother to dinner. The pretax bill was $54.50. He decided to leave a 20% tip. The sales tax rate is 7.75%. What was the final amount of the bill?

Source: Shutterstock (Monkey Business Images)

Installment plans allow someone to pay for a large purchase over time.

Section 5.2 Payment Options

Terms

- *payment card*
- *gift card*
- *charge account*
- *installment plan*
- *layaway plan*
- *digital cash*
- *online bill pay*

Objectives

- **Demonstrate how to make change.**
- **Describe the types and features of payment cards.**
- **Define the characteristics of a charge account.**
- **Summarize how electronic payments are used.**

Build Your Math Skills

Review these math skills to prepare for the lesson that follows.

1. Add decimals. Example: $81.15 + $205.67 = $286.82

A. $79.89 + $54.56 =

B. $103.48 + $97.39 =

C. $593.05 + $412.17 =

D. $76.91 + $205.46 =

2. Subtract decimals. Example: $540 − $125.10 = $414.90

A. $506.70 − $28.15 =

B. $718.11 − $405.85 =

C. $1,019.43 − $145.84 =

D. $819.14 − $99.45 =

Answer:
1. A. $134.45
   B. $200.87
   C. $1,005.22
   D. $282.37
2. A. $478.55
   B. $312.26
   C. $873.59
   D. $719.69

Cash

Cash is the most straightforward way to pay for a purchase. *Cash* is the physical form of money, represented by paper currency and coins. In the US, paper currency comes in several denominations, including $1, $2, $5, $10, $20, $50, and $100.

Making change is an important skill when transacting any business in cash. Rarely does a buyer have the exact amount in cash for the total price of a purchase. Instead, he or she might present a $20 bill as payment for a $17.50 purchase. Sellers have to know how to calculate the correct amount of change to give to buyers. Buyers also need to know how to calculate the correct amount of change so that they can be sure they receive the correct amount. You can use the following formula to calculate change due:

change due = amount of cash given to the clerk − purchase total

fyi

The $2 bill may not be a very popular currency, but it is still in circulation today. You can request $2 bills from your local bank.

Example 5-2A

See It

Isabella made a purchase totaling $75.18. She gave the clerk $100. How much change should Isabella receive?

Strategy

Use the formula:

change due = amount of cash given to the clerk – purchase total

Solution

Step 1: Identify the purchase total and the amount of cash given to the clerk.

purchase total = $75.18

amount of cash given = $100

Step 2: Determine the amount of cash Isabella should receive in change. Subtract the purchase total from the amount of cash given to the clerk.

amount of change = amount of cash given – purchase total

amount of change = $100 – $75.18

amount of change = $24.82

Check It

Aaron purchased $22.46 worth of vegetables at the supermarket. He gave the clerk $30 in cash. How much change should Aaron receive?

Answer:
$7.54

Payment Cards

Another way to transact a purchase is by using a substitute for cash, such as a payment card. A ***payment card*** is any card that is presented as payment for a purchase.

A payment card contains information that allows an electronic transaction to take place. When you use a debit card, your bank pays for the purchase with money taken electronically from your account. When you use a credit card, the credit card company actually buys the good or service for you and loans you the money.

A ***gift card*** is also a type of payment card that is preloaded with money that can be spent electronically. Gift cards can be for specific stores or may be accepted everywhere credit cards are. A smart card is another kind of payment card. A *smart card* has a computer chip embedded within the card that stores data regarding account and personal information.

Teaching Tip:
Engage students in a discussion about their own experiences with payment methods such as layaway, payment card, or gift cards. Ask: Would you rather operate only in cash or only by using a payment card? Why or why not?

Charge Accounts

A ***charge account*** is an arrangement in which a customer receives a good or service in exchange for the promise to pay at a later date. Some businesses offer charge accounts without a card. For example, an electrician might have a charge account with the company where he or she buys supplies. Because many supplies are purchased each month, the charge account makes it easier for both the electrician and the supplier to do business. At the end of each month, the supplier can collect the money for all the supplies purchased by the electrician that month. In most cases, a charge account involves a credit limit. A *credit limit* is the maximum amount that the business will allow you to carry on your charge account. To calculate an account balance, use the following formula:

account balance = cost of all purchases + sales tax

Example 5-2B

See It

Annette's Floral Shop has a charge account with Southern Flowers, a wholesaler where she buys her floral supplies. This month, Annette has purchased 16 dozen roses at $30.96 per dozen, 40 dozen chrysanthemums at $17.80 per dozen, and 20 dozen tulips at $21.10 per dozen. In her state, Annette must pay a 6% sales tax on all orders. At the end of the month, what is the balance on Annette's charge account?

Strategy

Use the formula:

account balance = cost of all purchases + sales tax

Solution

Step 1: Determine the total cost of roses. Multiply the cost per dozen by the number of dozen roses.

total cost = cost per dozen × number of dozen

total cost = $30.96 per dozen × 16 dozen

total cost = $495.36

Step 2: Determine the total cost of chrysanthemums. Multiply the cost per dozen by the number of dozen chrysanthemums.

total cost = cost per dozen × number of dozen

total cost = $17.80 per dozen × 40 dozen

total cost = $712

Step 3: Determine the total cost of tulips. Multiply the cost per dozen by the number of dozen tulips.

total cost = cost per dozen × number of dozen

total cost = $21.10 per dozen × 20 dozen

total cost = $422

Teaching Tip:
Explain that in addition to the cost of purchases and sales tax, accrued interest and other fees will affect an account balance and, consequently, available credit.

Step 4: Determine the total cost of all flowers. Add the total cost of each type of flower together.

total cost = cost of roses + cost of chrysanthemums + cost of tulips

total cost = $495.36 + $712 + $422

total cost = $1,629.36

Step 5: Convert the sales tax rate to a decimal by moving the decimal two places to the left.

$6\% \rightarrow 0.06$

Step 6: Determine the amount of sales tax. Multiply the sales tax rate by the total cost of the purchases. Round to the nearest cent ($0.01) if necessary.

sales tax = sales tax rate × total cost

sales tax = $0.06 \times \$1,629.36$

sales tax = $97.76

Step 7: Determine the account balance. Add the total cost of the flowers and the sales tax.

account balance = total cost of flowers + sales tax

account balance = $1,629.36 + $97.76

account balance = $1,727.12

Check It

Sung owns a plumbing supply store. One of his clients, Village Plumbers, has a charge account with his store. This month, Village Plumbers charged 200 feet of pipe at $0.40 per foot, 150 elbow joints at $0.75 per elbow joint, and 36 outdoor faucets at $2.49 per faucet. Sung must charge 5.5% sales tax on all items sold. What is the balance on Village Plumbers' charge account?

Answer:
$297.66

Installment plans are used by those who do not have a method to pay for the entire cost of an item when making a purchase. An *installment plan* is an agreement where the total amount owed is made in payments over time, also called *installments.* A car loan is the most common type of installment plan.

There are other examples of installment plans. Hospitals often allow patients to pay in installments toward a large hospital bill. The Internal Revenue Service allows taxes to be paid on installment plans, but penalties and interest will be charged. Vacations are sometimes paid for in installments as well.

A *layaway plan* is a type of installment plan where the store sets the item aside, or *lays the item away,* while the customer makes payments toward the purchase price. The customer also pays a small, nonrefundable fee for the convenience of using the service. Layaway fees are often a percentage of the price of the item. To calculate a layaway fee, use the following formula:

layaway fee = price of item × layaway charge rate

Once the customer has paid the entire cost of the item, the store releases the item to the customer. If the customer does not pay the entire cost by the stated time, the item is made available for others to purchase. The money the customer paid toward the purchase is returned. The fee is retained by the store.

Example 5-2C

See It

Marvin is placing a new game system on layaway at the local gaming store. The store charges a layaway fee of 10% of the price of the item. Marvin must pay a minimum of 20% of the price of the item each week. If the game system costs $189.99, determine the layaway fee and the amount of money that Marvin must pay each week.

Strategy

Use the formula:

layaway fee = price of item × layaway charge rate

Solution

Step 1: Convert the layaway charge rate from a percentage to a decimal by moving the decimal two places to the left.

10% → 0.10

Step 2: Determine the layaway fee. Multiply the price of the item by the layaway charge rate (as a decimal). Round to the nearest cent ($0.01) if necessary.

layaway fee = price of item × layaway charge rate

layaway fee = $189.99 × 0.10

layaway fee = $19

Step 3: Convert the weekly rate to a decimal by moving the decimal two places to the left.

20% → 0.20%

Step 4: Determine the weekly payment. Multiply the price of the item by the weekly rate (as a decimal). Round to the nearest cent ($0.01) if necessary.

weekly payment = (price of item + layaway fee) × weekly rate

weekly payment = ($189.99 + $19) × 0.20

weekly payment = $208.99 × 0.20

weekly payment = $41.80

Check It

Layla is placing a new sofa on layaway in a department store. The cost of the sofa is $599.95. The store charges a layaway fee, which is 5% of the item's purchase price. The store also requires that a minimum of 15% of the price of the item be paid each week until the item is fully paid. Determine both the layaway fee and the amount that Layla must pay each week.

Answer:
layaway fee = $30
weekly payment = $94.49

Electronic Payments

Technological advances and the innovation of previously used payment forms have made electronic payments possible. Whenever you use a credit card or debit card, you are making an electronic payment. Even if you are purchasing something from a store around the corner, your account information travels electronically to your bank, which authorizes a payment to the store from which you made the purchase.

Another important tool used to make electronic payments is digital cash. **Digital cash** is a form of currency that can be used online. The buyer transmits payment in the form of a digital certificate into the seller's account. Digital cash can be stored on your computer or your smartphone through a software application known as a *digital wallet*.

Another way to pay for goods and services is through online bill pay. **Online bill pay** is a service that allows you to direct payment from your bank account to companies and individuals. When offered through a bank, the service allows you to send money to virtually anyone. You can pay your phone bill or send money to an individual.

Career Discovery
Hospitality & Tourism Careers and Math Skills

With increasing leisure time and personal income, many people have more resources for dining out, travel, and recreation. Career options in the hospitality and tourism cluster focus on food and beverage services, lodging services, travel, and all types of recreation. Those who work in this industry must have exceptional customer service skills and like demanding and diverse work. These workers must also have a solid foundation in math, science, and technical skills.

Careers in hospitality and tourism require the frequent use of math skills to calculate sales and other business figures. Give examples in which math skills would be necessary for an individual with a career in this field.

Some companies provide an online bill pay service to pay your bill directly to the company. For example, an electric utility company may offer its customers a way to make payments online. Paying bills online saves time, postage, and paper. You can even set up bill payments to occur automatically each month.

Checkpoint 5.2

1. Hassan made a purchase at the convenience store for $22.19, including sales tax. He gave the clerk $40. How much change should Hassan receive?

2. Selena manages a landscaping company and purchases her materials from the local lumberyard, where she has a charge account. Last week, Selena's company purchased 48 landscaping timbers at $4.55 each, 80 cubic yards of mulch at $29.95 per cubic yard, and 90 flats of bedding plants at $4.88 per flat. She must also pay a 6.5% sales tax on all purchases. What was the balance of Selena's landscaping company's charge account at the end of the week?

3. Jacob owns a farm supply company. The chart that follows shows items purchased by one of his clients on a charge account. Assuming the sales tax rate is 4.5%, what is the client's charge account balance?

Item	Unit Price	Quantity
Baling Wire	$75.14	15 spools
Horse Feed	9.95	16 bags
Barbed Wire	52.15	6 spools

4. Renee placed some holiday gifts in layaway. The combined price of the items was $318.95. The store charges a 5% layaway fee and requires a 10% down payment. She must pay 15% of the item price each week for six weeks. Determine the layaway fee, down payment, and amount of Renee's weekly payments.

5. Hugo placed a necklace for his mother in layaway. The price of the necklace was $105.45. The store charges a $5 service charge, requires a 20% down payment, and requires weekly payments of 10% until the item is paid in full. Determine Hugo's down payment and weekly payments.

Section 5.3 Influences on Purchasing Decisions

Objectives

- **Calculate unit pricing.**
- **Describe the purpose of contracts.**
- **Explain extended warranties.**
- **Describe advertising.**

Terms

- *unit pricing*
- *contract*
- *warranty*
- *extended warranty*
- *advertising*
- *pay-per-click advertising*

Build Your Math Skills

Review these math skills to prepare for the lesson that follows.

1. Round decimals to the nearest cent ($0.01). Example: $516.784 = $516.78

A. $67.049 =

B. $118.193 =

C. $89.949 =

D. $1,017.947 =

2. Divide decimals. Round to the nearest cent ($0.01) if necessary. Example: $25.16 ÷ 14 = $1.80

A. $115 ÷ 8 =

B. $109.17 ÷ 5 =

C. $52 ÷ 1.8 =

D. $87.41 ÷ 1.35 =

3. Multiply decimals. Round to the nearest cent ($0.01) if necessary. Example: $5.58 × 8 = $44.64

A. $802.45 × 11 =

B. $8.75 × 98.4 =

C. $39.04 × 34 =

D. $80.09 × 10.05 =

Answer:
1. A. $67.05
   B. $118.19
   C. $89.95
   D. $1,017.95
2. A. $14.38
   B. $21.83
   C. $28.89
   D. $64.75
3. A. $8,826.95
   B. $861
   C. $1,327.36
   D. $804.90

Unit Pricing

There is more to making purchasing decisions than you may realize. In addition to deciding what you want to purchase, you may have to decide which brand and size to choose. Purchasing something as simple as dog food can involve several decisions. There are different types of dog food. Dog food can be for puppies, active dogs, or older dogs. Dog food comes in the form of wet food or dry food. There are also multiple brands of each type, and different sizes from which to choose. Making a decision to purchase something often requires more than answering the question: *How much does it cost?*

Unit pricing is the price per unit for a product. Unit pricing looks at the price of an item in units that can be compared across purchase options. For example, dry dog food comes in many different quantities. If you shop for dry dog food, you will find a wide array of bag weights. Some bags may hold 40 pounds of food, while other bags may contain less than five pounds of food. In order to compare the value of the purchase, you would need to calculate the price per pound, or unit price.

Teaching Tip:
Explain that unit pric-
ing is shown on price
stickers at most stores.
This is an easy way to
determine the best price
per unit of an item.

To calculate the unit price, divide the price of the item by the number of units:

$$\text{unit price} = \frac{\text{price}}{\text{number of units}}$$

Example 5-3A

See It

Southwestern Office Supply sells gel pens in packages of 12 for $6.99. What is the unit price of a gel pen?

Strategy

Use the formula:

$$\text{unit price} = \frac{\text{price}}{\text{number of units}}$$

Solution

Step 1: Identify the unit, the package price, and the number of units included in the package.

The unit is one gel pen.

The package price is $6.99.

The number of units included in one package is 12 gel pens.

Step 2: Determine the unit price. Divide the price of one package by the number of units included in one package. Round to the nearest cent ($0.01) if necessary.

$$\text{unit price} = \frac{\text{price}}{\text{number of units}}$$

$$\text{unit price} = \frac{\$6.99}{12 \text{ gel pens}}$$

unit price = $0.58 per gel pen

Check It

A discount warehouse club sells cloth diapers in packages of 24 for $15.99. What is the unit price of one cloth diaper?

Answer:
$0.67 per cloth diaper

Contracts

When you purchase a service, you may have to sign a contract with the party that provides the service. A **contract** is a formal agreement between two or more people or organizations. The purpose of a contract is to define an agreement in detail. Therefore, it is important to understand the details of the agreement. When calculating the cost of a mobile phone contract, for example, the following equation can be used:

total cost of contract = cost of units in contract + activation fee – discount on new phone

Services Provided

Make sure you understand all that you are getting for your money. With a mobile phone, for example, you should know what is included in the price and what costs extra. Does the contract include unlimited text messages? Does the plan include limits on data? How many minutes of talk time are included? What are the costs involved in exceeding a contract limit?

Length of Agreement

Typically, a contract has a period of time that is called a *term*. When you sign a contract, you are agreeing to continue to pay for the service through the entire term of the agreement. For example, a typical mobile phone contract has a two-year term. To end the contract early, you will have to pay a termination fee.

Price

The price of the service will generally be locked in for the length of the contract. That may be good if the service cost is going up for people signing new contracts. However, with some services, the cost may be trending downward. In that case, a two-year contract may be locking you in to paying more than what new customers are paying.

Teaching Tip:
Ask students to describe their experiences with mobile phone service plans or contracts.

Example 5-3B

See It

A mobile phone company sells a package that includes 750 minutes of talk time per month for a monthly fee of $44.99. If customers sign a two-year contract, they can receive a $150 discount on a new mobile phone. However, the contract includes a $250 early termination fee and a $35 activation fee. If Giselle signs a two-year contract with this company, what is the total cost of the contract, excluding the early termination fee?

Strategy

Use the formula:

total cost of contract = cost of units in contract + activation fee – discount on new phone

Solution

Step 1: Determine the unit of charge, amount of charge per unit, and the number of units in the contract.

unit of charge = 1 month

amount of charge per unit = $44.99 per month

number of units in contract = 2 years × 12 months = 24 months

Step 2: Determine any fixed costs or discounts.

activation fee = $35

discount on new phone = $150

Step 3: Determine the total cost of all units in the contract. Multiply the amount of charge per unit by the number of units in the contract.

total cost of units in contract = amount of charge per unit × number of units in contract

total cost of units in contract = $44.99 per month × 24 months

total cost of units in contract = $1,079.76

Step 4: Determine the total cost of the contract. Add the total cost of the units in the contract and any fixed fees. Subtract any fixed discounts.

total cost of contract = cost of units in contract + activation fee – discount on new phone

total cost of contract = $1,079.76 + $35 – $150

total cost of contract = $964.76

Check It

Ryan is shopping for a new mobile phone plan. Wireless-to-Go has a plan for 800 minutes of talk time for $35.99 per month. If Ryan signs an 18-month contract, he can get a $75 discount on a new phone. However, there is an activation fee of $55 and an early termination fee of $225. What is the total cost of the contract that Ryan was offered, excluding the early termination fee?

Answer:
$627.82

Extended warranties are often expensive. Before buying an extended warranty, consider the cost of the warranty and the likelihood that the product will need service during the warranty period. If you do purchase an extended warranty, don't forget that you purchased it. Many people forget they purchased an extended warranty and fail to take advantage of the warranty when a product breaks.

Extended Warranties

A **warranty** is a guarantee that the item purchased will perform to a certain standard or be free of defects for a specified period of time. A 90-day warranty is common on consumer electronics. Longer warranty periods may be available on more expensive items like large appliances and automobiles.

An *extended warranty* is an optional additional warranty that can be purchased by the consumer. An extended warranty *lengthens* the original product warranty by a specified period of time. For example, suppose you purchased a video game console that includes a one-year warranty. If the store offers a three-year extended warranty, it usually means that the warranty is being extended by two years for a total of three years.

Advertising

Everything you have read about in this chapter has been about how to make an informed purchasing decision. Sometimes people overlook the logic involved in purchasing and buy something solely based on an appealing advertisement. *Advertising* is the public promotion of a product, service, business, or event. Everywhere you go, you are bombarded by advertising. You see advertisements on buildings, on vehicles, in publications, online, and on television. Even movies embed advertising into the scenes. As consumers, we see thousands of advertisements each day.

Online advertising, such as a banner ad on a website or ad in a mobile app, is a way for advertisers to target the people they want to see their advertisement. For example, when a high school student uses Facebook, the ads are often about things in which teenagers are interested. An ad on a health website is more likely to be about pharmaceutical drugs that appeal to adults.

Even search engine results include paid advertisements. When you go to Google or Bing and search a phrase like *video games,* you will see ads alongside the search results. Ads on search sites are typically paid for based on the number of times a user clicks the link in the ad. *Pay-per-click advertising* charges the advertiser's account each time a viewer clicks the link in the advertisement. Website hosts can calculate advertising revenue based on the following formula:

advertising revenue = rate per click × number of clicks

The advertisers that pay more will have their ads appear more often. Advertisers are willing to pay for the click because the person clicking has indicated interest in a particular good or service. Be aware of the impact that advertisement may have on your purchasing decisions.

A lot of money is spent to generate all of this advertising. That alone should tell you that the companies buying this advertising are expecting it to have an effect on consumers. It is up to you to be aware of the impact that advertising has on people's behavior. When you receive a message through advertising, understand that it is a message provided by someone who will profit from persuading you to purchase his or her product. Do your own research before making a purchase. Do not rely solely on messages you receive through advertising.

In order for you to understand how advertising impacts you, be aware that advertisers use a technique called *dimensional analysis.* Dimensional analysis uses rates presented as fractions so that the units align and cancel as multiplication is

Be aware of what the extended warranty covers. Some may cover damage and others may only cover electronic or mechanical failure. Also, consider that during the extended warranty period, you will need to keep up with the receipt and warranty paperwork.

Teaching Tip:
Encourage students to describe their experiences with warranties. Has any student purchased an extended warranty?

completed. This analysis makes it easier to compute advertising rates. In Example 5-3C, dimensional analysis would look like this:

$$\frac{\$0.22}{1 \text{ click}} \times \frac{80 \text{ clicks}}{1 \text{ month}} = \frac{\$0.22 \times 80}{1 \text{ month}} = \frac{\$17.60}{1 \text{ month}} = \$17.60 \text{ per month}$$

Example 5-3C

See It

On a particular website, an advertiser pays $0.22 each time someone clicks on the company's web banner. Statistics for this website show that each advertisement receives about 80 clicks per month. How much advertising revenue will the website host receive from this advertiser in one month?

Strategy

Use the formula:

advertising revenue = rate per click × number of clicks

Solution

Step 1: Identify the rate per click and the number of clicks per month.

rate per click = $0.22 per click

number of clicks per month = 80 clicks per month

Step 2: Determine the advertising revenue. Multiply the rate per click by the number of clicks per month.

advertising revenue = rate per click × number of clicks

advertising revenue = $0.22 per click × 80 clicks per month

advertising revenue = $17.60 per month

Check It

In an online shopping directory, advertisers pay $0.61 when a customer clicks on their web banner. In one month, Armando's Pool Supply received 311 clicks on their web banner. How much advertising revenue did the website host receive from Armando's Pool Supply during this month?

Answer:
$189.71

Example 5-3D

See It

For a particular website, advertisers pay $0.44 per click. Usage statistics from this website show that viewers click on advertisements about 95 times per month. How much advertising revenue would this website host receive from advertisers in one year?

Strategy

Use the formula:

advertising revenue = rate per click × number of clicks

Solution

Step 1: Determine the monthly advertising revenue. Multiply the rate per click by the number of clicks per month.

monthly advertising revenue = rate per click × number of clicks

monthly advertising revenue = $0.44 per click × 95 clicks per month

monthly advertising revenue = $41.80 per month

Step 2: Determine the yearly advertising revenue. Multiply the monthly advertising revenue by 12 (the number of months in a year).

yearly advertising revenue = monthly advertising revenue × 12 months per year

yearly advertising revenue = $41.80 per month × 12 months

yearly advertising revenue = $501.60 per year

Check It

A website charges $0.27 for each click on an advertiser's web banner. Central City Urban Clothing Store received an average of 62 clicks per month during the months of July, August, and September. What is Central City Urban Clothing Store's advertising bill for this quarter?

Answer:
$50.22

Checkpoint 5.3

1. A package of orange juice contains 96 fluid ounces and costs $5.29. What is the unit price per ounce?

2. A package of three boxes of facial tissue sells for $9.82. Each box contains 250 facial tissues. What is the unit price per facial tissue?

3. Haley is shopping for a new mobile phone plan. Her mobile phone company has a plan for 500 minutes of talk time for $19.99 per month. If Haley signs a two-year contract, she will receive a $135 discount on a new phone. However, there is also an activation fee of $45 and an early termination fee of $250. What is the total cost of the mobile phone contract, excluding the early termination fee?

4. Lorenzo signed a two-year contract with his wireless tablet computer company for a data plan that costs $15.99 per month. There is an early termination fee of $249. After Lorenzo was five months into his contract, he cancelled his service. Including the early termination fee, what was the total cost of Lorenzo's contract?

5. A website charges $0.39 for each click on an advertiser's web banner. Red River Valley Bookstore received 75 clicks in January, 68 clicks in February, and 104 clicks in March. What is Red River Valley Bookstore's advertising bill for this quarter?

Teaching Tip:
Checkpoint questions offer opportunities for formative assessment.

Answer:
1. $0.06 per fluid ounce
2. $0.01 per facial tissue
3. $389.76
4. $488.85
5. $96.33

Chapter Review

Build Your Vocabulary

As you progress through this course, develop a personal glossary of financial literacy terms and add it to your portfolio. This will help you build your financial literacy vocabulary. Write out a definition for each of the following terms, and add it to your personal glossary.

market	charge account
good	installment plan
service	layaway plan
market size	digital cash
sales tax	online bill pay
coupon	unit pricing
rebate	contract
tip	warranty
comparison shopping	extended warranty
payment card	advertising
gift card	pay-per-click advertising

 ## Teamwork

In teams of two, research hard-sell sales tactics and create two short one-act plays. The first should depict the salesperson making the sale using hard-sell tactics. The second should depict the customer deflecting the salesperson's hard-sell sales tactics.

Review Your Math Skills

Practice and build on the math skills that you have learned.

1. Convert percentages to decimals by moving the decimal two places to the left. Example: 15% → 0.15

A. 9.8% →

B. 13% →

C. 7.625% →

D. 10.5% →

2. Add decimals. Example: $81.15 + $205.67 = $286.82

A. $81.43 + 63.50 =

B. $406.85 + $120.11 =

C. $612.74 + $351.86 =

D. $15.33 + $99.97 =

Answer:
1. A. 0.098
   B. 0.13
   C. 0.07625
   D. 0.105
2. A. $144.93
   B. $526.96
   C. $964.60
   D. $115.30

3. Subtract decimals. Example: $540 − $125.10 = $414.90

A. $377.85 − $61.77 =

B. $806 − $53.14 =

C. $492.69 − $244.28 =

D. $500.30 − $79.90 =

4. Convert percentages to decimals by moving the decimal two places to the left. Example: 4% → 0.04

A. 8.1% →

B. 4.4% →

C. 36.23% →

D. 71.25% →

5. Subtract decimals. Example: $720 − $25.10 = $694.90

A. $41.92 − $18.13 =

B. $745.80 − $15.27 =

C. $28.17 − $2.89 =

D. $87.97 − $19.63 =

6. Multiply decimals. Round to the nearest cent ($0.01) if necessary. Example: $45 × 0.08 = $3.60

A. $105 × 0.08 =

B. $18.34 × 0.09 =

C. $36 × 0.15 =

D. $265 × 0.105 =

7. Round decimals to the nearest cent ($0.01). Example: $516.784 = $516.78

A. $45.632 =

B. $1,745.816 =

C. $92.749 =

D. $523.125 =

8. Divide decimals. Round to the nearest cent ($0.01) if necessary. Example: $25.16 ÷ 14 = $1.80

A. $235 ÷ 7 =

B. $39.05 ÷ 4 =

C. $102.67 ÷ 1.65 =

D. $85.56 ÷ 1.2 =

9. Add decimals. Example: $78.13 + $2.19 = $80.32

A. $906.10 + $27.25 =

B. $52.87 + $8.63 =

C. $235.96 + $102.01 =

D. $764.20 + $18.03 =

10. Multiply decimals. Round to the nearest cent ($0.01) if necessary. Example: $5.58 × 8 = $44.64

A. $618.35 × 11 =

B. $8.97 × 68.32 =

C. $35.81 × 58 =

D. $337.20 × 13 =

3. A. $316.08
   B. $752.86
   C. $248.41
   D. $420.40
4. A. 0.081
   B. 0.044
   C. 0.3623
   D. 0.7125
5. A. $23.79
   B. $730.53
   C. $25.28
   D. $68.34
6. A. $8.40
   B. $1.65
   C. $5.40
   D. $27.83
7. A. $45.63
   B. $1,745.82
   C. $92.75
   D. $523.13
8. A. $33.57
   B. $9.76
   C. $62.22
   D. $71.30
9. A. $933.35
   B. $61.50
   C. $337.97
   D. $782.23
10. A. $6,801.85
    B. $612.83
    C. $2,076.98
    D. $4,383.60

Section 5.1 Basics of Purchasing

11. Nicole purchased new lawn furniture for $279.90. She used a coupon to get a 15% discount. What was the final purchase price, excluding sales tax, of the lawn furniture?

12. Conner took his sister and their mother to breakfast, and the pretax bill was $38.25. He decided to leave an 18% tip. The sales tax rate is 5.25%. What was the final amount of the bill?

Answer:
11. $237.91
12. $47.15

Section 5.2 Payment Options

13. Namir purchased fuel for his farm truck that cost $79.17. He gave the clerk a $100 bill. How much change should Namir receive?

14. Delia owns a bowling alley and orders the necessary supplies for her concession stand from a restaurant supply store using a charge account. The items she ordered this week are in the chart that follows. Delia must pay 8.25% sales tax. What is her charge account balance?

Item	Unit Price	Quantity
Fruit Cups	$5.99	8
Fruit Juice Concentrate	32.18	11
Granola Bars	8.37	20

Answer:
13. $20.83
14. $569.30
15. layaway fee = $11.00
   down payment = $32.99
   weekly payment = $32.99

15. Caleb placed a bicycle in layaway. The price of the bicycle was $219.90. The store charges a 5% layaway fee and requires a 15% down payment. Equal installments must be paid each week for six weeks. Determine the layaway fee, down payment, and amount of Caleb's weekly payments.

Section 5.3 Influences on Purchasing Decisions

16. A 24-pound package of Hi-Gro kitten food sells for $28.84. What is the unit price per pound of kitten food?

17. Chen is shopping for a new mobile phone plan. Her mobile phone company has a plan for 600 minutes of talk time for $29.99 per month. If Chen signs a two-year contract, she will receive a $95 discount on a new phone. However, there is also an activation fee of $35 and an early termination fee of $175. What is the total cost of the contract, excluding the early termination fee?

Answer:
16. $1.20 per pound
17. $659.76
18. $184.68

18. A website charges $0.19 for each click on an advertiser's web banner. Western Farm and Ranch Supply received an average of 81 clicks per month. What is Western Farm and Ranch Supply's advertising bill for the year?

Reinforce Your Understanding

Answer:
19. $37,160.68

19. Latoya works as an automobile technician, earning $37,360 per year. Her employer contributes an additional $95 per month to her retirement plan and pays $250 per month toward her health insurance. Latoya pays $41.79 per month in labor union dues and $319.82 per month in health insurance premiums. Determine the net annual value of Latoya's job.

20. Gia wants to place a catalog order from Franklin's Spirit Wear. Use the catalog form provided to calculate the total cost of the order, including shipping and handling and sales tax. The sales tax is 7.5%. Shipping and handling can be calculated using the chart that follows. Gia is ordering the following items:

- 1 red fleece blanket (item #1652) for $39.99

- 2 blue hooded sweatshirts (item #1499) for $29.99 each

- 4 silver car decals (item #1224) for $5.99 each

If Your Order Totals...	Please Add...
$10 or less	$6.50
$10.01 to $25	$9.50
$25.01 to $50	$11
$50.01 to $75	$12.25
$75.01 to $125	$13.25
$125.01 or more	$16.75

Teaching Tip:
The reproducible master for the catalog order form in question 20 is available on the Instructor's Resource CD.

20. $146.47

Apply Your Technology Skills

Teaching Tip:
The Apply Your Technology Skills activities offer project-based authentic assessment opportunities.

Access the G-W Learning companion website for this text at www.g-wlearning.com. Download each data file for this chapter. Follow the instructions to complete financial literacy activities to practice what you have learned in this chapter.

Data File 5-1—Calculating Sales Tax

Data File 5-2—Completing an Online Catalog Form

Data File 5-3—Calculating Tips

Data File 5-4—Completing a Rebate Form

6 Budgeting

Materials:
Instructor's Resource CD
Student Workbook
G-W Learning companion website
EXAMVIEW® Assessment Suite
Microsoft Excel®–compatible software
Calculator with advanced-math functions

One of the most difficult parts of handling finances is managing spending. Spending in a way that is in-line with your income, while maintaining your priorities, is not always easy. Creating a budget is a way to balance the two. A budget is simply a plan for how your income is going to be saved and spent. In this chapter, you will learn how to analyze expenses, make a budget, understand cash flow, and create financial goals.

Section 6.1	**Creating a Budget**
Section 6.2	**Cash Flow**
Section 6.3	**Setting Financial Goals**

College and Career Readiness

Reading Prep. As you read the chapter, think about why it is important to set financial goals. Do you think setting goals, financial or otherwise, makes it easier for you to meet them? Use examples from the text to support your opinion.

> *"Budgeting is one of the important ways to save money. I plan to begin budgeting soon." ~ Guadalupe I.*

Money Matters
Gold

- Gold coins date back to around 600 BC.

- Until 1934, the paper bills used in the United States were certificates that could be traded for gold coins.

- A monetary system in which the currency is based on actual stored gold is called a *gold standard*.

- Investors typically buy gold in the form of a stock certificate, rather than actual gold pieces. The certificates are backed by gold deposits.

- In 1934, the United States Congress passed the Gold Reserve Act, which required that all gold and gold certificates be turned over to the US Department of the Treasury.

- The Gold Reserve Act also required that most privately held gold be sold to the US Treasury. Only a small amount of gold, such as jewelry, could be owned legally.

- It was not until 1975 that Americans could legally own gold in any quantity.

- In 1968, gold traded for $35 per ounce.

- In 2011, gold reached an all-time high of $1,900 per ounce.

Section 6.1 Creating a Budget

Objectives

- **Explain various means of recordkeeping.**
- **Describe how competing financial needs can affect your financial health.**
- **Create a budget.**
- **Explain the difference between needs and wants.**
- **Describe the financial benefits of combining household expenses.**

Terms

- *recordkeeping*
- *budget*
- *fixed expense*
- *fixed income*
- *need*
- *want*

Build Your Math Skills

Review these math skills to prepare for the lesson that follows.

1. Add decimals. Example: $14.57 + $108.74 = $123.31

A. $56.17 + $118.93 =

B. $604.15 + $87.04 =

C. $187.93 + $402.08 =

D. $97 + $115.16 =

2. Divide decimals. Round to the nearest cent ($0.01) if necessary. Example: $115.30 ÷ 3 = $38.43

A. $512.45 ÷ 4 =

B. $810.40 ÷ 5 =

C. $278.48 ÷ 2 =

D. $1,118.94 ÷ 3 =

3. Find the average of a set of numbers. Round to the nearest cent ($0.01) if necessary. Example: The average of $112, $57, and $181 is ($112 + $57 + $181) ÷ 3 = $116.67

A. $119, $55, $108

B. $512, $180, $217, $55

C. $125.25, $75.86

D. $756.95, $496.69, $554.97

Answer:
1. A. $175.10
   B. $691.19
   C. $590.01
   D. $212.16
2. A. $128.11
   B. $162.08
   C. $139.24
   D. $372.98
3. A. $94
   B. $241
   C. $100.56
   D. $602.87

Recordkeeping

Good money management cannot be achieved unless you know how much money you have and what you are doing with it. *Recordkeeping* is keeping track of your money. It is important to keep records of how much money you have, what you are earning, what you are saving, and what you are spending.

Some recordkeeping is done on paper. A written check register is one example of recordkeeping on paper. Saving printed receipts and bills you receive in the mail is also recordkeeping.

Financial Smarts

Many people keep their records online and pay bills electronically. Even so, it is important to keep paper and electronic copies of important records. If for some reason you can't retrieve the files online, you will need to have access to them elsewhere. For example, some banks only provide three months of transaction data online. If you need information from four months earlier, you wouldn't be able to find it online. Make sure that you create a backup system so you can always access your banking records.

Today, however, more recordkeeping is done electronically than on paper. Financial records are often tracked using computer software. Software that helps keep track of finances is called *accounting software* or *personal finance software.* Some financial records are kept in electronic spreadsheets. Bank statements, credit card statements, and bills are often delivered electronically.

Competing Financial Needs

Just about everyone has experienced not having enough money to do all the things they want or need to do. This can be very serious if you cannot pay all your bills. However, you may not always be able to buy what you want because you have higher priorities. Or, you may have two items you wish to purchase but only enough money for one of the two. There is a lot of competition for the dollars under your control.

For example, suppose Audra has been keeping records of her spending. Figure 6-1 shows a portion of the records she has kept. Audra spent $142, $206, and $81 on things that are considered entertainment. Entertainment includes things like buying music, going to movies, bowling, and going out with friends. Because Audra is keeping records, she notices that during the month of May she did not put $100 in her savings account as she normally does. Her increased spending on entertainment is likely part of the reason she did not have the money available to save. Because setting aside savings is an important financial goal, savings should be given priority over other less-important spending. This less-important spending is sometimes called *discretionary spending.*

By keeping a spending record, you can see what you have already spent. The next step is to *project,* or estimate, what your expenses are likely to be in future months. You can do this by calculating the *average* of known expenses over a certain period. In math, the average is known as the *mean.* To calculate Audra's average monthly entertainment expenditures, use the following formula:

mean = sum of amounts ÷ number of amounts added

Example 6-1A

See It

Using the information in Figure 6-1, what was Audra's mean monthly spending on entertainment for April, May, and June?

	April	May	June
Entertainment	$142	$206	$81
Savings	100	0	100

Figure 6-1. Audra's Record of Spending

Strategy

Use the formula:

mean = sum of amounts ÷ number of amounts added

Solution

Step 1: Using the table, determine Audra's spending on entertainment for April, May, and June.

spending in April = $142

spending in May = $206

spending in June = $81

Step 2: Determine the sum of Audra's spending on entertainment for April, May, and June.

sum of spending on entertainment = spending in April + spending in May + spending in June

sum of spending on entertainment = $142 + $206 + $81

sum of spending on entertainment = $429

Step 3: Determine the mean of Audra's spending on entertainment for April, May, and June. Divide the sum by three (the number of amounts you added).

mean = sum of amounts ÷ number of amounts added

mean = $429 ÷ 3

mean = $143

fyi

There are several types of means in mathematics. The mean that is also called the *average* of a set of numbers is an *arithmetic mean*.

Check It

Simon uses a gasoline company charge card to make his gasoline purchases. The following table shows his total gasoline purchases per month for four months. Determine Simon's mean monthly amount of spending on gasoline during this four-month period.

August	September	October	November
$248.75	$197.50	$305.48	$267.89

Answer:
$254.91

Creating a Budget

To meet your financial priorities, you must plan how you are going to use your money before you receive it. A *budget* is a plan for saving and spending your money. A budget helps you balance competing financial goals and priorities. For Audra, spending $200 on entertainment is not going to allow her other priorities to be met. A budget would help Audra plan her spending and ensure that she has funds to meet her commitment to save money.

Teaching Tip:
The complete solutions to the Check It problems can be found on the Instructor's Resource CD.

In a budget, you should account for every dollar of your income. Figure 6-2 is an example of a very simple budget. In the budget, there is a line item for:

- each source of income;

- planned savings; and

- each type of expense.

Also notice that there is a category for miscellaneous. Realistically, you are going to want to spend some money on things that are not in your budget. In this budget, you are allowing yourself $64 to spend freely. There is nothing wrong with spending money on something you want, even if it is not specifically planned. Because you have a specified amount for that purpose, that unplanned purchase does not take money away from another priority.

Sample Budget		
Category	**Amount**	**Totals**
Income:		
Wages (Ross Bowl-A-Rama)	$980	
Dog Walking Service	200	
Total Income		$1,180
Savings:		
Savings account	200	
Total Savings		200
Expenses:		
Rent	300	
Utilities	140	
Phone	46	
Gas and oil	55	
Food	275	
Clothing	30	
Entertainment	70	
Miscellaneous	64	
Total Expenses		980
Total Savings and Expenses		$1,180

Figure 6-2.
Sample Budget

One of the challenges in budgeting is that life does not always fit into neat and predictable line items. Some expenses are the same each month, but most are not. And for many people, income also varies.

Income or expenses that do not vary are called *fixed*. **Fixed expenses** are those expenses that stay the same each month. A rent payment is an example of a fixed expense. A **fixed income** is an income that stays the same each month. A paycheck from a salaried job is an example of a fixed income.

Other expenses and incomes are *variable,* meaning the amount can change. Food is a *variable expense*. You will rarely spend exactly the same amount on food each month. If you work by the hour, it is likely that you will not have exactly the same number of hours worked on each paycheck. This would mean you have *variable income.*

When creating your own budget, you first must have a record of your income and spending habits to know how much you earn on average and how much you spend in each category. When you track your own spending, you will likely be surprised by how much you spend on certain things. An important part of budgeting is to control your spending habits. For example, people who eat out a lot may be surprised to see how much those meals cost monthly. Once you see all your spending in expense categories, you may decide your priorities are not reflected in your spending habits.

A budget needs to include enough expense categories to help you plan spending, but not so many that it becomes hard to manage. For example, you will occasionally need to change the oil in your car. The expense for an oil change is probably included in your budget category called *gas and oil*. Dental and medical expenses are also commonly combined into a *health care* category. Ultimately, there is no single way to create a budget. Your budget should reflect your life.

Events will arise that cause you to revise your budget. You might find that you need to spend more on gas than you had originally budgeted. If your income does not increase by the same amount, you will need to spend less in another category of your budget to free up more money for gas. Use the following formulas to calculate this realignment. You will have to modify these formulas to align with the demands of your particular budget:

difference in gas and oil budget = new gas and oil budget amount – current gas and oil budget amount

new clothing budget = current clothing budget amount – difference in gas and oil budget

> **Teaching Tip:**
> Explain to students that most financial experts suggest saving 10% of your income per month.

> **fyi**
>
> When you spend more money on discretionary items than you allowed for in your budget, you will not have enough money for essentials, such as food and shelter.

Example 6-1B

See It

Abdul has a part-time job. His monthly budget is shown in the table that follows. Abdul changed his cell phone plan to a different plan that costs $34 per month. He wants to allocate those savings to his clothing budget. What will Abdul's new monthly clothing budget be?

Abdul Monthly Budget		
Category	**Amount**	**Totals**
Income:		
Wages	$1,060	
Total Income		$1,060
Savings:		
Savings account	120	
Total Savings		120
Expenses:		
Rent	250	
Utilities	110	
Phone	58	
Gas and oil	72	
Food	280	
Clothing	35	
Entertainment	75	
Miscellaneous	60	
Total Expenses		940
Total Savings and Expenses		$1,060

Strategy

Use the formulas:

difference in phone budget = current phone budget amount – new phone budget amount

new clothing budget = current clothing budget amount + difference in phone budget

Solution

Step 1: Determine the difference in Abdul's phone budget. Subtract the new phone expense amount from the current phone expense amount.

difference in phone budget = current phone budget amount – new phone budget amount

difference in phone budget = $58 – $34

difference in phone budget = $24

Step 2: Add the difference in Abdul's phone budget to his clothing budget.

new clothing budget = current clothing budget amount + difference in phone budget

new clothing budget = $35 + $24

new clothing budget = $59

Check It

Because of an increase in gas prices, Abdul must increase his gas and oil budget to $98 per month. How much money must Abdul take out of his miscellaneous budget amount to make sure his expenses do not exceed his income?

Answer:
$26

Needs and Wants

To set proper financial priorities, it is important to know the difference between a need and a want. *Needs* are things required to survive. Food and shelter are needs. *Wants* are things that a person desires but that are not essential to survival. While it may sound simple to distinguish between necessities and optional expenses, it is not always that clear.

Food is a necessity. Eating out is optional. Buying groceries is a more cost-effective way to meet the need for food than eating out. Shelter is a necessity. Most people live somewhere that provides them more than the minimal need for shelter. Clothing is a necessity. But a closet filled with clothes is not necessary to meet the need for clothing.

You may think that a cell phone is a necessity. For some, it is a necessity due to a particular job or some other factor. However, for most people, a cell phone is a convenience rather than a necessity. And, most people want more than a basic cell phone.

Financial $marts

There is nothing wrong with spending money on optional expenses, as long as you can afford them. As you set financial priorities, it is most important to examine all of your expenses. For example, when you are comparing places to live, consider whether the apartment that costs $200 more each month is more important than applying that $200 per month somewhere else. The financially smart person considers these kinds of things when making financial decisions.

Entertainment is an enjoyable part of life and can contribute to your health and well-being. The cost of the forms of entertainment you choose can affect your financial well-being.

You will have a certain level of expenses that are necessary to provide for necessities. But the optional expenses are where your important decision making will take place.

Teaching Tip:
Discuss how much the budget of a household would be affected by adding a roommate. Ask students to describe some benefits and disadvantages of adding a roommate to a household.

Combining Households

One way to save on expenses is to share a household with another person. College students commonly have one or more roommates to share rent and utility expenses. Look at the following example to see the advantage of combining households.

In Figure 6-3, Kaley and Amanda are each maintaining their own apartments, or *households*. Both are paying similar rent and utilities. Amanda eats out more often, so she has a larger budget for food. Overall, their budgets are similar.

By becoming roommates and renting a slightly larger apartment, Kaley and Amanda can save more money. Rent and utilities become shared expenses, which generates savings. By sharing their food expenses, Kaley and Amanda also save money. Cooking for two can reduce waste and encourage more eating at home rather than eating out. Carpooling, when possible, can save on gasoline expenses. As shown in Figure 6-4, by combining households, they can save a lot of money. To determine rent savings, use the following formula:

rent savings = previous rent expenses – individual shared rent expense

Kaley and Amanda Monthly Budget Separate Households				
	Kaley Living Alone		**Amanda Living Alone**	
Category	**Amount**	**Totals**	**Amount**	**Totals**
Expenses:				
Rent	$550		$600	
Utilities	110		120	
Cell phone	43		51	
Gas and oil	55		48	
Food	260		310	
Clothing	40		50	
Entertainment	50		90	
Miscellaneous	65		70	
Total Expenses		$1,173		$1,339
Total Expenses for Both Households				$2,512

Figure 6-3. Kaley and Amanda's Separate Household Expenses

	Kaley's Direct Expenses		Shared Expenses		Amanda's Direct Expenses	
Category	Amount	Totals	Amount	Totals	Amount	Totals
Expenses:						
Rent	—		$700		—	
Utilities	—		140		—	
Cell phone	43		—		51	
Gas and oil	48		—		40	
Food	80		300		140	
Clothing	40		—		50	
Entertainment	50		—		90	
Miscellaneous	65		—		70	
Total Expenses		$326		$1,140		$441
Total Expenses for the Combined Household						$1,907

Table title: **Kaley and Amanda Monthly Budget Combined Household**

Figure 6-4. Kaley and Amanda's Combined Household Expenses

Example 6-1C

See It

How much will Kaley and Amanda each save in rent by sharing an apartment? Assume their shared expenses are split evenly.

Strategy

Use Figures 6-3 and 6-4 and the formula:

rent savings = previous rent expenses − individual shared rent expense

Solution

Step 1: Determine Kaley's and Amanda's individual rent if they share an apartment. Divide the shared rent by two.

individual rent expense = shared rent ÷ 2

individual rent expense = $700 ÷ 2

individual rent expense = $350

Teaching Tip:
Project or otherwise display Figures 6-3 and 6-4 as the See It portion of Example 6-C is demonstrated.

Step 2: Determine Kaley's rent savings. Subtract her new rent expense from her previous rent expense.

rent savings = previous rent expense – new rent expense

rent savings = $550 – $350

rent savings = $200

Step 3: Determine Amanda's rent savings. Subtract her new rent expense from her previous rent expense.

rent savings = previous rent expense – new rent expense

rent savings = $600 – $350

rent savings = $250

Check It

You just calculated Kaley and Amanda's overall savings. Now, calculate how much Kaley and Amanda will each save in utilities by sharing an apartment. Assume that shared expenses are split evenly.

Checkpoint 6.1

Lian's actual monthly spending for gasoline and entertainment are shown in the table that follows. Use this information to answer questions 1 and 2.

	April	May	June
Gasoline	$116	$153	$148
Entertainment	104	167	72

1. What is Lian's mean monthly spending for gasoline during this three-month period?

2. What is Lian's mean monthly spending for entertainment during this three-month period?

Mason's monthly budget is shown in the table that follows. Use this information to answer question 3.

Mason Monthly Budget			
Category		**Amount**	**Totals**
Income:			
Wages		$1,434	
Total Income			$1,434
Savings:			
Savings account		115	
Total Savings			115
Expenses:			
Rent		600	
Utilities		135	
Cell phone		58	
Gas and oil		81	
Food		280	
Clothing		25	
Entertainment		80	
Miscellaneous		60	
Total Expenses			1,319
Total Savings and Expenses			$1,434

3. If Mason changes to a mobile phone plan that only costs $39.50 per month, by what amount could he increase his savings?

3. $18.50

Mason and Esteban decide to share an apartment to help decrease their household expenses, as shown in the following table. Use this information to answer questions 4 and 5.

Category	Mason's Direct Expenses		Shared Expenses		Esteban's Direct Expenses	
	Amount	Totals	Amount	Totals	Amount	Totals
Expenses:						
Rent	—		$750		—	
Utilities	—		155		—	
Cell phone	58		—		48	
Gas and oil	81		—		73	
Food	28		300		65	
Clothing	25		—		35	
Entertainment	80		—		66	
Miscellaneous	<u>60</u>		—		<u>53</u>	
Total Expenses		$332		$1,205		$340
Total Expenses for the Combined Household						$1,877

Table title: Mason and Esteban Monthly Budget Combined Household

4. Mason saves $225 per month, and Esteban saves $260.
5. Mason saves $57.50 per month, and Esteban saves $62.50.

4. Prior to sharing an apartment, Mason spent $600 per month in rent. Esteban spent $635 per month. By sharing an apartment, how much are Mason and Esteban each saving in rent per month?

5. Prior to sharing an apartment, Mason spent $135 per month on utilities. Esteban spent $140 per month on utilities. By sharing an apartment, how much are Mason and Esteban each saving on utilities per month?

Section 6.2 Cash Flow

Objectives

- **Describe the difference between cash inflow and outflow.**
- **Create a cash flow statement.**

Terms

- *cash flow*
- *cash inflow*
- *cash outflow*
- *net cash flow*
- *cash flow statement*

Build Your Math Skills

Review these math skills to prepare for the lesson that follows.

1. Subtract integers. Example: $16 – $18 = –$2

A. $25 – $40 =

B. $53 – $77 =

C. $116 – $415 =

D. $1,045 – $1,476 =

2. Add and subtract decimals. Example: $164.79 + $74.09 = $238.88

A. $312.58 + $71.69 =

B. $1,045.17 + $709.01 =

C. $415.71 – $173.04 =

D. $503.15 – $99.73 =

Integers are all positive and negative whole numbers and zero.

Answer:
1. A. $15
   B. –$24
   C. –$299
   D. –$431
2. A. $384.27
   B. $1,754.18
   C. $242.67
   D. $403.42

Cash Inflow and Outflow

Cash flow describes the movement of cash. When you have income and expenses, you are dealing with cash flow. Cash can move in, or it can move out.

Cash inflow is any money that comes in. Income is a type of cash inflow. The word *income* itself is descriptive; when you make money, *in comes* the cash. Anything that brings in cash is cash inflow. A paycheck, proceeds from the sale of an asset, cash gifts, returns on an investment, or even borrowed money creates cash inflow. An *asset* is anything you own that has monetary value.

Expenses are a type of cash outflow. A *cash outflow* is anything that takes cash away. Examples of cash outflows include purchases, paying bills, making a cash investment, paying taxes, loaning someone money, or repaying a loan.

During a specified period of time, you will have a certain amount of cash inflow and a certain amount of cash outflow. The *net cash flow* is the balance remaining after cash outflows are deducted from cash inflows. Net cash flow can be determined using this formula:

net cash flow = cash inflows – cash outflows

Teaching Tip:
Have students compare and contrast the uses for a budget and a cash flow statement.

Example 6-2A

See It

Aaron's monthly banking statement contains a summary of deposits and withdrawals. His summary for the month of May is shown in the chart that follows. What is Aaron's net cash flow for May?

Aaron		
Checking Account Summary for the Month of May, 20--		
	Transactions	**Amount**
Deposits and Additions	2	$4,166.14
Checks Paid	5	815.96
ATM & Debit Card Withdrawals	12	1,746.37
Electronic Withdrawals	6	1,348.47

Strategy

Use the formula:

net cash flow = cash inflows – cash outflows

Solution

Step 1: Determine Aaron's cash inflows and cash outflows.

cash inflows:

deposits and additions = $4,166.14

cash outflows:

checks paid = $815.96

ATM & debit card withdrawals = $1,746.37

electronic withdrawals = $1,348.47

Step 2: Determine Aaron's total cash outflows. Find the sum of the cash outflows.

cash outflow = checks paid + ATM & debit card withdrawals + electronic withdrawals

cash outflow = $815.96 + $1,746.37 + $1,348.47

cash outflow = $3,910.80

Step 3: Determine Aaron's net cash flow. Subtract his cash outflows from his cash inflows.

net cash flow = cash inflows – cash outflows

net cash flow = $4,166.14 – $3,910.80

net cash flow = $255.34

Check It

Chantal's monthly banking statement includes a summary of deposits and withdrawals. Her summary for the month of January is shown as follows. What is Chantal's net cash flow for January?

Chantal Checking Account Summary for the Month of January, 20--		
	Transactions	Amount
Deposits and Additions	2	$3,716.18
Checks Paid	6	948.19
ATM & Debit Card Withdrawals	15	1,394.86
Electronic Withdrawals	4	1,206.38

Answer:
$166.75

Example 6-2B

See It

Logan's monthly banking statement includes a summary of deposits and withdrawals. His summary for the month of September is shown as follows. What is Logan's net cash flow for September?

Logan Checking Account Summary for the Month of September, 20--		
	Transactions	Amount
Deposits and Additions	1	$3,409.74
Checks Paid	4	1,218.84
ATM & Debit Card Withdrawals	16	949.60
Electronic Withdrawals	5	1,619.04

Strategy

Use the formula:

net cash flow = cash inflows – cash outflows

Solution

Step 1: Determine Logan's cash inflows and cash outflows.

cash inflows:

deposits and additions = $3,409.74

cash outflows:

checks paid = $1,218.84

ATM & debit card withdrawals = $949.60

electronic withdrawals = $1,619.04

Step 2: Determine Logan's total cash outflows. Find the sum of the cash outflows.

cash outflow = checks paid + ATM & debit card withdrawals + electronic withdrawals

cash outflow = $1,218.84 + $949.60 + $1,619.04

cash outflow = $3,787.48

Step 3: Determine Logan's net cash flow. Subtract his cash outflows from his cash inflows.

net cash flow = cash inflows − cash outflows

net cash flow = $3,409.74 − $3,787.48

net cash flow = −$377.74

Teaching Tip:
Explain the difference between a cash flow statement and a budget.

Check It

Padma's monthly banking statement includes a summary of deposits and withdrawals. Her summary for the month of June is shown as follows. What is Padma's net cash flow for June?

Answer:
−$778.73

Padma Checking Account Summary for the Month of June, 20--		
	Transactions	**Amount**
Deposits and Additions	3	$4,318.19
Checks Paid	5	1,018.47
ATM & Debit Card Withdrawals	12	1,583.29
Electronic Withdrawals	8	2,495.16

Cash Flow Statements

Managing cash flow is something independent people deal with even if they have not used the term *cash flow*. Even children who receive an allowance learn the basics of cash flow. For example, Carlos receives a $5 weekly allowance. When Carlos walks into a store, he quickly learns that having more cash would enable him to buy more. And when Carlos walks out with a pack of gum and very little change, cash flow starts to become real to him.

A cash flow statement is a tool for managing money. A cash flow statement is very similar to a budget. Whereas a budget is a plan for your money, a ***cash flow statement*** is a report of how much money actually came in and how much went out during a given period.

A cash flow statement for an entire year is shown in Figure 6-5. In this cash flow statement, there are several sources of cash: wages, interest income, sale of a boat, and a gift from a family member. Most of the outflows are typical, including some loan repayment.

Sample Cash Flow Statement		
Category	**Amount**	**Totals**
Inflow:		
Wages	$52,500	
Interest income	540	
Sale of boat	6,700	
Gift from grandma	1,000	
Total Inflow		$60,740
Outflow:		
Fixed Expenses		
Investment contributions	8,000	
Rent	7,200	
Loan payments	3,980	
Insurance	2,160	
Total Fixed Expenses		21,340
Variable Expenses		
Utilities	3,960	
Phone	630	
Gas and oil	974	
Charitable giving	5,520	
Food	4,455	
Clothing	1,511	
Medical care	490	
Maintenance/repairs	609	
Education	2,000	
Entertainment	1,367	
Gifts	822	
Miscellaneous	2,181	
Total Variable Expenses		24,519
Total Outflow		45,859
Net Cash Flow		$14,881

Figure 6-5.
Sample Cash
Flow Statement

In a cash flow statement, fixed expenses are often separated from variable expenses. The reason for this is that you have more control over the variable expenses. By grouping the variable expenses, you can see how much of your outflow involves items that you may be able to control.

Example 6-2C

See It

Minerva's cash flow statement for last year is shown as follows. Use this statement to calculate Minerva's total inflow, total fixed expenses, total variable expenses, total outflow, and net cash flow.

Minerva Cash Flow Statement		
Category	**Amount**	**Totals**
Inflow:		
Wages	$48,419	
Interest income	510	
Dividends	1,285	
Cash gifts	750	
Total Inflow		
Outflow:		
Fixed Expenses		
Investment contributions	7,600	
Rent	9,000	
Student loans	2,580	
Renters insurance	1,216	
Life insurance	264	
Health insurance	4,560	
Savings	1,440	
Total Fixed Expenses		
Variable Expenses		
Utilities	1,680	
Phone	780	
Gas and oil	2,064	
Food	3,960	
Clothing	431	
Medical care	616	
Entertainment	1,415	
Pets	2,315	
Gifts	944	
Miscellaneous	756	
Total Variable Expenses		
Total Outflow		
Net Cash Flow		

Strategy

Use Minerva's cash flow statement and the formula:

net cash flow = cash inflows − cash outflows

Solution

Step 1: Determine Minerva's total inflow. Find the sum of each of Minerva's cash inflow items.

total inflow = wages + interest + dividends + cash gifts

total inflow = $48,419 + $510 + $1,285 + $750

total inflow = $50,964

Step 2: Determine Minerva's total fixed expenses. Find the sum of Minerva's fixed expense items.

total fixed expenses = investment contributions + rent + student loans + renters insurance + life insurance + health insurance + savings

total fixed expenses = $7,600 + $9,000 + $2,580 + $1,216 + $264 + $4,560 + $1,440

total fixed expenses = $26,660

Step 3: Determine Minerva's total variable expenses. Find the sum of Minerva's variable expense items.

total variable expenses = utilities + phone + gasoline and auto + food + clothing + medical + entertainment + pets + gifts + miscellaneous

total variable expenses = $1,680 + $780 + $2,064 + $3,960 + $431 + $616 + $1,415 + $2,315 + $944 + $756

total variable expenses = $14,961

Step 4: Determine Minerva's total outflow. Add Minerva's total fixed expenses and total variable expenses.

total outflow = total fixed expenses + total variable expenses

total outflow = $26,660 + $14,961

total outflow = $41,621

Step 5: Determine Minerva's net cash flow. Subtract Minerva's total outflow from her total inflow.

net cash flow = total inflow − total outflow

net cash flow = $50,964 − $41,621

net cash flow = $9,343

Check It

Payden's cash flow statement for last year is shown as follows. Use this statement to calculate Payden's total inflow, total fixed expenses, total variable expenses, total outflow, and net cash flow.

Payden Cash Flow Statement		
Category	**Amount**	**Totals**
Inflow:		
Wages	$42,670	
Interest income	225	
Sale of car	3,700	
Cash gifts	550	
Total Inflow		
Outflow:		
Fixed Expenses		
Investment contributions	6,400	
Rent	8,700	
Student loans	2,340	
Renters insurance	552	
Life insurance	300	
Health insurance	5,076	
Savings	1,440	
Total Fixed Expenses		
Variable Expenses		
Utilities	2,160	
Phone	660	
Gas and oil	3,024	
Food	3,480	
Clothing	371	
Medical care	496	
Entertainment	1,560	
Charitable giving	4,200	
Gifts	1,015	
Miscellaneous	944	
Total Variable Expenses		
Total Outflow		
Net Cash Flow		

Checkpoint 6.2

1. Bradley examined his bank account. He determined that his cash inflows are $3,018.95, and his cash outflows are $2,716.17. What is Bradley's net cash flow?

2. Quintessa studied her monthly bank account. She determined that her cash inflows are $4,516.17, and her cash outflows are $4,985.03. What is Quintessa's net cash flow?

3. Santiago's bank statement for February included the following checking account summary. What is Santiago's net cash flow for February?

Santiago Checking Account Summary for the Month of February, 20--		
	Transactions	Amount
Deposits and Additions	2	$3,994.83
Checks Paid	6	1,415.67
ATM & Debit Card Withdrawals	13	1,043.41
Electronic Withdrawals	7	1,973.37

4. Santiago's bank statement for March included the following checking account summary. What is Santiago's net cash flow for March?

Santiago Checking Account Summary for the Month of March, 20--		
	Transactions	Amount
Deposits and Additions	3	$5,992.25
Checks Paid	5	1,567.67
ATM & Debit Card Withdrawals	16	1,597.75
Electronic Withdrawals	8	2,016.38

Answer:
1. $302.78
2. –$468.86
3. –$437.62
4. $810.45

5. Sani's cash flow statement for last year is shown as follows. Use this statement to calculate Sani's total inflow, total fixed expenses, total variable expenses, total outflow, and net cash flow.

Sani Cash Flow Statement		
Category	Amount	Totals
Inflow:		
Wages	$51,370	
Interest income	479	
Sale of motorcycle	2,500	
Dividends	1,476	
Total Inflow		
Outflow:		
Fixed Expenses		
Investment contributions	9,100	
Mortgage	12,360	
Car payment	4,860	
Homeowners insurance	1,050	
Life insurance	300	
Health insurance	6,144	
Savings	2,400	
Total Fixed Expenses		
Variable Expenses		
Utilities	3,840	
Phone	660	
Gas and oil	2,544	
Food	3,960	
Clothing	492	
Medical care	517	
Entertainment	2,314	
Gifts	1,443	
Miscellaneous	1,483	
Total Variable Expenses		
Total Outflow		
Net Cash Flow		

5. total inflow = $55,825
total fixed expenses = $36,214
total variable expenses = $17,253
total outflow = $53,467
net cash flow = $2,358

Source: Shutterstock (Tyler Olson)

Creating a budget will help you analyze your expenses.

Section 6.3 Setting Financial Goals

Objectives

- **Define measurable financial goals.**
- **Calculate a budget adjustment.**
- **Calculate rate of inflation.**

Build Your Math Skills

Review these math skills to prepare for the lesson that follows.

1. Convert decimals to percentages by moving the decimal two places to the right. **Example:** 0.15 → 15%

A. 0.0156 →

B. 0.12 →

C. 0.035 →

D. 0.0417 →

2. Divide decimals and whole numbers. Round to the nearest cent ($0.01) if necessary. **Example:** $1,250.50 ÷ 12 = $104.21

A. $754.14 ÷ 6 =

B. $1,045 ÷ 10 =

C. $3.56 ÷ $65.15 =

D. $5.14 ÷ $110 =

3. Add or subtract decimals. **Example:** $114.57 − $65.18 = $49.39

A. $516.73 + $114.18 =

B. $1,053.14 + $970.40 =

C. $87.14 − $83.14 =

D. $104.38 − $93.76 =

Answer:

1. A. 1.56%
   B. 12%
   C. 3.5%
   D. 4.17%
2. A. $125.69
   B. $104.50
   C. 0.05
   D. 0.05
3. A. $630.91
   B. $2,023.54
   C. $4
   D. $10.62

Setting Measurable Financial Goals

Earlier in this chapter, you learned about prioritizing competing financial demands. An important part of budgeting is setting financial goals so that you may have continued financial success. *Financial goals* are measurable objectives related to acquiring or spending money. *SMART goals* should be specific, measurable, attainable, relevant, and timely, as shown in Figure 6-6.

Preparing for a financial emergency is a common financial goal. Suppose a married couple, Dane and Katie, want to be prepared to handle financial emergencies and times of negative net cash flow. They currently have $125 in an emergency fund. In their budget, they have determined that they can set aside $300 per month for their emergency fund. They have two goals. Their short-term goal is to have at least $1,000 in their emergency fund in three months. Their long-term goal is to have more than $5,000 in the fund in 18 months. By having a measurable goal, Dane and Katie will be able to see the progress of their goals each month.

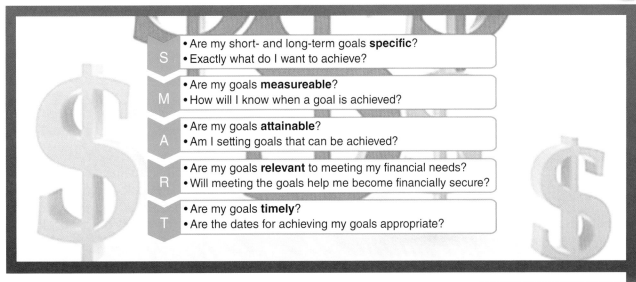

S
- Are my short- and long-term goals **specific**?
- Exactly what do I want to achieve?

M
- Are my goals **measureable**?
- How will I know when a goal is achieved?

A
- Are my goals **attainable**?
- Am I setting goals that can be achieved?

R
- Are my goals **relevant** to meeting my financial needs?
- Will meeting the goals help me become financially secure?

T
- Are my goals **timely**?
- Are the dates for achieving my goals appropriate?

Background source: Shutterstock (sn4ke)

Figure 6-6. SMART Goals

Other measurable financial goals may include paying down debt, saving for a down payment on a house, or preparing to send a child to college. In order to calculate how long it will take to reach a financial goal, use the formula that follows:

number of months = total amount needed ÷ savings per month

Teaching Tip:
Encourage students to describe their financial goals. Then, have students identify some of the tools they have learned that may help them achieve those goals.

Example 6-3A

See It

Marco and Caroline want to save money for a down payment on a new house. They received a gift of $5,000 toward the down payment. However, they need a total of $17,000. If Marco and Caroline save $750 per month toward the down payment, how many months will it take for them to reach their goal?

Strategy

Use the formula:

number of months = total amount needed ÷ savings per month

Solution

Step 1: Determine the total amount of money Marco and Caroline need to save. Subtract what they currently have from their goal savings amount.

total amount needed = goal savings amount – current funds

total amount needed = $17,000 – $5,000

total amount needed = $12,000

fyi

If you have a remainder after calculating the number of months you will need to save, just round up to the next month. This means that you will need to save for one additional month to meet, and exceed, your savings goal.

Step 2: Determine the number of months required to meet the savings goal. Divide the amount needed by the amount saved per month.

number of months = total amount needed ÷ savings per month

number of months = $12,000 ÷ $750 per month

number of months = 16

Check It

Sunna met with her financial planner and determined that she needs to have an emergency fund of six months of living expenses. They calculated that her monthly living expenses are $1,950. Sunna currently has $3,000 in her savings account. If she can save $850 per month toward the emergency fund, how long will it take to meet her goal?

Answer:
Sunna will need to save $850 per month for 11 months to meet her goal.

Adjusting a Budget

Budgets must be adjusted, just like many other plans that you make. A budget might need to be adjusted because you realize your spending in some categories is more or less than you expected. An expense may also increase. Or, you may have a change in income that requires you to adjust your budget.

Career Discovery
Human Services Careers and Math Skills

Careers in human services relate to family and human needs. If you like to help others, one of these careers may be for you. People who enter these careers often desire to protect, nurture, or provide services for others in need. Career pathways include services in early childhood development, counseling and mental health, family and community, personal care, and consumer services.

For careers that involve direct contact with people who need help finding a job or looking for housing, it can be helpful to have strong math skills. Describe situations where you might need to use math skills if you had a career in consumer services or another human services field.

Example 6-3B

See It

Earlier in this chapter, you met Abdul. His monthly budget was shown in Example 6-1B. Due to an increase in gasoline costs, Abdul determined that he needs to increase his gas and oil budget to $95. He wants to take that amount evenly from his entertainment and miscellaneous budgets. What will be Abdul's adjusted budget amounts for entertainment and miscellaneous?

Teaching Tip:
To help students recall the information about Abdul's budget, project or otherwise display the figure on page 188 showing Abdul's monthly budget.

Strategy

Use the monthly budget found in Example 6-1B and the formulas:

difference in gas and oil budget = new gas and oil budget amount – current gas and oil budget amount

new entertainment budget = current entertainment budget amount – difference in gas and oil budget

Solution

Step 1: Determine the amount of increase in Abdul's gas and oil budget. Subtract the original amount from the adjusted amount.

difference in gas and oil budget = new gas and oil budget amount – current gas and oil budget amount

difference in gas and oil budget = $95 – $72

difference in gas and oil budget = $23

Step 2: Determine by what amount Abdul will decrease the other budget categories. Divide the increase in the gas and oil budget by two, since Abdul is splitting this evenly between two categories.

decrease in other budget categories = difference in gas and oil budget ÷ 2

decrease in other budget categories = $23 ÷ 2

decrease in other budget categories = $11.50

Step 3: Determine the new budget amount for entertainment. Subtract the difference in the gas and oil budget from the current budget amount.

new entertainment budget = current entertainment budget amount – difference in gas and oil budget

new entertainment budget = $75 – $11.50

new entertainment budget = $63.50

Step 4: Determine the new budget amount for miscellaneous. Subtract the difference in the gas and oil budget from the current budget amount.

new miscellaneous budget = current miscellaneous budget amount – difference in gas and oil budget

new miscellaneous budget = $60 – $11.50

new miscellaneous budget = $48.50

fyi

Later in this text, you will
learn more about inflation
and how to protect your
money and your future
from the effects of
inflation.

Check It

Suppose that Abdul reconsiders how to allocate money within his budget. He still has to budget $95 for gas and oil. Now he wants to evenly reduce his budget for clothing and miscellaneous. What will be Abdul's adjusted budget amounts for clothing and miscellaneous?

Inflation

Over time, prices tend to trend upward. You have probably heard people talk about how groceries are more expensive than they were several years ago. *Inflation* is a general rise in prices.

For example, a loaf of bread cost about a nickel in the year 1900. By 1970, the cost was about a quarter. By 2011, the cost of a loaf of bread was over $2. But, people in 1970 did not necessarily find it easier to afford the cost of bread. This is because inflation causes wages to rise, as well. The average income in 2011 was about four times the average income in 1970.

Inflation is not just about prices and wages going up. Inflation is about cash being worth less. If you had $30,000 in cash in 1970, you could have bought about eight average-priced brand new cars. By 2011, that same $30,000 would only get you one average-priced car with little money left over.

The *consumer price index (CPI)* is a measure of the change in the price of goods and services purchased by households. It includes a wide range of commonly purchased goods and services. The CPI is widely used as a measure of overall inflation.

While the rate of inflation is usually expressed as an annual percentage, you can calculate the rate of inflation for any period of time. The rate of inflation for a specific period can be calculated using the following formula:

$$\textbf{inflation rate} = \left(\frac{\textbf{ending price – beginning price}}{\textbf{beginning price}} \right) \times \textbf{100\%}$$

Rates of inflation are usually reported on an annual basis, so it is sometimes helpful to think of an *annual* inflation rate instead of an inflation rate over a longer period of time. There are many factors that influence the price of goods or services over time, and inflation is only one of those factors. Other factors may include changes in the availability of an item and the number of customers who want the item. Availability can be affected by weather events, such as floods, droughts, or an early freeze that decreases production in food products. A simplified formula for calculating the annual inflation rate is as follows:

$$\textbf{average annual inflation rate} = \frac{\textbf{inflation rate}}{\textbf{number of years}}$$

Example 6-3C

See It

A clothes dryer in 1980 sold for $228. A similar clothes dryer in 2010 sold for $429. What is the overall inflation rate for this 30-year period? Assuming that the rate of inflation was constant, what is the average annual inflation rate?

Strategy

Use the formulas:

$$\textbf{inflation rate} = \left(\frac{\textbf{ending price – beginning price}}{\textbf{beginning price}} \right) \times \textbf{100\%}$$

$$\textbf{average annual inflation rate} = \frac{\textbf{inflation rate}}{\textbf{number of years}}$$

Solution

Step 1: Determine the change in price. Subtract the beginning price from the ending price.

change in price = ending price – beginning price

change in price = $429 – $228

change in price = $201

Step 2: Determine the rate of price increase. Divide the change in price by the beginning price.

$$\text{rate of price increase} = \frac{\text{change in price}}{\text{beginning price}}$$

$$\text{rate of price increase} = \frac{\$201}{\$228}$$

rate of price increase ≈ 0.882

Step 3: Determine the overall inflation rate. Multiply by 100% to convert the decimal to a percentage.

0.882 × 100% = 88.2%

Step 4: Determine the average annual inflation rate. Divide the overall inflation rate by the number of years.

$$\text{average annual inflation rate} = \frac{\text{inflation rate}}{\text{number of years}}$$

$$\text{average annual inflation rate} = \frac{88.2\%}{30 \text{ years}}$$

average annual inflation rate = 2.94% per year

> Multiplying by 100% adds the % notation. Moving the decimal point two places to the right converts the decimal to a percentage.

Check It

In 1980, an average new car sold for $7,200. In 2011, an average new car sold for $29,602. What is the overall inflation rate for this 31-year period? Assuming that the rate of inflation was constant, what is the average annual inflation rate?

Answer:
overall inflation rate = 311.11%
average annual inflation rate = 10.04% per year

Checkpoint 6.3

1. Phoebe wants to save for a down payment on a new house. She currently has $5,500 in savings and needs to save a total of $20,000. She plans to save $725 each month for her down payment. How long will it take Phoebe to reach her goal?

2. Amin and Tori have decided that they need to save $22,000 for their daughter's college fund. They have 12 years before they will need the money. How much will they need to save each month to reach their goal?

Autumn has a part-time job doing contract work for a local temporary agency. Her monthly budget is shown. Use Autumn's monthly budget to answer questions 3 and 4.

Autumn Monthly Budget		
Category	**Amount**	**Totals**
Income:		
Wages	$1,434	
Contract work	750	
Total Income		$2,184
Savings:		
Savings account	210	
Total Savings		210
Expenses:		
Rent	850	
Utilities	195	
Phone	78	
Gas and oil	91	
Food	350	
Charitable giving	140	
Clothing	35	
Entertainment	145	
Miscellaneous	90	
Total Expenses		1,974
Total Savings and Expenses		$2,184

3. Due to an increase in gasoline costs, Autumn needs to adjust her gasoline and oil budget to $110 per month. She wants to adjust her entertainment budget to reflect that change. What is Autumn's new entertainment budget?

4. Autumn also learned that next month her rent will increase to $925. She would like to split that budget adjustment between miscellaneous and charitable giving. What will be the new budget amounts for those two categories?

5. In 2008, a gallon of whole milk cost $2.65. In 2011, a gallon of whole milk cost $3.39. What is the overall rate of inflation for this three-year period? What is the approximate average annual rate of inflation?

Chapter Review

Build Your Vocabulary

As you progress through this course, develop a personal glossary of financial literacy terms and add it to your portfolio. This will help you build your financial literacy vocabulary. Write out a definition for each of the following terms, and add it to your personal glossary.

recordkeeping	cash inflow
budget	cash outflow
fixed expense	net cash flow
fixed income	cash flow statement
need	financial goal
want	inflation
cash flow	consumer price index (CPI)

 ## Teamwork

Working with a teammate, select two of the occupations discussed in one of the Career Discovery features in this text. Conduct research on the salary range associated with each occupation. Next, develop a monthly budget for a married couple assuming each has one of these careers. Assume they have a combined household and live in your state.

Review Your Math Skills

Practice and build on the math skills that you have learned.

1. Convert percentages to decimals by moving the decimal two places to the left. Example: 27% → 0.27

A. 11.2% →   B. 8% →

C. 6.572% →   D. 16.8% →

2. Divide decimals. Round to the nearest cent ($0.01) if necessary. Example: $115.30 ÷ 3 = $38.43

A. $1,332.10 ÷ 6 =   B. $509.58 ÷ 3 =

C. $198.71 ÷ 4 =   D. $655.16 ÷ 8 =

Answer:
1. A. 0.112
   B. 0.08
   C. 0.06572
   D. 0.168
2. A. $222.02
   B. $169.86
   C. $49.68
   D. $81.90

3. Find the average of a set of numbers. **Round to the nearest cent ($0.01) if necessary.** Example: The average of $112, $57, and $181 is ($112 + $57 + $181) ÷ 3 = $116.67

A. $345.68, $664.82, $546

B. $182.47, $196.75

C. $545, $125, $399, $276

D. $357.25, $159.86, $87.68

4. Subtract integers. Example: $16 – $18 = –$2

A. $97 – $113 =

B. $42 – $81 =

C. $1,652 – $1,809 =

D. $251 – $508 =

5. Convert decimals to percentages by moving the decimal two places to the right. Example: 0.15 → 15%

A. 0.0856 →

B. 0.44 →

C. 0.064 →

D. 0.0697 →

6. Find the average of a set of numbers. **Round to the nearest cent ($0.01) if necessary.** Example: The average of $152, $57, and $206 is ($152 + $57 + $206) ÷ 3 = $138.33

A. $685.32, $721.08, $690

B. $427.88, $231.51

C. $305, $91, $256, $47

D. $138.85, $197.62, $100.34

7. Add and subtract decimals. Example: $164.79 + $74.09 = $238.88

A. $443.89 + $175.10 =

B. $852.35 – $1,124.04 =

C. $614.93 – $382.01 =

D. $741.22 – $227.64 =

8. Convert decimals to percentages by moving the decimal two places to the right. Example: 0.02 → 2%

A. 0.499 →

B. 0.81 →

C. 0.013 →

D. 0.557 →

9. Divide decimals and whole numbers. **Round to the nearest cent ($0.01) if necessary.** Example: $1,250.50 ÷ 12 = $104.21

A. $214.23 ÷ 4 =

B. $2,632.06 ÷ 11 =

C. $6.91 ÷ $77.18 =

D. $3.21 ÷ $140 =

10. Add and subtract decimals. Example: $206.43 + $110.09 = $316.52

A. $974.51 + $32.11 =

B. $1,213.02 + $569.39 =

C. $168.05 – $144.70 =

D. $298.75 – $159.81 =

3. A. $518.83
   B. $189.61
   C. $336.25
   D. $201.60
4. A. –$16
   B. –$39
   C. –$157
   D. –$257
5. A. 8.56%
   B. 44%
   C. 6.4%
   D. 6.97%
6. A. $698.80
   B. $329.70
   C. $174.75
   D. $145.60
7. A. $618.99
   B. –$271.69
   C. $232.92
   D. $513.58
8. A. 49.9%
   B. 81%
   C. 1.3%
   D. 55.7%
9. A. $53.56
   B. $239.28
   C. 0.09
   D. 0.02
10. A. $1,006.62
    B. $1,782.41
    C. $23.35
    D. $138.94

Section 6.1 Creating a Budget

11. Estrella's record of spending for utilities and gasoline is shown as follows. What is Estrella's mean monthly spending for gasoline during this three-month period?

	July	August	September
Utilities	$215.67	$285.89	$190.47
Gasoline	149.35	184.06	161.63

12. Dennis' monthly budget is shown as follows. He is able to reduce his entertainment budget to $60 per month and his utilities budget to $145 per month. Dennis wants to allocate these funds to his monthly savings budget. Determine Dennis' new monthly savings budget.

Dennis Monthly Budget		
Category	Amount	Totals
Income:		
Wages	$2,115	
Total Income		$2,115
Savings:		
Savings account	300	
Total Savings		300
Expenses:		
Rent	450	
Utilities	160	
Phone	70	
Gas and oil	85	
Food	300	
Clothing	250	
Charitable giving	200	
Entertainment	75	
Miscellaneous	225	
Total Expenses		1,815
Total Savings and Expenses		$2,115

Section 6.2 Cash Flow

13. Arthur's cash inflows for one month were $1,618.74. His cash outflows for the same month were $1,719.23. What was Arthur's net cash flow for that month?

14. Chet is the secretary for a club. During one month, the club's statement showed cash inflows of $2,587.49 and cash outflows of $2,306.73. What was the club's net cash flow for that month?

15. Shirley's bank statement for October included the following checking account summary. What is Shirley's net cash flow for October?

Answer:
13. –$100.49
14. $280.76
15. –$573.40

Shirley Checking Account Summary for the Month of October, 20--		
	Transactions	**Amount**
Deposits and Additions	2	$4,018.74
Checks Paid	4	945.83
ATM & Debit Card Withdrawals	21	2,230.94
Electronic Withdrawals	6	1,415.37

Section 6.3 Setting Financial Goals

16. When Jill and Dakota got married, Jill's grandparents gave them $7,000 toward a down payment for a new house. In order to buy a house in the neighborhood where they would like to live, Jill and Dakota need to have a down payment of $21,000. They can afford to save $550 per month. How long will it take them to save enough money for their down payment?

17. Dennis learned that his rent expense will increase to $480. He wants to evenly split the budget adjustment to reduce his entertainment and clothing budgets. Using Dennis' monthly budget shown in question 12, determine his new entertainment and clothing budget amounts.

18. In 1930, a loaf of bread cost $0.09. In 2011, a similar loaf of bread cost $2.79. What is the overall rate of inflation for this 78-year period? What was the approximate annual rate of inflation?

Answer:
16. 26 months
17. new entertainment
      budget = $60
   new clothing budget =
      $15
18. overall rate of
      inflation = 3,000%
   annual inflation rate =
      38.5% per year

Reinforce Your Understanding

19. Jermaine is a salesclerk at a furniture store. He receives a base salary of $500 biweekly plus 6.5% commission of his sales. The following table shows his sales for one two-week period. Determine Jermaine's gross pay for the two-week period.

Item	Item Price	Number of Items Sold
Sofa	$1,200	5
Chair	325	8
Bedroom Set	1,015	2
Dining Room Table Set	950	3

20. Araceli had an emergency plumbing repair and transferred $550.16 from her savings account to her checking account. Before the transfer, her checking account balance was $229.46 and her savings account balance was $4,187.23. What are Araceli's new savings and checking account balances?

Answer:
19. $1,378.20
20. savings account balance = $3,637.07 checking account balance = $779.62

Apply Your Technology Skills

Access the G-W Learning companion website for this text at www.g-wlearning.com. Download each data file for this chapter. Follow the instructions to complete financial literacy activities to practice what you have learned in this chapter.

Data File 6-1—Tracking Your Spending

Data File 6-2—Creating a Budget

Data File 6-3—Creating a Cash Flow Statement

Data File 6-4—Creating Circle Graphs

Unit 2 Summative Assessment

On a separate sheet of paper or in a word processing document, apply what you have learned in this unit to answer the questions that follow.

Multiple Choice Questions

1. Use the rule of 72 to find the number of years it will take you to _____.

   A. pay off a debt

   B. reduce the principal you own on a loan

   C. have all of the retirement savings you need

   D. double an initial investment

2. Jared has put a video game system on layaway. The cost of the system before taxes is $299. The layaway fee is 1.25% of that price. How much will Jared have to pay before taxes for his new system?

   A. $300.25   B. $302.74

   C. $311.50   D. $373.75

3. To *reconcile* a bank statement means to _____.

   A. clear up any overdrafts

   B. calculate simple interest charges

   C. verify that you and the bank agree on your account balance

   D. check your account balance on the bank's website

4. Net cash flow is the _____.

   A. total of all cash inflows

   B. total of all cash outflows

   C. the difference between cash inflows and outflows

   D. the difference between cash inflows and income

5. Fixed expenses _____.

   A. stay the same each month

   B. are the same as variable expenses

   C. should exceed fixed income

   D. are the same for everybody

Answer:
1. D
2. B
3. C
4. C
5. A

Matching

Match the letter beside each equation to the situation to which it applies.

A. net deposit = currency + coins + check amount – less cash received

B. adjusted balance = statement balance + outstanding deposits – outstanding payments

C. $I = Prt$

D. $M = P(1 + i)^n$

E. $M = P(1 + \dfrac{i}{n})^{nt}$

F. change due = amount of cash given to the clerk – purchase total

G. unit price = $\dfrac{\text{price}}{\text{number of units}}$

H. advertising revenue = rate per click × number of clicks

I. mean = sum of amounts ÷ number of amounts added

J. net cash flow = cash inflows – cash outflows

6. Kareem wants to determine his interest charges for a credit card that compounds interest daily.

7. Christina wants to reconcile her checkbook.

8. Ellen gave the cashier three $10 bills for a $23.76 purchase.

9. Hari wants to determine his average grocery bill.

10. Lien is filling out a deposit slip.

11. Julia wants create a cash flow statement to track her expenses.

12. Rosanne likes to buy her favorite gum by the case to save money.

13. Sanat wants to make money on the website he hosts.

14. Shaun wants to calculate simple interest.

15. Victoria wants to calculate interest compounded yearly.

Answer:
6. E
7. B
8. F
9. I
10. A
11. J
12. G
13. H
14. C
15. D

True/False Questions

16. *True or False?* The Internet can serve as a market.

17. *True or False?* A budget is a plan for saving and spending.

18. *True or False?* By purchasing a warranty, you are guaranteed that whatever you purchased will not break.

19. *True or False?* Digital cash can be stored on a computer or smartphone.

20. *True or False?* Sales tax is a type of progressive tax.

Answer:
16. True
17. True
18. False
19. True
20. False

Mastery Questions

21. Troy has seven months remaining on his mobile phone contract. The monthly payment is $59.99 per month. His contract includes an early termination fee of $225. He wants to change mobile phone providers. He found an equivalent plan for $25.99 per month with no contract. Will Troy save money if he cancels his current contract and moves to the new provider? Explain your answer.

22. Tony is studying his quarterly bank statement to understand his net cash flow. His bank account summary for the three months is shown as follows. Determine Tony's net cash flow for each month, and then determine his total cash flow for the quarter. Based on these data, does Tony need to adjust his spending habits? Why or why not?

21. Yes. If Troy continues paying on his current contract, he will pay $419.93 in the next seven months. However, if he cancels his current contract, pays the early termination fee, and moves to the new provider, he will pay $406.93, a savings of $13.

22. July net cash flow = –$145.37
   August net cash flow = $271.87
   September net cash flow = –$86.78
   quarterly net cash flow = $39.72
   Over the quarter, Tony is barely breaking even. If Tony wants to save additional money, he may need to adjust his spending habits.

	Tony **Checking Account Summary** **Second Quarter, 20--**					
	July		**August**		**September**	
	Trans-actions	**Amount**	**Trans-actions**	**Amount**	**Trans-actions**	**Amount**
Deposits and Additions	2	$4,085.67	3	$4,785.67	2	$4,085.67
Checks Paid	4	750.85	5	1,012.16	4	718.38
ATM & Debit Card Withdrawals	21	1,919.36	24	2,085.69	22	1,879.46
Electronic Withdrawals	6	1,560.83	5	1,415.95	5	1,574.61

23. Alta received a bonus check from her employer for $4,230.85. She decided to invest the money in an account that yields 4.45% compound interest annually. If Alta leaves the money in the account and makes no additional deposits, what will be the balance of the account in 10 years?

24. Eric deposited $4,000 into an account that earns 3% interest. How many years will it take for his investment to double?

25. Lona needs to purchase new tires for her vehicle. The cost before sales tax is $425.29. She has a coupon from the tire shop for a 20% discount. The tire manufacturer is offering a mail-in rebate of $75. Because of restrictions on the coupon and mail-in rebate, she cannot take both discounts. If the sales tax rate is 7%, which will give Lona the lowest final cost: the coupon, or the mail-in rebate?

23. $6,539.20
24. 24 years
25. The coupon; the final cost of $364.05 from the coupon is lower than the final cost of $380.06 from the mail-in rebate.

Unit 3
Credit, Debt, and Major Purchases

A growing number of people have gotten into serious financial trouble by borrowing money they were unable to repay. Borrowed money can come in the form of loans or credit cards, which themselves are a type of loan. Saving for the things you want will make it easier for you to afford the things you need. Without the burden of debt, you will be better able to achieve your personal and financial goals.

7 Credit Cards

Materials:
Instructor's Resource CD
Student Workbook
G-W Learning companion website
EXAMVIEW® Assessment Suite
Microsoft Excel®–compatible software
Calculator with advanced-math functions

Credit cards are widely used financial tools. It is important, however, to learn how to use credit cards wisely. Building good credit can help you achieve your financial goals. On the other hand, poor credit can stand in the way of achieving those goals.

Section 7.1	**Credit Basics**
Section 7.2	**Finance Charges and Fees**
Section 7.3	**Debt Management**

College and Career Readiness

Reading Prep. As you read, determine two or three central ideas of the chapter. How do these ideas build on each other throughout the text?

"I always thought credit cards were free money. I didn't think about having to pay it back until I got older." ~ Amanda B.

Money Matters
Credit Cards

- The first credit cards were issued in the 1920s. Oil companies and department stores were the first to issue cards that would allow customers to pay without cash and be billed later for their purchases. The cards were primarily offered to build customer loyalty.

- In the 1940s, banks began to introduce credit cards. With a bank card, purchases could be made with any merchant who accepted the card. Early bank cards could only be used locally.

- In 1950, the Diners Club card was introduced as the first national credit card. It was originally a credit card used in restaurants only, hence its name.

- Many early credit cards had to be paid in full each month and would not allow the cardholder to carry over a balance.

- Early credit cards were made of cardboard or paper. In 1959, the first plastic credit card was made.

- The Credit CARD Act of 2009 provides consumer protection against unfair fees and regulations imposed by credit card issuers.

Section 7.1 Credit Basics

Objectives

- **Describe how a credit card works.**
- **Explain how to apply for a credit card.**
- **Describe the difference between a credit score and a credit report.**
- **Explain the purpose of a credit limit.**
- **Calculate available credit.**

Build Your Math Skills

Review these math skills to prepare for the lesson that follows.

1. Subtract whole numbers. Example: $19.63 – $7.27 = $12.36

A. $2,000 – $373 =   B. $3,500 – $1,453 =

C. $2,500 – $717 =   D. $3,000 – $2,045 =

2. Add decimals. Example: $520.38 + $102.94 = $623.32

A. $304.18 + $80.06 =   B. $94.14 + $8.93 =

C. $1,117.07 + $30.47 =   D. $298.17 + $73.55 =

3. Subtract decimals. Example: $104.29 – $45.16 = $59.13

A. $391.49 – $107.48 =   B. $500.50 – $287.24 =

C. $1,200 – $512.33 =   D. $1,800 – $970.38 =

Terms

- *credit*
- *credit card*
- *line of credit*
- *credit report*
- *credit score*
- *FICO score*
- *credit limit*
- *current balance*
- *available credit*
- *credit card statement*
- *grace period*

Answer:
1. A. $1,627
   B. $2,047
   C. $1,783
   D. $955
2. A. $384.24
   B. $103.07
   C. $1,147.54
   D. $371.72
3. A. $284.01
   B. $213.26
   C. $687.67
   D. $829.62

Credit Card Basics

Credit is a term that describes the contractual agreement between a borrower and a lender. The borrower agrees to pay back the lender for money that the borrower receives, usually with interest. If you *extend* credit to someone, you are allowing that person to use your money with the agreement that it will be repaid. If someone extends credit to you, then you are using that person's money and agreeing to pay him or her back.

A *credit card* is a plastic card that allows you to borrow money from the bank or financial institution that issued you the card. The credit card allows you to borrow a limited amount of money called a *line of credit.* Each month, you must send at least a minimum amount of money to the credit card company as a payment toward the money you have borrowed on the line of credit. You also agree to pay the bank a certain amount of interest for the money you borrowed.

A credit card is different from a debit card. You will recall that a debit card is connected to a checking account. When you use your debit card to make a purchase, the money is withdrawn almost immediately from your account at the bank.

The transaction process of a credit card is similar to a debit card. When you make a purchase, the card is swiped electronically, and the bank that issued the card is contacted to approve the purchase. If you have available funds on your line of credit, the purchase will be approved. If your spending exceeds the maximum level on the line of credit, the card will be declined.

Many credit cards offer rewards or incentives for using the card for purchases. For example, a credit card company may offer to pay you a small percentage of your purchases back in cash or to give you airline miles for using their card. Credit cards can also include insurance and other consumer protections for using the card.

The Credit CARD Accountability Responsibility and Disclosure Act of 2009 is also known as the *Credit CARD Act* or the *Credit Card Bill of Rights*. The act is one of the most extensive sets of credit card regulations ever enacted. Among other things, the CARD Act protects cardholders from arbitrary rate increases, requires payments to be applied to highest interest rate balances first, makes certain fees illegal, and gives the consumer at least 21 days to make a payment after a statement is mailed.

Some credit card companies attempt to increase your use of their card by offering promotional rates. For example, they may offer 0% interest for a period of time on a new credit card. These *promotional rates* usually expire after a specified number of months.

Applying for a Credit Card

Receiving a credit card requires that you complete an application. The application will ask you to share personal information with the company that is issuing you the card. You will be asked for your name, Social Security number, date of birth, and address. You will be asked about your employment and income. You may be asked how much money you have in the bank and whether you own or rent your home.

Using the personal information you provide, the credit card company will analyze your credit history by requesting and paying for a credit report. A **credit report** is a summary of all the companies that have extended you credit. The credit report shows how much you owe, how often you make payments on time, and other information that tells the lender whether it is safe or risky to loan you money.

A credit bureau will run a credit report on your credit history. They will charge the credit card company a fee for this report. There are three credit bureaus that keep track of an individual's credit: Equifax, Experian, and TransUnion. You can receive a free copy of your credit report every 12 months.

The credit card company uses the information from the application and credit report to determine whether to extend credit to you. Access to credit has changed significantly since the economic downturn that began in 2008. Some people who would have qualified for credit before that time are no longer considered creditworthy. Being *creditworthy* means that you are likely to repay a loan.

Lenders look at three factors when determining whether someone is creditworthy. Together, they are known as the *three C's of credit:*

- character

- capacity

- capital

Character

Paying your debts in full and on time is a sign of character. Lenders look to your credit history to see how you have dealt with your debts in the past. A *credit history* is a record of your prior experience with debt.

Without a credit history, lenders have nothing to evaluate. So, those who seek credit for the first time often need a cosigner on their loans. A *cosigner* is a creditworthy person who agrees to be responsible for repayment of the debt in the event that the borrower does not repay it.

Capacity

It would not make sense to give someone a $100,000 line of credit if he or she earns $10,000 a year. This person would not have the ability to repay it. *Capacity* is the ability to repay a loan. Your capacity to repay a loan is determined by your cash flow. To determine this, the lender looks at your cash inflows as well as your cash outflows.

Capital

Capital is all of your assets, including savings, property, and other things of value that you own. The less capital a borrower has, the riskier the loan will be to the lender. Sometimes lenders require that a borrower pledge an asset as a type of insurance. The pledged asset is known as *collateral*. In the event that the loan is not repaid, the lender can take the pledged asset as payment.

fyi

Never provide your personal information to a company without knowing exactly where the information is going. Find out what the credit card company's policies are about protecting your information and identity.

Credit Scores

A **credit score** is a number that shows how well you handle credit. The score is calculated by credit bureaus that run the credit report. A credit score is not the same as a credit report. A credit report is a snapshot of an individual's credit history. A credit score is a number that is calculated based on the credit report.

A credit score is based on your history of making payments on time, the amount of debt you owe, the extent of your credit history, as well as other information. The **FICO score** is the most common credit score. It is named for the Fair Isaac Corporation, which provides the calculation for the score. A FICO score is between 300 and 850. What is considered a good score varies by lender and economic conditions. However, a score above 700 is generally considered good or very good credit. The better your score, the more likely you are to be given credit. Better scores also qualify borrowers for better interest rates in many cases.

Teaching Tip:
Have students brainstorm some ways in which they can achieve a high FICO score and increase their creditworthiness.

Credit Limits

A line of credit usually has a limit, called a **credit limit.** A college student, for example, may be issued a credit card with a $500 credit limit. This means the total owed to the credit card company can never exceed $500. A salaried employee making $50,000 annually, however, may qualify for a credit card with a $5,000 credit limit. Each person's credit limit is determined by the amount of money the credit card company feels comfortable extending to the borrower.

The **current balance** is the total amount of money owed to the lender. This is similar to the balance in a bank account. A bank account balance shows how much money you have. The current balance of a credit card indicates how much money you owe.

Available credit refers to the amount of money that can still be used for purchases with the credit card. For example, a credit card with a $500 credit limit and a current balance of $200 would have $300 in available credit. The following formula can be used to calculate available credit:

$$\text{available credit} = \text{credit limit} - \text{current balance}$$

Example 7-1A

See It

Irene has a credit limit of $2,300. She checked her current account balance online and saw that it was $1,473.90. She made a purchase today of $75.16 that is not listed on the account balance. What is Irene's remaining available credit on this account?

Strategy

Use the formula:

$$\text{available credit} = \text{credit limit} - \text{current balance}$$

Solution

Step 1: Determine Irene's current balance. Add her online balance and the amount of the recent purchase.

current balance = online balance + amount of purchase

current balance = $1,473.90 + $75.16

current balance = $1,549.06

Step 2: Determine Irene's available credit. Subtract her current balance from her credit limit.

available credit = credit limit – current balance

available credit = $2,300 – $1,549.06

available credit = $750.94

Check It

Cameron has a credit limit on his gasoline company credit card of $500. He has no initial balance, but has charged gasoline purchases of $79.15 and $63.45. What is Cameron's remaining available credit?

Example 7-1B

See It

Iris has a balance of $1,340.39 on her credit card account. The bank recently lowered her credit limit to $2,200. What is Iris' available credit on this account?

Strategy

Use the formula:

available credit = credit limit – current balance

Solution

Step 1: Determine Iris' credit limit and current balance.

credit limit = $2,200

current balance = $1,340.39

Step 2: Determine Iris' available credit. Subtract her current balance from her credit limit.

available credit = credit limit – current balance

available credit = $2,200 – $1,340.39

available credit = $859.61

Check It

Wen has a balance of $2,045.67 on his credit card account. His bank recently raised his credit limit to $3,500. What is Wen's available credit on this account?

Answer:
$1,454.33

Credit Card Statements

Like a bank account, a credit card also has a monthly statement. A *credit card statement* is a report that shows the purchases you made, your current balance, and the amount of money that you must pay by the due date. Most credit card statements are sent monthly.

On a credit card statement, the balance indicates how much you owe rather than how much you have. The credit card statement shows purchases and payments made since the last statement, along with your current balance.

Figure 7-1 shows a sample credit card statement. As you can see, in addition to the current balance, the statement also shows when the next payment is due and the minimum payment that must be made to avoid penalties.

When you receive your credit card statement each month, you must make at least the minimum payment to the credit card company. The statement, as shown in Figure 7-1, specifies the minimum payment due. The minimum payment must reach the credit card company by the due date to avoid penalties.

Similar to bank accounts, credit card activity and statements may be viewed online through a secure website.

Teaching Tip:
Walk through the credit card statement in Figure 7-1. Discuss each item and encourage students to ask questions.

Account Statement

For the period ending Aug 9, 20-- Days in billing cycle: 31
Questions or lost/stolen card? Call Customer Service 1-800-555-1234

1234 1234 1324 1234

Account Number: XXXX-XXXX-XXXX-XXXX

Summary of Account Activity

Previous Balance	$0.00
Payments	$0.00
Other Credits/Adjustments	$0.00
Purchases	+$152.33
Cash Advances	$0.00
Fees Charged	$0.00
Interest Charged	$0.00
Total New Balance	**$152.33**
Past Due Amount	$0.00
Credit Limit	$3000.00
Credit Available	$2847.00

Payment Information

Total New Balance	$152.33
Minimum Payment Due	$5.00
Payment Due Date	Sep 9, 20--

Late Payment Warning: If we do not receive your minimum payment by the date listed above, you may have to pay a Late Payment Fee of up to $25.00.

Minimum Payment Warning: If you make only the minimum payment each period, you will pay more in interest and it will take you longer to pay off your balance. For example:

If you make no additional charges using this card and each month you pay...	You will pay off the balance shown on this Statement in about...	And you will end up paying an estimated total of...
Only the minimum payment	5 years	$275
$6	3 years	$217 (Savings=$58)

If you are experiencing financial difficulty and would like information about credit counseling or debt management services, you may call 1-800-123-4567.

Figure 7-1. Credit Card Statement

fyi

The periodic rate is determined by dividing the number of billing periods by the annual percentage rate. You will learn more about this in section 7.2.

You can pay any amount over the minimum payment up to your full balance. You can also make more than one payment to a credit card company during one month. For example, if you are paid twice a month, you may want to make two payments per month to your credit card company.

Most credit cards do not charge interest if you pay your entire balance each month. A ***grace period*** is a time during which you can pay off the balance of your card and not incur finance charges. To avoid finance charges, you must pay the full statement balance by the payment due date. The purchases made after your statement processes will not be due until the next statement. If you carry over a balance from the previous statement, all purchases begin accruing finance charges immediately.

To calculate the finance charge if the balance is not paid in full prior to the grace period, use the following formula:

$$\textbf{finance charge} = \textbf{new balance} \times \textbf{periodic rate}$$

Example 7-1C

See It

Suravi has a gasoline company credit card that charges 2.2917% on an unpaid balance for a given month. Last month, she paid off her balance so the previous balance on this month's statement is $0. This month, she charged a total of $328.19 on her credit card. If she pays the balance prior to the grace period, she will not incur a finance charge. Calculate the finance charge Suravi will pay if she does not pay the balance in full prior to the grace period.

Strategy

Use the formula:

finance charge = new balance × periodic rate

Solution

Step 1: Convert the periodic rate to a decimal by moving the decimal two places to the left.

2.2917% → 0.022917

Step 2: Determine Suravi's finance charge. Multiply the new balance by the periodic rate.

finance charge = new balance × periodic rate

finance charge = $328.19 × 0.022917

finance charge = $7.52

Check It

Jack has a gasoline company credit card where 2.2083% is charged to any unpaid balance for a given month. Last month, he paid off his balance so the previous balance on this month's statement is $0. This month, he charged a total of $279.84 on his credit card. If he pays the balance prior to the grace period, then he will not incur a finance charge. Calculate the finance charge Jack will pay if he does not pay the balance in full prior to the grace period.

fyi

Some people describe a credit card that has reached its limit with no remaining available credit as *maxed out*.

Answer:
$6.18

Checkpoint 7.1

1. Armando checked his department store credit account balance online and learned that it was $375.16. He charged a pair of shoes to his account for $83.47. If his credit limit is $500, what is the remaining available credit on this account?

2. Ana received her credit card bill in the mail, and it showed an account balance of $679.35. She made a purchase of $114.64 that is not shown on the bill. If her credit limit is $1,500, what is Ana's remaining available credit on this account?

3. Garrett has a gasoline company credit card. He has a balance of $110.43, and the bank raised his credit limit to $750. What is Garrett's remaining available credit on this account?

4. Yolanda has a credit card with a balance of $743.15 and a credit limit of $1,500. She also has a second credit card with no balance and a credit limit of $2,000. What is Yolanda's combined available credit?

5. Rishi checked his credit card account online and noticed that he has a current balance of $1,620.77 and remaining available credit of $2,879.23. What is the credit limit on Rishi's account?

Answer:
1. $41.37
2. $706.01
3. $639.57
4. $2,756.85
5. $4,500

Section 7.2 Finance Charges and Fees

Objectives

- **Compare and contrast annual percentage rate (APR) and periodic rate.**
- **Describe the purpose of a disclosure statement.**
- **Explain how to receive a cash advance on credit.**
- **Calculate balance transfer fees.**

Build Your Math Skills

Review these math skills to prepare for the lesson that follows.

1. Convert percentages to decimals by moving the decimal point two places to the left. Example: 8.25% → 0.0825

A. 18.1% →

B. 9.25% →

C. 17.5% →

D. 5.3% →

2. Multiply decimals. Round to the nearest cent ($0.01) if necessary. Example: $115.64 × 0.08 = $9.25

A. $845.60 × 0.04 =

B. $110.48 × 0.12 =

C. $430.75 × 0.15 =

D. $408.39 × 0.015 =

3. Divide decimals. Round to the nearest hundredth (0.01) if necessary. Example: 18.5 ÷ 12 = 1.54

A. 24.5 ÷ 12 =

B. 28.3 ÷ 12 =

C. 14.8 ÷ 8 =

D. 20.4 ÷ 16 =

Terms

- *finance charge*
- *annual percentage rate (APR)*
- *revolving line of credit*
- *periodic rate*
- *unpaid balance method*
- *previous balance*
- *average daily balance (ADM) method*
- *annual fee*
- *late fee*
- *disclosure statement*
- *cash advance*
- *convenience check*

Answer:
1. A. 0.181
   B. 0.0925
   C. 0.175
   D. 0.053
2. A. $33.82
   B. $13.26
   C. $64.61
   D. $6.13
3. A. 2.04
   B. 2.36
   C. 1.85
   D. 1.28

Finance Charges

As you learned in chapter 4, those who loan money earn interest, and those who borrow money pay interest. It works the same way when credit is extended through a credit card. When using a credit card, one of the most important things to understand is finance charges. A **finance charge** is a fee associated with credit. A finance charge is primarily interest, but it can also include transaction fees or any other fee that makes up the cost of the credit.

A finance charge usually begins with an annual percentage rate. The **annual percentage rate (APR)** is the rate of interest that you would pay to borrow a given amount of money for one year. For example, a typical credit card APR is 18%. If you think of the finance charge as simple interest, that means that for every $100 borrowed, the finance charge would be $18 per year. A finance charge can be calculated by using the simple interest formula:

$$\text{finance charge} = \text{APR} \times \text{balance}$$

Example 7-2A

See It

Zimra has a credit card with an APR of 21.4%. If she charges a purchase for $750, what is the estimated amount Zimra will pay in finance charges on that purchase?

Strategy

Use the formula:

$$\text{finance charge} = \text{APR} \times \text{balance}$$

Solution

Step 1: Convert the APR from a percentage to a decimal by moving the decimal two places to the left.

$21.4\% \rightarrow 0.214$

Step 2: Multiply the APR (as a decimal) by the balance.

finance charge = APR × balance

finance charge = $0.214 \times \$750$

finance charge = $160.50

Check It

Franklin has a credit card with an APR of 23.2%. If he charges a purchase for $1,220, what is the estimated amount Franklin will pay in finance charges on that purchase?

Teaching Tip:
Have students discuss the reality of paying 18% interest over an extended period of time on a purchase. Suggest that prior to making a credit purchase, they ask themselves the following question: Is this product worth paying an extra 18%? What if it takes months or years to pay off? Explain that sometimes paying cash is better for smaller purchases.

Answer:
$283.04

Borrowing money with a credit card is not considered simple borrowing. A credit card is a ***revolving line of credit,*** which means that the balance is constantly changing. Each month a credit card may be used for purchases, which increases the balance, and payments are made that decrease the balance. The term *revolving* indicates that money is going in and out like a revolving door.

The amount of extended credit varies from day to day. This means that calculating the finance charge is not as straightforward as simply multiplying a balance by an interest rate.

The first step in calculating a credit card finance charge is to convert the annual percentage rate into a periodic rate. The ***periodic rate*** is the APR divided by the number of periods in the year that finance charges will be applied. For example, if finance charges will be calculated monthly, then the periodic rate is the APR divided by 12. To determine the periodic rate, use the following formula:

$$\text{periodic rate} = \frac{\text{APR}}{\text{number of periods}}$$

Example 7-2B

See It

Consider Zimra's credit card with a 21.4% APR. If her finance charges are calculated monthly, what is the periodic rate on Zimra's credit card?

Strategy

Use the formula:

$$\text{periodic rate} = \frac{\text{APR}}{\text{number of periods}}$$

Solution

Step 1: Determine the APR and the number of periods.

APR = 21.4%

Since the finance charge is calculated monthly, and there are 12 months in a year, there are 12 periods.

Step 2: Calculate the periodic rate. Divide the APR by the number of periods. Round your answer to the nearest ten-thousandth (0.0001).

$$\text{periodic rate} = \frac{\text{APR}}{\text{number of periods}}$$

$$\text{periodic rate} = \frac{21.4\%}{12 \text{ months}}$$

period rate = 1.7833% per month

Check It

Consider Franklin's credit card with a 23.2% APR. If his finance charges are calculated monthly, what is the periodic rate on Franklin's credit card?

Answer:
1.9333%

Once you have determined the periodic rate, there are several ways that the finance charge can be calculated. Two common methods are used to calculate the finance charge: the unpaid balance method and the average daily balance method.

Unpaid Balance Method

The *unpaid balance method* is a way to calculate finance charges based on the portion of the previous balance that is unpaid at the time of the calculation. The *previous balance* refers to the balance the last time the finance charge was calculated, typically the last time a statement was issued. In this method, purchases made since the last time the finance charge was calculated are not included. The formula for calculating finance charges using the unpaid balance method is as follows:

unpaid balance = previous balance – payments – other credits

Example 7-2C

See It

Recall that Zimra's credit card has a 21.4% APR. Her finance charge is calculated monthly. The balance shown on her last statement was $1,118.93. Since that time, she made a payment of $225. What is the finance charge on Zimra's current statement? Use the information that you have already calculated to solve this problem.

Strategy

Use the formulas:

unpaid balance = previous balance – payments – other credits

finance charge = unpaid balance × periodic rate

Solution

Step 1: Identify Zimra's previous balance, payment, and periodic rate.

previous balance = $1,118.93

payment = $225

periodic rate = 1.7833% per month

Step 2: Determine Zimra's unpaid balance. Subtract her payment from the previous balance.

unpaid balance = previous balance – payments

unpaid balance = $1,118.93 – $225

unpaid balance = $893.93

Step 3: Convert the periodic rate from a percentage to a decimal by moving the decimal two places to the left.

1.7833% → 0.017833

Step 4: Determine Zimra's finance charge. Multiply the unpaid balance by the periodic rate (as a decimal). Round to the nearest cent ($0.01).

finance charge = unpaid balance × periodic rate

finance charge = $893.33 × 0.017833

finance charge = $15.94

Check It

Franklin's credit card has a 23.2% APR. His finance charge is calculated monthly. The balance shown on his last statement was $2,074.19. He made a payment of $285. What is the finance charge on Franklin's current statement?

Once a finance charge is calculated, it becomes part of the new account balance, along with new purchases made during the period. The formula for determining the new balance, including finance charges and new purchases, is as follows:

new balance = unpaid balance + finance charge + new purchases

Example 7-2D

See It

Zimra's credit card, with an APR of 21.4%, has an unpaid balance of $893.93 and a finance charge of $15.94. She also made new purchases that total $418.30. What is Zimra's new balance?

Strategy

Use the formula:

new balance = unpaid balance + finance charge + new purchases

Solution

Step 1: Identify Zimra's unpaid balance, finance charge, and new purchases.

unpaid balance = $893.93

finance charge = $15.94

new purchases = $418.30

Step 2: Determine Zimra's new balance. Find the sum of the unpaid balance, finance charge, and new purchases.

new balance = unpaid balance + finance charge + new purchases

new balance = $893.93 + $15.94 + $418.30

new balance = $1,328.17

Teaching Tip:
Reinforce the concept by having students write the steps for the unpaid balance method of finance charge calculation in their own words.

Check It

Since his last credit card statement, Franklin made new purchases that total $530.87. Use the information about Franklin's credit card from Example 7-2C to determine his new balance.

Average Daily Balance Method

Another common method for calculating finance charges is the average daily balance method. The *average daily balance (ADM) method* uses an average balance for the period as a basis for the finance charge. The ADM method includes new purchases made since the last time the finance charge was calculated. The following formula can be used to calculate ADM:

average daily balance = sum of daily balances ÷ days in period

Example 7-2E

See It

Camila has a credit card with an 18.7% APR and a 30-day billing period. Her daily balances for one billing period are shown in the following chart. Determine Camila's average daily balance.

Days 1–3	Days 4–7	Days 8–13	Days 14–20	Days 21–28	Days 29–30
$350.79	$443.28	$530.17	$664.97	$870.13	$904.92

Strategy

Use the formula:

average daily balance = sum of daily balances ÷ days in period

Solution

Step 1: Determine balance for each day of Camila's billing cycle.

day 1: $350.79	day 11: $530.17	day 21: $870.13
day 2: $350.79	day 12: $530.17	day 22: $870.13
day 3: $350.79	day 13: $530.17	day 23: $870.13
day 4: $443.28	day 14: $664.97	day 24: $870.13
day 5: $443.28	day 15: $664.97	day 25: $870.13
day 6: $443.28	day 16: $664.97	day 26: $870.13
day 7: $443.28	day 17: $664.97	day 27: $870.13
day 8: $530.17	day 18: $664.97	day 28: $870.13
day 9: $530.17	day 19: $664.97	day 29: $904.92
day 10: $530.17	day 20: $664.97	day 30: $904.92

Step 2: Determine the sum of Camila's daily balances. Add all 30 of the daily balances together.

sum of daily balances = $350.79 + $350.79 + $350.79 + $443.28 +
$443.28 + $443.28 + $443.28 + $530.17 + $530.17 + $530.17 +
$530.17 + $530.17 + $530.17 + $664.97 + $664.97 +
$664.97 + $664.97 + $664.97 + $664.97 + $664.97 +
$870.13 + $870.13 + $870.13 + $870.13 + $870.13 +
$870.13 + $870.13 + $870.13 + $904.92 + $904.92

sum of daily balances = $19,432.18

Step 3: Determine Camila's average daily balance. Divide the sum of the daily balances by the number of days in the billing period. Round to the nearest cent ($0.01) if necessary.

average daily balance = sum of daily balances ÷ days in period

average daily balance = $19,432.18 ÷ 30

average daily balance = $647.74

Check It

Yasir has a credit card with a 19.7% APR and a 30-day billing period. His daily balances for one billing period are shown in the chart that follows. Determine Yasir's average daily balance.

Days 1–3	Days 4–7	Days 8–13	Days 14–21	Days 22–27	Days 28–30
$556.73	$683.14	$729.84	$810.15	$940.81	$1,060.73

Fees and Disclosure Statements

It is important to understand all the fees charged for any card you have. Finance charges also include annual fees, late fees, and other fees associated with the use of credit.

Many credit cards have an ***annual fee*** that is charged for the privilege of having the card. Typically, annual fees range from $19 to $59. Be aware that some cards may have even larger annual fees.

Late fees are fees charged if you fail to make at least a minimum payment before the due date. A typical late fee is $35. In addition to a late fee, a late payment can also cause the interest rate to increase on the card.

There can be many fees associated with a credit card. To know exactly what fees apply to a particular credit card, the credit card company provides a disclosure statement. A ***disclosure statement*** is a document that details your card's finance charges, annual percentage rate, and cardholder rights. When you accept a credit card, you are accepting the terms of the disclosure statement.

Figure 7-2 is a sample disclosure statement. The disclosure statement includes a table that is designed to make it easy for the cardholder to quickly find the most important information, such as interest rates and fees.

Teaching Tip:
To help students better visualize the arithmetic, show the daily balance amounts in a column aligned by the decimal points. This may also be illustrated through the use of a spreadsheet.

Teaching Tip:
A solution spreadsheet for Example 07-02E Check It appears on the Instructor's Resource CD.

Answer:
$803

fyi

If a charge is not added to the account each day, then for some days the daily balance does not change. It may be easier to multiply the daily balance by the number of days with that daily balance, and then add the products together to get the sum of the daily balances.

Teaching Tip:
Encourage students to use the Internet to conduct research about the fees and finance charges of credit cards. Engage them in a discussion about the pros and cons of certain fees.

Annual percentage rate (APR) for purchases	18%
Grace period for repayment of balances for purchases	25 days for purchases
Method of computing the balance for purchases	Average daily balance (including new purchases)
Annual fee	$29
Minimum finance charge	$0.50
Late fee	$19
Cash advance fee	2% of amount requested, minimum $5, maximum $15
Over the credit limit fee	$29

Figure 7-2. Credit Card Disclosure Statement

Career Discovery
Marketing Careers and Math Skills

If you crave variety and enjoy a fast-paced environment, a career in marketing may be perfect for you. Careers in this cluster include all the jobs involved in buying, distributing, marketing, and selling products, and providing follow-up service to customers. Related jobs include finding new customers and tracking marketing data.

The ability to evaluate numbered data is a very strong quality for marketing employees to have. Describe situations in which a person in this field would need good math skills.

Example 7-2F

See It

Lin has a credit card that uses the disclosure statement in Figure 7-2. The billing cycle is monthly. Her average daily balance for October was $2,194.39. Use the information in the disclosure statement to calculate Lin's finance charge for the October billing cycle.

Strategy

Use the formulas:

$$\text{periodic rate} = \frac{\text{APR}}{\text{number of periods}}$$

finance charge = average daily balance × periodic rate

Solution

Step 1: Determine Lin's periodic rate. Divide the APR by 12 (the number of billing cycles in a year).

$$\text{periodic rate} = \frac{APR}{\text{number of periods}}$$

$$\text{periodic rate} = \frac{18\%}{12 \text{ months}}$$

periodic rate = 1.5% per month

Step 2: Convert the periodic rate to a decimal by moving the decimal two places to the left.

$1.5\% \rightarrow 0.015$

Step 3: Determine Lin's finance charge. Multiply her average daily balance by the periodic rate. Round to the nearest cent ($0.01) if necessary.

finance charge = average daily balance × periodic rate

finance charge = $2,194.39 × 0.015

finance charge = $32.92

Teaching Tip:
Remind students that the formula calls for the APR to be divided by the number of periods.

Check It

Richard has a credit card that uses the disclosure statement in Figure 7-2. The billing cycle is monthly. His average daily balance for February was $3,019.37. Use the information in the disclosure statement to calculate Richard's finance charge for the February billing cycle.

Answer:
$45.29

Borrowing Cash from a Credit Card

Most credit cards offer a way to borrow cash from the card's line of credit, called a *cash advance*. A ***cash advance*** is a loan against the available credit on your card. One way to obtain a cash advance is by calling the credit card company and having them issue you a check.

Another way to get a cash advance is by writing a blank check sent to you by your credit card company. ***Convenience checks*** allow you to write a paper check that will be charged against your credit card account. Some of these checks are specifically for transferring balances, but some of these checks can be used to make a purchase, pay a bill, or write a check for cash.

A common and popular way to get a cash advance is through an *automated teller machine (ATM)*. To access cash from an ATM using a credit card, you will need to set up a personal identification number (PIN) with the credit card company to allow access to cash through the card.

The amount of the cash advance is added to the existing credit balance. A cash advance has its own fee that is applied immediately. A charge of 2% to 4%

is common on a cash advance. The fee is in addition to finance charges incurred by adding the cash advance to your credit card balance. Also, note that cash advances do not usually have a grace period and will begin accruing interest charges immediately. The fee for a cash advance can be calculated using the formula:

cash advance fee = amount of cash advance × cash advance rate

Sometimes a credit card will not allow all of your available credit to be used for a cash advance. On your statement or when viewing your account online, you will often see two numbers for available credit. One amount is credit available for purchases. The other amount is credit available for cash advances.

Example 7-2G

See It

Denise has a credit card that charges a 3% fee for a cash advance. Due to an unexpected home repair, she decided to obtain a $1,100 cash advance on her credit card. What is the fee that Denise will pay for the cash advance? Round to the nearest cent ($0.01) if necessary.

Strategy

Use the formula:

cash advance fee = amount of cash advance × cash advance rate

Solution

Step 1: Convert the cash advance rate to a decimal by moving the decimal point two places to the left.

$3\% \rightarrow 0.03$

Step 2: Determine the cash advance fee. Multiply the amount of the cash advance by the cash advance rate.

cash advance fee = amount of cash advance × cash advance rate

cash advance fee = $1,100 × 0.03

cash advance fee = $33

Check It

Miguel has a credit card that charges a 3.5% fee for cash advances. Miguel had a car accident and decided to get a $750 cash advance to pay his insurance deductible. What is the fee he will pay for the cash advance? Round to the nearest cent ($0.01) if necessary.

For the example that follows, you will calculate finance charges over time. You will use the same set of math operations multiple times in the same problem, such as multiplication and addition, which is called recursion. *Recursion* is the application of the same set of operations to the answer of the previous step. When using recursion, a spreadsheet is often a helpful tool.

Example 7-2H

See It

Maureen wants to use a credit card to purchase a new clothes washer and dryer. Her standard APR is 21.1%, but her credit card is offering a promotional rate of 4.5% for six months. The cost of the washer and dryer, including sales tax, is $879. Assume that Maureen has a previous unpaid balance, and her monthly payments apply to that balance. How much will the promotional rate save Maureen in finance charges during the six-month period?

Strategy

Use the formulas:

$$\text{periodic rate} = \frac{\text{APR}}{\text{number of periods}}$$

$$\text{finance charge} = \text{new balance} \times \text{periodic rate}$$

Solution

Step 1: Determine Maureen's standard periodic rate and promotional periodic rate.

$$\text{standard periodic rate} = \frac{\text{APR}}{\text{number of periods}}$$

$$\text{standard periodic rate} = \frac{21.1\%}{12}$$

$$\text{standard periodic rate} = 1.7583\%$$

$$\text{promotional periodic rate} = \frac{\text{APR}}{\text{number of periods}}$$

$$\text{promotional periodic rate} = \frac{4.5\%}{12}$$

$$\text{promotional periodic rate} = 0.375\%$$

Step 2: Convert both periodic rates to decimals by moving the decimals two places to the left.

$1.7583\% \rightarrow 0.017583$

$0.375\% \rightarrow 0.00375$

Step 3: Calculate the first month's finance charge using the standard periodic rate and the promotional periodic rate. Multiply the cost of the clothes washer and dryer by the periodic rate. Round to the nearest cent ($0.01) if necessary.

standard APR:

finance charge = new balance × periodic rate

finance charge = $879 × 0.017583

finance charge = $15.46

promotional APR:

finance charge = new balance × periodic rate

finance charge = $879 × 0.00375

finance charge = $3.30

Step 4: Determine the new credit card balance at the end of the first month. Add the finance charge to the cost of the clothes washer and dryer.

Teaching Tip:
Engage students in a dis-
cussion regarding how a
low promotional rate can
draw someone into using
a credit card when they
otherwise would not.

standard APR:

new balance = original cost + finance charge

new balance = $879 + $15.46

new balance = $894.46

promotional APR:

new balance = original cost + finance charge

new balance = $879 + $3.30

new balance = $882.30

Step 5: Calculate the second month's finance charge using the standard periodic rate and the promotional periodic rate. Multiply the new balance by the periodic rate. Round to the nearest cent ($0.01) if necessary.

standard APR:

finance charge = new balance × periodic rate

finance charge = $894.46 × 0.017583

finance charge = $15.73

promotional APR:

finance charge = new balance × periodic rate

finance charge = $882.30 × 0.00375

finance charge = $3.31

Step 6: Determine the new credit card balance at the end of the second month. Add the finance charge to the previous month's new balance.

standard APR:

new balance = month one balance + finance charge

new balance = $894.46 + $15.73

new balance = $910.19

- promotional APR:

- new balance = month two balance + finance charge

- new balance = $882.30 + $3.31

- new balance = $885.61

- **Step 7:** Repeat steps 5 and 6 to complete the information through month six.

- **Step 8:** Determine the sum of the finance charges for the standard APR and the sum of the finance charges for the promotional APR.

- standard APR:

- total finance charge = month one + month two + month three + month four + month five + month six

- total finance charge = $15.46 + $15.73 + $16 + $16.29 + $16.57 + $16.86

- total finance charge = $96.91

- promotional APR:

- total finance charge = month one + month two + month three + month four + month five + month six

- total finance charge = $3.30 + $3.31 + $3.32 + $3.33 + $3.35 + $3.36

- total finance charge = $19.97

- **Step 9:** Determine the difference between the total finance charges for the standard APR and the total finance charges for the promotional APR.

- difference in finance charges = total for standard APR – total for promotional APR

- difference in finance charges = $96.91 – $19.97

- difference in finance charges = $76.94

Check It

Kendall wants to use a credit card to purchase new furniture. His standard APR is 22.65%, but his credit card is offering a promotional rate of 3% for six months. The cost of the furniture, including sales tax, is $1,014. Assume that Kendall has a previous unpaid balance, and his monthly payments apply to that balance. How much will the promotional rate save Kendall in finance charges during the six-month period?

Teaching Tip:
A solution spreadsheet for Example 07-02H Check It appears on the Instructor's Resource CD.

Answer:
$105.09

Transferring Balances

Most credit card companies allow you to transfer the balance from another credit card to their card. This is sometimes done to consolidate balances from multiple accounts. It can also be done to take advantage of a lower rate made available by another card, possibly as part of a promotional rate offer.

You can initiate a balance transfer by contacting the credit card company that will be receiving the balance transfer. The receiving card company will send payment to the other card and apply that amount to your balance.

Teaching Tip:
Have students describe
a situation where they
might need to write
a convenience check
rather than use a credit
card.

You can also transfer a credit card balance using a convenience check. There is often a fee associated with using a credit card check, especially if you use it to transfer a balance or get a cash advance. A typical fee balance transfer fee is 3%. The amount of the fee can be determined using the formula:

check fee amount = amount of check × fee rate

Example 7-21

See It

Stella received a set of convenience checks with her last credit card statement. She decided to use one of the checks to pay her property tax bill for $2,467. There is a 3.2% fee for using the convenience check. Determine the fee that Stella will pay for using the convenience check.

Strategy

Use the formula:

check fee amount = amount of check × fee rate

Solution

Step 1: Convert the fee rate from a percentage to a decimal by moving the decimal two places to the left.

$3.2\% \rightarrow 0.032$

Step 2: Determine the check fee amount. Multiply the amount of the check by the fee rate. Round to the nearest cent ($0.01) if necessary.

check fee amount = amount of check × fee rate

check fee amount = $2,467 × 0.032

check fee amount = $78.94

Check It

Darren received a set of convenience checks with his last credit card statement. He decided to use one of the checks to transfer a balance from another credit card to this credit card account. The check has a fee of 2.8%, and Darren wrote the check for $1,830.28. Calculate the fee that Darren will pay for using the convenience check.

Answer:
$51.25

Checkpoint 7.2

1. Sabrina has a credit card with an APR of 22.7%. What is her monthly periodic rate? Round to the nearest ten-thousandth (0.0001) if necessary.

2. Byron has a credit card with an APR of 17.6%. The billing cycle is monthly, and an unpaid balance method is used to calculate the finance charge. His previous balance was $1,658.73. During the month, he made a $175 payment. What is Byron's new balance?

3. Lee has a credit card with a 22.3% APR and a 30-day billing period that uses the average daily balance method to calculate the finance charge. His daily balances for one billing period are shown in the following chart. Lee had a previous balance of $445.93, made a payment of $350, and has new purchases that total $1,643.57. Determine Lee's average daily balance.

Days 1–2	Days 3–6	Days 7–13	Days 14–16	Days 17–25	Days 26–30
$445.93	$612.87	$1,083.16	$1,110.34	$1,418.30	$1,739.50

4. Padma has a credit card with a 21.9% APR and a 30-day billing period that uses the average daily balance method to calculate the finance charge. Her daily balances for one billing period are shown in the following chart. Padma had a previous balance of $263.71. She made a payment of $225 and new purchases that total $1,270.88. Determine Padma's average daily balance.

Days 1–4	Days 5–8	Days 9–12	Days 13–18	Days 19–27	Days 28–30
$263.71	$445.93	$984.19	$1,045.17	$1,243.68	$1,309.59

5. Alexandria received a set of convenience checks with her last credit card statement. She decided to use one of the checks to transfer a balance from another credit card to this credit card account. The check has a fee of 1.75%, and Alexandria wrote the check for $769.42. Calculate the fee that Alexandria will pay for using the convenience check.

Section 7.3 Debt Management

- *nominal APR*
- *effective annual rate (EAR)*
- *debt-to-income ratio*

Objectives

- **Demonstrate understanding of the impact of effective APR.**
- **Calculate a debt-to-income ratio.**
- **Describe ways to manage and reduce debt.**

Build Your Math Skills

Review these math skills to prepare for the lesson that follows.

1. Convert decimals to percentages by moving the decimal two places to the right. Example: 0.0825 → 8.25%

A. 0.1587 →

B. 0.126 →

C. 0.0791 →

D. 0.497 →

2. Divide whole numbers and decimals. Round to the nearest thousandth (0.001) if necessary. Example: $2,168.50 ÷ $25,000 = 0.087

A. $2,516.80 ÷ $40,000 =

B. $16,793 ÷ $32,600 =

C. $159.65 ÷ $1,018.93 =

D. $5,134 ÷ $25,000 =

3. Add and subtract decimals. Example: $678.17 − $79.38 = $598.79

A. $7,891.07 + $187.09 =

B. $1,578.74 + $974.43 =

C. $704.81 − $96.07 =

D. $1,178.04 − $971.46 =

Answer:

1. A. 15.87%
   B. 12.6%
   C. 7.91%
   D. 49.7%
2. A. 0.063
   B. 0.515
   C. 0.157
   D. 0.205
3. A. $8,078.16
   B. $2,553.17
   C. $608.74
   D. $206.58

Teaching Tip:
Refer students to the section about compounding interest in section 4.3, and then discuss the benefits of compounding interest. Ask students to describe how compounding interest works against them when credit cards are involved.

Effective annual rate (EAR) is also known as *effective APR.*

Understanding the Cost of Debt

An important part of managing your debt is understanding the actual cost of that debt. The annual percentage rates (APRs) discussed in this chapter do not necessarily reflect the total cost of financing. In fact, credit card debt is one of the more expensive forms of debt. When carrying a balance on a credit card, finance charges can exceed the amount of the original purchases.

The percentage rate quoted in credit card ads and solicitations is often the nominal annual percentage rate. The ***nominal APR*** is the simple interest rate for the year. The ***effective annual rate (EAR)*** is the nominal rate compounded. The EAR is higher than the nominal APR. The EAR more accurately reflects the true cost of the debt than does nominal APR. To calculate the effective annual rate, use the following formula, where *n* is the number of compounding periods per year:

$$EAR = \left(1 + \frac{\text{nominal APR}}{n}\right)^n - 1$$

Example 7-3A

See It

Stephen has a credit card with a nominal APR of 11.99%. The interest on unpaid balances compounds daily. What is the EAR?

Teaching Tip:
Explain that *nominal* means low cost.

Strategy

Use the formula:

$$EAR = \left(1 + \frac{\text{nominal APR}}{n}\right)^n - 1$$

Solution

Step 1: Determine the number of compounding periods per year.

n = number of compounding periods per year

n = 365

Step 2: Follow the order of operations in the formula. First, divide the nominal APR by the number of compounding periods per year, n. Round to the nearest hundred-thousandth (0.00001).

$$\frac{\text{nominal APR}}{n} = \frac{11.99\%}{365} = 0.03285\%$$

Step 3: Convert the percentage to a decimal by moving the decimal two places to the left.

0.03285% → 0.0003285

Step 4: To account for the original balance (or principal), add 1.

1 + nominal APR = 1 + 0.0003285 = 1.0003285

Step 5: Compound the interest using this rate. Raise the addend to the nth power. Round to the nearest ten-thousandth (0.0001).

$(1.0003285)^{365} = 1.1274$

Step 6: To identify only the rate, remove the original balance. Subtract 1.

EAR = 1.1274 − 1

EAR = 0.1274

Step 7: Convert the decimal to a percentage by moving the decimal two places to the right.

0.1274 → 12.74%

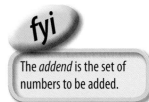

The *addend* is the set of numbers to be added.

Check It

Susanna has a credit card with a nominal APR of 18%. The interest on unpaid balances compounds daily. What is the effective annual rate (EAR)?

Answer:
19.71%

Using credit cards can make it more difficult to stick to your budget. Studies have shown that people spend more money when they pay with a credit card, rather than paying with cash. Debit cards have the same effect as credit cards on spending. Many people have credit card debt that was acquired through wasteful and unplanned spending.

Debt-to-Income Ratio

One way to determine if your debt is too high is to calculate your debt-to-income ratio. Your *debt-to-income ratio* is the amount of money required each month to pay debts divided by your monthly gross income. Many financial experts recommend that your debt-to-income ratio not exceed 36%. A ratio above 50% is very dangerous. Your debt-to-income ratio can be calculated using the formula:

$$\text{debt-to-income ratio} = \frac{\text{sum of monthly debt payments}}{\text{monthly income}}$$

Example 7-3B

See It

A *ratio* is a relationship between two quantities. A ratio can be expressed as a fraction, a decimal, or a percentage.

Gloria works as a librarian and earns $56,360 per year. She made a list of her current debt payments per month, which are listed as follows. What is Gloria's debt-to-income ratio?

mortgage = $1,014.57

car loan = $489.35

student loans = $214.39

credit cards = $437.18

Strategy

Use the formula:

$$\text{debt-to-income ratio} = \frac{\text{sum of monthly debt payments}}{\text{monthly income}}$$

Solution

Step 1: Determine the sum of Gloria's monthly debt payments. Add each of her monthly debt payments together.

sum of monthly debt payments = mortgage + car loan + student loans + credit cards

sum of monthly debt payments = $1,014.57 + $489.35 + $214.39 + $437.18

sum of monthly debt payments = $2,155.49

Step 2: Determine Gloria's monthly income. Divide her annual salary by 12. Round to the nearest cent ($0.01) if necessary.

$$\text{monthly income} = \frac{\text{annual salary}}{12 \text{ pay periods}}$$

$$\text{monthly income} = \frac{\$56,360}{12}$$

monthly income = $4,696.67

Step 3: Determine Gloria's debt-to-income ratio. Divide her sum of monthly debt payments by her monthly income. Round to the nearest thousandth (0.001).

$$\text{debt-to-income ratio} = \frac{\text{sum of monthly debt payments}}{\text{monthly income}}$$

$$\text{debt-to-income ratio} = \frac{\$2,155.49}{\$4,696.67}$$

debt-to-income ratio = 0.459

Step 4: Change the decimal to a percentage by moving the decimal point two places to the right.

$0.459 \rightarrow 45.9\%$

Teaching Tip:
Have students write a paragraph describing the steps taken to determine debt-to-income ratio.

Check It

Robert works as a curator at the local historical museum and earns $53,160 per year. He made a list of his current debt payments per month, as follows. What is Robert's debt-to-income ratio?

Answer:
39.5%

    mortgage = $989.74

    car loan = $315.76

    student loans = $177.85

    credit cards = $267.19

Managing and Reducing Debt

Learning to manage and reduce debt is one of the most important financial skills to learn. Your goal should be to become debt free because money that isn't being spent on interest could be reallocated to other expenses or investments.

Pay more than minimum payments whenever possible to reduce debt as quickly as possible. If you have multiple debts, concentrate on paying off one debt at a time while making minimum payments on the others. As you pay off debts, apply the money you were sending to the paid-off debts to the ones you have yet to pay off. Some recommend paying off the smallest debts first in order to achieve victory sooner. This method is sometimes called the *debt snowball method.*

Teaching Tip:
Assign students into groups to create a chart outlining the various methods available for managing and reducing debt. Have student discuss ways to avoid getting into debt.

Using cash rather than cards is another way to manage debt by avoiding debt. Taking a budget seriously is also important to free up money to apply to debt reduction.

There are individuals and companies that offer debt counseling. In many cases, the advice of an independent third party can help you make a plan and stick to it. Think of debt counselors as personal trainers for your finances.

You might have heard advertisements for debt consolidation loans. In a debt consolidation loan, debts are combined into one larger debt. This can be a good option if you can get a lower interest rate on the consolidated loan than on the individual loans you wish to combine. You can use the following formula to help you decide whether debt consolidation is a good idea:

difference in interest charges = debt consolidation interest charges – combined interest charges

Source: Shutterstock (AVAVA)

Many companies do not charge interest if a credit card balance is paid off each month.

Example 7-3C

See It

Jemina has two credit cards. She used her credit card statements to make the summary table that follows. Jemina is also eligible for a debt consolidation loan with an APR of 11% that reduces her monthly payments to $133.24. This loan will take six years to pay off, and Jemina will pay a total of $2,593.14 in interest charges. How much more in interest charges will the debt consolidation loan cost Jemina?

	APR	Balance	Monthly Payment	Time to Pay in Full	Total Interest Charges
Bank of the Plains	18.9%	$5,000	$200	3 years	$1,406
Western Bank	21.5%	$2,000	$80	3 years	$677

Strategy

Use the formula:

difference in interest charges = debt consolidation interest charges – combined interest charges

Solution

Step 1: Determine the combined interest charges Jemina will pay on both credit cards. Add the total interest charges for each credit card together.

combined interest charges = total interest charge for credit card one + total interest charges for credit card two

combined interest charges = $1,406 + $677

combined interest charges = $2,083

Step 2: Determine the difference between the combined interest charges and the interest charges for the debt consolidation loan. Subtract the combined interest charges from the debt consolidation interest charges.

difference in interest charges = debt consolidation interest charges – combined interest charges

difference in interest charges = $2,593.14 – $2,083

difference in interest charges = $510.14

Check It

Qadir has two credit cards. He used his credit card statements to make the summary table that follows. Qadir is also eligible for a debt consolidation loan with an APR of 12.3% that reduces his monthly payments to $145.58. This loan will take five years to pay off, and Qadir will pay a total of $2,234.49 in interest charges. How much more in interest charges will the debt consolidation loan cost Qadir?

	APR	Balance	Monthly Payment	Time to Pay in Full	Total Interest Charges
Central Bank	21.3%	$4,000	$160	3 years	$1,335
Bank of the Lakes	17.6%	$2,500	$100	3 years	$638

Checkpoint 7.3

1. Jason has a credit card with a nominal APR of 17.65%. The interest on unpaid balances compounds daily. What is the EAR?

For questions 2–4, the list of current debt payments per month and information about income is provided for each individual. Using this information, calculate the person's debt-to-income ratio. Express your answer as a percentage rounded to the nearest tenth (0.1).

2. Lashawna works as a travel agent and earns $33,950 per year.

   mortgage = $560.92

   car loan = $239.76

   credit cards = $163.74

3. Rolando works as an agricultural inspector and earns $1,628.46 biweekly.

   mortgage = $858.16

   car loan = $217.94

   student loans = $207.73

   credit cards = $185.76

4. Melanie works as an aircraft repair technician and earns $2,220 semimonthly.

   mortgage = $749.16

   car loan = $178.63

   student loans = $201.74

   credit cards = $148.77

5. Sheng has two credit cards. He used his credit card statements to make the summary table that follows. Sheng is also eligible for a debt consolidation loan with an APR of 10.7% that reduces his monthly payments to $179.37. This loan will take six years to pay off, and Sheng will pay a total of $3,414.39 in interest charges. How much more in interest charges will the debt consolidation loan cost Sheng?

4. 28.8%
5. $765.39

	APR	Balance	Monthly Payment	Time to Pay in Full	Total Interest Charges
Bank of the Levee	19.4%	$6,000	$240	3 years	$1,750
City Bank	17.7%	$3,500	$140	3 years	$899

Chapter Review

Build Your Vocabulary

As you progress through this course, develop a personal glossary of financial literacy terms and add it to your portfolio. This will help you build your financial literacy vocabulary. Write out a definition for each of the following terms, and add it to your personal glossary.

credit	revolving line of credit
credit card	periodic rate
line of credit	unpaid balance method
credit report	previous balance
credit score	average daily balance (ADM) method
FICO score	annual fee
credit limit	late fee
current balance	disclosure statement
available credit	cash advance
credit card statement	convenience check
grace period	nominal APR
finance charge	effective annual rate (EAR)
annual percentage rate (APR)	debt-to-income ratio

Teamwork

Working in teams of three, conduct research online regarding agencies that deal with consumer problems. Make a chart that shows at least five agencies, the problems they specialize in solving, and statistics regarding the number of consumer problems they handle each year. Reflect on your findings. What problems seem to be the most common? What advice would you give consumers about avoiding financial problems?

Review Your Math Skills

Practice and build on the math skills that you have learned.

1. Convert decimals to percentages by moving the decimal point two places to the right. Example: 0.0825 → 8.25%

A. 0.0527 →   B. 0.139 →

C. 0.0812 →   D. 0.375 →

2. Add decimals. Example: $520.38 + $102.94 = $623.32

A. $981.05 + $56.27 =   B. $782.49 + $43.69 =

C. $2,076.52 + $50.03 =   D. $688.30 + $211.09 =

Answer:
1. A. 5.27%
   B. 13.9%
   C. 8.12%
   D. 37.5%
2. A. $1,037.32
   B. $826.18
   C. $2,126.55
   D. $899.39

3. Divide decimals. Round to the nearest hundredth (0.01) if necessary.
Example: 18.5 ÷ 12 = 1.54

A. 35.8 ÷ 11 =   B. 39.2 ÷ 9 =

C. 19.5 ÷ 4 =   D. 40.7 ÷ 15 =

4. Add and subtract decimals. Example: $678.17 − $79.38 = $598.79

A. $8,505.32 + $152.97 =   B. $2,148.33 + $872.30 =

C. $612.76 − $96.07 =   D. $1,842.12 − $866.74 =

5. Multiply decimals. Round to the nearest cent ($0.01) if necessary. Example:
$97.25 × 0.08 = $7.78

A. $645.08 × 0.06 =   B. $230.65 × 0.14 =

C. $594.77 × 0.18 =   D. $178.39 × 0.028 =

6. Convert percentages to decimals by moving the decimal point two places
to the left. Example: 8.25% → 0.0825

A. 11.2% →   B. 8.93% →

C. 8% →   D. 21.7% →

7. Divide whole numbers and decimals. Round to the nearest thousandth
(0.001) if necessary. Example: $2,168.50 ÷ $25,000 = 0.087

A. $3,356 ÷ $50,000 =   B. $15,201 ÷ $64,522 =

C. $187.05 ÷ $2,040 =   D. $4,399 ÷ $19,000 =

8. Add decimals. Example: $1,024.91 + $102.94 = $1,127.85

A. $687.02 + $74.20 =   B. $45.78 + $8.01 =

C. $2,325 + $52.73 =   D. $329.47 + $50.32 =

9. Multiply decimals. Round to the nearest cent ($0.01) if necessary. Example:
$115.64 × 0.08 = $9.25

A. $425 × 0.05 =   B. $149.24 × 0.06 =

C. $813.26 × 0.09 =   D. $289.22 × 0.035 =

10. Subtract decimals. Example: $104.29 − $45.16 = $59.13

A. $500.31 − $198.84 =   B. $637.02 − $126.61 =

C. $2,700 − $1,420.38 =   D. $1,200 − $485.76 =

3. A. 3.25
   B. 4.36
   C. 4.88
   D. 2.71
4. A. $8,658.29
   B. $3,020.63
   C. $516.69
   D. $975.38
5. A. $38.70
   B. $32.29
   C. $107.06
   D. $4.99
6. A. 0.112
   B. 0.0893
   C. 0.08
   D. 0.217
7. A. 0.067
   B. 0.236
   C. 0.092
   D. 0.232
8. A. $761.22
   B. $53.79
   C. $2,377.73
   D. $379.79
9. A. $21.25
   B. $8.95
   C. $73.19
   D. $10.12
10. A. $301.47
    B. $510.41
    C. $1,279.62
    D. $714.24

Section 7.1 Credit Basics

11. Cheyenne checked her department store credit account balance online and learned that it was $108.38. Afterward, she made a purchase in the amount of $117.42. If her credit limit is $800, what is Cheyenne's remaining available credit on this account?

12. Jesse has a credit card with a balance of $918.87. The bank lowered his credit limit to $1,750. What is Jesse's remaining available credit on this account?

Answer:
11. $574.20
12. $831.13

Section 7.2 Finance Charges and Fees

13. Sandra has a credit card with an APR of 24.7%. What is her monthly periodic rate? Round to the nearest ten-thousandth (0.0001) if necessary.

14. Traci has a credit card with a 17.6% APR and a 30-day billing period. The average daily balance method is used to calculate the finance charge. Her daily balances for one billing period are shown in the following chart. Traci had a previous balance of $716.34, made a payment of $650, and has new purchases that total $632.39. Determine Traci's average daily balance.

Teaching Tip:
The spreadsheet solutions for questions 14 and 16 appear on the Instructor's Resource CD.

Days 1–2	Days 3–6	Days 7–11	Days 12–22	Days 23–29	Day 30
$716.34	$289.43	$414.93	$543.75	$640.27	$698.73

15. Ian has a credit card that charges a 2.75% fee for a cash advance. Because of a family emergency, he decided to get an $800 cash advance. What is the fee that Ian will pay for the cash advance? Round to the nearest cent ($0.01) if necessary.

16. Jill wants to use her credit card for a vacation package. The standard APR is 18.75%, but the credit card company is offering a promotional rate of 1.75% for six months. The cost of the vacation package, including taxes and fees, is $1,526. Assume that Jill has a previous unpaid balance and her monthly payments apply to that balance. How much will the promotional rate save Jill in finance charges during the six-month period?

Answer:
13. 2.0583%
14. $527.56
15. $22
16. $135.37

Section 7.3 Debt Management

17. Fatima has a credit card with a nominal APR of 22.1%. The interest on unpaid balances compounds daily. What is the EAR?

18. Marquez, who works as a technical writer for a software company and earns $66,240 per year, made a list of his current debt payments per month, which is shown as follows. What is Marquez' debt-to-income ratio?

mortgage = $1,189.46

car loan = $435.08

student loans = $214.96

Answer:
17. 24.72%
18. 39.5%

Reinforce Your Understanding

19. A website charges $0.17 for each click on an advertiser's web banner. Mountain Snow Vacations received an average of 62 clicks per month for the last quarter. What is Mountain Snow Vacations advertising bill for the last quarter?

20. Jeanetta works as an independent contractor providing dog-walking services. Her monthly earnings from several clients last month totaled $3,025. Calculate the self-employment taxes that Jeanetta will pay on her earnings. Assume the self-employment tax rate is 13.3%.

Answer:
19. $31.62
20. $402.33

Apply Your Technology Skills

Companion
Website
www.g-wlearning.com

Access the G-W Learning companion website for this text at www.g-wlearning.com. Download each data file for this chapter. Follow the instructions to complete financial literacy activities to practice what you have learned in this chapter.

Teaching Tip:
The Apply Your Technology Skills activities offer project-based authentic assessment opportunities.

Data File 7-1—Completing a Credit Card Application

Data File 7-2—Evaluating Your Three C's of Credit

Data File 7-3—Completing a Credit Report Application

Data File 7-4—Calculating Finance Charges

8 Loans

Materials:
Instructor's Resource CD
Student Workbook
G-W Learning companion website
EXAMVIEW® Assessment Suite
Microsoft Excel®–compatible software
Calculator with advanced-math functions

Loans and credit are important to our economy. Few people can say they have never borrowed money. Most homes and cars today are purchased with borrowed money. Understanding how loans can be used to help achieve financial goals, as well as when they can derail financial plans, is very important in today's economy.

Section 8.1 **Loans and Interest**

Section 8.2 **Installment Loans**

Section 8.3 **High-Interest Loans**

Section 8.4 **Student Loans**

College and Career Readiness

Reading Prep. As you read the chapter, think about the role interest plays in borrowing money. Consider why banks pay you less to borrow your money, which comes in the form of your deposits, than they charge you to borrow theirs.

"Student loans are incredibly helpful as long as you plan ahead and don't get in over your head. If used wisely, student loans can help get you through college and into the real world." ~ Vince N.

Money Matters
Student Debt

- Eighty-two percent of college students are carrying a credit card balance and are incurring finance charges each month.

- The average college undergraduate student carries over $3,000 in credit card debt.

- College freshman carry an average of more than $900 in credit card debt.

- Only 15% of college freshmen have zero balances on their credit cards.

- Sixty percent of college students are surprised at how high their credit card balances are.

- Forty percent of college students admit they had purchased items with a credit card even when they did not have the money to pay the credit card bill.

- In addition to credit card debt, the average graduating senior has more than $20,000 in student loans.

- The Credit CARD Act of 2009 restricts credit card issuers from giving a credit card to anyone under the age of 21 unless they can prove they have enough income to repay credit card debt. Without this proof, a cosigner is needed.

Section 8.1 Loans and Interest

Objectives

- **Describe single-payment loans.**
- **Calculate ordinary interest.**
- **Calculate exact interest.**
- **Determine the interest rate of a loan.**

Terms

- *single-payment loan*
- *principal*
- *term*
- *promissory note*
- *collateral*
- *lien*
- *ordinary interest method*
- *exact interest method*

Build Your Math Skills

Review these math skills to prepare for the lesson that follows.

1. Convert percentages to decimals by moving the decimal two places to the left. Round to the nearest cent ($0.01) if necessary. Example: 5.25% → 0.0525

A. 9.25% →

B. 12.1% →

C. 8.375% →

D. 5.5% →

2. Multiply decimals. Round to the nearest cent ($0.01) if necessary. Example: $975 × 0.07 = $68.25

A. $565 × 0.04 =

B. $1,114 × 0.05 =

C. $768 × 0.075 =

D. $405.75 × 1.05 =

3. Divide decimals. Round to the nearest cent ($0.01) if necessary. Example: $14.50 ÷ 0.02 = $725

A. $750 ÷ 25.5 =

B. $1050 ÷ $500 =

C. $465.50 ÷ $750.80 =

D. $75 ÷ $125 =

4. Simplify fractions. Example: $\frac{16}{32} = \frac{1}{2}$

A. $\frac{20}{25} =$

B. $\frac{14}{49} =$

C. $\frac{18}{81} =$

D. $\frac{21}{56} =$

5. Convert fractions to decimals by dividing the numerator by the denominator. Round to the nearest hundredth if necessary (0.01). Example: $\frac{11}{23} = 0.48$

A. $\frac{15}{56} =$

B. $\frac{24}{49} =$

C. $\frac{9}{25} =$

D. $\frac{7}{10} =$

Answer:
1. A. 0.0925
   B. 0.121
   C. 0.08375
   D. 0.055
2. A. $22.60
   B. $55.70
   C. $57.60
   D. $426.04
3. A. $29.41
   B. 2.1
   C. 0.62
   D. 0.6
4. A. $\frac{4}{5}$
   B. $\frac{2}{7}$
   C. $\frac{2}{9}$
   D. $\frac{3}{8}$
5. A. 0.27
   B. 0.49
   C. 0.36
   D. 0.7

Single-Payment Loans

There are many ways that money can be borrowed and repaid. The simplest is a **single-payment loan,** which is a loan that is repaid in one payment with interest. The **principal** is the original sum of money borrowed. The **term** is the length of time that the money will be borrowed. At the end of the term, the loan must be repaid.

As with the other examples of interest in this text, loan interest is also expressed as an annual rate. In a single-payment loan, the interest is paid at the end of the term, along with the principal repayment. If money is borrowed for exactly one year, the formula for simple interest can be used. In this formula, $t = 1$, because there is only one payment period in a single payment loan. If, for example, the annual rate is 10%, the interest due at the end of the year is 10% of the principal. For a single-payment loan, the following formula can be used to calculate interest:

$$I = Prt$$

fyi

In the formula for simple interest: *I* is for interest paid; *P* is for principal; *r* is interest rate; and *t* is term.

Example 8-1A

See It

Martha borrowed $1,600 from her parents. They agreed that at the end of one year, Martha would repay the entire amount plus 8.5% interest. How much interest will Martha owe her parents?

Strategy

Use the formula:

$$I = Prt$$

Solution

Step 1: Convert the annual interest rate to a decimal by moving the decimal two places to the left.

8.5% → 0.085

Step 2: Determine the annual interest amount. Multiply the principal by the annual interest rate.

interest owed = principal × rate × term

interest owed = $1,600 × 0.085 × 1

interest owed = $136

Check It

Jerome borrowed $2,500 from his grandparents to pay his fall semester college tuition payment. They agreed that at the end of one year, Jerome would repay the entire amount plus 4.75% interest. How much interest will Jerome owe his grandparents?

Teaching Tip:
The complete solutions to the Check It problems can be found on the Instructor's Resource CD.

Answer:
$118.75

A loan is usually formalized by a legal document called a promissory note. A *promissory note* is a written *promise, or contract,* to pay back a loan. The amount of the principal, the interest rate, and the terms of the loan are all specified in the promissory note. Figure 8-1 shows an example of a promissory note.

Sometimes a lender requires something of value to be pledged as security for a loan. For example, suppose Natalie wants to borrow $5,000. She owns a car with a value of $8,000, which is paid in full. Before granting the loan, the lender may require that the car be pledged as security. The car is being used as collateral for the loan. *Collateral* can be any asset worth money, including a house, a car, or a possession. Securing a loan with collateral means that in the event you default on the loan, the lender will receive the asset pledged as collateral.

When property is used as collateral, the lender will place a lien on it. A *lien* is a legal agreement giving the lender the right to claim assets of the borrower if necessary to repay a loan. In Natalie's case, this means that if the lender is not repaid, the car could be sold to repay the loan.

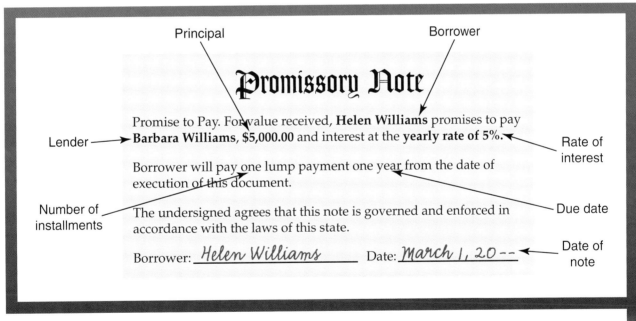

*Figure 8-1.
Promissory Note*

Example 8-1B

See It

Teaching Tip:
Remind students that lenders use the three C's of credit when evaluating whether a person is creditworthy.

Serafina received a loan from her bank and signed a promissory note as shown. Determine the amount of interest that Serafina will pay based on the information from her promissory note.

𝔓𝔯𝔬𝔪𝔦𝔰𝔰𝔬𝔯𝔶 𝔑𝔬𝔱𝔢

Serafina Johanssen borrows from the lender, Coastal Bank, the sum of $6,500 for a period of one year.

Ms. Johanssen will pay an annual interest rate of 6.75%.

She promises to pay the loan in full, including all applicable interest, at the end of one year.

Strategy

Use the formula:

$$I = Prt$$

Solution

Step 1: Identify the principal and annual interest rate.

principal = $6,500

annual interest rate = 6.75%

Step 2: Convert the annual interest rate to a decimal by moving the decimal two places to the left.

6.75% → 0.0675

Step 3: Determine the annual interest amount. Multiply the principal by the annual interest rate.

annual interest amount = principal × annual interest rate

annual interest amount = $6,500 × 0.0675

annual interest amount = $438.75

Check It

Mikhail loaned his nephew money to purchase a used car. Mikhail's nephew agreed to pay the sum of $3,300 and 5.35% interest. The full amount is due in one year. Determine the amount of interest that Mikhail's nephew will pay based on the information in the promissory note.

Answer:
$176.55

Promissory Note

The borrower, Mikhail Nikolai, borrows from the lender, Dmitri Nikolai, the sum of $3,300 for a period of one year.

Mikhail will pay an annual interest rate of 5.35%, and promises to pay the loan in full, including all applicable interest, at the end of one year.

Ordinary Interest Method

When money is borrowed for less than a year, calculating the interest is not as simple as calculating a single payment loan.

One common way to calculate loan interest for fractions of a year is to use the ordinary interest method. In the **ordinary interest method,** the interest is calculated assuming that each month has 30 days, for a total of 360 days in the year. This is done to make calculation easier than if all 365 days are considered. For most applications, this method is accurate enough for the calculation. The ordinary interest method is sometimes called the *banker's interest method* or simply the *banker's rule*.

To calculate ordinary interest, the number of ordinary interest days is divided by 360. The result will be the fraction of the year that will be multiplied by the annual interest rate. This idea can be expressed as shown in the formulas that follow:

$$\text{term} = \frac{\text{number of days of the loan}}{360}$$

$$I = Prt$$

fyi

Before committing to a loan, make sure you understand the interest and how many payments you will be making.

Teaching Tip:
Ask students to think about whether simple interest or ordinary interest is more beneficial to the borrower.

Example 8-1C

See It

Shelby borrowed $1,750 from her cousin using the ordinary interest method. They agreed that Shelby would pay an annual interest rate of 4.5%. She would repay the loan in seven months. How much interest will Shelby pay on the loan?

Strategy

Use the formulas:

$$\text{term} = \frac{\text{number of days of the loan}}{360}$$

$$I = Prt$$

Solution

Step 1: Determine the number of days of the loan. Multiply the number of months by 30 days.

number of days of the loan = number of months × number of days per month

number of days of the loan = 7 × 30

number of days of the loan = 210

Step 2: Convert the annual interest rate to a decimal by moving the decimal two places to the left.

4.5% → 0.045

Step 3: Determine the term of the loan. Divide the number of days of the loan by 360.

$$\text{term} = \frac{\text{number of days of the loan}}{360}$$

$$\text{term} = \frac{210}{360}$$

Step 4: Convert the fraction to a decimal. Divide the numerator by the denominator.

term = 210 ÷ 360 ≈ 0.5833

Step 5: Determine the amount of interest. Multiply the principal, annual interest rate, and term of the loan. Round to the nearest cent ($0.01) if necessary.

amount of interest = principal × rate × term

amount of interest = $1,750 × 0.045 × 0.5833

amount of interest = $45.93

Check It

Aadi borrowed $850 using the ordinary interest method. He agreed to pay an annual interest rate of 6.25%. He will repay the loan in eight months. Calculate the amount of interest that Aadi will pay.

Example 8-1D

See It

Shania has agreed to borrow money from her aunt using the ordinary interest method. She wants to borrow $1,500 for six months at an annual interest rate of 6.5%. Determine the total amount of money that Shania will need to pay back at the end of the six-month loan period.

Strategy

Use the formulas:

$$\text{term} = \frac{\textbf{number of days of the loan}}{\textbf{360}}$$

$$I = Prt$$

Solution

Step 1: Determine the number of days of the loan. Multiply the number of months by 30 days per month.

number of days of the loan = number of months × number of days per month

number of days of the loan = 6 × 30

number of days of the loan = 180

Step 2: Convert the annual interest rate to a decimal by moving the decimal two places to the left.

6.5% → 0.065

Step 3: Determine the term of the loan. Divide the number of days of the loan by 360.

$$\text{term} = \frac{\text{number of days of the loan}}{360}$$

$$\text{term} = \frac{180}{360}$$

Step 4: Convert the fraction to a decimal. Divide the numerator by the denominator.

term = 180 ÷ 360 = 0.5

Step 5: Determine the amount of interest. Multiply the principal, annual interest rate, and term of the loan.

amount of interest = principal × annual interest rate × term

amount of interest = $1,500 × 0.065 × 0.5

amount of interest = $48.75

Step 6: Determine the total amount of money that Shania will pay back. Add the principal and amount of interest.

total amount of money paid = principal + amount of interest

total amount of money paid = $1,500 + $48.75

total amount of money paid = $1,548.75

fyi

When using the ordinary interest method, you may choose to write the term of the loan as a fraction or as a decimal, whichever makes the arithmetic easier.

Check It

Kameron has agreed to borrow $2,200 from his parents using the ordinary interest method. He will borrow the money for nine months. The annual interest rate is 5.85%. Calculate the total amount of money that Kameron will pay back at the end of the nine-month loan period.

Answer:
$2,296.53

Exact Interest Method

The exact interest method is similar to the ordinary interest method. The *exact interest method* calculates the loan interest by using the exact number of days divided by 365 to get an exact fraction of the year. This method is more complicated because you have to account for the varying length of actual months. There are four months with 30 days. Seven months have 31 days. And, of course, February has 28 days. These days total 365.

The formulas for exact interest are similar to those for ordinary interest. However, the more exact number of 365 days in a year is used instead of the general 360 days:

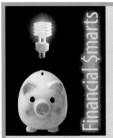

Loans are a commitment that should be taken seriously. Once you sign for a loan, you are responsible for making payments on time. Before you apply for a loan, do your homework. Interest rates change regularly, so shop for the best interest rate and repayment plans. Make sure that a loan payment fits into your budget as you will be making payments for an extended amount of time. Using an online calculator can help you estimate your payments while you are doing your research.

$$\text{term} = \frac{\text{number of days of the loan}}{365}$$

$$I = Prt$$

Example 8-1E

See It

Nita borrowed $2,450 from her credit union. The annual percentage rate is 7.6%. She repaid the loan 65 days after she borrowed the money. Calculate the amount of interest that Nita paid for the loan.

Strategy

Use the formulas:

$$\text{term} = \frac{\text{number of days of the loan}}{365}$$

$$I = Prt$$

Solution

Step 1: Convert the annual interest rate to a decimal by moving the decimal two places to the left.

7.6% → 0.076

Step 2: Determine the term of the loan. Divide the number of days of the loan by 360. Round to the nearest thousandth (0.001) if necessary.

$$\text{term} = \frac{\text{number of days of the loan}}{365}$$

$$\text{term} = \frac{65}{365}$$

$$\text{term} \approx 0.178$$

Step 3: Determine the amount of interest. Multiply the principal, annual interest rate, and term of the loan.

amount of interest = principal × annual interest rate × term

amount of interest = $2,450 × 0.076 × 0.178

amount of interest = $33.14

Check It

Mikel borrowed $1,675 from his credit union at an annual percentage rate of 8.3%. He repaid the loan 77 days after he borrowed the money. Calculate the amount of interest that Mikel paid for the loan.

Answer:
$29.33

Example 8-1F

See It

On April 17, Robert obtained a loan for $1,150 from his bank. The annual percentage rate was 9.25%. He repaid the loan in one payment on July 2. Determine the amount of interest that Robert paid on the loan.

Strategy

Use the formulas:

$$\textbf{term} = \frac{\textbf{number of days of the loan}}{\textbf{365}}$$

$$\textbf{I} = \textbf{Prt}$$

If the beginning date and ending date of a loan are known, then the number of days of the loan can be calculated.

Solution

Step 1: Determine the number of days of Robert's loan. Use the calendar to count the number of days between April 17 and July 2.

number of days of loan = April + May + June + July

number of days of loan = (30 − 17) + 31 + 30 + 2

number of days of loan = 13 + 31 + 30 + 2

number of days of loan = 76

Step 2: Determine the term of Robert's loan. Divide the number of days of the loan by 365.

$$\text{term} = \frac{\text{number of days of the loan}}{365}$$

$$\text{term} = \frac{76}{365}$$

$$\text{term} \approx 0.208$$

Step 3: Convert the annual interest rate to a decimal by moving the decimal two places to the left.

$$9.25\% \rightarrow 0.0925$$

Step 4: Determine the amount of interest. Multiply the principal, annual interest rate, and term.

amount of interest = principal × annual interest rate × term

amount of interest = $1,150 × 0.0925 × 0.208

amount of interest = $22.12

Check It

On August 21, Cheryl obtained a loan for $2,215 from her bank. The annual percentage rate was 7.35%. She repaid the loan in one payment on November 11. Determine the amount of interest that Cheryl paid on the loan.

Answer:
$36.63

Finding the Interest Rate

If you know the principal of a loan and the interest owed for a one-year term, you can calculate the interest rate. The following formula can be used:

annual interest rate = annual interest amount ÷ principal

Example 8-1G

See It

Maribel borrowed $4,450 for a one-year term loan. Maribel paid a total of $317.06 in annual interest. What was Maribel's annual interest rate?

Strategy

Use the formula:

annual interest rate = annual interest amount ÷ principal

Solution

Step 1: Divide the annual interest amount by the principal. Round to the nearest hundred-thousandth (0.00001) if necessary.

annual interest rate = annual interest amount ÷ principal

annual interest rate =$317.06 ÷ $4,450

annual interest rate ≈ 0.07125

Step 2: Convert the annual interest rate to a percentage by moving the decimal two places to the right.

0.07125 → 7.125%

Check It

Danielle borrowed $3,175 for a one-year term loan. She paid a total of $254 in annual interest. What was Danielle's annual interest rate?

Answer:
8%

Checkpoint 8.1

1. Marvella received a loan from her bank in the sum of $5,165 for a period of one year. The annual interest rate for the loan is 5.75%. The full amount of the principal and interest are due at the end of one year. Determine the amount of interest that Marvella will pay.

2. Alvin borrowed $1,050 using the ordinary interest method. He agreed to pay an annual interest rate of 4.85%. He will repay the loan in six months. Calculate the amount of interest that Alvin will pay.

3. Dina borrowed $2,890 using the method of exact interest. She will pay an annual interest rate of 6.45% and will repay the loan in 85 days. Calculate the total amount that Dina will pay back when she repays the loan.

4. Rafik borrowed $1,600 for a one-year loan. He paid $131.20 in interest. What was the annual interest rate on Rafik's loan?

5. Panna borrowed $2,715 for a one-year term loan. She paid a total of $162.90 in annual interest. What was Panna's annual interest rate?

Teaching Tip:
Checkpoint questions offer opportunities for formative assessment.

Answer:
1. $296.99
2. $25.46
3. $2,933.43
4. 8.2%
5. 6%

Section 8.2 Installment Loans

Objectives

- **Describe installment loans.**
- **Define down payment.**
- **Calculate an early loan repayment amount.**

Build Your Math Skills

Review these math skills to prepare for the lesson that follows.

1. Convert percentages to decimals by moving the decimal two places to the left. Example: 12% → 0.12

A. 13% →

B. 1.5% →

C. 8.35% →

D. 9.2% →

2. Multiply decimals. Round to the nearest cent ($0.01) if necessary. Example: $1,155 × 0.07 = $80.85

A. $164 × 0.04 =

B. $608.94 × 0.25 =

C. $217.46 × 0.025 =

D. $665.37 × 1.07 =

3. Add and subtract decimals. Example: $945.74 – $85.71 = $860.03

A. $87.45 + $7.41 =

B. $145.96 + $107.04 =

C. $560.42 – $78.83 =

D. $770.04 – $207.16 =

Installment Loans

Most loans are not single-payment loans. A more common way to repay a loan is in periodic payments, usually monthly. In an ***installment loan,*** payments are made at predetermined intervals. Each payment includes the interest accrued since the last payment and a portion of the principal. For example, suppose you borrow $1,000 and plan to pay it back in 12 monthly installments. The term of the loan would be 12 months because the loan is not fully repaid until the final payment is made.

Typically, installment loans are level payment plans. ***Level payment plans*** are designed to have the same payment amount in each installment. With each payment, a portion of the payment covers interest due for the most recent period. The remainder of the payment reduces the principal.

Figure 8-2 shows a table of payments, called an *amortization table,* for a $1,000 installment loan using an interest rate of 9%. An ***amortization table*** is a schedule that shows the amount of interest and principal for each payment so that a loan can be repaid within a specific period of time.

Month	Payment	Principal	9% Interest	Principal Balance
1	$87.45	$79.95	$7.50	$920.05
2	87.45	80.55	6.90	839.50
3	87.45	81.15	6.30	758.35
4	87.45	81.76	5.69	676.59
5	87.45	82.38	5.07	594.21
6	87.45	82.99	4.46	511.22
7	87.45	83.62	3.83	427.60
8	87.45	84.24	3.21	343.36
9	87.45	84.87	2.58	258.49
10	87.45	85.51	1.94	172.98
11	87.45	86.15	1.30	86.83
12	87.48	86.83	0.65	0.00

Figure 8-2.
Amortization Table

Because the principal is reduced with each payment, the interest owed for each successive period is less. Because the payment stays the same, each payment applies more money to the principal.

Notice in Figure 8-2 that the final payment is three cents more than the other payments. Many times, the final payment is slightly more or less than the other payments as the remaining interest and principal are paid.

Interest payments are calculated by dividing the annual interest rate by the number of payments per year, then multiplying that ratio by the principal balance:

$$\textbf{interest payment} = \frac{\textbf{annual interest rate} \times \textbf{principal balance}}{\textbf{number of payments per year}}$$

Because the payments in Figure 8-2 are monthly, the 9% interest is divided by 12 and applied to the remaining balance after the previous payment.

Calculating a level monthly payment for an installment loan is very complex. Bankers and other professional lenders use loan amortization software or special handheld calculators. There are also many loan amortization calculators on the Internet.

Teaching Tip:
Call students' attention to Figure 8-2. Ask them to try to discern any patterns in the data. They should note that while the amount of the payment stays the same until the last month, the portion of the payment that goes toward interest goes down. Why is this?

Graphing calculators have finance applications that can be used to calculate payments for amortization.

Example 8-2A

See It

Carla has a $2,000 loan with a 9% annual interest rate. Each monthly installment is $349.80. Calculate the amount of interest and principal that are paid with her first monthly payment.

Strategy

Use the formula:

$$\text{interest payment} = \frac{\text{annual interest rate} \times \text{principal balance}}{\text{number of payments per year}}$$

Solution

Step 1: Determine the monthly interest rate. Divide the annual interest rate by 12 (the number of payments per year).

$$\text{monthly interest rate} = \frac{\text{annual interest rate}}{\text{number of payments per year}}$$

$$\text{monthly interest rate} = \frac{9\%}{12}$$

Step 2: Convert the fraction to a decimal. Divide the numerator by the denominator.

monthly interest rate = 9% ÷ 12 = 0.75%

Step 3: Convert the monthly interest rate to a decimal by moving the decimal two places to the left.

0.75% → 0.0075

Step 4: Determine Carla's interest payment for the first month. Multiply the monthly interest rate by the principal balance.

interest payment = monthly interest rate × principal balance

interest payment = 0.0075 × $2,000

interest payment = $15

Step 5: Determine the amount of the monthly payment that will be applied to the principal. Subtract the interest payment from the monthly payment amount.

principal payment = monthly payment amount − interest payment

principal payment = $349.80 − $15

principal payment = $334.80

Check It

After Carla makes her first monthly payment, her principal balance is reduced by $334.80 to $1,665.20. Use this new principal balance to determine how much of Carla's second monthly payment is an interest payment and how much of Carla's second monthly payment is applied to the principal balance. Round to the nearest cent ($0.01) if necessary.

Down Payment

An installment loan is often used to finance the purchase of an asset. The asset could be a house, a car, or a piece of equipment. The asset could even be a

fyi

The steps used in the See It portion of Example 8-2A can be used to create an amortization table.

Answer:
interest payment =
$12.49
principal payment =
$337.31

business. It is common for a lender to require that some of the purchase amount be paid up front by the borrower, rather than financing the entire purchase price. The **down payment** is the amount the borrower pays up front. The **amount financed** is the remaining cost that will be covered by the loan. The amount financed is calculated as follows:

amount financed = purchase price – down payment

There is no consistent rule governing the amount of a down payment. Depending on what is being purchased, a lender may require as much as 20% down. Some loans require a smaller down payment. You probably have heard advertisements promising no down payment on purchases.

Installment loans are different than other types of loans because they generally do not require collateral. Most installment loans are used to purchase items such as furniture or equipment. These loans are usually short-term and range from 3 to 24 months for repayment. Installment loans are fairly easy to obtain but may not be available in all states. Generally, there is no prepayment penalty if the loan is paid before the end of the term.

You may be asking why a down payment is required. The reason is that when you finance a purchase with an installment loan, the item purchased is generally used as collateral for the loan. The down payment reduces the risk for the lender. Should the borrower not be able to pay back the loan and the lender has to sell the asset to cover the loan, the lender hopes that the asset is worth more than the balance on the loan. The higher the down payment, the more likely the asset's value will cover the balance of the loan. Also, as payments are made each month, the principal is further reduced, which makes it more likely that the value of the asset is higher than the principal balance.

fyi

During the financial crises that began in 2008, the value of many houses fell to less than the amount left to be paid on the mortgage loans. When the value of an asset is worth less than the amount owed on the loan, it is often referred to as being *under water*.

Example 8-2B

See It

Mali wants to purchase a new boat that costs $14,995. She wants to finance her purchase. The bank wants a down payment of 15%. Determine both Mali's down payment and the amount that Mali will be financing.

Strategy

Use the formulas:

down payment = purchase price × down payment rate

amount financed = purchase price – down payment

Solution

Step 1: Convert the down payment percentage to a decimal by moving the decimal two places to the left.

15% → 0.15

Step 2: Determine the amount of the down payment. Multiply the purchase price by the down payment rate.

down payment = purchase price × down payment rate

down payment = $14,995 × 0.15

down payment = $2,249.25

Step 3: Determine the amount that Mali will finance. Subtract the down payment from the purchase price.

amount financed = purchase price – down payment

amount financed = $14,995 – $2,249.95

amount financed = $12,745.75

Check It

Riley and Marie want to purchase a lake house for $243,500. The bank is requiring a down payment of 20%. Determine both the down payment and the amount that Riley and Marie will be financing.

Early Loan Repayment

fyi

Some lenders charge a penalty if a loan is paid off early. The prepayment penalty is usually based on a percentage of the remaining balance or a certain number of months' worth of interest. Recent legislation has sought to limit lenders' ability to charge early repayment penalties.

Many loans allow for early repayment. *Early repayment* means that the borrower pays off the installment loan sooner than the original term. This can be done in two ways. One way involves the borrower making more than the planned payment each month. Because a normal level payment plan pays all the interest due first and the rest is applied to principal, paying more than the planned level payment reduces the principal even more. Therefore, the loan will be paid off early.

Early repayment can also be made by making a single payment that will pay off the remaining balance. To pay off an installment loan early, you must pay the remaining principal and any interest due. An early payoff quote usually must be obtained from the lender. However, you can estimate the amount of the early payoff using the following formulas:

Teaching Tip:
Discuss the pros and cons of paying off a loan early.

$$\textbf{monthly interest rate} = \frac{\textbf{annual interest rate}}{\textbf{number of payments per year}}$$

$$\textbf{interest due} = \textbf{monthly interest rate} \times \textbf{principal balance}$$

$$\textbf{early payoff amount} = \textbf{principal balance} + \textbf{interest due}$$

Example 8-2C

See It

Kayla has a loan that she used to buy a new computer. She originally borrowed $1,200 at an annual interest rate of 7.5%. Kayla has been making monthly payments of $54 and wants to pay her loan off early. There are six remaining payments, and the principal balance is $317.03. What will be Kayla's final payment if she pays the loan off early?

Strategy

Use the formulas:

$$\text{monthly interest rate} = \frac{\textbf{annual interest rate}}{\textbf{number of payments per year}}$$

$$\textbf{interest due} = \textbf{monthly interest rate} \times \textbf{principal balance}$$

$$\textbf{early payoff amount} = \textbf{principal balance} + \textbf{interest due}$$

Solution

Step 1: Determine the monthly interest rate. Divide the annual interest rate by 12 (the number of payments per year).

$$\text{monthly interest rate} = \frac{\text{annual interest rate}}{\text{number of payments per year}}$$

monthly interest rate = 0.625%

Step 2: Convert the monthly interest rate to a decimal by moving the decimal two places to the left.

$0.625\% \rightarrow 0.00625$

Step 3: Determine the interest due. Multiply the monthly interest rate by the principal balance. Round to the nearest cent ($0.01) if necessary.

interest due = monthly interest rate × principal balance

interest due = 0.00625 × $317.03

interest due = $1.98

Step 4: Determine the early payoff amount. Add the remaining principal balance and the interest due.

early payoff amount = principal balance + interest due

early payoff amount = $317.30 + $1.98

early payoff amount = $319.28

Check It

Jiang has a car loan. He originally borrowed $5,200 at an annual interest rate of 6.25% for three years. Jiang's monthly payments are $158.79. With five remaining payments, his principal balance is $781.66. He wants to pay the balance of the loan. Calculate an estimate of Jiang's early payoff amount.

Checkpoint 8.2

1. Bianca has a car loan with monthly payments of $381.86. She originally borrowed $16,500 for four years at an annual interest rate of 5.25%. For her first monthly payment, calculate the amount that was paid in interest and the amount that was applied to the principal balance.

2. Aaron financed his new motorcycle for $18,250. He has a three-year loan at a 6.3% annual interest rate. The monthly payments are $557.68. For his first monthly payment, calculate the amount that was paid in interest and the amount that was applied to the principal balance.

3. Martina and Luis want to purchase a new recreational vehicle for $29,450. The bank requires a down payment of 12%. How much will Martina and Luis need to provide for a down payment? What is the amount they will need to finance?

4. Maiko has a car loan. He originally borrowed $7,850 at an annual interest rate of 5.45% for three years. Maiko's monthly payments are $237.86. With six remaining payments, his principal balance is $1,398.85, and he wants to pay the balance of the loan. Calculate an estimate of Maiko's early payoff amount.

5. Safia has a truck loan. She originally borrowed $14,950 at an annual interest rate of 5.65% for five years. Safia's monthly payments are $286.60. With nine remaining payments, her principal balance is $2,519.70. She wants to pay the balance of the loan. Calculate an estimate of Safia's early payoff amount.

Section 8.3 High-Interest Loans

Objectives

- **Describe how payday loans work.**
- **Explain how title loans work.**
- **Describe the nature of pawnshop loans.**
- **Identify resources for overcoming financial difficulties.**

Terms

- *payday loan*
- *title*
- *title loan*
- *pawnshop*
- *foreclosure*
- *bankrupt*
- *bankruptcy*

Build Your Math Skills

Review these math skills to prepare for the lesson that follows.

1. Convert percentages to decimals by moving the decimal two places to the left. Example: 15.8% → 0.158

A. 2.34% →

B. 17.1% →

C. 10.4% →

D. 0.95% →

2. Add decimals. Example: $15.80 + $3.90 = $19.70

A. $570.49 + $85 =

B. $409.07 + $391.09 =

C. $1,178.06 + $940.98 =

D. $507.57 + $346.82 =

3. Multiply decimals. Round to the nearest cent ($0.01) if necessary. Example: $154 × 0.14 = $21.56

A. $112 × 0.06 =

B. $340.50 × 0.09 =

C. $418.62 × 0.0045 =

D. $350 × 1.25 =

Answer:
1. A. 0.0234
   B. 0.171
   C. 0.104
   D. 0.0095
2. A. $655.49
   B. $800.16
   C. $2,119.04
   D. $854.39
3. A. $6.72
   B. $30.65
   C. $1.88
   D. $437.50

Payday Loans

A *payday loan* is a short-term loan designed to be repaid when the borrower gets his or her next paycheck. A payday loan is usually for an amount ranging from fifty to a few hundred dollars. A typical use for a payday loan is to pay a bill that is due before the borrower's next paycheck or to make an emergency repair. With a payday loan, the borrower writes a check to the lender for the amount of the loan plus a fee. The lender agrees to hold the check until the borrower gets paid and gives the borrower cash for the amount of the loan.

Financial $marts

The financially smart person knows that payday loans are a very expensive way to borrow money. If you think you need a payday loan, you should analyze your budget. Make a plan to begin building some savings that will help you avoid expensive emergency financing. Payday loans can become a trap because part of your next paycheck is pledged to repay the payday loan. This can also create continued financial stress. Avoiding payday loans is the financially smart thing to do.

The fees for payday loans are extremely high. Most payday loans are paid back within a week or two. It is typical for the fee to be between $10 and $20 for each $100 borrowed. APRs on payday loans can be over 900%, depending on how long the money is borrowed. Different states have different regulations that determine the minimum or maximum time for the terms of a payday loan. If the fee is a percentage of the loan amount, the fee can be determined using the following formula:

loan fee = loan amount × fee rate

The total cost of the loan, or the full amount that must be paid back at the end of the term of the loan, is calculated using the following formula:

payback amount = loan amount + loan fee

fyi

Payday loans are sometimes called paycheck advances.

Example 8-3A

See It

A payday loan company offers a 14-day term loan. They charge 22% of the principal as a brokerage fee and an additional 0.38% in interest charges. Greg had an unexpected car repair and decided to obtain a payday loan for $150. How much will Greg pay back at the end of the 14-day loan term?

Strategy

Use the formulas:

loan fee = loan amount × fee rate

payback amount = loan amount + loan fee

Solution

Step 1: Determine the total fee rate for the payday loan. Add the brokerage fee and the interest rate.

fee rate = brokerage fee + interest rate

fee rate = 22% + 0.38%

fee rate = 22.38%

Step 2: Convert the fee rate to a decimal by moving the decimal two places to the left.

22.38% → 0.2238

Step 3: Determine the loan fee. Multiply the loan amount by the fee rate.

loan fee = loan amount × fee rate

loan fee = $150 × 0.2238

loan fee = $33.57

Step 4: Determine the full loan payback amount. Add the loan amount to the loan fee.

payback amount = loan amount + loan fee

payback amount = $150 + $33.57

payback amount = $183.57

Check It

Jennessa decided that she needed to get a payday loan for $225. The payday lender charges 25% for a brokerage fee plus 0.4% in interest charges for a 14-day term loan. How much will Jennessa pay back at the end of the 14 days?

Payday loans are made by institutions called *payday lenders*. Payday lenders typically operate from storefront locations and often perform a variety of services such as check cashing, money orders, and title loans.

Title Loans

Because automobiles are significant assets, there is a special kind of document, called a **title,** which legally establishes the owner of the automobile. A **title loan** is a form of loan where a lender takes possession of the title of your car as collateral until a short-term loan is repaid. Most title loans are for one month or less. At the end of the term, the entire loan is due in one payment with fees. If the borrower cannot repay the loan at the end of the term, the lender may *roll the loan over* for another month and add more fees. The lender may also choose to sell the car if the borrower cannot repay the loan.

Title loans, like payday loans, are typically high-interest loans. APR on a title loan can be 300% or more. Some states have made it illegal to charge an APR over 36% on a title loan. To determine the true cost of a title loan, use the following formulas:

loan fee = loan amount $\times$ **fee rate**

payback amount = loan amount + loan fee

Example 8-3B

See It

Hasty Cash Xpress offers title loans. They will lend up to 20% of the value of a vehicle for a 30-day loan term. Hasty Cash Xpress charges a fee of 28% of the loan amount. Pete has a car that is worth $4,300 and wants to get a title loan for the maximum amount possible. Calculate Pete's loan amount and the amount that he will have to pay back in 30 days.

Strategy

Use the formulas:

loan fee = loan amount × fee rate

payback amount = loan amount + loan fee

Solution

Step 1: Convert the loan percentage to a decimal by moving the decimal two places to the left.

20% → 0.20

Step 2: Determine the loan amount. Multiply the value of the car by the loan percentage.

loan amount = value of car × loan percentage

loan amount = $4,300 × 0.20

loan amount = $860

Step 3: Convert the fee rate to a decimal by moving the decimal two places to the left.

28% → 0.28

Step 4: Determine the loan fee. Multiply the loan amount by the fee rate.

loan fee = loan amount × fee rate

loan fee = $860 × 0.28

loan fee = $240.80

Step 5: Determine the full loan payback amount. Add the loan amount to the loan fee.

payback amount = loan amount + loan fee

payback amount = $860 + $240.80

payback amount = $1,100.80

Check It

Maya is trying to decide if she wants to get a title loan on her car that is worth $3,500. Loans-R-Us offers title loans. They will lend up to 20% of the value of a vehicle for a 30-day loan term. Loans-R-Us charges a fee of 24% of the loan amount. If she decides to get the full amount of the loan, how much would Maya have to pay back at the end of the 30 days?

Answer:
$868

Pawnshop Loans

Pawnshops are businesses that offer loans requiring personal property as collateral. An individual with something of value can go to a pawnshop and borrow money after handing over possession of the item to the shop. Interest rates charged by pawnshops are much higher than those charged by banks or credit unions. If the borrower pays back the loan and interest, the item is released back to the borrower. If the borrower does not pay the loan back within a specified period of time, the pawnshop becomes the owner of the collateral and can sell the item to earn back the money.

Pawnshops also buy items with the intent of reselling them. If you sell an item to a pawnshop, you walk out the door with cash that does not have to be repaid.

To determine the total amount to be paid back on a loan from a pawnshop, use the following formula:

total payback amount = loan amount + amount of fees

Example 8-3C

See It

Veronica needs cash for an emergency, so she decided to take her electric guitar to a pawnshop. The pawnbroker took the electric guitar as collateral and gave Veronica $75. In 30 days, Veronica must pay 2% interest as well as 22% in storage and handling fees in order to get her electric guitar back. How much will Veronica pay back if she returns in 30 days to reclaim her electric guitar?

Strategy

Use the formula:

total payback amount = loan amount + amount of fees

Solution

Step 1: Determine the total rate for fees and interest. Add the interest rate to the storage and handling fee rate.

total fee rate = interest rate + storage and handling rate

total fee rate = 2% + 22%

total fee rate = 24%

Step 2: Convert the total fee rate to a decimal by moving the decimal two places to the left.

24% → 0.24

Step 3: Determine the amount of fees and interest. Multiply the loan amount by the total fee rate.

amount of fees = loan amount × total fee rate

amount of fees = $75 × 0.24

amount of fees = $18

Step 4: Determine the total payback amount. Add the loan amount and the amount of fees.

total payback amount = loan amount + amount of fees

total payback amount = $75 + $18

total payback amount = $93

Check It

Takeo decided to take his television to a pawnshop because he needed money. The pawnbroker gave him $85. They agreed to a 30-day contract. He would pay a 2.2% interest fee and 21% service fee in order to reclaim his television. How much will Takeo pay back if he returns in 30 days to reclaim his television?

Answer:
$104.72

Borrow Wisely

Borrowing money should be taken seriously. When you commit to a loan or incur credit card debt, you are promising to repay money for an extended period of time. These payments will make an impact on your budget and your life. Don't be tempted to get a loan or credit that you cannot afford and get in a situation where you are living paycheck to paycheck.

Sometimes individuals owe more on their cars and houses than these assets are worth. If an individual's assets are worth less than they owe, his or her liabilities are probably higher than his or her assets. Since the onset of the financial downturn in 2008, many people have found themselves in situations where they have more debt than they can afford. Some borrowers have discovered that their loans are higher than their houses or cars are worth. This is known as an *upside down loan*. With the downturn in the economy, many assets have lost part of their value. Borrowers are finding that they owe more money on their assets than they would get if they sold those assets.

Foreclosure

As discussed earlier in this chapter, loans generally require collateral. When the loan is not repaid under the terms of the agreement, the property pledged as collateral can be seized. This type of seizure of assets is called *repossession*. When a home is repossessed, it is referred to as foreclosure. **Foreclosure** is when the ownership interest in a piece of real estate is transferred to the lender. During the financial crises that began in 2008, those who could not afford monthly payments defaulted on their mortgages in record numbers. This led to high rates of foreclosure. With demand for homes severely depressed, banks were unable to sell foreclosed houses, leading to excess supply and lower prices.

Bankruptcy

If a person or entity gets into a situation in which it is not possible to pay debts as the payments are due, the person or entity is considered **bankrupt.** In legal terminology, a person or business can enter bankruptcy either to settle debt or allow for repayment under court protection. ***Bankruptcy*** is a court order that excuses the debtor from having to repay some or all of his or her debts. The court appoints a bankruptcy trustee to decide how to use the debtors' assets to repay those owed.

There are two main types of bankruptcy—Chapter 7 and Chapter 13. *Chapter 7 bankruptcy* requires that the assets of the person or business be sold and the proceeds used to pay as much debt as can be repaid. Then, the remaining debt is cancelled. The debtor may be allowed to keep some personal items, but must make an attempt to pay off his or her bills. Chapter 7 bankruptcy stays on the debtor's credit report for ten years.

Chapter 13 bankruptcy sets up a payment plan for the debtor, rather than requiring that he or she sell all of his or her assets. The court gives protection to the debtor from those to which money is owed while the debt is being repaid. Chapter 13 bankruptcy stays on the debtor's credit report for seven years.

Bankruptcy is a drastic step and should not be undertaken without a great deal of thought. The consequences of filing bankruptcy have a significant impact on an individual's financial goals as well as his or her ability to get credit in the future.

Checkpoint 8.3

1. Rita is considering a payday loan for $330. The payday lender charges 24% for a brokerage fee plus 0.3% in interest charges for a 14-day term loan. How much will Rita pay back at the end of the 14 days?

2. Sherman is considering a payday loan for $295. The payday lender charges 23.5% for a brokerage fee plus 0.4% in interest charges for a 14-day term loan. How much will Sherman pay back at the end of the 14 days?

3. Lynda is trying to decide if she wants to get a title loan on her car that is worth $4,150. Check City will lend up to 18% of the value of a vehicle for a 30-day loan term. Check City charges a fee of 22.5% of the loan amount. If Lynda decides to get the full amount of the loan, how much would she have to pay back at the end of the 30 days?

4. Keenan pawns his trombone and receives $65. Pawn Towne offers 30-day loans for a 1.65% interest charge and a 23.5% fee for storage and handling. How much will Keenan have to pay back in 30 days in order to reclaim his trombone?

5. Joyetta pawns a gold necklace and receives $115. Best City Pawn offers 30-day loans for a 1.85% interest charge and a 21% fee for storage and handling. How much will Joyetta have to pay back in 30 days in order to reclaim her necklace?

Teaching Tip:
Checkpoint questions offer opportunities for formative assessment.

Answer:
1. $410.19
2. $365.51
3. $915.08
4. $79.85
5. $143.92

Section 8.4 Student Loans

Terms

- *Free Application for Federal Student Aid (FAFSA)*
- *grant*
- *scholarship*
- *merit-based scholarship*
- *529 plan*

Objectives

- **Explain the types of student loans.**
- **Define the methods of student loan repayment.**
- **Define various means for paying for college.**

Build Your Math Skills

Review these math skills to prepare for the lesson that follows.

1. Convert percentages to decimals by moving the decimal two places to the left. Example: 5.35% → 0.0535

A. 8.1% →

B. 9.75% →

C. 6.3% →

D. 7.65% →

2. Multiply decimals. Round to the nearest cent ($0.01) if necessary. Example: $1,265 × 0.055 = $69.58

A. $1,675 × 0.05 =

B. $955 × 0.0475 =

C. $2,450 × 0.07 =

D. $2,050 × 0.085 =

3. Add and subtract decimals. Example: $2,534.18 − ($975 + $414.50) = $1,144.68

A. $1,784.36 − ($375 + $718.35) =

B. $1,450 − ($875 + $105.50) =

C. $1,650.75 − ($576 + $819.35) =

D. $2,657.75 − ($425.65 + $830.84) =

Answer:
1. A. 0.081
   B. 0.0975
   C. 0.063
   D. 0.0765
2. A. $83.75
   B. $45.36
   C. $171.50
   D. $174.25
3. A. $691.01
   B. $469.50
   C. $255.40
   D. $1,401.26

Loan Options

Student loans are one way to pay for education beyond high school. For most students, borrowing some or all of the money to pay for college is the way they choose to finance their education. Student loans are different than standard loans because they have special features that make them ideal for students. For example, student loans typically offer lower interest rates and you may be able to postpone making payments until after graduation.

Student loan options vary based on financial need. The financial condition of the student's family is considered when determining the kind of loan for which a student qualifies. The following formula can be used to determine student loan eligibility:

student loan eligibility = total tuition and fees × student loan eligibility rate

Families must complete a special form called a Free Application for Federal Student Aid. The *Free Application for Federal Student Aid (FAFSA)* is a form issued by the federal government that is used by schools to determine a

Teaching Tip:
Give students the opportunity to share their thoughts on what percentage of post-secondary school costs should be the responsibility of the student. This can be done through discussion or a short essay.

student's need for financial aid. The information required on the FAFSA is similar to the information required for a tax return. In addition to the FAFSA form, the FAFSA website also has a great deal of information about ways to fund your post-high school education.

There are different types of student loans. Some loans, like the *Perkins Loan*, require that the student demonstrate a higher-than-average financial need. *Stafford loans* are easier to receive and are also based on need. *PLUS loans* offer higher loan amounts, but the loan is made to a parent or guardian, rather than to the student.

Example 8-4A

See It

Carlota is attending her local community college and has applied for financial aid. Based on her family's income, the college's financial aid office estimates that her family should pay for 35% of the $2,780 that one year of tuition and fees will cost. Carlota is eligible for student loans for the remaining portion of her tuition and fees. How much in student loans is Carlota eligible for?

Strategy

Use the formula:

student loan eligibility = total tuition and fees × student loan eligibility rate

Solution

Step 1: Determine the percentage of the total tuition and fees that Carlota's family does not have to pay. Subtract the percentage that her family should pay from 100%.

student loan eligibility rate = 100% – family contribution rate

student loan eligibility rate = 100% – 35%

student loan eligibility rate = 65%

Step 2: Convert Carlota's student loan eligibility rate to a decimal by moving the decimal two places to the left.

65% → 0.65

Step 3: Determine the portion of the total tuition and fees that Carlota's family does not have to pay. Multiply Carlota's student loan eligibility rate by the total amount of tuition and fees.

student loan eligibility = total tuition and fees × student loan eligibility rate

student loan eligibility = $2,780 × 0.65

student loan eligibility = $1,807

Answer:
$2,922.60

Check It

Kwon plans to attend a technical school, and his first year's tuition and fees are an estimated $4,871. Based on his family's income, Kwon and his family are responsible for 40% of the tuition and fees. How much in student loans is Kwon eligible for?

Answer:
$2,922.60

Loan Repayment

Student loan repayment varies depending on the type of loan. Some loans must be repaid within ten years. Most loans require that repayment begin six months after you stop attending school. Specific requirements vary, so make sure you understand the terms of the loan.

In most cases, payments are expected each month. You can pay off student loans early with no penalty, which can save on interest. To determine the amount of interest that you will pay, use the following formulas:

total amount owed = monthly payment × number of payments

amount of interest paid = total amount owed − principal

Source: Shutterstock (Supri Suharjoto)

There are several ways to finance college tuition, including loans, scholarships, and grants.

Example 8-4B

See It

Ignacio recently graduated from college and has a total student loan amount of $16,245. His monthly payments will be $165.13. He will make those payments for ten years. How much interest will Ignacio pay on his student loans when they are completely paid off?

Strategy

Use the formulas:

total amount owed = monthly payment × number of payments

amount of interest paid = total amount owed − principal

Solution

Step 1: Determine the number of payments Ignacio will make. Multiply the length of his loans, in years, by 12.

number of payments = length of loans (years) × 12

number of payments = 10 × 12

number of payments = 120

Step 2: Determine the total amount of money that Ignacio will pay for his student loans. Multiply his monthly payment by the number of payments.

total amount owed = monthly payment × number of payments

total amount owed = $165.13 × 120

total amount owed = $19,815.60

Step 3: Determine the amount of interest paid. Subtract the principal from the total amount owed.

amount of interest paid = total amount owed − principal

amount of interest paid = $19,815.60 − $16,245

amount of interest paid = $3,570.60

Check It

Hansa recently graduated from college. She has a total student loan amount of $21,379. Her monthly payments will be $196.73, and she will make those payments for ten years. How much interest will Hansa have paid when her student loans are paid in full?

Answer:
$2,228.60

Other Means of Funding

Loans are not the only way to pay for college. The best way to pay for college is with money that is not borrowed. There are multiple alternatives to student loans.

A *grant* is money that does not have to be repaid. There are many grants available, and you should always search for any grants for which you may qualify. For example, if you are a first-generation college student, there are probably grants available to you. Low-income students are eligible for grants. There are grants for military families, grants for attending graduate school, and even grants for students majoring in fields where there is a high need for graduates. These are just some examples. You should always search for all available grants for which you may qualify.

A scholarship is another way to pay for school. A *scholarship* is an amount of money awarded to a student that must be used toward payment for college. A scholarship can be a *merit-based scholarship,* which means the student earns it based on ability. For example, an athletic scholarship or a scholarship based on academic achievement is merit-based. Scholarships can also be need-based or can be set up to encourage a specific field of study. They can also be student specific. For example, a donor could provide a scholarship that is awarded to a student from the donor's hometown. A donor can specify almost any criteria as eligibility for a scholarship. Many scholarships go unclaimed because a qualifying student may not search diligently enough to find it.

Many students use work to pay for all or part of their college education. Students often work while going to school, either on or off campus. And students may also work full-time during the summer to save up money to offset college expenses. *Work-study programs* are another funding option. These programs fund part-time jobs for qualifying students. The schools themselves or the government provides all or part of the funding for these programs.

Career Discovery
Education & Training Careers and Math Skills

Do you have the ability to inspire and motivate others? Are you sensitive to the needs of others? If so, a career in education and training may be an option for you. This area includes teaching, training, professional support services, administration, and administrative support.

Some people who are in an education career help students navigate the financial decisions necessary to attend college. Good math skills are crucial to making sure students have the information they need. Give several examples of when a financial aid counselor would use basic math skills.

Some states have a plan for saving for college called a 529 plan. A **529 plan** is a savings plan for college that requires that payments be made over time for use in the distant future. The funds from these plans can be used to pay for colleges all over the country. They are not meant for a specific college. One drawback of money placed in a 529 plan is that it can only be used for educational purposes. For instance, these funds cannot be used to purchase a car after you graduate.

Financial $marts

As you are preparing for education after high school, you will need to include funding for your education as part of your financial plan. There are many different ways to fund college or other types of training needed to pursue a career. One funding source is a work-study program. These programs are available on some campuses and enable students to work part-time while going to school. Work-study programs are often funded by the government. Check with your counselor for other sources of funding.

You may need to take out a student loan if these alternatives do not cover all of your college tuition costs. Use the following formula to find your remaining tuition costs after your tuition assistance options have been exhausted:

student loan balance = total cost − total tuition assistance

Example 8-4C

See It

Holly is attending a university. The estimated cost of tuition and fees will be $6,750 per year. She has earned a $2,000 per year scholarship and has been accepted into a work-study program that will pay $3,125 per year toward her tuition and fees. Holly plans to use student loans to pay for the remaining tuition and fees. At the end of her four-year program, what will Holly's student loan balance be?

Strategy

Use the formula:

student loan balance = total cost − total tuition assistance

Solution

Step 1: Determine the total costs of tuition and fees for Holly's four-year program. Multiply the annual cost by four.

total cost = annual cost × number of years

total cost = $6,750 per year × 4 years

total cost = $27,000

Step 2: Determine the combined annual amount of tuition assistance Holly will receive. Add the amounts of the annual scholarship and value of the work-study program.

annual tuition assistance = annual scholarship + annual work-study value

annual tuition assistance = $2,000 + $3,125

annual tuition assistance = $5,125

Step 3: Determine the four-year value of the tuition assistance. Multiply the annual tuition assistance by four.

total tuition assistance = annual tuition assistance × number of years

total tuition assistance = $5,125 per year × 4 years

total tuition assistance = $20,500

Step 4: Determine the student loan balance. Subtract the total tuition assistance from the total four-year cost.

student loan balance = total cost – total tuition assistance

student loan balance = $27,000 – $20,500

student loan balance = $6,500

Check It

Jose is attending a technical college to obtain a two-year certificate. The annual costs of tuition and fees are $5,435. Jose has obtained an annual scholarship of $1,750 and annual grants in the amount of $2,300. The remainder of Jose's tuition and fees will be paid for using student loans. At the end of the two-year program, what will Jose's student loan balance be?

Answer:
$2,770

Checkpoint 8.4

1. Aasaf plans to attend the local community college. His first year's tuition and fees are an estimated $2,245. Based on his family's income, Aasaf and his family are responsible for 35% of the tuition and fees. The remaining balance can be paid for using student loans. How much in student loans is Aasaf eligible for?

2. Carmen is attending a vocational school. Her tuition and fees for one year are $4,318. Based on her family's income, Carmen and her family are responsible for 30% of the tuition and fees. The remaining balance can be paid for using a mixture of student loans and grants. How much tuition assistance is Carmen eligible for?

Answer:
1. $1,459.25
2. $3,022.60

3. Darya recently graduated from college and has a total student loan amount of $20,498. Her monthly payments will be $204.98, and she will make those payments for ten years. How much interest will Darya pay on her student loans when they are completely paid off?

4. Marcel recently graduated from medical school and has a total student loan amount of $110,475. His monthly payments will be $1,104.75, and he will make those payments for ten years. How much interest will Marcel pay on his student loans when they are completely paid off?

5. Susita is attending an out-of-state university to obtain a four-year degree. The annual costs of tuition and fees are $27,936. Susita has obtained an annual scholarship of $2,500, annual grants in the amount of $12,450, and a work-study program in the amount of $6,550 per year. The remainder of Susita's tuition and fees will be paid for using student loans. At the end of the four-year degree, what will Susita's student loan balance be?

3. $4,099.60
4. $22,095
5. $25,744

Chapter Review

Build Your Vocabulary

As you progress through this course, develop a personal glossary of financial literacy terms and add it to your portfolio. This will help you build your financial literacy vocabulary. Write out a definition for each of the following terms, and add it to your personal glossary.

single-payment loan

principal

term

promissory note

collateral

lien

ordinary interest method

exact interest method

installment loan

level payment plan

amortization table

down payment

amount financed

early repayment

payday loan

title

title loan

pawnshop

foreclosure

bankrupt

bankruptcy

Free Application for Federal Student
   Aid (FAFSA)

grant

scholarship

merit-based scholarship

529 plan

 ## Teamwork

Working in teams, conduct research on the Internet to determine the costs of several different types of loans from different lending institutions. Create a table of the information. Share with the class any conclusions you can draw from the data you collected.

Review Your Math Skills

Practice and build on the math skills that you have learned.

1. Simplify fractions. Example: $\frac{16}{32} = \frac{1}{2}$

A. $\frac{22}{121} =$

B. $\frac{49}{105} =$

C. $\frac{18}{27} =$

D. $\frac{58}{87} =$

2. Convert percentages to decimals by moving the decimal point two places to the left. **Round to the nearest hundredth (0.01) if necessary. Example:** 5.25% → 0.05

A. 201% →

B. 54% →

C. 0.61% →

D. 1.33% →

3. Multiply decimals. **Round to the nearest cent ($0.01) if necessary. Example:** $975 × 0.07 = $68.25

A. $7.20 × 0.05 =

B. $4.26 × 0.02 =

C. $20.80 × 0.04 =

D. $50.10 × 0.10 =

4. Convert fractions to decimals by dividing the numerator by the denominator. **Round to the hundredth place if necessary. Example:**
$$\frac{1}{5} = 1 \div 5 = 0.20$$

A. $\frac{2}{5} =$

B. $\frac{1}{16} =$

C. $\frac{5}{9} =$

D. $\frac{4}{7} =$

5. Add and subtract decimals. **Example:** $945.74 − $85.71 = $860.03

A. $17.21 + $19.10 =

B. $98.90 + $1.10 =

C. $8.16 − $0.66 =

D. $2.35 − $1.75 =

6. Multiply decimals. **Round to the nearest cent ($0.01) if necessary. Example:** $482 × 0.08 = $38.56

A. $14.77 × 3.25 =

B. $1.99 × 0.075 =

C. $2.69 × 0.03 =

D. $3,250 × 0.08 =

7. Divide decimals. **Round to the nearest cent ($0.01) if necessary. Example:** $14.50 ÷ 0.02 = $725

A. $63.24 ÷ 0.03 =

B. $58.06 ÷ 0.05 =

C. $85.34 ÷ 0.17 =

D. $49.21 ÷ 0.07 =

8. Convert fractions to decimals by dividing the numerator by the denominator. **Round to the hundredth place if necessary. Example:**
$$\frac{9}{7} = 9 \div 7 = 1.29$$

A. $\frac{1}{4} =$

B. $\frac{1}{2} =$

C. $\frac{1}{3} =$

D. $\frac{3}{4} =$

2. A. 2.01
   B. 0.54
   C. 0.01
   D. 0.01
3. A. $0.36
   B. $0.09
   C. $0.83
   D. $5.01
4. A. 0.40
   B. 0.06
   C. 0.56
   D. 0.57
5. A. $36.31
   B. $100
   C. $7.50
   D. $0.60
6. A. $48
   B. $0.15
   C. $0.08
   D. $260
7. A. $2,108
   B. $1,161.20
   C. $502
   D. $703
8. A. 0.25
   B. 0.50
   C. 0.33
   D. 0.75

9. A. $23
   B. $97.50
   C. $28.90
   D. $20.90

10. A. $\frac{1}{2}$
    B. $\frac{1}{5}$
    C. $\frac{5}{27}$
    D. $\frac{3}{5}$

9. Divide decimals. Round to the nearest cent ($0.01) if necessary. Example: $20.62 ÷ 0.2 = $103.10

A. $5.75 ÷ 0.25 =

B. $39 ÷ 0.4 =

C. $14.45 ÷ 0.5 =

D. $6.27 ÷ 0.3 =

10. Simplify fractions. Example: $\frac{16}{32} = \frac{1}{2}$

A. $\frac{70}{140} =$

B. $\frac{16}{80} =$

C. $\frac{15}{81} =$

D. $\frac{57}{95} =$

Section 8.1 Loans and Interest

11. Kathleen received a loan from her bank for $4,085 for a period of one year. The interest rate is 4.95%. The original loan amount and the interest must be repaid in full at the end of the year. Determine the amount of interest that Kathleen will pay.

12. Derek borrowed $2,150 using the exact interest method. He will pay an annual interest rate of 5.29% and will repay the loan in 58 days. Calculate the total amount that Derek will pay back when he repays the loan.

Answer:
11. $202.21
12. $2,168.07

Section 8.2 Installment Loans

13. Seth financed a purchase of a used car for $6,750. He has a four-year loan at a 7.125% annual interest rate with monthly payments of $162.03. For his first monthly payment, calculate the amount that was paid in interest and the amount that was applied to the principal balance.

14. Marisol has a loan that she used for vision correction surgery. She originally borrowed $3,680 at an annual interest rate of 8.45% for three years. Marisol's monthly payments are $286.60. With five remaining payments, her principal balance is $568.35, and she wants to pay the balance of the loan. Calculate an estimate of Marisol's early payoff amount.

Answer:
13. interest payment = $40.08
    principal payment = $121.95
14. $572.35

Section 8.3 High-Interest Loans

15. Fatir is considering a payday loan for $245. The payday lender charges 24.5% for a brokerage fee, plus 0.43% in interest charges for a 14-day term loan. How much will Fatir pay back at the end of the 14 days?

16. Neela decided to take her DVD player to a pawnshop because she needed money. The pawnbroker gave her $63, and they agreed to a contract in which Neela would need to return the cash in 30 days and pay a 2.4% interest fee and 22.3% service fee in order to reclaim her DVD player. How much will Neela pay back if she returns in 30 days to reclaim her DVD player?

Answer:
15. $306.08
16. $78.56

Section 8.4 Student Loans

17. Janis is attending graduate school, and her tuition and fees for one year are $9,390. Based on her family's income, Janis and her family are responsible for 60% of the tuition and fees. The remaining balance can be paid for using student loans. How much in student loans per year is Janis eligible for?

18. Mason is attending a community college to obtain a two-year degree. The annual costs of tuition and fees are $3,750. Mason has obtained an annual scholarship of $1,250 and annual grants in the amount of $835. The remainder of Mason's tuition and fees will be paid for using student loans. At the end of the two-year degree, what will Mason's student loan balance be?

Answer:
17. $3,756
18. $3,330

Reinforce Your Understanding

19. When Tom and Eve got married, Eve's grandparents gave them $5,000 toward a down payment for a new house. In order to buy a house in the neighborhood where they would like to live, Tom and Eve need to have a down payment of $17,850. They can afford to save $450 per month. How long will it take them to save enough money for their down payment?

20. Keisha has a checking account balance of $471.19. She wrote a check to Central Department Store for $104.84. What is Keisha's new checking account balance?

Answer:
19. 29 months
20. $366.35

Apply Your Technology Skills

Companion Website
www.g-wlearning.com

Access the G-W Learning companion website for this text at www.g-wlearning.com. Download each data file for this chapter. Follow the instructions to complete financial literacy activities to practice what you have learned in this chapter.

Teaching Tip:
The Apply Your Technology Skills activities offer project-based authentic assessment opportunities.

Data File 8-1—Creating an Amortization Table

Data File 8-2—Calculating Monthly Loan Payments

Data File 8-3—Researching Teen Credit

Data File 8-4—Filling Out a Financial Aid Application

9 Housing

Materials:
Instructor's Resource CD
Student Workbook
G-W Learning companion website
EXAMVIEW® Assessment Suite
Microsoft Excel®–compatible software
Calculator with advanced-math functions

Moving out on your own is an important milestone for most people. There are many important considerations to keep in mind when deciding to rent or own. Knowing the effect housing costs will have on your financial plan will help you make better housing decisions.

Section 9.1 **Renting**

Section 9.2 **Purchasing a Home**

Section 9.3 **Mortgage Payments**

College and Career Readiness

Reading Prep. In preparation for reading this chapter, perform preliminary research on how the idea of shelter has evolved. Consider the various types of places in which people live today when compared to how people lived 100 years ago.

"Since I am going to be in college next year, I am going to live in the dorms. Once I get started with a steady job, I may get a small apartment with my friends and split the rent and utilities." ~ Ashlee H.

Money Matters
Homeownership

- Owning a home has been called *The American Dream.*

- Data from the US Census Bureau shows that you are more likely to become a homeowner as you get older. Only 22.8% of individuals under 25 own their home.

- The rate of homeownership steadily increases up until the age of 75, when homeownership begins to decline.

- When buying a house, the house payment should not be more than 28% of your income.

- Homeowners must buy homeowners insurance to maintain a mortgage.

- Yearly property taxes must be paid on a home and land.

- To buy a home, you will likely need at least 20% as a down payment on the purchase price.

- As a homeowner, it is a good idea to set aside a percentage of your income each year for home maintenance.

- The economic downturn that began in 2008 had a negative impact on some homeowners. Many people were forced into foreclosure.

- In 2012, mortgage interest rates were at a 50-year low.

Section 9.1 Renting

Objectives
- **Explain the purpose of a lease agreement.**
- **Describe a security deposit.**
- **Define renters insurance.**

Build Your Math Skills

Review these math skills to prepare for the lesson that follows.

1. Add decimals. Example: $1,659.64 + $803.08 = $2,462.72

A. $518.09 + $498.37 =

B. $780.17 + $207.65 =

C. $57.91 + $530.17 =

D. $107.18 + $1,186.39 =

2. Subtract decimals. Example: $88.45 − $8.19 = $80.26

A. $506.78 − $50.68 =

B. $84.19 − $71.83 =

C. $804.76 − $194.63 =

D. $1,145.16 − $914.58 =

3. Divide decimals. Round to the nearest cent ($0.01) if necessary. Example: $587.41 ÷ 3 = $195.80

A. $1,150.25 ÷ 2 =

B. $945.23 ÷ 3 =

C. $540.17 ÷ 3 =

D. $950.37 ÷ 6 =

Leases

Right now, you are likely living in a house or apartment that is being provided for you by a parent or guardian. When it comes time to be out on your own, you will most likely rent a place to live. You might do this by yourself or with roommates. The term used to describe the legal agreement when renting property is a *lease*.

Renting describes any agreement to pay for the use of someone else's property. Leasing obligates the person leasing the property to a specific period of time and inflexible price, in exchange for use of the property. For example, you can rent a building for a day to hold an event. You can also rent a building for a year to house a business.

A *lease agreement* is a contract used to lease property for a prolonged period of time. The *term* of the lease is the length of time the agreement will be in effect. A typical lease on a house or apartment is one year, but the term may be shorter or longer. Payments from the lessee to the lessor are usually made monthly on a specified date each month.

The *lessor* is the owner of the property. The *lessee* is the person renting the property under the lease. A *property owner* is the person or entity managing the

Terms
- *lease agreement*
- *lessor*
- *lessee*
- *tenant*
- *security deposit*
- *renters insurance*
- *actual cash value policy*
- *replacement cost policy*
- *claim*
- *premium*
- *deductible*

Answer:
1. A. $1,016.46
   B. $987.82
   C. $588.08
   D. $1,293.57
2. A. $456.10
   B. $12.36
   C. $610.13
   D. $230.58
3. A. $575.13
   B. $315.08
   C. $180.06
   D. $158.40

fyi

When it comes to housing, the verbs *rent* and *lease* are often used interchangeably.

property being rented. A *tenant* is the occupant of the property being rented. In most cases, the tenant and lessee are the same.

A lease agreement can be a fairly long and complex document, but it is important to read and understand the entire agreement. Don't accept anyone's word that the lease is *standard*. You should know exactly what you are agreeing to. For example, even though a lease period may be closing at the end of May, the lease may require 30 days notice that you intend to move out when your lease is complete. This means that you may have to pay an extra month's rent for that 30-days' notice whether you live there or not.

A lease agreement is a legally binding contract between a lessor and a lessee and usually includes some common elements:

- description of the property being leased

- amount being paid to lease the property

- length of time the lessee will be renting the property

- renewal options

The lease will also specify what happens at the end of the lease term. In some leases, the tenant may be allowed to stay and pay rent on a month-to-month basis. *Paying month to month* means the tenant may decide each month whether to continue to extend the rental of the property. Other leases may require that a new lease agreement be signed to continue renting the property.

A lease may be signed by multiple people who share the rented house or apartment. This is very common with college students and single people. It is usually more economical for two or more people to share a place than for each person to rent a separate place. To determine each person's share of rent, the following formula can be used:

share of rent = total monthly rent ÷ number of people

Example 9-1A

See It

Teaching Tip:
Remind students of the importance of reading and understanding any lease that they sign. If they have a roommate, make sure that they both understand the terms of the lease, since both will be responsible for upholding the terms.

Frank and Emmett are college students who agreed to share an apartment. They decided to rent a two-bedroom apartment with a monthly rent of $949. If they split the cost evenly, what is each person's share of the monthly rent?

Strategy

Use the formula:

share of rent = total monthly rent ÷ number of people

Solution

Step 1: Identify the total monthly rent and the number of people sharing the rent.

total monthly rent = $949

number of people = 2

Step 2: Determine each person's share of the rent. Divide the total monthly rent by the number of people.

share of rent = total monthly rent ÷ number of people

share of rent = $949 ÷ 2

share of rent = $474.50

Check It

Monique and Donna are college students who agreed to share an apartment in order to help reduce their costs of living. They decided to rent a two-bedroom apartment with a monthly rent of $865. If they split the cost evenly, what is each person's share of the monthly rent?

Teaching Tip:
The complete solutions to the Check It problems can be found on the Instructor's Resource CD.

Answer:
$432.50

Deposits

A *security deposit* is a payment held by the lessor to cover the costs of potential damage to the property during the term of the lease. Tenants with pets may also be required to pay a *pet deposit* in addition to the security deposit. At the end of the lease, the lessee gets the deposit back if everything is in good condition when he or she moves out. However, if a tenant leaves the property dirty, for example, the property owner may deduct the cost of cleaning from the tenant's deposit. A tenant may also lose all or part of the security deposit if he or she damaged the property.

A lessor may also require that the tenant pay the first and last month's rent before moving in. This is additional security for the lessor. Some lessors have problems with lessees not paying the last month's rent. If you pay first and last month's rent when you move in, you will not pay rent the last month you occupy the property.

When calculating the costs of moving into rental property, be sure to consider deposits and first and last month's rent. The following formula can be used to calculate total move-in costs:

move-in costs = security deposit + pet deposit + first month's rent + last month's rent

Teaching Tip:
Direct students to brainstorm things that might make them lose a security deposit on an apartment. How can they ensure they get their security deposit back?

fyi

A lease may specify an increase in monthly rent after lease termination for continuing month-to-month occupancy. This is often done to encourage the renter to sign a new lease agreement.

Example 9-1B

See It

Margaret and Edgar Henry are moving into a new apartment. There is a security deposit of $350 and a pet deposit of $200. The monthly rent is $750. According to their lease, they must pay all deposits and the first and last month's rent up front. What are the Henry family's total move-in costs?

Strategy

Use the formula:

move-in costs = security deposit + pet deposit + first month's rent + last month's rent

Solution

Step 1: Identify each charge for the apartment move-in.

security deposit = $350

pet deposit = $200

first month's rent = $750

last month's rent = $750

Step 2: Determine the sum of all deposits and rent payments. Add the four charges together.

move-in costs = security deposit + pet deposit + first month's rent + last month's rent

move-in costs = $350 + $200 + $750 + $750

move-in costs = $2,050

Check It

Kabira got a new job in a different part of town and is moving into a new apartment with a monthly rent of $625. According to her lease, there is a security deposit of $275. She must pay her first and last month's rent up front. What are Kabira's total move-in costs?

Renters Insurance

When you rent a place to live, you place many, if not all, of your belongings in that house or apartment. If the property is robbed or if there is a fire or other disaster, the owner's insurance will not replace your belongings. That is why it is important to consider renters insurance to protect your personal property when renting a place to live. *Renters insurance* is a type of insurance tenants can purchase, which provides financial protection should the tenant's personal property be damaged or stolen.

Some people do not think they have enough items of value to insure. However, you probably have more than you think. When you consider what it would cost to replace your clothes, electronics, appliances, jewelry, and furniture, it probably is enough to make renters insurance a good idea.

There are two types of renters insurance policies: actual cash value and replacement cost. An *actual cash value policy* pays what the property was worth at the time it was damaged or stolen. For example, if you paid $800 for a laptop computer, the cash value today may only be $200. Were the laptop damaged or stolen, the actual cash value policy would pay $200.

A ***replacement cost policy*** will pay what it actually costs to replace the item. For example, the laptop that originally cost $800 would be replaced with an equivalent product. This would happen even if the cost today is more or less than when originally purchased. A replacement cost insurance policy will cost more than a policy that pays actual cash value. However, if you have property damaged or stolen, the replacement cost policy will make it easier for you to replace all that you lost.

When you experience a loss that is covered by insurance, you file a ***claim*** to the insurance company, which details your losses. The money paid to cover an insured loss is called a *settlement.*

The amount paid to purchase insurance is called a ***premium.*** People often choose to pay for their insurance by the month or quarter rather than in a lump sum one time per year. Insurance companies often charge a *partial payment fee* when the premium is paid in installments. To calculate a monthly insurance payment, including a partial payment fee, use the following formula:

monthly payment = monthly premium + partial payment fee

Example 9-1C

See It

Maria lives in an apartment. She pays a $310 yearly premium for a renters insurance replacement cost policy. If Maria chooses to pay monthly, she will also have to pay an additional partial payment fee of $2.50 per month. What will be Maria's monthly payments for renters insurance?

Strategy

Use the formula:

monthly payment = monthly premium + partial payment fee

Solution

Step 1: Determine the monthly premium of Maria's renters insurance policy. Divide the annual premium by 12. Round to the nearest cent ($0.01) if necessary.

monthly premium = annual premium ÷ 12

monthly premium = $310 ÷ 12

monthly premium = $25.83

Step 2: Determine the monthly payment for Maria's renters insurance. Add the monthly premium and the partial payment fee.

monthly payment = monthly premium + partial payment fee

monthly payment = $25.83 + $2.50

monthly payment = $28.33

Check It

Glenn rents a house from his aunt. He pays a $395 yearly premium for a renters insurance replacement cost policy. If he chooses to pay monthly, his insurance company will charge him an additional partial payment fee of $1.75 per month. What will be Glenn's monthly payments for renters insurance?

Whether you have an actual cash value policy or a replacement cost policy, you are required to pay for part of any loss. The ***deductible*** is the part of the loss for which you are responsible. For example, your policy may have a $250 deductible. If your $800 laptop is stolen and you have a replacement cost policy, the deductible is *deducted* from the payment made to you by the insurance company. To determine the amount of money you will receive from a covered claim, use the following formula:

amount of payment = amount of claim – deductible

Example 9-1D

See It

Javier's laptop was stolen last week. Fortunately, he has a replacement cost insurance policy that covers the loss of the laptop. It will cost $800 to replace Javier's laptop, and his insurance policy includes a $250 deductible. Calculate the payment that Javier will receive from his insurance company.

Strategy

Use the formula:

amount of payment = amount of claim – deductible

Solution

Step 1: Identify the amount of the claim and the deductible.

amount of claim = $800

deductible = $250

Step 2: Determine the insurance company payment. Subtract the deductible from the amount of the claim.

amount of payment = amount of claim – deductible

amount of payment = $800 – $250

amount of payment = $550

Check It

Kelli's diamond ring was stolen. Fortunately, she has a replacement cost insurance policy that covers her loss. It will cost Kelli $975 to replace her ring, and her insurance policy includes a $500 deductible. Calculate the payment that Kelli will receive from her insurance company.

Checkpoint 9.1

Teaching Tip:
Checkpoint questions offer opportunities for formative assessment.

1. Viola, Kerry, and Ida agreed to share an apartment in order to reduce their living expenses. They found a three-bedroom apartment with a monthly rent of $1,435. If they divide the rent evenly, what is each person's share of the rent? Round your answer to the nearest cent ($0.01) if necessary.

2. Nadir and Jennifer Salazar are moving into a new apartment with a monthly rent of $950. They must pay a security deposit of $400 and a pet deposit of $250. According to their lease, they must pay the first and last month's rent up front. What will be the move-in costs for the Salazar's new apartment?

3. Tola is moving into a rental house. The owner wants Tola to pay a security deposit of $500 as well as the first and last month's rent. Tola's monthly rent is $865. What will be Tola's move-in costs for the rental house?

4. Keith lives in a rented condo and wants to purchase renters insurance with a premium of $285 per year. If he pays monthly, there will be an additional partial payment fee of $1.50. What will be Keith's monthly insurance bill? Round your answer to the nearest cent ($0.01) if necessary.

5. Shelley's apartment was recently burglarized. Her television and DVD player were stolen. Fortunately, Shelley has replacement cost renters insurance with a $250 deductible. The cost to replace her television and DVD player will be $695. Calculate the payment that Shelley will receive from her insurance company.

Answer:
1. $478.33
2. $2,550
3. $2,230
4. $25.25
5. $445

Source: Shutterstock (Goodluz)

In order to rent an apartment, you must often sign a lease agreement.

Section 9.2 Purchasing a Home

Terms

- *mortgage*
- *appraisal*
- *closing costs*
- *title insurance*
- *escrow account*
- *homeowners insurance*
- *property tax*
- *assessed value*
- *utilities*
- *home warranty*

Objectives

- **Explain the role a mortgage loan plays in the purchase of a home.**
- **Calculate a down payment amount.**
- **Identify closing costs associated with purchasing a home.**
- **Describe how an escrow account works.**
- **Explain how expenses associated with homeownership add to monthly housing costs.**

Build Your Math Skills

Review these math skills to prepare for the lesson that follows.

1. Convert percentages to decimals by moving the decimal two places to the left. Example: 1.15% → 0.0115

A. 1.45% →

B. 2.8% →

C. 0.56% →

D. 0.78% →

2. Multiply decimals. Round to the nearest cent ($0.01) if necessary. Example: $1,985 × 0.065 = $129.03

A. $975 × 0.025 =

B. $1,485 × 0.08 =

C. $1,705 × 0.038 =

D. $55,718 × 0.011 =

3. Add decimals. Example: $95.74 + $107.14 = $202.88

A. $409.22 + $75.93 =

B. $840.27 + $197.89 =

C. $655.70 + $109.45 =

D. $1,074.06 + $450.96 =

Answer:
1. A. 0.0145
   B. 0.028
   C. 0.0056
   D. 0.0078
2. A. $24.38
   B. $118.80
   C. $64.79
   D. $612.90
3. A. $485.15
   B. $1,038.16
   C. $765.15
   D. $1,525.02

Mortgages

The purchase of a home is the largest financial transaction many people will ever make. A person's home is usually his or her single most valuable asset.

Most homes are not paid for with cash. Instead, people take out a mortgage. A **mortgage** is a contract between a home buyer and a lender in which the property being purchased is held as collateral. A mortgage loan is similar to any other installment loan. The term of a mortgage is typically 15, 20, or 30 years because of the large amount of money borrowed to purchase a home. The home itself serves as collateral for the loan.

In order to get a loan, the bank will require an appraisal. An **appraisal** is a professional assessment of the value of the home. An appraisal is necessary to ensure that the property is sufficient collateral for the loan.

There is a lot of paperwork involved in transferring ownership from one owner to the next. People often hire an attorney to help them with this and many other details.

fyi

Housing costs, including mortgage, taxes, insurance, and any homeowners association fees or dues, should not exceed 28% of your gross monthly income.

Career Discovery
Manufacturing Careers and
Math Skills

Careers in the manufacturing cluster involve skills in planning, managing, and making raw materials into quality products. Careers in this area involve production, process development, equipment maintenance and installation, and inventory control. They also include quality, health, safety, and environmental assurance.

Strong math skills are key qualities for manufacturing workers. One skill that is necessary for this career is the ability to use decimals, fractions, and metric conversions. Describe a situation in which someone pursuing a career in this field would need to be able to use basic math skills.

For many years, home values steadily increased. However, beginning in 2008, the value of many houses fell. The value of some fell to a level where the amount owed on the mortgage was greater than the home was worth. This situation is often referred to as being *under water*.

Down Payment

As with any installment loan, a percentage of the total cost of the home may be required as a down payment. Today, zero down payment loans are available to military veterans and very few others. The Federal Housing Administration (FHA) has a guaranteed loan program for first-time home buyers where only a 3.5% down payment is required. A standard mortgage may require 20% down. Those who do secure mortgage loans with less than 20% down may be required to pay private mortgage insurance. *Private mortgage insurance (PMI)* is insurance paid by the borrower to insure the lender against the risk of default.

Teaching Tip:
Remind students that a mortgage is just a part of the expense of owning a home. Homeowners insurance, utilities, repairs, and other maintenance should also be included when calculating monthly costs.

Example 9-2A

See It

Ohanna wants to purchase a new house for $185,000. Her bank requires a 20% down payment. How much will Ohanna's down payment be for this house? How much will Ohanna need to finance with her mortgage?

Strategy

Use the formula:

amount of mortgage = purchase price – down payment

Solution

Step 1: Convert 20% to a decimal by moving the decimal two places to the left.

20% → 0.20

Step 2: Multiply the purchase price by the down payment rate.

down payment = purchase price × down payment rate

down payment = $185,000 × 0.20

down payment = $37,000

Step 3: Determine the amount Ohanna will finance. Subtract the down payment from the purchase price.

amount of mortgage = purchase price − down payment

amount of mortgage = $185,000 − $37,000

amount of mortgage = $148,000

Check It

Darin wants to purchase a house as an investment property. He wants to make a down payment of 30% in order to reduce the mortgage costs. If the investment property is purchased for $115,500, what is Darin's down payment? How much will Darin need to finance with a mortgage?

Closing Costs

When you purchase a home, closing costs are part of the transaction. *Closing costs* are special fees that cover a variety of things, including:

- attorney's fees;

- document filing fees;

- loan application fees;

- appraisal fees;

- title insurance; and

- other fees.

A *title* is a legal document that proves who owns a particular piece of property. When real estate is purchased, the title is transferred from the old owner to the new owner. As mentioned earlier, most real estate purchases require a mortgage. Because this is the case, the mortgage lender needs to be certain that the person selling the property actually has the right to do so. Lenders require that buyers purchase title insurance for just this reason. *Title insurance* protects the lender in case any questions arise regarding who has title, or ownership, of a piece of real estate.

To calculate closing costs, use the following formula:

total closing costs = legal fees + document legal fees + loan application fees + appraisal fees + inspection fee + title insurance

Example 9-2B

See It

Emi and Omar Renaldi are buying a new house. Their closing costs are itemized in the following table provided by the mortgage broker. What are the Renaldis' total closing costs?

Type of Fee	Amount
Legal	$750.00
Document filing	315.50
Loan application	939.45
Appraisal	515.50
Inspection	550.00
Title insurance	617.25

Strategy

Use the formula:

total closing costs = legal fees + document legal fees + loan application fees + appraisal fees + inspection fee + title insurance

Solution

Step 1: Identify each closing cost from the table.

Step 2: Calculate the sum of all of the closing costs. Add each closing cost together.

total closing costs = legal fees + document legal fees + loan application fees + appraisal fees + inspection fee + title insurance

total closing costs = $750 + $315.50 + $939.45 + $515.50 + $550 + $617.25

total closing costs = $3,687.70

Check It

Alejandro and Alma Sanchez are buying a new house. Their closing costs are itemized in the following table. What are the Sanchez family's total closing costs?

Type of Fee	Amount
Legal	$ 855.00
Document filing	323.40
Loan application	1,015.67
Appraisal	495.00
Inspection	395.00
Title insurance	705.46

Answer:
$3,789.53

Escrow

Property tax is a tax levied against the value of personal property. If the homeowner does not pay property taxes, the government agency that is owed the tax may seize the property.

If homeowners insurance premiums are not paid, the insurance will be cancelled or suspended. Should the house be damaged while insurance is not in force, the lender may end up losing money.

If property taxes or homeowners insurance premiums are not paid, the lender providing the mortgage is at risk. Therefore, the bank or mortgage company will usually require that the borrower have an escrow account. An **escrow account** is an account that adds an amount of money to the mortgage payment to cover taxes and insurance. An escrow account is managed by a third party called an *escrow agent*.

The money is held in the escrow account until tax and insurance bills are due. The escrow agent then pays the bills on the owner's behalf from the money that has been deposited into the escrow account. Because taxes and insurance rates change, the lender will reevaluate the amount of the escrow payment annually to adjust for changes. The following formula can be used to determine monthly escrow payments:

monthly escrow payments = total annual costs ÷ 12

fyi

In addition to protecting the lender, an escrow account can help the borrower by automatically budgeting for property taxes and homeowners insurance.

Example 9-2C

See It

Jeffrey and Pam Wong are purchasing a new home. Their annual property taxes are estimated to be $3,148.38, and their homeowners insurance policy has an annual cost of $1,418. They must also purchase earthquake insurance, since they live in an active earthquake zone, at an additional cost of $1,974 per year. How much will be put into their escrow account each month in order to cover these costs?

Strategy

Use the formula:

monthly escrow payments = total annual costs ÷ 12

Solution

Step 1: Determine the sum of the annual costs. Add the annual property taxes, cost of homeowners insurance, and earthquake insurance.

total annual costs = property taxes + homeowners insurance + earthquake insurance

total annual costs = $3,148.38 + $1,418 + $1,974

total annual costs = $6,540.38

Step 2: Determine the monthly escrow payments. Divide the total annual costs by 12 months. Round to the nearest cent ($0.01) if necessary.

monthly escrow payments = total annual costs ÷ 12

monthly escrow payments = $6,540.38 ÷ 12

monthly escrow payments = $545.03

Check It

Morgan and Elizabeth Martinez are purchasing a new home. Their estimated annual property taxes will be $2,187.47, and their homeowners insurance policy will cost $1,568.38 per year. Their new home requires flood insurance, which is an additional $653.95 per year. How much will be put into their escrow account each month in order to cover these costs?

Answer:
$367.48

Homeowners Insurance

Homeowners insurance is similar to renters insurance. *Homeowners insurance* includes coverage for the structure of the house as well as its contents. Homeowners insurance is not optional if you have a mortgage. This is because the bank loaning the money wants to ensure that their collateral is protected.

Homeowners insurance can include options to cover the property of others at your home. For example, if your friend's car is vandalized while on your property, your homeowners insurance may cover that damage. Also, you can get coverage from when your personal property is not at your home. For example, if you have belongings stolen or damaged while on vacation, your insurance may cover the loss.

Teaching Tip:
Have students conduct research on what role a claims adjuster plays after a claim is made.

Property Taxes

Homeowners are subject to property tax. Remember that property tax is a tax levied against the value of personal property. Property tax is usually an annual tax that is used to fund local activities, such as public schooling. One property may be within several different taxing jurisdictions, such as city, state, library, and school districts.

fyi

The term *percentage* means one part per 100, and is shown using the % symbol. The term *millage* means one part per 1,000, and is shown using the ‰ symbol.

The amount of property tax paid is determined by the *assessed value* of your home. A home's **assessed value** is its worth as determined by a tax assessor. The property tax rate may be expressed as a decimal that is multiplied by the assessed value as shown in the following formula:

property tax = assessed value × tax rate

Often, however, the tax rate is expressed as a tax per $100 or $1,000 of value. For example, a tax rate might be $1.91 per $100, meaning that for each $100 in assessed value, you must pay $1.91 in tax. To calculate the amount of property tax, multiply the property's assessed value by the tax rate (as a decimal).

Example 9-2D

See It

Marcus and Tamika Ingram own a home in Rocketville. A portion of their tax statement is shown in the table that follows. According to their statement, they pay property taxes to eight different taxing authorities, or taxing jurisdictions. Taxable values differ depending on the jurisdiction and property tax exemptions. Use the table to calculate the portion of the property tax that will be paid to the Independent School District.

Taxing Jurisdiction	Taxable Value	Tax Rate (%)
Independent School District	$ 88,793	1.1567
Eastman County	103,793	0.39117
County Flood Control District	103,793	0.02809
Port Authority	103,793	0.01856
County Hospital District	103,793	0.19216
County Dept. of Education	103,793	0.006581
Community College System	116,767	0.097222
City of Rocketville	103,793	0.63875

Strategy

Use the formula:

property tax = assessed value × tax rate

Solution

Step 1: For the Independent School District, identify the assessed value and the tax rate as a percentage.

assessed value = $88,793

tax rate = 1.1567%

Step 2: Convert the tax rate from a percentage to a decimal by moving the decimal point two places to the left.

1.1567% → 0.011567

Step 3: Determine the amount of property tax. Multiply the assessed value by the tax rate. Round to the nearest cent ($0.01) if necessary.

property tax = assessed value × tax rate

property tax = $88,793 × 0.011567

property tax = $1,027.07

Check It

Use the same table to calculate the portion of the property tax that will be paid to the city of Rocketville.

Answer:
$662.98

Example 9-2E

See It

Oscar and Angelica Molina own a home in Steeltown. A portion of their tax statement is shown in the table that follows. According to their statement, they pay property taxes to four different taxing jurisdictions. Use the table to calculate the portion of the property tax that will be paid to the school district.

Taxing Jurisdiction	Assessed Value	Tax Rate (‰)
Steeltown School District	$162,000	13.92
Valleyview County	162,000	4.69
County Community College District	162,000	9.17
City of Steeltown	162,000	10.8

Teaching Tip:
Point out that a taxing jurisdiction can impose sales taxes on items and services as well as on real estate. Gas tax rates differ from taxing jurisdiction to taxing jurisdiction, for example.

Strategy

Use the formula:

$$\text{property tax} = \text{assessed value} \times \text{tax rate}$$

Solution

Step 1: For Steeltown School District, identify the assessed value and the tax rate (as a millage).

assessed value = $162,000

tax rate = 13.92‰

Step 2: Convert the tax rate from a millage to a decimal by moving the decimal point *three* places to the left.

13.92‰ → 0.01392

Teaching Tip:
Remind students that *millage* means per 1,000.

Step 3: Determine the amount of property tax. Multiply the assessed value by the tax rate. Round to the nearest cent ($0.01) if necessary.

property tax = assessed value × tax rate

property tax = $162,000 × 0.01392

property tax = $2,250.04

Check It

Answer:
$759.78

Use the same table to calculate the portion of the property tax that will be paid to Valleyview County.

Expenses

A mortgage, taxes, and insurance are just a portion of your monthly expenses as a homeowner. Utilities and maintenance must be accounted for in any budget or financial plan.

Utilities

Teaching Tip:
Explain to students that utilities vary in different regions of the country. In addition, what may be commonly available in an urban area, such as high speed Internet or city water service, may not be available in rural areas.

Utilities are a major expense related to housing. *Utilities* are basic services such as telephone service, cable and Internet services, electricity, natural gas, and water for a home.

While you cannot control the rates the various utility companies charge, you can compare companies and plans to see which is most economical for you and your family. When purchasing appliances, you should also compare their efficiency ratings. The more efficient an appliance, the less you will have to pay in utility costs to run the appliance.

Electric service is the most common utility bill. Electricity is paid based on usage, measured in a unit of energy called a *kilowatt hour (kWh)*. It is not necessary that you understand what a kilowatt hour is, but you should understand how much you pay for a kilowatt hour of electricity. The cost per kilowatt hour of electricity varies depending on where you live. To calculate your electricity usage, use the following formula:

electricity usage = current meter reading – previous meter reading

The company that sells you electricity places a meter on the power running to your house. The meter displays the amount of kilowatt hours of electricity used. The company reads the meter monthly and charges you for the amount of power used. To calculate the cost of electricity, use the following formula:

cost of electricity = electricity usage × cost per kilowatt hour + fees

Example 9-2F

See It

Shalonda received her electric bill. The previous electric meter reading was 35,712, and the current meter reading is 39,121. How many kilowatt hours of electricity did Shalonda use for this billing period?

Strategy

Use the formula:

electricity usage = current meter reading – previous meter reading

Solution

Step 1: Identify the current meter reading and the previous meter reading.

current meter reading = 39,121

previous meter reading = 35,712

Step 2: Determine the number of kilowatt hours used. Subtract the previous meter reading from the current meter reading.

electricity usage = current meter reading – previous meter reading

electricity usage = 39,121 – 35,712

electricity usage = 3,409 kilowatt hours

Check It

Jose received his electric bill. The previous electric meter reading was 38,471, and the current meter reading is 41,940. How many kilowatt hours of electricity did Jose and his family use for this billing period?

Answer:
3,469 kilowatt hours

Example 9-2G

See It

According to her electricity bill, Aponi used 2,846 kilowatt hours last month. Her electric company charges $0.109 per kilowatt hour plus a state-mandated fee of $6.95 for maintaining the power lines. What is the amount of Aponi's electricity bill?

Strategy

Use the formula:

cost of electricity = electricity usage × cost per kilowatt hour + fees

Solution

Step 1: Determine the cost of the electricity that Aponi used. Multiply the electricity usage by the cost per kilowatt hour. Round to the nearest cent ($0.01) if necessary.

cost of electricity = electricity usage × cost per kilowatt hour

cost of electricity = 2,846 kilowatt hours × $0.109

cost of electricity = $310.21

Step 2: Determine the amount of the bill. Add the cost of the electricity and the additional fees.

amount of bill = cost of electricity + maintenance fee

amount of bill = $310.21 + $6.95

amount of bill = $317.16

Check It

Dexter's recent electricity bill shows that he used 2,429 kilowatt hours of electricity last month. His electric company charges $0.084 per kilowatt hour, plus a state tax of $4.38. What is the total amount of Dexter's electricity bill?

Answer:
$208.42

In many homes, natural gas is used to heat rooms, cooktops, and ovens. Similar to electricity, natural gas is measured with a meter and billed for actual use. Natural gas may be measured in units called *therms, CCFs,* or *MCFs.* Natural gas bills are often made up of several different kinds of charges.

If your home is in a city or town, you may also get your water from the city or some other entity. A water bill is typically based on how much you use. Because water bills often come from the city, the same bill may include charges for garbage collection or sewer usage.

To calculate the cost for total monthly utility expenses, use the following formula.

monthly utility expense = electricity + natural gas + telephone + Internet + television + water

Example 9-2H

See It

Melea's utility bills are summarized in the table that follows. What is Melea's total monthly utilities expense?

Utility Bill	Amount
Electricity	$271.43
Natural gas	38.49
Telephone/Internet	88.37
Cable television	114.35
Water	94.82

Strategy

Use the formula:

monthly utility expense = electricity + natural gas + telephone + Internet + television + water

Teaching Tip:
Ask students to offer ways to conserve energy and thus reduce utility bills.

Solution

Step 1: Calculate the sum of the set of utility bills. Add the amount of each bill together.

monthly utility expense = $271.43 + $38.49 + $88.37 + $114.35 + $94.82

monthly utility expense = $607.46

Check It

Russell's utility bills are summarized in the table that follows. What is Russell's total monthly utilities expense?

Utility Bill	Amount
Electricity	$173.29
Natural gas	44.83
Telephone/Internet	65.17
Cell phone	112.38
Cable television	85.33
Water	60.36

Answer:
$541.36

Maintenance

When you rent a place to live, any needed repairs are typically the responsibility of the property owner. When you own a home, repairs are your responsibility. Some repairs are fairly simple, like interior painting and patching. But many home repairs are complex and costly. The units that provide heat and air conditioning must be repaired by trained professionals. Carpeting and other flooring also wears and will eventually need replacing.

The roof of a home may have a life of 14 to 50 years or more, depending on the type of roof. Weather, trees, sun, or even humidity may shorten the life of the roof. Hail storms are a common source of roof damage in many parts of the country. Homeowners insurance covers damage from natural events such as windstorms, hail, and lightning. However, the homeowner is still responsible for replacement of a roof when age causes the need for a replacement.

Financial $marts

An adjustable rate mortgage, known as an ARM, is a loan in which the interest changes during the life of the loan. The interest rate may go down, in which case your payment will decrease. However, the interest could increase, making your monthly payment higher. ARMs can be risky if your payment goes up and you do not have the additional money to pay the increased amount each month. If you are offered this type of loan, make sure your budget is flexible and you can afford monthly payments that may change. Otherwise, you could get in a negative financial situation.

Plumbing is one of the most common systems needing repairs. Faucets and toilets will develop problems over time. Freezing temperatures can sometimes cause more serious plumbing issues.

One way homeowners attempt to lessen the risk of an expensive home repair is by purchasing a home warranty. A ***home warranty*** is a service contract that covers the repair and replacement costs of appliances and systems that commonly need repair. A home warranty typically covers heating and air conditioning systems, dishwashers, water heaters, garbage disposals, electrical systems, plumbing, and some other major appliances beyond manufacturers' warranties. The home warranty covers the major portion of needed repairs or replacement. The homeowner pays a service fee that is typically less than $100 per repair.

On existing homes, a home warranty can be purchased from a variety of companies that offer home warranty policies. Keep in mind that on a new home, the systems and appliances are generally covered by manufacturers' warranties. However, for new homes, the builder often provides an additional warranty for a period of time.

Teaching Tip:
Checkpoint questions offer opportunities for formative assessment.

Answer:
1. down payment = $29,841.30
   amount of mortgage = $135,943.70
2. down payment = $42,470
   amount of mortgage = $169,880

Checkpoint 9.2

1. Samir wants to purchase a house that has a selling price of $165,785. His bank requires a down payment of 18%. Calculate Samir's down payment and the amount that Samir will finance with his mortgage.

2. Huan and Mary Li want to purchase a house that has a selling price of $212,350. Their bank requires a down payment of 20%. Calculate the Li family's down payment and the amount that they will finance with their mortgage.

3. Grant and Deborah Collins are buying a new house. Their closing costs are itemized by their lender in the list that follows. What are the Collins' total closing costs?

Type of Fee	Amount
Legal	$659.00
Document filing	228.95
Loan application	894.76
Appraisal	445.00
Inspection	425.00
Title insurance	810.37

4. Danek and Moira McPherson own a home. A portion of their tax statement is shown in the table that follows. According to their statement, they pay property taxes to five different taxing jurisdictions. Use the table to calculate the portion of the property taxes for each taxing jurisdiction.

Taxing Jurisdiction	Assessed Value	Tax Rate (‰)
Norman Public Schools	$25,780	67.02
Cleveland County	25,780	16.96
Multi-County Library Fund	25,780	6.11
Moore-Norman Vo-Tech Schools	25,780	14.38
City of Norman	25,780	9.47

5. According to his recent electricity bill, Giovanni's electricity meter had a previous reading of 68,738 kilowatt hours and a current reading of 70,043 kilowatt hours. If his electric company charges $0.077 per kilowatt hour, what is the amount of Giovanni's electricity bill?

3. $3,463.08
4. Norman Public Schools = $1,727.78
   Cleveland County = $437.23
   Multi-County Library Fund = $157.52
   Moore-Norman Vo-Tech Schools = $370.72
   City of Norman = $244.14
5. $100.49

Section 9.3 Mortgage Payments

Terms

- *amortization*
- *balloon payment*
- *equity*
- *home equity loan*
- *refinancing*

Objectives

- **Determine a monthly payment on a mortgage.**
- **Calculate a balloon payment.**
- **Describe a home equity loan.**
- **Explain mortgage refinancing.**

Build Your Math Skills

Review these math skills to prepare for the lesson that follows.

1. Convert percentages to decimals by moving the decimal two places to the left. Example: 5.5% → 0.055

A. 7.25% →

B. 10.5% →

C. 3.75% →

D. 6.85% →

2. Multiply decimals. Round to the nearest cent ($0.01) if necessary. Example: $2.35 \times \$115.63 = \$271.73$

A. $\$512 \times 4.4 =$

B. $\$308.50 \times 2.71 =$

C. $4.5 \times \$418.75 =$

D. $3.8 \times \$275.63 =$

3. Subtract decimals. Example: $\$564.17 - \$468.09 = \$96.08$

A. $\$714.82 - \$498.76 =$

B. $\$496.45 - \$385.72 =$

C. $\$75.81 - \$35.94 =$

D. $\$1,095.47 - \$846.75 =$

Answer:

1. A. 0.0725
   B. 0.105
   C. 0.0375
   D. 0.0685
2. A. $2,252.80
   B. $836.04
   C. $1,884.38
   D. $1,047.39
3. A. $216.06
   B. $110.73
   C. $39.87
   D. $248.72

Amortization

Amortization is the process of paying down a loan by making regular payments of interest and principal. As you learned in Chapter 8, each payment on an installment loan pays the interest due and then reduces the principal. Because the principal is reduced, the next payment will have slightly less interest due and more of the payment will be applied to principal. In Chapter 8, you saw an example of a simple amortization table.

To create an amortization table for a mortgage, you first must calculate the amount of the monthly payment required to achieve payoff in a specific period. Figure 9-1 is a helpful starting point. In Figure 9-1, you can look up the monthly payment required for a $1,000 loan given the interest rate and the length of the loan in years.

Once you look up the appropriate payment for a $1,000 loan, you can calculate the monthly payment for a mortgage loan using the following formula:

Teaching Tip:
To help students understand the concept of amortization tables, direct them to an online mortgage calculator. These are very useful tools for determining mortgage payments and comparing mortgages.

$$\text{monthly payment} = \frac{\text{amount of mortgage}}{\$1,000} \times \text{monthly payment for \$1,000 loan}$$

Monthly Payment per $1,000 of Loan Amortization			
Interest Rate	**15 years**	**20 years**	**30 years**
4.0%	$ 7.40	$ 6.06	$ 4.78
4.5%	7.65	6.34	5.08
5.0%	7.91	6.60	5.37
5.5%	8.18	6.88	5.68
6.0%	8.44	7.17	6.00
6.5%	8.72	7.46	6.32
7.0%	8.99	7.76	6.66
7.5%	9.28	8.06	7.00
8.0%	9.56	8.37	7.34
8.5%	9.85	8.68	7.69
9.0%	10.15	9.00	8.05
9.5%	10.45	9.33	8.41
10.0%	10.75	9.66	8.78
10.5%	11.06	9.99	9.15
11.0%	11.37	10.33	9.53
11.5%	11.69	10.67	9.91
12.0%	12.01	11.02	10.29

Figure 9-1. Monthly Payment per $1,000 of Loan Amortization

Example 9-3A

See It

Daaliah is purchasing a new home. After making her down payment, she will need to obtain a mortgage for $110,000. Based on her credit score, Daaliah qualifies for a fixed rate 30-year mortgage with a 5.5% APR. Calculate Daaliah's monthly payment.

Teaching Tip:
Explain that the monthly payment multiplier is the number of times 1,000 goes into the amount of the mortgage.

Strategy

Use Figure 9-1 and the formula:

$$\text{monthly payment} = \frac{\text{amount of mortgage}}{\$1,000} \times \text{monthly payment for \$1,000 loan}$$

Solution

Step 1: Determine the monthly payment for a $1,000 loan at 5.5% APR for 30 years.

monthly payment for $1,000 loan = $5.68

Step 2: Determine the monthly payment multiplier. Divide the amount of Daaliah's mortgage by $1,000.

$$\text{monthly payment multiplier} = \frac{\text{amount of mortgage}}{\$1,000}$$

Teaching Tip:
Project or otherwise display Figure 9-1. Ask students what patterns and conclusions they can discern.

$$\text{monthly payment multiplier} = \frac{\$110,000}{\$1,000}$$

monthly payment multiplier = 110

Step 3: Determine Daaliah's monthly payment. Multiply the monthly payment for a $1,000 loan by the monthly payment multiplier.

monthly payment = monthly payment multiplier × monthly payment for $1,000 loan

monthly payment = 110 × $5.68

monthly payment = $624.80

Check It

Answer:
$688.34

Martin is purchasing a new home. After making his down payment, he will need a mortgage for $135,500. Based on his credit score, he qualifies for a fixed rate 30-year mortgage with a 4.5% APR. Calculate Martin's monthly payment.

Example 9-3B

See It

Consider Daaliah's mortgage from the previous example. Calculate the amount of her second monthly payment that is an interest payment, the amount that is applied to the principal, and the loan balance after the second monthly payment. After making her first monthly payment, the principal balance is $109,879.33.

Strategy

Use the formulas:

$$\textbf{interest payment} = \frac{\textbf{annual interest rate}}{\textbf{number of payments per year}} \times \textbf{principal balance}$$

$$\textbf{principal payment} = \textbf{monthly payment amount} - \textbf{interest payment}$$

$$\textbf{new loan balance} = \textbf{previous loan balance} - \textbf{principal payment}$$

Solution

Step 1: Calculate the portion of Daaliah's second monthly payment that is applied toward interest. Multiply the monthly interest rate by the new loan balance after the first monthly payment.

interest payment = monthly interest rate × new loan balance

interest payment = 0.004583 × $109,879.33

interest payment = $503.58

Step 2: Calculate the portion of Daaliah's second monthly payment that is applied toward the loan balance. Subtract the interest payment from the monthly payment.

principal payment = monthly payment amount − interest payment

principal payment = $624.80 − $503.58

principal payment = $121.22

Step 3: Calculate Daaliah's new loan balance. Subtract the principal payment from the previous loan balance.

new loan balance = previous loan balance − principal payment

new loan balance = $109,879.33 − $121.22

new loan balance = $109,758.11

Check It

Consider Martin's mortgage from the previous example. After making his first monthly payment, the principal balance is $135,319.79. Calculate the amount of his second monthly payment that is an interest payment, the amount that is applied to the principal, and the loan balance after the second monthly payment.

Answer:
interest payment =
$507.45
principal payment =
$180.89
new loan balance =
$135,138.90

Balloon Payments

Some loans include a large final payment called a ***balloon payment.*** For example, a mortgage might begin amortizing as if it were a 30-year mortgage. But after seven years, the remainder of the principal is due in one payment. However, the borrower may not have the money to pay off the loan at that time. For that reason, many balloon notes include a plan to begin another amortization of the balloon amount if the borrower is not prepared to pay off the principal.

A mortgage with a balloon payment is more common when houses are consistently rising in value. Mortgages with balloon payments tend to have lower interest rates and lower payments. The borrower most often plans to either sell the house before the balloon payment is due or enter into another agreement to finance the balloon payment.

To find the amount of a balloon payment, use the following formula:

amount of balloon payment = remaining principal + interest due

fyi

Few cities have seen increased housing values in recent years.

Example 9-3C

See It

Lamar and Gabriella Luna purchased a home using a $225,000 mortgage at 5.5% APR for a seven-year term with a balloon payment. The last portion of their amortization schedule is shown. Calculate the amount of the Lunas' balloon payment.

Payment Number	Payment Amount	Interest	Principal	Balance
83	$1,277.53	$919.21	$ 358.32	$200,195.71
84		917.56	200,195.71	0.00

Strategy

Use the formula:

amount of balloon payment = remaining principal + interest due

Solution

Step 1: Identify the remaining principal and the interest due for the final payment from the table.

remaining principal = $200,195.71

interest due = $917.56

Step 2: Calculate the amount of the balloon payment. Add the remaining principal and the interest due.

amount of balloon payment = remaining principal + interest due

amount of balloon payment = $200,195.71 + $917.56

amount of balloon payment = $201,113.27

Check It

Luis and Anala Bridges purchased a house using an $185,000 mortgage with a 5.25% APR. They chose a mortgage with a five-year term and a balloon payment. A portion of their amortization schedule is shown. Calculate the amount of the Bridges' balloon payment.

Payment Number	Payment Amount	Interest	Principal	Balance
59	$1,021.58	$748.23	$ 273.34	$170,751.09
60		747.04	170,751.09	0.00

Answer:
$171,498.13

Home Equity Loans

When a person buys a home, he or she hopes that the value of the home increases while owning the home. However, this is not always the case. If the value of the home rises as the principal is paid down, the home will be worth more than the principal owed on the mortgage. The *equity* is the amount that the value of the home exceeds what is owed.

A *home equity loan* is a loan in which the homeowner borrows money using the equity as collateral. Home equity loans are often used to finance repairs on the home, pay medical bills, or for emergency cash needs.

Some people use a home equity loan to pay off credit card debt. In effect, they shift debt from credit cards to a home equity loan. The danger of using a home equity loan to pay off credit card debt is that the credit cards are made available for new debt. The end result can be a worse debt situation than existed before the home equity loan.

Financial $marts

It is possible for house values to drop, which can erase any equity a homeowner may have in a home. It is even possible to owe more than the home is worth, which is called *negative equity*. The longer you plan to live in a house, the less risk you take in purchasing it. You cannot always predict when you will need to move or sell your home. Experts recommend as a general rule that you do not buy a home unless you plan to live in it for more than two or three years.

Refinancing

Refinancing replaces one mortgage with another. A mortgage with a higher interest rate is often replaced by one with a lower rate. The house being refinanced is used as collateral for the new mortgage. The original mortgage is paid off with the new mortgage. The borrower then begins making payments on the new mortgage.

Teaching Tip:
Engage students in a discussion about why a homeowner might refinance his or her mortgage.

Example 9-3D

See It

Joyce currently has a 30-year mortgage on her home with a 7.5% APR and a balance of $85,316.73. Her monthly payments are $769.14. She decided to refinance her mortgage with a 15-year mortgage that has a 5% APR. Calculate Joyce's new monthly payment.

Strategy

Use Figure 9-1 and the formula:

$$\text{monthly payment} = \frac{\text{amount of mortgage}}{\$1,000} \times \frac{\text{monthly payment}}{\text{for \$1,000 loan}}$$

Solution

Step 1: Determine the monthly payment for a 15-year $1,000 loan and an APR of 5%.

monthly payment for $1,000 loan = $7.91

Step 2: Determine the monthly payment multiplier. Divide the amount of Joyce's new mortgage by $1,000.

$$\text{monthly payment multiplier} = \frac{\text{amount of mortgage}}{\$1,000}$$

$$\text{monthly payment multiplier} = \frac{\$85,316.73}{\$1,000}$$

monthly payment multiplier = 85.31673

Step 3: Determine Joyce's monthly payment. Multiply the monthly payment for a $1,000 loan by the monthly payment multiplier.

monthly payment = monthly payment multiplier × monthly payment for $1,000 loan

monthly payment = 85.31673 × $7.91

monthly payment = $674.86

Check It

Ranita currently has a 20-year mortgage on her home with an 8.3% APR and a balance of $125,603.86. Her monthly payments are $1,282.81. She decided to refinance her mortgage with a 20-year mortgage that has a 4% APR. Calculate Ranita's new monthly payment.

Answer:
$761.16

Checkpoint 9.3

1. Jaleel is purchasing a new home. After making his down payment, he will need a mortgage for $165,750. Based on his credit score, he qualifies for a fixed rate 30-year mortgage with a 4.5% APR. Calculate Jaleel's monthly payment.

2. Rhonda is purchasing a new home. After making her down payment, she will need a mortgage for $140,490. Based on her credit score, she qualifies for a fixed rate 30-year mortgage with a 6.5% APR. Calculate Rhonda's monthly payment.

3. Arianne is purchasing a new home. After making her down payment, she will need to obtain a mortgage for $90,000. Based on her credit score, she qualifies for a fixed rate 30-year mortgage with a 5% APR. Calculate her monthly payment, the amount of her first monthly payment that is an interest payment, the amount that is applied to the principal, and the new loan balance.

4. Logan is purchasing a new home. After making his down payment, he will need to obtain a mortgage for $120,000. Based on his credit score, he qualifies for a fixed rate 15-year mortgage with a 4.5% APR. Calculate his monthly payment, the amount of his first monthly payment that is an interest payment, the amount that is applied to the principal, and the new loan balance.

5. Yvette currently has a 30-year mortgage with a 7.7% APR and a balance of $107,972.20. Her monthly payments are $784.26. She decided to refinance her mortgage with a 20-year mortgage that has a 4.5% APR. Calculate Yvette's new monthly payment.

Answer:
1. $842.01
2. $887.90
3. monthly payment = $483.30
   interest payment = $375.03
   principal payment = $108.27
   new loan balance = $89,891.73
4. monthly payment = $918
   interest payment = $450
   principal payment = $468
   new loan balance = $119,532
5. $684.54

Chapter Review

Build Your Vocabulary

As you progress through this course, develop a personal glossary of financial literacy terms and add it to your portfolio. This will help you build your financial literacy vocabulary. Write out a definition for each of the following terms, and add it to your personal glossary.

lease agreement

lessor

lessee

tenant

security deposit

renters insurance

actual cash value policy

replacement cost policy

claim

premium

deductible

mortgage

appraisal

closing costs

title insurance

escrow account

homeowners insurance

property tax

assessed value

utilities

home warranty

amortization

balloon payment

equity

home equity loan

refinancing

 ## Teamwork

In teams of two, interview a number of people who own a home. Develop interview questions that relate to the advantages and disadvantages of homeownership. After conducting your interviews, create a chart that visually depicts the results of your interviews. Share with the class any conclusions you can draw from the interviews.

Review Your Math Skills

Practice and build on the math skills that you have learned.

1. Convert decimals to percentages by moving the decimal two places to the right. Example: 0.055 → 5.5%

A. 0.579 →

B. 0.1642 →

C. 2.31 →

D. 0.09 →

2. Subtract whole numbers. Example: 14,516 – 11,307 = 3,209

A. 38,719 – 36,796 =

B. 50,734 – 47,864 =

C. 908 – 176 =

D. 60,468 – 46,836 =

Answer:
1. A. 57.9%
   B. 16.42%
   C. 231%
   D. 9%
2. A. 1,923
   B. 2,870
   C. 732
   D. 13,632

3. Add decimals. Example: $241.19 + $40.89 = $282.08

A. $40.56 + $174.28 =

B. $107.08 + $99.46 =

C. $341.18 + $140.07 =

D. $662.34 + $78.19 =

4. Subtract decimals. Example: $88.45 – $8.19 = $80.26

A. $332.48 – $43.98 =

B. $604.78 – $73.07 =

C. $1,167.08 – $40.73 =

D. $918.67 – $445.85 =

5. Add a series of numbers. Example: $186.26 + $642.99 + $14.58 + $314.04 = $1,157.87

A. $864.84 + $42.08 + $379.60 + $127.57 =

B. $326.16 + $162.42 + $126.20 + $98.56 =

C. $38.21 + $29.29 + $14.67 + $9.50 =

D. $54.10 + $44.25 + $78.14 + $29.71=

6. Convert percentages to decimals by moving the decimal two places to the left. Example: 4.24% → 0.0424

A. 8.4% →

B. 7.36% →

C. 4% →

D. 12.3% →

7. Multiply decimals. Round to the nearest cent ($0.01) if necessary. Example: 2,019 × $0.08 = $161.52

A. 1,198 × $0.065 =

B. 2,481 × $0.10 =

C. 4,489 × $0.11 =

D. 3,867 × $0.135 =

8. Subtract decimals. Example: $564.17 – $468.09 = $96.08

A. $288.50 – $48 =

B. $474.82 – $3 =

C. $531.71 – $36 =

D. $1,126.35 – $29 =

9. Add decimals. Example: $125.76 + $205.83 = $331.59

A. $332.48 + $43.98 =

B. $604.78 + $73.07 =

C. $1,167.08 + $40.73 =

D. $445.85 + $918.67 =

10. Multiply decimals. Round to the nearest cent ($0.01) if necessary. Example: $175.64 × 0.03 = $5.27

A. $248 × 0.03 =

B. $186.85 × 0.04 =

C. $708.48 × 0.07 =

D. $307.75 × 0.035 =

3. A. $214.84
   B. $206.54
   C. $481.25
   D. $740.53
4. A. $288.50
   B. $531.71
   C. $1,126.35
   D. $472.82
5. A. $1,414.09
   B. $713.34
   C. $91.67
   D. $206.20
6. A. 0.084
   B. 0.0736
   C. 0.04
   D. 0.123
7. A. $77.87
   B. $248.10
   C. $493.79
   D. $522.05
8. A. $240.50
   B. $471.82
   C. $495.71
   D. $1,097.35
9. A. $376.46
   B. $677.85
   C. $1,207.81
   D. $1,364.52
10. A. $7.44
    B. $7.47
    C. $49.59
    D. $10.77

Section 9.1 Renting

11. José, Mark, and Terrell decided to share an apartment in order to reduce their living expenses. They found a three-bedroom apartment with a monthly rent of $1,385. If they divide the rent evenly, what is each person's share of the rent? Round your answer to the nearest cent ($0.01) if necessary.

12. Kayla lives in a rented condo and wants to purchase renters insurance that will cost $348 per year. If she pays monthly, there will be an additional partial payment fee of $2.50. What will be Kayla's monthly insurance bill? Round your answer to the nearest cent ($0.01) if necessary.

Answer:
11. $461.67
12. $31.50

Section 9.2 Purchasing a Home

13. Derrick and Claudia Walker want to purchase a house that has a selling price of $194,870. Their bank requires a down payment of 17.5%. Calculate the Walkers' down payment and the amount that they will finance through their mortgage.

14. Rasheed is buying a new house. His closing costs are itemized in the following table provided by the mortgage broker. What are Rasheed's total closing costs?

Type of Fee	Amount
Legal	$ 771.45
Document filing	304.59
Loan application	1,048.95
Appraisal	505.00
Inspection	430.00
Title insurance	708.46

15. Anita owns a home in Dogwood. A portion of her tax statement is shown in the following table. According to her statement, she pays property taxes to five different taxing authorities, or taxing jurisdictions. Use the table to calculate the portion of the property tax that will be paid to each taxing jurisdiction.

Taxing Jurisdiction	Taxable Value	Tax Rate (‰)
City of Dogwood	$96,000	11.44
Dogwood Parks District	66,000	0.5
Newtown Public Schools	66,000	21.694
Newtown County	63,169	10.551
State of Georgia	94,000	0.25

Answer:
13. down payment = $34,102.25
amount of mortgage = $160,767.75
14. $3,768.45
15. City of Dogwood = $1,098.24
Dogwood Park District = $33
Newtown Public Schools = $1,431.80
Newtown County = $666.50
State of Georgia = $23.50

Section 9.3 Mortgage Payments

16. Blanca is purchasing a new home. After making her down payment, she will need a mortgage for $136,750. Based on her credit score, she qualifies for a fixed rate 30-year mortgage with a 4.5% APR. Calculate Blanca's monthly payment.

17. Darrell is purchasing a new home. After making his down payment, he will need to obtain a mortgage for $118,800. Based on his credit score, he qualifies for a fixed rate 15-year mortgage with a 4.5% APR. Calculate his monthly payment, the amount of his first monthly payment that is an interest payment, the amount that is applied to the principal, and the new loan balance.

18. Kim currently has a thirty-year mortgage with a 6.75% APR and a balance of $110,749.46. Her monthly payments are $972.90. She decided to refinance her mortgage with a 30-year mortgage that has a 5.5% APR. Calculate Kim's new monthly payment.

Answer:
16. $694.69
17. monthly payment = $908.82
    interest payment = $445.50
    principal payment = $463.32
    new loan balance = $363.68
18. $629.06

Reinforce Your Understanding

19. Marshall has a credit card with a nominal APR of 19.35%. The interest on unpaid balances compounds daily. What is the EAR?

20. Dawn is a courier for a local delivery company. She purchases health insurance and dental insurance for herself and her husband. Her total monthly premiums are $512.49. Dawn's federal income tax rate is 15%. Determine Dawn's monthly tax savings by having her insurance premiums withheld before taxes are calculated.

Answer:
19. 21.34%
20. $76.87

Apply Your Technology Skills

www.g-wlearning.com

Access the G-W Learning companion website for this text at www.g-wlearning.com. Download each data file for this chapter. Follow the instructions to complete financial literacy activities to practice what you have learned in this chapter.

Data File 9-1—Using an Online Mortgage Calculator

Data File 9-2—Estimating Mortgage Payments

Data File 9-3—Researching an Apartment

Data File 9-4—Completing an Application for Rental Property

Teaching Tip:
The Apply Your Technology Skills activities offer project-based authentic assessment opportunities.

10 Automobiles

Materials:
Instructor's Resource CD
Student Workbook
G-W Learning companion website
EXAMVIEW® Assessment Suite
Microsoft Excel®–compatible software
Calculator with advanced-math functions

Transportation costs can take up a significant portion of your budget. Making wise decisions about how you will get to and from all the places you go will determine what remains in your budget for other things, such as entertainment.

Section 10.1 Owning or Leasing a Car

Section 10.2 Cost of Owning a Car

College and Career Readiness

Reading Prep. In preparation for this chapter, research information on leasing or buying a car. What are some things to keep in mind when making this decision? As you read, consider how this information is reflected in the text.

"Some people may think that owning a car is all fun and games, but there are a lot of expenses that come along with it." ~ Juanito P.

Money Matters
Car Facts

- People in the US own more cars than almost any other country in the world. There are 828 cars for every 1,000 people.

- Edmunds, Inc. and Kelly Blue Book are two popular publishers of information to help educate consumers on buying cars.

- The economic recession of 2008 put automobile manufacturers in jeopardy. The government helped bail out General Motors and Chrysler to keep the manufacturers in business.

- In 1950, gasoline cost $0.25 a gallon.

- In many states, it is illegal to talk on the phone while driving.

- Keep your proof of car insurance card and the car's registration in the glove compartment.

Section 10.1 Owning or Leasing a Car

Objectives
- **Describe the process of purchasing a car.**
- **Explain typical auto financing.**
- **Calculate depreciation.**
- **Define auto leasing.**

Terms
- *automobile dealer*
- *sticker price*
- *manufacturer's suggested retail price (MSRP)*
- *trade-in allowance*
- *tax, title, and license (TT & L)*
- *depreciation*
- *straight-line*

Build Your Math Skills

Review these math skills to prepare for the lesson that follows.

1. Convert percentages to decimals by moving the decimal two places to the left. **Example: 7.5% → 0.075**

A. 5.25% →

B. 8.9% →

C. 14.5% →

D. 22.7% →

2. Subtract decimals. **Example: $452.74 – $74.96 = $377.78**

A. $418.74 – $284.76 =

B. $1,147.83 – $914.52 =

C. $706.48 – $482.55 =

D. $148.56 – $65.88 =

3. Divide decimals. **Round to the nearest hundredth (0.01) if necessary. Example: $1,501.58 ÷ $2,517.92 = 0.6**

A. $3,542.60 ÷ $5,128.17 =

B. $4,417.02 ÷ $8,828.92 =

C. $3,610.32 ÷ $9,608.42 =

D. $5,328.05 ÷ $15,975.19 =

Answer:
1. A. 0.0525
   B. 0.089
   C. 0.145
   D. 0.227
2. A. $133.98
   B. $233.31
   C. $223.93
   D. $82.68
3. A. 0.691
   B. 0.5
   C. 0.376
   D. 0.334

Purchasing a Car

Purchasing a car is more complicated than most purchases, other than the purchase of a home. Before you consider shopping for your dream vehicle or even a serviceable vehicle, you have to give your budget and cash flow a careful look.

Although some car buyers pay with cash, most cars are financed with an installment loan. To finance a car purchase, you will need to provide detailed personal information so the car dealership can request a credit report. As you learned in chapter 7, a credit report gives information on how you have paid other debts. The information on your credit report will affect if the loan will be granted and at what interest rate the loan will be financed. People with better credit get lower interest rates to borrow money because they are considered more likely to repay the loan. Those without good credit will be charged a higher rate, or may not be granted a loan at all.

An ***automobile dealer*** is an individual or company whose business is selling cars. If you purchase a car from an automobile dealer, the car usually has a

A car with an unfixable defect, which prevents you from driving it safely, is often called a *lemon*. *Lemon laws* allow consumers to receive a refund, replacement, or other cash payment from a dealer who sold the defective vehicle.

suggested price, called a *sticker price.* If the car is new, the sticker price may be the *manufacturer's suggested retail price (MSRP),* which means that it is set by the manufacturer. Whatever the sticker price, most people negotiate with the seller to get the best price.

Often, a buyer trades in one car for another. The dealer may discount the price of the car being purchased based on the value of the trade-in. A *trade-in allowance* is a discount in price resulting from the trade-in of one car for another car.

Another way the price of a car can be discounted is through a rebate. A rebate comes in the form of a refund after a purchase has been made. To find the final price of an automobile purchase after the trade-in allowance and rebates, use the following formula:

final price = sale price − (trade-in allowance + rebate)

Example 10-1A

See It

Charlotte is buying a new car with an MSRP of $21,995. She has negotiated a sale price of $19,500 with the dealer. She will receive a trade-in allowance of $4,100 in exchange for her old car. What is the final price that Charlotte will pay for her new car?

Strategy

Use the formula:

final price = sale price − (trade-in allowance + rebate)

Solution

Step 1: Identify the negotiated sale price of the car and any discounts or allowances.

sale price = $19,500

trade-in allowance = $4,100

Step 2: Calculate the difference between the sale price and the trade-in allowance. Subtract the trade-in allowance from the negotiated sale price.

final price = sale price − trade-in allowance

final price = $19,500 − $4,100

final price = $15,400

Check It

Eduardo is buying a new truck with an MSRP of $31,450. He has negotiated a sale price of $27,500 with the dealer. He will receive a trade-in allowance of $5,650 in exchange for his old truck. What is the final price that Eduardo will pay for his new truck?

Example 10-1B

See It

Sula is purchasing a new car. The MSRP is $23,469, and she has negotiated a sale price of $21,050. The dealer is offering a cash rebate of $1,500 and has offered Sula a $3,600 trade-in allowance for her old car. What will be the final price for Sula's new car?

Strategy

Use the formula:

final price = sale price − (trade-in allowance + rebate)

Solution

Step 1: Identify the negotiated sale price of the car and any discounts or allowances.

sale price = $21,050

trade-in allowance = $3,600

rebate = $1,500

Step 2: Calculate the difference between the sale price and the trade-in allowance. Subtract the trade-in allowance from the negotiated sale price.

final price = sale price − (trade-in allowance + rebate)

final price = $21,050 − ($3,600 + $1,500)

final price = $21,050 − $5,100

final price = $15,950

Check It

Ishmael is purchasing a new car. The MSRP is $26,718, and he has negotiated a sale price of $23,750. The dealer is offering a cash rebate of $1,500 and has offered Ishmael a $4,150 trade-in allowance for his old car. What will be the final price for Ishmael's new car?

Answer:
$18,100

Once the cash price is calculated, there are multiple fees that must be paid by the buyer. Some common fees include:

- sales tax;
- title transfer fee; and
- license fee.

Sales tax is calculated as a percentage of the cash price of the sale. A *title transfer fee* is paid to transfer the title to the name of the new owner. If there is an outstanding loan on the car, the title will be recorded in the lender's name until the loan is fully repaid. When the car changes hands, the new owner pays for the car's *registration*. The car's registration can also be called the car's license. This should not be confused with a driver's license. License plates are issued along with a vehicle's registration, which help make the car readily identifiable.

Together these fees are often referred to as *tax, title, and license (TT & L)*. In addition, there may be a state inspection fee, a documentation fee, and other miscellaneous fees. To find the total price of a car, including all applicable fees, use the following formula:

total price = sale price + sales tax + title fee + license fee

Example 10-1C

See It

Lance is purchasing a used car and has negotiated a sale price of $14,325. He must pay 6.25% sales tax, a license fee of $60, and a title transfer fee of $35. What is the price of the car, including TT & L?

Strategy

Use the formula:

total price = sale price + sales tax + title fee + license fee

Solution

Step 1: Convert the sales tax rate to a decimal by moving the decimal two places to the left.

6.25% → 0.0625

Step 2: Determine the amount of sales tax. Multiply the sale price by the sales tax rate. Round to the nearest cent ($0.01) if necessary.

sales tax = sale price × sales tax rate

sales tax = $14,325 × 0.0625

sales tax = $895.31

Step 3: Determine the total price of the car. Add the sale price, sales tax, title fee, and license fee.

total price = sale price + sales tax + title fee + license fee

total price = $14,325 + $895.31 + $60 + $35

total price = $15,315.31

Check It

Misa is purchasing a used car and has negotiated a sale price of $11,350. She must pay 7.5% sales tax, a license fee of $55, and a title transfer fee of $30. What is the price of the car, including TT & L?

Cost of Financing

With any installment loan, a percentage of the total cost may be required as a down payment. In some cases, the buyer pays cash for the down payment. In other cases, the trade-in value may cover the requirement for a down payment.

Car loan terms are usually three, four, or five years, and are expressed in months (36, 48, or 60 months). Some car loans are available on a six-year term. Because automobiles drop in value rapidly, when a buyer chooses a five- or six-year term, the value of the car may decline faster than the balance on the loan. When that happens, the buyer is said to be *upside down* on the value of the car because the buyer owes more than the car is worth.

When determining which financing option to choose, compare interest rates and terms of loans. The following equation can be used to compare car loans:

difference = amount of interest paid for first loan – amount of interest paid for second loan

Teaching Tip: Explain to students that a person can be *under water* with a car loan in the same way as with a home loan.

Example 10-1D

See It

Malika is purchasing a new truck and has negotiated a final price of $18,450. She has qualified for two loans. The first is a three-year car loan at 4.5% APR, with monthly payments of $548.83. The second is a five-year car loan at 4.1% APR, with monthly payments of $340.62. How much more in interest will Malika pay for the five-year car loan than the three-year car loan?

Strategy

Use the formula:

difference = amount of interest paid for first loan – amount of interest paid for second loan

Solution

Step 1: Determine the total amount that Malika will pay on the three-year loan. Multiply the monthly payment by the number of years and 12 months per year.

total paid = monthly payment × number of years × 12 months per year

total paid = $548.83 per month × 3 years × 12 months per year

total paid = $19,757.88

Step 2: Determine the amount of interest paid for the three-year loan. Subtract the final price from the total amount paid.

amount of interest paid = total paid – final price of truck

amount of interest paid = $19,757.88 – $18,450

amount of interest paid = $1,307.88

Step 3: Determine the total amount that Malika will pay on the five-year loan. Multiply the monthly payment by the number of years and 12 months per year.

total paid = monthly payment × number of years × 12 months per year

total paid = $340.62 per month × 5 years × 12 months per year

total paid = $20,437.20

Step 4: Determine the amount of interest paid for the five-year loan. Subtract the final price from the total amount paid.

amount of interest paid = total paid – final price of truck

amount of interest paid = $20,437.20 – $18,450

amount of interest paid = $1,987.20

Step 5: Determine the difference in the amounts of interest paid. Subtract the amount of interest paid for the three-year loan from the amount of interest paid for the five-year loan.

difference = amount of interest paid for five-year loan – amount of interest paid for three-year loan

difference = $1,987.20 – $1,307.88

difference = $679.32

Check It

Jared is purchasing a new truck and has negotiated a final price of $21,325. He has qualified for two loans. The first is a three-year car loan at 5.5% APR, with monthly payments of $643.93. The second is a 5-year car loan at 4.5% APR, with monthly payments of $397.56. How much more interest will Jared pay for the five-year car loan than the three-year car loan?

Answer:
$672.12

Calculating Depreciation

Cars lose their value as they age. When an asset loses value, the loss of value is called *depreciation.* With a car, much of the depreciation occurs in the first few months of the car's life. A car depreciates more when it is newer—up to 25% in the first five years. The rate of depreciation varies from year to year.

Future depreciation can only be estimated based on historical information. Actual depreciation is only known after a car is sold. Depreciation is calculated by subtracting the value of the asset when sold from the value of the asset when purchased. The following formula can be used to calculate depreciation:

depreciation = purchase price – resale price

To calculate the average annual depreciation, you must take into consideration the number of years the

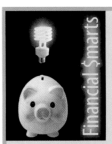

Financial $marts

Because a car depreciates so quickly in the first few years, purchasing a pre-owned car may be a more financially smart decision. It is common to find five-year-old cars are in very good condition with many years of life remaining. For example, if you can purchase a car for $8,000 that was $20,000 new, you would save $12,000. The sales tax would be based on $8,000 instead of $20,000, so you would save money from lower taxes. Also, the depreciation rate would be much slower. And, if you saved your money and paid cash for the car, you would not have to pay finance charges.

car was owned. By dividing the depreciation by the years owned, an average annual depreciation can be calculated. The following formula can be used to calculate average annual depreciation:

$$\text{average annual depreciation} = \frac{\text{depreciation}}{\text{number of years}}$$

Once you calculate the average annual depreciation, you can calculate the percentage of depreciation. The rate of straight-line depreciation percentage can be found by dividing the average annual depreciation by the original purchase price as shown in the following formula:

$$\text{depreciation rate} = \frac{\text{average annual depreciation}}{\text{purchase price}}$$

fyi

When an asset increases in value over time, it is called *appreciation*.

Example 10-1E

See It

Tia bought a car for $14,500 and sold it four years later for $5,500. What was the average annual depreciation of Tia's car?

Strategy

Use the formulas:

$$\text{depreciation} = \text{purchase price} - \text{resale price}$$

$$\text{average annual depreciation} = \frac{\text{depreciation}}{\text{number of years}}$$

Solution

Step 1: Identify the purchase price, resale price, and number of years the car was owned.

purchase price = $14,500

resale price = $5,500

number of years owned = four years

Step 2: Determine the amount of depreciation. Subtract the resale price from the purchase price.

depreciation = purchase price – resale price

depreciation = $14,500 – $5,500

depreciation = $9,000

Step 3: Determine the average annual depreciation. Divide the amount of depreciation by the number of years the car was owned.

$$\text{average annual depreciation} = \frac{\text{depreciation}}{\text{number of years}}$$

$$\text{average annual depreciation} = \frac{\$9,000}{4 \text{ years}}$$

average annual depreciation = $2,250 per year

Check It

Lawrence paid $8,650 for a used car. He sold it three years later for $4,125. What was Lawrence's average annual depreciation?

The straight-line method is the most commonly used approach for determining depreciation of a personal car. *Straight-line* means that the asset depreciates the same amount each year it is used.

To calculate the average annual depreciation, you must take into consideration the number of years the car was owned. By dividing the depreciation by the years owned, an average annual depreciation can be calculated. The following formula can be used to calculate average annual depreciation:

$$\textbf{depreciation rate} = \frac{\textbf{average annual depreciation}}{\textbf{purchase price}}$$

Career Discovery

Transportation, Distribution, & Logistics Careers and Math Skills

Transportation by road, rail, water, and air offers many employment options. These careers focus on effective planning, efficient management, and safe movement of products and people. Related careers focus on planning, managing, and maintaining the equipment, facilities, and systems used.

Strong math skills are key qualities for these workers. Describe a situation in which someone pursuing a career in this cluster must be able to perform accurate math calculations.

Example 10-1F

See It

For Tia's car in the previous example, calculate the rate of straight-line depreciation.

Strategy

Use the formula:

$$\text{depreciation rate} = \frac{\text{average annual depreciation}}{\text{purchase price}}$$

Solution

Step 1: Divide the average annual depreciation by the original purchase price. Round to the nearest thousandth (0.001) if necessary.

$$\text{depreciation rate} = \frac{\text{average annual depreciation}}{\text{purchase price}}$$

$$\text{depreciation rate} = \frac{\$2,250}{\$14,500}$$

$$\text{depreciation rate} \approx 0.155$$

Step 2: Convert the rate from a decimal to a percentage by moving the decimal two places to the right.

$$0.155 \rightarrow 15.5\%$$

Check It

Use the information in the previous example to calculate the rate of straight-line depreciation for Lawrence's car.

Answer:
17.4%

Leasing a Car

An alternative to purchasing a car is leasing. With an automobile lease, the customer signs a contract to use the car in exchange for payment. Typically, there is a down payment and a monthly payment, similar to purchasing a car.

Lease payments must cover the depreciation, finance charges, and other costs. At the end of the lease period, the car is returned to the company that owns it. From there, the car will likely be sold as a used car. Most auto leases are two, three, or four years.

A major part of the lease agreement is the limit on the number of miles a lessee can drive the car. If the lessee exceeds the mileage limit, additional fees will be charged. Also, any damage to the vehicle beyond normal wear will also be charged to the lessee.

Teaching Tip:
Remind students that the *lessee* is the person who holds the lease and the *lessor* is who owns the property being leased.

Source: Shutterstock (Levent Konuk)

Monthly payments on a leased car are generally less than an auto loan.

There are multiple reasons why a lease may be selected over purchasing a car. The monthly payment on a lease is often lower than on an installment loan, and qualifying for a lease is often easier than qualifying for an auto loan. Luxury cars are more likely to be leased than lower-cost cars. Many people find they can afford a nicer car and have a new car every few years by leasing, rather than purchasing. Another advantage of leasing is that the car is covered under a warranty through the lease period, and maintenance is often included in the lease price.

When a lease term is over, the lessee has the option of purchasing the car he or she had been leasing. However, it is more likely that the person will begin leasing another car. Because the owner has no equity in the car at the end of the lease, entering into another lease is often the most affordable option. This is especially true for someone who does not have the cash to buy a car or to make a down payment.

Financial $marts

The downside to a lease on a car is similar to the downside of purchasing a new car. In a lease, the lessee is driving the car during the period of greatest depreciation. So while a lease may offer an attractive monthly payment, the lessee is simply renting a car with nothing to show for it at the end of the lease. In a lease, you are making a monthly payment close to what you would pay if purchasing the car, but you don't own the vehicle. If you choose to lease a car, you should recognize that there are more financially smart ways to provide for transportation.

To determine the cost-effectiveness of leasing a car, use the following formula:

difference in total cost = total purchase cost – total lease cost

Example 10-1G

See It

Oralee and her car dealer negotiated a price of $25,400 for a new car. She can lease the car for $319 per month for 36 months. She can buy the car at the end of the lease for its residual value of $14,490. If she purchases the car now, her monthly loan payment will be $718 for 36 months after making a $2,000 down payment. What is the total cost under each plan? Which plan is less expensive?

Strategy

Use the formula:

difference in total cost = total purchase cost – total lease cost

Solution

Step 1: For the lease, determine the total cost of the lease payments. Multiply the monthly payment amount by the number of monthly payments.

total lease payments = monthly payment × number of payments

total lease payments = $319 per month × 36 months

total lease payments = $11,484

Step 2: Determine the total cost of the lease. Add the total lease payments to the residual value.

total lease cost = total lease payments + residual value

total lease cost = $11,484 + $14,490

total lease cost = $25,974

Step 3: For the purchase, determine the total cost of the loan payments. Multiply the monthly payment amount by the number of monthly payments.

total loan payments = monthly payment × number of payments

total loan payments = $718 per month × 36 months

total loan payments = $25,848

Step 4: Determine the total cost of the purchase. Add the total loan payments to the down payment.

total purchase cost = total loan payments + down payment

total purchase cost = $25,848 + $2,000

total purchase cost = $27,848

Step 5: Determine the difference between the total lease cost and the total purchase cost. Subtract the two values.

difference in total cost = total purchase cost − total lease cost

difference in total cost = $27,848 − $25,974

difference in total cost = $1,874

The lease plan is less expensive by $1,874.

Check It

Sal and his auto dealer have negotiated a price of $30,290 for a new truck. The dealer presents Sal with two options. He can lease the truck for $419 per month for 36 months and then purchase the truck at the end of the lease for the residual value of $16,258. Or, Sal can purchase the truck with a down payment of $5,000 and monthly payments of $782 for 36 months. What is the total cost of purchasing the truck under each plan? Which plan is less expensive?

Checkpoint 10.1

Use the following information for questions 1–3. Kristopher is purchasing a new car. The MSRP is $28,850, and he has negotiated a sale price of $25,250. The dealer is offering a cash rebate of $1,250 and has offered Kristopher a $3,600 trade-in allowance for his old car.

1. What will be the final price of Kristopher's new car?

2. Kristopher must pay 8.25% sales tax, a license fee of $75, and a title transfer fee of $40. What is the price of the car, including TT & L?

3. Kristopher qualifies for either a three-year car loan at 5.9% APR, with monthly payments of $674.30, or a five-year car loan at 4.75% APR, with monthly payments of $416.37. How much more interest will Kristopher pay for the five-year car loan than the three-year car loan?

4. Tasha purchased a new car five years ago for $31,450. She sold it this year for $9,950. Calculate the average annual depreciation and the depreciation rate for Tasha's car.

5. Mona and her auto dealer have negotiated a price of $29,200 for a new sport-utility vehicle (SUV). The dealer presents Mona with two options. She can lease the SUV for $349 per month for 36 months and purchase the SUV at the end of the lease for the residual value of $19,697. Or, Mona can purchase the SUV with a down payment of $4,000 and monthly payments of $730 for 36 months. What is the total cost of purchasing the SUV under each plan? Which plan is less expensive?

Section 10.2 Cost of Owning a Car

Objectives
- **Calculate the cost of maintaining a car.**
- **Explain the purpose of extended warranties.**
- **Describe automobile insurance coverage.**

Terms
- *manufacturer's warranty*
- *extended warranty*
- *automobile insurance*
- *liability coverage*
- *collision coverage*
- *uninsured motorist coverage*
- *comprehensive coverage*
- *full coverage*
- *totaled*

Build Your Math Skills

Review these math skills to prepare for the lesson that follows.

1. Add decimals. Example: $139.18 + $208.04 = $347.26

A. $78.10 + $312.75 =

B. $804.16 + $97.86 =

C. $286.73 + $196.71 =

D. $1,190.03 + $607.19 =

2. Multiply decimals. Round to the nearest cent ($0.01) if necessary. Example: $80 \times \$3.56 = \$284.80$

A. $115 \times \$2.99 =$

B. $216 \times \$1.57 =$

C. $95 \times \$2.50 =$

D. $120 \times \$3.74 =$

3. Divide decimals. Round to the nearest cent ($0.01) if necessary. Example: $716.50 \div 4 = $179.13

A. $506.78 \div 4 =$

B. $941.85 \div 12 =$

C. $412.19 \div 4 =$

D. $541.32 \div 6 =$

Answer:
  1. A. $390.85
     B. $902.02
     C. $483.44
     D. $1,797.22
  2. A. $343.85
     B. $339.12
     C. $237.50
     D. $448.80
  3. A. $126.70
     B. $78.49
     C. $103.05
     D. $90.22

Maintenance

Like anything mechanical, cars require maintenance and repair. Common maintenance expenses include changing the oil, changing filters, servicing brakes, and maintaining tires. Other unexpected problems could develop with the engine or other parts of the car.

It is important to anticipate the total cost of owning and operating a car. The first obvious cost is gasoline. The price of gas fluctuates regularly and can even change on a daily basis. That is why you want your car to get as many miles per gallon of gas as possible. To calculate the cost of gas, use the following formulas:

annual number of gallons = number of annual miles ÷ fuel efficiency

total cost = annual number of gallons × average cost per gallon

Teaching Tip:
Give students an opportunity to share their thoughts about what makes a particular car desirable.

Example 10-2A

See It

Nikhita is purchasing a new car. Because she drives back and forth to work every day, fuel efficiency is an important consideration for Nikhita. She is considering a car that gets 28 miles per gallon. Nikhita estimates that she drives 14,000 miles per year. If gasoline costs an average of $3.60 per gallon, calculate Nikhita's annual fuel costs.

Strategy

Use the formulas:

annual number of gallons = number of annual miles ÷ fuel efficiency

total cost = annual number of gallons × average cost per gallon

Solution

Step 1: Determine the number of gallons of gasoline that Nikhita will need in a year. Divide the number of annual miles driven by the fuel efficiency.

annual number of gallons = number of annual miles ÷ fuel efficiency

annual number of gallons = 14,000 miles ÷ 28 miles per gallon

annual number of gallons = 500

Step 2: Determine the cost of the gasoline. Multiply the annual number of gallons of gasoline by the average cost of gasoline per gallon.

total cost = annual number of gallons × average cost per gallon

total cost = 500 gallons × $3.60 per gallon

total cost = $1,800

Check It

Brad has a truck that gets 21 miles per gallon. He drives about 12,000 miles per year. If the average cost of gasoline is $3.50 per gallon, calculate Brad's annual gasoline cost.

Answer:
$2,000

fyi

Fuel efficiency is a unit rate, so you could also use a proportion to solve fuel-efficiency problems:

$$\frac{\text{number of miles}}{1 \text{ gallon}} = \frac{\text{annual miles driven}}{\text{annual gasoline consumption}}$$

Routine maintenance, such as changing the oil, is a cost that you must anticipate. Your car's manufacturer will make a recommendation for how often you should change the engine oil. It is important to change the oil when recommended in order to extend the life of the car. Recommendations will range from every 3,000 miles to 7,500 miles or more depending on the car that you drive.

To determine the total annual cost of fuel and maintenance for a vehicle, use the following formula:

total annual cost = annual cost of oil changes + annual cost of gasoline

Example 10-2B

See It

The car that Nikhita is considering requires an oil change every 3,000 miles. Each oil change will cost $36.50, including sales tax and environmental fees. Use the information from the previous example to determine the total cost of fuel and maintenance for Nikhita's car.

Strategy

Use the formula:

total annual cost = annual cost of oil changes + annual cost of gasoline

Teaching Tip:
Explain that failure to adequately maintain a car can cause its value to decrease and may even void the manufacturer's warranty.

Solution

Step 1: Determine the number of oil changes required in a year. Divide the number of annual miles driven by the number of miles between oil changes. Round to the nearest whole number.

number of oil changes = number of annual miles ÷ mileage between oil changes

number of oil changes = 14,000 ÷ 3,000

number of oil changes ≈ 5

Step 2: Determine the annual cost of oil changes. Multiply the cost per oil change by the number of oil changes per year.

annual cost of oil changes = cost per oil change × number of oil changes

annual cost of oil changes = $36.50 × 5

annual cost of oil changes = $182.50

Step 3: Determine the total cost of fuel and maintenance. Add the annual cost of gasoline and the annual cost of oil changes.

total annual cost = annual cost of oil changes + annual cost of gasoline

total annual cost = $182.50 + $1,800

total annual cost = $1,982.50

Check It

The manufacturer of Brad's truck recommends an oil change every 4,000 miles. For this vehicle, an oil change costs $47.85, including sales tax and environmental fees. Determine the total annual cost of fuel and maintenance for Brad's truck.

Answer:
$2,143.55

Warranties

One of the attractions of buying a new car is the manufacturer's warranty. A *manufacturer's warranty* is a promise by the car manufacturer to cover specified repairs to the car for a specific amount of time or number of miles driven. Most new cars come with at least a three year/36,000 mile warranty. That means that if anything goes wrong with the car during the first three years or 36,000 miles (whichever comes first), the auto dealer will repair it at no cost. Many new cars come with five year/60,000 mile warranties and may include an even longer warranty on the engine and related parts. The manufacturer's warranty is included in the price of the car.

There is some disagreement over whether an extended warranty is a good purchase. Typically, any repairs that are needed to a new car will happen during the original warranty. However, if something happens and a major repair is needed after the original warranty expires, the repair cost could be high. Always research the cost of an extended warranty, specifically what it covers, and decide if it is worth the additional cost.

Some car owners purchase an extended warranty from the manufacturer through a third-party company. *Extended warranties* are warranties that pick up where the manufacturer's warranty leaves off. An extended warranty will generally cover less than the original warranty. Think of an extended warranty as an insurance policy for major repairs.

Automobile Insurance

Automobile insurance is insurance to protect your vehicle and to protect you in accidents involving your vehicle. The required insurance coverage for an automobile varies from state to state, but there are some common components to most auto insurance coverage.

Liability coverage pays for bodily injury or property damage that you or your automobile cause. For example, if you are responsible for an accident that damages someone else's car and causes someone to need medical attention, your liability insurance will pay expenses for which you would be responsible. Your state requires you to carry liability coverage in order to operate a vehicle on the public roadways in order to protect others.

Collision coverage is insurance that covers damage to your own car. This coverage pays to repair your car in an accident that is your fault or damage that is not covered by other insurance. This type of coverage is not required by the state. However, it may be required by a lender who is providing an auto loan on the vehicle. The lender requires the coverage to protect the value of the automobile that is serving as collateral for the loan.

Uninsured motorist coverage covers damage and bodily injury in cases where a driver without insurance is at fault. This insurance provides protection in an accident where the driver of the other vehicle has no liability insurance to pay for your damage or injuries.

Comprehensive coverage protects your car from a wide range of other hazards, such as theft, storm and hail damage, vandalism, and broken windows. Comprehensive coverage is sometimes referred to as *full coverage.*

Some auto insurance coverage includes a deductible. Recall from chapter 9 that a deductible is the part of the expense that you are responsible for before insurance begins paying. Coverage that pays others, such as liability, does not have a deductible. Coverage that pays you, such as collision or comprehensive, will have a deductible. Auto insurance deductibles are typically $100 to $1,000 per incident.

Like any other insurance, the insured pays premiums to purchase and maintain coverage. Auto insurance premiums vary based on location, age of the driver, and other factors. Drivers under the age of 25 commonly pay higher premiums because younger drivers tend to have more accidents. Figure 10-1 contains some sample coverage and premiums. To determine your monthly insurance cost, use the following formula:

Teaching Tip:
Reinforce students' understanding of this section by having students summarize its contents in their own words.

monthly payment = monthly premium + partial-payment fee

It is important to understand that auto insurance only pays up to the depreciated value of the car. For example, if a car has a current value of $4,000, the most the insurance will pay to repair or replace the car is $4,000 minus any deductibles that may apply.

Often, the maximum the insurance company will pay is not enough to replace the vehicle. When the damage to a vehicle reaches or exceeds the value of the car, the car is said to be *totaled,* meaning it would cost more to fix it than the car is worth.

Example 10-2C

See It

Gina has auto insurance with the coverage shown in Figure 10-1. She has decided to pay her insurance premium in monthly payments. Her insurance company charges a $2.50-per-payment partial-payment fee. What will be Gina's monthly insurance payment?

Coverage Type	Coverage Limits	Annual Premium
Liability (bodily injury)	$250,000/person, $500,000/accident	$239.26
Liability (property damage)	$100,000/accident	274.60
Collision	$1,000 deductible	219.64
Uninsured motorist (bodily injury)	$100,000/person, $300,000/accident	58.86
Uninsured motorist (property damage)	$25,000/accident ($250 deductible)	33.78
Comprehensive	$1,000 deductible	57.56

Figure 10-1. Sample Automobile Insurance Premiums

Strategy

Use the formula:

monthly payment = monthly premium + partial-payment fee

Solution

Step 1: Determine the total annual premium. Find the sum of the premiums of all coverage types shown in the table.

total annual premium = liability (bodily injury) + liability (property damage) + collision + uninsured motorist (bodily injury) + uninsured motorist (property damage) + comprehensive

total annual premium = $239.26 + $274.60 + $219.64 + $58.86 + $33.78 + $57.56

total annual premium = $883.70

Step 2: Determine the amount of the monthly premium. Divide the total annual premium by 12. Round to the nearest cent ($0.01) if necessary.

monthly premium = total annual premium ÷ 12

monthly premium = $883.70 ÷ 12

monthly premium = $73.64

Step 3: Determine the monthly payment. Add the monthly premium and the partial-payment fee.

monthly payment = monthly premium + partial-payment fee

monthly payment = $73.64 + $2.50

monthly payment = $76.14

Check It

Alfredo has the following auto insurance coverage and corresponding annual premiums. Alfredo has chosen to pay his auto insurance premium quarterly. His insurance company charges a $2.50 fee for each partial-payment. What will be Alfredo's quarterly insurance payment?

Coverage Type	Annual Premium
Liability (bodily injury)	$167.60
Liability (property damage)	186.80
Collision	180.80
Uninsured motorist (bodily injury)	61.20
Uninsured motorist (property damage)	53.20
Comprehensive	91.60

Checkpoint 10.2

Teaching Tip:
Checkpoint questions
offer opportunities for
formative assessment.

1. Prem owns a car with a fuel efficiency of 26 miles per gallon. She drives about 11,000 miles per year, and the average cost of gasoline where she lives is $3.80 per gallon. Calculate Prem's annual fuel costs.

2. Crystal owns a van with a fuel efficiency of 14 miles per gallon. She drives about 12,000 miles per year, and the average cost of gasoline where she lives is $4.10 per gallon. Calculate Crystal's annual fuel costs.

3. Hakim drives a truck with a fuel efficiency of 21 miles per gallon. He drives about 15,000 miles per year, and the average cost of gasoline where he lives is $3.90. The truck manufacturer recommends an oil change every 5,000 miles, which costs $51.50, including sales tax and environmental fees. Calculate the total annual cost of fuel and maintenance for Hakim's truck.

Use the information that follows for questions 4 and 5: Annemarie's declarations page from her auto insurance policy is shown. Her insurance company charges a $3.50-per-payment partial-payment fee.

Coverage Type	Annual Premium
Liability (bodily injury)	$107.80
Liability (property damage)	96.60
Collision	347.40
Uninsured motorist (bodily injury)	61.20
Uninsured motorist (property damage)	53.20
Comprehensive	153.80

4. If Annemarie decides to pay quarterly, calculate her quarterly auto insurance payment.

5. If Annemarie decides to pay monthly, calculate her monthly auto insurance payment.

Chapter Review

Build Your Vocabulary

As you progress through this course, develop a personal glossary of financial literacy terms and add it to your portfolio. This will help you build your financial literacy vocabulary. Write out a definition for each of the following terms, and add it to your personal glossary.

automobile dealer

sticker price

manufacturer's suggested retail price (MSRP)

trade-in allowance

tax, title, and license (TT & L)

depreciation

straight-line

manufacturer's warranty

extended warranty

automobile insurance

liability coverage

collision coverage

uninsured motorist coverage

comprehensive coverage

full coverage

totaled

 ## Teamwork

With a partner, research the cost-effectiveness of traveling by car or using public transportation. First, use a mapping website, such as www.mapquest.com or maps.google.com, to find the distance between your school and a point at least five miles away. Then, consult local transportation authority websites to find out which bus or train routes run between the locations. Calculate the cost per month of driving and of taking public transportation. Remember to add in the cost of auto insurance, gas, parking, and any additional costs. In addition to cost, what are some other considerations when deciding which method of transportation to use? Taking all available data into account, which transportation method is the best? Explain your conclusion.

Review Your Math Skills

Practice and build on the math skills that you have learned.

1. Convert percentages to decimals by moving the decimal two places to the left. Example: 7.5% → 0.075

A. 105.5% →

B. 2.87% →

C. 47.8% →

D. 0.054% →

2. Subtract decimals. Example: $452.74 – $74.96 = $377.78

A. $12.765 – $2.458 =

B. $14.85 – $3.07 =

C. $125.642 – $214.108 =

D. $457.38 – $628.12 =

Answer:
1. A. 1.055
   B. 0.0287
   C. 0.478
   D. 0.00054
2. A. $10.307
   B. $11.78
   C. –$88.466
   D. –$170.74

3. Divide decimals. Round to the nearest hundredth (0.01) if necessary.
Example: $1.503 \div 2.514 \approx 0.60$

A. $5.64 \div 2.04 \approx$

B. $1.118 \div 0.03 \approx$

C. $508.1 \div 632.8 \approx$

D. $65.47 \div 0.0125 \approx$

4. Add decimals. Example: $\$139.18 + \$208.04 = \$347.22$

A. $109.427 + 9.54 =$

B. $\$1,024.32 + \$111.18 =$

C. $0.058 + 1.357 =$

D. $\$92.87 + \$35.41 =$

5. Multiply decimals. Round to the nearest cent (\$0.01) if necessary. Example:
$80 \times \$3.56 = \$284.80$

A. $5.356 \times \$5.24 =$

B. $\$12.14 \times \$3.29 =$

C. $\$98.27 \times 0.045 =$

D. $12.45 \times \$102.58 =$

6. Divide decimals. Round to the nearest cent (\$0.01) if necessary. Example:
$\$716.50 \div 4 = \$179.13$

A. $\$28.54 \div 3.05 =$

B. $23.65 \div \$1.28 =$

C. $\$1.78 \div 3.27 =$

D. $\$132.92 \div 14.108 =$

7. Subtract decimals. Example: $\$132.49 - \$4.32 = \$128.17$

A. $\$552.1078 - \$35.28 =$

B. $\$1,475.62 - \$117.507 =$

C. $\$24.78 - \$108.54 =$

D. $\$110,217.51 - \$12,048.49 =$

8. Convert decimals to percentages by moving the decimal two places to
the right. Example: $0.075 \rightarrow 7.5\%$

A. $2.058 \rightarrow$

B. $0.04052 \rightarrow$

C. $0.6058 \rightarrow$

D. $10.1549 \rightarrow$

9. Add decimals. Example: $19.108 + 806.02 = 825.128$

A. $\$30.57 + \$23.54 =$

B. $1.4075 + 0.04687 =$

C. $\$901.46 + \$852.31 =$

D. $0.0257 + 0.7502 =$

10. Multiply decimals. Round to the nearest cent (\$0.01) if necessary.
Example: $17 \times \$2.52 = \$42.84$

A. $0.045 \times \$504.75 =$

B. $\$1,483.47 \times 1.0357 =$

C. $1.0975 \times \$351.58 =$

D. $\$101,347.92 \times 0.0137 =$

3. A. 2.77
   B. 37.27
   C. 0.80
   D. 5,237.60
4. A. 118.967
   B. $1,135.50
   C. 1.415
   D. $128.28
5. A. $28.07
   B. $39.94
   C. $4.42
   D. $1,277.12
6. A. $9.36
   B. $18.48
   C. $0.54
   D. $9.42
7. A. $516.8278
   B. $1,358.113
   C. −$83.76
   D. $98,169.02
8. A. 205.8%
   B. 4.052%
   C. 60.58%
   D. 1,015.49%
9. A. $54.11
   B. 1.45437
   C. $1,753.77
   D. 0.7759
10. A. $22.71
    B. $1,536.43
    C. $385.86
    D. $1,388.47

Section 10.1 Owning or Leasing a Car

Use the following information for questions 11 and 12. Sam is purchasing a new car. The MSRP is $35,250, and he has negotiated a sale price of $31,900. The dealer is offering a cash rebate of $1,500, and has offered Sam a $4,500 trade-in allowance for his old car. Sam must pay 7.5% sales tax, a license fee of $125, and a title transfer fee of $60.

11. Calculate the final price of the car, as well as the total cost of the car, including TT & L.

12. Sam qualifies for either a three-year car loan at 6.5% APR, with monthly payments of $859.01, or a five-year car loan at 7.5% APR, with monthly payments of $561.61. How much more in interest will Sam pay for the five-year car loan than the three-year car loan?

13. Lauren purchased a new car six years ago for $28,190. She sold it this year for $5,200. Calculate the average annual depreciation and the depreciation rate for Lauren's car.

14. Delma and her auto dealer have negotiated a price of $43,810 for a new sports car. The dealer presents Delma with two options. She can lease the sports car for $939 per month for 36 months and then purchase it at the end of the lease for the residual value of $28,419. Or, Delma can purchase the car with a down payment of $5,000 and monthly payments of $1,347 for 36 months. What is the total cost of purchasing the car under each plan? Which plan is less expensive?

Answer:
11. final price = $25,900
    total cost =
        $28,027.50
12. $2,772.24
13. average annual
    depreciation =
        $3,831.67 per year
    depreciation rate =
        13.6%
14. The purchase plan
    is $8,731 less
    expensive than the
    lease plan.

Section 10.2 Cost of Owning a Car

15. Ricky drives a convertible with a fuel efficiency of 25 miles per gallon. He drives about 13,000 miles per year, and the average cost of gasoline where he lives is $3.65. The manufacturer recommends an oil change every 3,000 miles, which costs $34.75, including sales tax and environmental fees. Calculate the total annual cost of fuel and maintenance for Ricky's convertible.

16. Ramani's coverage and annual premium information follows. She has chosen to pay her auto insurance premium monthly. Her insurance company charges a $1.75-per-payment partial-payment fee. What will be Ramani's monthly insurance payment?

Coverage Type	Annual Premium
Liability (bodily injury)	$219.86
Liability (property damage)	224.75
Collision	185.76
Uninsured motorist (bodily injury)	66.45
Uninsured motorist (property damage)	55.39
Comprehensive	115.74

Answer:
15. $2,037
16. $74.08

17. If Ramani changes insurance companies, she can decrease her annual premium in each coverage type by 12%. What would Ramani's annual savings be if she changed companies?

18. Jordan had $7,212 left to repay on his car loan when he was in an accident and the car was totaled. The value of his car at the time was $6,124. He has a $500 deductible. How much will Jordan have to pay out of pocket to resolve the outstanding balance?

17. $104.15
18. $1,588

Reinforce Your Understanding

19. Conrad is considering a payday loan for $355. The payday lender charges 22.5% for a brokerage fee, plus 0.62% in interest charges for a 14-day term loan. How much will Conrad pay back at the end of the 14 days?

20. Sung received a bonus check from her employer in the amount of $5,165.74. She decided to invest the money in an account that yields 3.6% compound interest annually. If Sung leaves the money in the account, and makes no additional deposits, what will be the balance of the account in eight years?

Answer:
19. $437.08
20. $6,854.94

Apply Your Technology Skills

www.g-wlearning.com

Access the G-W Learning companion website for this text at www.g-wlearning.com. Download each data file for this chapter. Follow the instructions to complete financial literacy activities to practice what you have learned in this chapter.

Teaching Tip:
The Apply Your Technology Skills activities offer project-based authentic assessment opportunities.

Data File 10-1—Estimating Annual Gallons of Gas Purchased

Data File 10-2—Completing an Application for a Car Loan

Data File 10-3—Researching Car Values

Data File 10-4—Calculating the Cost of Owning a Car

Unit 3 Summative Assessment

On a separate sheet of paper or in a word processing document, apply what you have learned in this unit to answer the questions that follow.

Multiple Choice Questions

1. Deon recently graduated from college. He has a total student loan amount of $12,400. His monthly payments will be $165.13. He will make those payments for ten years. How much interest will Deon have paid on his student loans when they are completely paid off?

    A. $1,651.30

    B. $7,415.60

    C. $19,815.60

    D. $32,215.60

2. Using cash, rather than credit cards, is a way to manage debt by ____.

    A. avoiding debt

    B. paying a lower interest rate

    C. creating a budget

    D. transferring risk

3. Sondra loaned her sister $7,500 to start a small business. Her sister agreed to pay back the original amount plus 5% interest. The full amount is due in one year. Determine the amount of interest that Sondra's sister will pay.

    A. $375

    B. $3,750

    C. $787.50

    D. $7,875

4. Which method of calculating interest assumes each month has 30 days?

    A. Compound interest method.

    B. Exact interest method.

    C. Ordinary interest method.

    D. Average daily balance method.

5. Kiena, Jessica, and Sierra agreed to share an apartment to help reduce their costs of living. The rent on their three-bedroom apartment is $1,075. If divided evenly, what is each person's share of the monthly rent?

    A. $538.34

    B. $537.50

    C. $337.50

    D. $358.33

Answer:
1. B
2. A
3. A
4. C
5. D

Matching

Match the letter beside each equation to the situation to which it applies.

A.   interest payment = $\dfrac{\text{annual interest rate} \times \text{principal balance}}{\text{number of payments per year}}$

B.   average daily balance = sum of daily balances ÷ days in period

C.   debt-to-income ratio = $\dfrac{\text{sum of monthly debt payments}}{\text{monthly income}}$

D.   I = Prt

E.   down payment = purchase price × down payment rate

F.   share of rent = total monthly rent ÷ number of people

G.   amount of mortgage = purchase price − down payment

H.   amortization table

I.   average annual depreciation = $\dfrac{\text{depreciation}}{\text{number of years}}$

J.   monthly payment = monthly premium + partial-payment fee

6. Aaron wants to know how much of his monthly mortgage payment is interest.

7. Blanca wants to calculate how much value per year her car has lost since she bought it.

8. Jackie wants to determine her monthly principal and interest payment.

9. Chuck is taking out a loan to purchase a motorcycle. He wants to know by what percentage this loan will increase his debt obligations.

10. Samir wants to find out what his monthly insurance payment will be.

11. Jon wants to take the first step to finding out how much interest he is charged daily on unpaid balances.

12. Mateo wants to know how much he will have to pay if he shares a house with two roommates.

13. Michelle wants to calculate a 20% down payment on a house.

14. Niesha wants to find out how much simple interest she will pay over the course of her loan.

15. Ray wants to find out how much of a mortgage loan he will need.

Answer:
6. A
7. I
8. H
9. C
10. J
11. B
12. F
13. E
14. D
15. G

True/False Questions

16. *True or False?* The better your FICO score, the more likely you are to be given credit.

17. *True or False?* The effective annual interest rate is the simple interest rate for the year.

18. *True or False?* A 529 plan helps first-time homebuyers get mortgage loans.

19. *True or False?* Exclude the cost of deposits and first month's rent when calculating move-in costs for a rental property.

20. *True or False?* An actual cash value policy pays what the property was worth at the time it was damaged or stolen.

Answer:
16. True
17. False
18. False
19. False
20. True

Mastery Questions

21. Callista, Kim, and Mei are college students who decided to share an apartment in order to save money. The monthly rent for their three-bedroom apartment will be $1,240. They must also pay a security deposit of $450. According to their lease, they must pay the first and last month's rent in advance. What is each roommate's share of the move-in costs for their apartment?

22. Nisha and Lee Nguyen are purchasing a new home with monthly mortgage payments of $740.16. Their annual property taxes are estimated to be $3,047.16, and their homeowners insurance policy has an annual cost of $2,149.76. They must also purchase wind insurance with an annual cost of $850.72. If the Nguyen family chooses to have these costs included in an escrow account, calculate their total monthly house payments.

Answer:
21. $976.67
22. $1,244.13

23. Noreen has three credit cards. She used her credit card statements to make the summary table that follows. Noreen is also eligible for a debt consolidation loan with an APR of 11.2% that reduces her monthly payments to $238.83. This loan will take six years to pay off, and Noreen will pay a total of $4,715.32 in interest charges. How much more in interest charges will the debt consolidation loan cost Noreen?

	APR	Balance	Monthly Payment	Time to Pay in Full	Total Interest Charges
Bayou Bank	18.75%	$4,000	$160	3 years	$1,112
Tumbleweed Bank	14.6%	6,500	260	3 years	1,297
Bank of the Swamp	21.7%	1,980	79	3 years	682

24. Juanita received her electricity bill for one month during the summer. Her previous meter reading was 56,019 kilowatt hours, and her current reading is 59,283 kilowatt hours. Her electric company charges $0.064 for the first 1,400 kilowatt hours and $0.113 for each additional kilowatt hour. What is the amount of Juanita's electricity bill?

25. Tarik has a credit card that charges a 3.75% fee for cash advances. Tarik had an unexpected electrical repair on his home and decided to get a $925 cash advance. What is the fee that he will pay for the cash advance? Round to the nearest cent ($0.01) if necessary.

23. $1,624.32
24. $300.23
25. $34.69

Unit 4
Building and Protecting Wealth

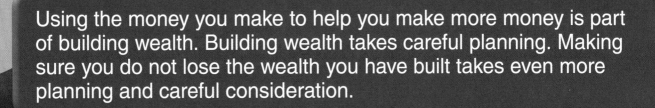

Using the money you make to help you make more money is part of building wealth. Building wealth takes careful planning. Making sure you do not lose the wealth you have built takes even more planning and careful consideration.

11 Building Wealth

Materials:
Instructor's Resource CD
Student Workbook
G-W Learning companion website
EXAMVIEW® Assessment Suite
Microsoft Excel®–compatible software
Calculator with advanced-math functions

Up to this point in the text, most of the focus has been on short-term money management. It is important, however, to plan for your financial future. To prepare for your future financial needs, you must set aside some of the money you are earning today. In this chapter, you will learn how taking some of your money and *putting it to work* will help you build wealth for your future.

Section 11.1 What Is Wealth?

Section 11.2 Bonds

Section 11.3 Stocks and Mutual Funds

College and Career Readiness

Reading Prep. In preparation for this chapter, read the portion of the Declaration of Independence that discusses *the pursuit of happiness*. What do you think the authors of this document meant by this phrase? As you read the chapter, consider what happiness means to Americans today.

> *"You should think about financial planning when you're younger, even though you may think that you don't need it."* ~ Courtney H.

 Money Matters
Stocks and Bonds

- The Philadelphia Stock Exchange, established in 1790, was the first stock exchange in the US.

- The stock market was created in 1792, when 24 stockbrokers and merchants signed the Buttonwood Agreement.

- Until 1817, the New York Stock Exchange (NYSE) conducted business at the Tontine Coffee House on the corner of Water and Wall Streets.

- The lowest volume day on the NYSE was March 16, 1830, when 31 shares of stock were traded.

- Since 1953, no less than 1 million shares have been traded daily on the NYSE. Since 1997, no less than 1 *billion* shares have been traded daily.

- The NASDAQ purchased the Philadelphia Stock Exchange in 2007 for $652 million.

- The smallest bond is the Louisiana Baby Bond, which was issued in the 1800s. The bond costs $5, is the size of an index card, and features a picture of a baby.

- Some companies have been creative with their stock symbols: BOOT for LaCrosse Footwear, Inc.; CASH for Meta Financial Group, Inc.; BABY for Natus Medical, Inc.; and GRRR for Lion Country Safari, Inc.

Section 11.1 What Is Wealth?

Objectives
- **Describe how wealth is accumulated.**
- **Calculate net worth.**
- **Identify the two most common types of bankruptcy.**

Terms
- *wealth*
- *financial plan*
- *active income*
- *passive income*
- *net worth*
- *bankrupt*

Build Your Math Skills

Review these math skills to prepare for the lesson that follows.

1. Add decimals. Example: $1,189.48 + $398.15 = $1,587.63

A. $973.56 + $704.08 =   B. $703.95 + $1,489.47 =

C. $2,746.52 + $17,840.19 =   D. $907.96 + $16,749.85 =

2. Subtract decimals. Example: $80,405.74 – $9,587.69 = $70,818.05

A. $8,704.65 – $6,741.76 =   B. $885.41 – $603.74 =

C. $7,463.15 – $955.23 =   D. $11,706.09 – $8,407.19 =

3. Add and subtract integers. Example: –$650 + $1,250 = $600

A. –$750 – $625 =   B. –$95 + $150 =

C. $800 – (–$150) =   D. $620 – (–$640) =

Answer:
1. A. $1,677.64
   B. $2,193.42
   C. $20,586.71
   D. $17,657.81
2. A. $1,962.89
   B $281.67
   C. $6,507.92
   D. $3,298.90
3. A. –$1,375
   B. $55
   C. $950
   D. $1,260

How Is Wealth Built?

Wealth is an abundance of resources or possessions that you own. As you begin your working career, one of your goals will probably be to build enough wealth to retire at a reasonable age with a lifestyle that you desire. Having enough money to maintain your lifestyle without working is known as *financial independence*. A **financial plan** is your road map to acquiring, saving, and spending money. A financial plan will help you build financial independence.

Active income is the money you earn from your work. To build wealth, you need to budget a portion of your active income as savings and investment. An *investment* is an asset that is purchased with the expectation of making a profit. Wealth is built by consistently investing so that you are putting a portion of your money to work for you. The goal is to use your money to make money.

Passive income is the income you receive from an investment. By taking a portion of your active income and investing it in assets that produce a passive income, you begin to create a snowball effect. As you reinvest the passive income into additional assets and continue to invest a portion of your active income, you can reach a point where your passive income is approaching or exceeding your active income.

There are many ways you can invest your money. Buying a home has been a good investment for many families over the years. However, in recent years,

Teaching Tip: Emphasize to students that the way they manage their money has a big impact on the type of lifestyle they will have.

home values have declined. Some people purchase land, gold, antiques, or other assets. Assets purchased as investments have traditionally increased in value over time.

For example, if you believe that the value of land in your area is going to increase, you might buy land as an investment in hopes that in the future the value of the land will be greater. The land can then be sold at a higher price to provide cash for other purposes.

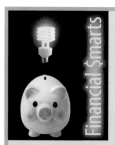

Financial $marts

Building wealth requires planning and patience. Very few people become wealthy overnight. One of the first steps in building wealth is to learn to be responsible with your money. It is important to create a budget for your paycheck that includes saving money. *Pay yourself first* is a phrase used in personal finance that means to save some of your money before you start spending. If you don't deposit money into savings or investments, you may spend all of your money and forget about saving for your future.

Other investments might generate immediate cash without having to be sold. For example, buying a house with the intention of renting it to others is a type of investment. The goal is that the rent paid by tenants will generate cash. In addition, you hope that the house will increase in value in the future.

There are many reasons to make investments. Investments are commonly used to build money for college and retirement. Many parents begin saving when a child is a baby in preparation for sending the child to college. Rather than just putting cash in a jar, most people invest their money with the expectation that it will grow.

Net Worth

Things you own that have value are *assets*. The money in your checking account, cash you have on hand, your car, real estate, and anything else that has monetary value are your assets. Money that you owe others is a form of *liability*. Credit card balances, the principal owed on loans, and any other money you owe anyone are your liabilities. Your **net worth** is your total assets minus your total liabilities:

$$\text{net worth} = \text{total assets} - \text{total liabilities}$$

Example 11-1A

See It

Mindy and Joaquin Smith made a list of their assets and liabilities, as shown in the table that follows. Calculate the Smiths' net worth.

Mindy and Joaquin Smith Net Worth		
Category	**Amount**	**Totals**
Assets:		
Checking account	$ 1,587.38	
Savings account	6,078.34	
Investment account	16,073.59	
Retirement account	55,670.93	
Home	162,000.00	
Automobile	18,450.00	
Other assets	33,650.00	
Total Assets		
Liabilities:		
Mortgage	98,502.19	
Credit card debt	6,498.36	
Auto loan	17,041.66	
Total Liabilities		
Net Worth		

Strategy

Use the formula:

net worth = total assets – total liabilities

Solution

Step 1: Determine the total assets. Add the value of each asset.

total assets = checking account + savings account + investment account +
retirement account + home + car + other assets

total assets = $1,587.38 + $6,078.34 + $16,073.59 + $55,670.93 + $162,000 +
$18,450 + $33,650

total assets = $293,510.24

Step 2: Determine the total liabilities. Add the value of each liability.

total liabilities = mortgage + credit card debt + auto loan

total liabilities = $98,502.19 + $6,498.36 + $17,041.66

total liabilities = $122,042.21

Step 3: Determine the net worth. Subtract the total liabilities from the total assets.

net worth = total assets – total liabilities

net worth = $293,510.24 – $122,042.21

net worth = $171,468.03

Check It

Leticia met with her financial planner and made a list of her assets and liabilities, as shown in the following table. Calculate Leticia's net worth.

Leticia Net Worth		
Category	**Amount**	**Totals**
Assets:		
Checking account	$ 2,743.62	
Savings account	2,951.04	
Retirement account	13,780.45	
Home	143,000.00	
Automobile	6,540.00	
Other assets	12,400.00	
Total Assets		
Liabilities:		
Mortgage	75,623.96	
Credit card debt	7,945.16	
Total Liabilities		
Net Worth		

An individual's wealth is commonly measured by his or her net worth. Many people you know may appear to be wealthy because they have a high-paying job, live in a nice house, and drive an expensive car. They could have a lot of debt and use much of their income to repay loans for a house and car. Others you know who live in a modest home and drive inexpensive cars may actually have a higher net worth and more accumulated wealth.

But, how could that be? Think of net worth as the cash you would have if you sold everything you own and then paid off all your debts.

Jordan and Makalah are two good examples of net worth, as shown in Figure 11-1. Jordan lives in a more expensive home and drives a more expensive car than Makalah. Jordan's assets add up to more than Makalah's. But when their liabilities are considered, you see that Makalah has no credit card debt and no auto loan. That may be part of the reason that Makalah has paid down her mortgage and has more equity in her home than Jordan.

Makalah has been putting more money toward retirement. Overall, Makalah has a much better net worth than Jordan. If both Jordan and Makalah faced a financial challenge, Makalah has no car payment to make, no credit card debt, and real equity in her home. Makalah's smart budgeting has helped her build up almost $13,000 in savings to face those financial challenges.

To determine an increase or decrease in net worth, use the following formula:

new net worth = previous net worth + new assets – new liabilities

	Jordan and Makalah Net Worth				
	Jordan			**Makalah**	
Category	**Amount**	**Totals**		**Amount**	**Totals**
Assets:					
Checking account	$ 3,288.10			$ 2,143.17	
Savings account	1,107.22			12,888.30	
Retirement account	45,321.88			77,645.35	
Home	320,000.00			205,000.00	
Automobile	23,900.00			9,600.00	
Other assets	24,300.00			22,650.00	
Total Assets		$ 417,917.20			$329,926.82
Liabilities:					
Mortgage	301,789.22			118,329.78	
Credit card debt	9,344.12			—	
Auto loan	26,644.25			—	
Total Liabilities		337,777.59			118,329.78
Net Worth		$ 80,139.61			$211,597.04

Figure 11-1. Jordan and Makalah's Net Worth

Example 11-1B

See It

Jordan pays off his credit card debt and increases his savings by $8,000. What is Jordan's new net worth?

Strategy

Use Figure 11-1 and the formula:

new net worth = previous net worth + new assets – new liabilities

Solution

Step 1: Identify the changes in Jordan's assets and liabilities.

assets: savings account increased by $8,000

liabilities: credit card debt reduced by $9,344.12

Step 2: Use a positive number to represent an increase and a negative number to represent a decrease.

assets: +$8,000

liabilities: –$9,344.12

Step 3: Add new assets to, and subtract new liabilities from, the previous net worth.

new net worth = previous net worth + new assets − new liabilities

new net worth = $80,139.61 + $8,000 − (−$9,344.12)

new net worth = $80,139.61 + $8,000 + $9,344.12

new net worth = $97,483.73

Check It

Calculate Jordan's net worth if he also pays off his auto loan and increases his retirement account by $5,000. Use the net worth from the See It portion of Example 11-1B as Jordan's previous net worth.

Bankruptcy

Is it possible to have a negative net worth? Absolutely. Remember that many individuals owe more on their cars and houses than these assets are worth. If an individual's assets have decreased in value since they were purchased, or he or she has a lot of credit card debt, the liabilities are probably more than assets. This can create a situation where the person is living paycheck to paycheck, hoping the debts will eventually be paid.

If a person or entity gets into a situation in which it is not possible to pay debts as the payments are due, the person or entity is considered **bankrupt.** Consider the situation of Jordan in Figure 11-1. The payments on that nice home and car are likely to be a combined total of well over $2,000 per month. Jordan is also making credit card debt payments. He has less than $4,500 total in his checking and savings. If Jordan loses his job, he will quickly be in financial trouble. As Jordan falls behind on making loan payments, it becomes harder to back up even if he gets another job. Because Jordan does not have a large net worth and he has large liabilities, he could be in danger of bankruptcy.

In legal terminology, a person or business can enter bankruptcy either to settle debt or allow for repayment under court protection. There are two main types of bankruptcy—Chapter 7 bankruptcy and Chapter 13 bankruptcy.

Chapter 7 bankruptcy requires that the assets of the person or business are sold and the proceeds are used to pay as much debt as can be repaid. Then, the remaining debt is cancelled. The debtor may be allowed to keep some personal items, but must make an attempt to pay off his or her bills. Chapter 7 bankruptcy stays on a consumer's credit report for ten years.

Chapter 13 bankruptcy sets up a payment plan rather than requiring that you sell all of your assets. The court gives protection to a person or business from those to which money is owed while the debt is repaid. Chapter 13 bankruptcy stays on a consumer's credit report for seven years.

Checkpoint 11.1

Use the information in the table to answer questions 1–5.

	Marc and Latoya Net Worth				
	Marc		Latoya		
Category	Amount	Totals	Amount	Totals
Assets:				
Checking account	$3,708.94		$2,761.23	
Savings account	7,046.45		15,708.46	
Retirement account	43,874.96		65,718.79	
Home	196,500.00		310,000.00	
Automobile	25,500.00		12,500.00	
Other assets	24,300.00		16,780.00	
Total Assets				
Liabilities:				
Mortgage	110,079.63		146,349.57	
Credit card debt	4,780.14		—	
Auto loan	27,465.18		—	
Total Liabilities				
Net Worth				

1. Calculate Marc's net worth.

2. Calculate Latoya's net worth.

3. Marc receives a $6,500 bonus check from work. He decides to pay off his credit card debt and put the remainder of the bonus in his savings account. What is Marc's new net worth?

4. Latoya had a $7,500 family emergency and had to spend $4,000 from her savings account and sell $3,500 worth of other assets. What is Latoya's new net worth?

5. Latoya received an inheritance of $3,300. She added the money to her investment account. What is Latoya's new net worth compared to that calculated in question 4?

Answer:
1. $158,605.40
2. $277,118.91
3. $165,105.40
4. $269,618.91
5. $272,918.91

Section 11.2 Bonds

Objectives

- **Calculate interest over the life of a bond.**
- **Explain bond income and bond yield.**
- **Describe savings bonds.**

Build Your Math Skills

Review these math skills to prepare for the lesson that follows.

1. Convert percentages to decimals by moving the decimal two places to the left. Example: 4.5% → 0.045

A. 8.1% →

B. 12.3% →

C. 5.65% →

D. 10.74% →

2. Multiply decimals. Round to the nearest cent ($0.01) if necessary. Example: $115 × 0.06 = $6.90

A. $541 × 0.045 =

B. $970 × 0.08 =

C. $5,100 × 0.07 =

D. $4,675 × 0.035 =

3. Add and subtract decimals. Example: $714.62 + $86.43 = $801.05

A. $1,735.29 + $637.41 =

B. $465.17 + $904.78 =

C. $904.78 − $85.39 =

D. $6,708.63 − $4,890.07 =

Answer:
1. A. 0.081
   B. 0.123
   C. 0.0565
   D. 0.1074
2. A. $24.35
   B. $77.60
   C. $357
   D. $163.63
3. A. $2,372.70
   B. $1,369.95
   C. $819.39
   D. $1,818.56

Bonds

A *bond* is a debt issued by a government or company. When you purchase a bond, you are actually making a loan to the company or government that issued the bond. The loan is repaid at the bond's maturity date. The *maturity date* is the date when the amount borrowed plus the agreed to interest is payable. The *face value* of the bond is the amount borrowed. The face value is also known as the *par value*. The *coupon rate* of a bond is the annual interest rate. To determine the total interest received on a bond, the following formula can be used:

interest = face value × coupon rate × time

For example, suppose you purchased a bond with a face value of $1,000, at an annual interest rate of 5%, and a maturity of ten years. Assuming the bond pays interest semiannually, you will receive $50 (5% of $1,000) each year ($25 every six months). In addition to the interest payments, when the bond matures in ten years, the face value of $1,000 will be returned to you.

Teaching Tip:
Remind students that the formula *interest = face value × coupon rate × time* is the same thing as *I = Prt*, the formula for simple interest.

Example 11-2A

See It

Ming purchased a corporate bond with a face value of $4,000 at a coupon rate of 4.5% that will mature in ten years. If Ming keeps the bond for ten years, how much total interest will she receive?

Strategy

Use the formula:

interest = face value × coupon rate × time

Solution

Step 1: Convert the interest rate to a decimal by moving the decimal two places to the left.

4.5% → 0.045

Step 2: Determine the amount of annual interest. Multiply the face value (principal) by the coupon rate and the amount of time.

interest = face value × annual interest rate × time

interest = $4,000 × 0.045 × 10 years

interest = $1,800

Check It

Ricardo purchased a municipal bond with a face value of $3,500 at a coupon rate of 3.75% that will mature in eight years. If Ricardo keeps the bond for eight years, how much total interest will he receive?

Answer:
$1,050

Career Discovery
Information Technology Careers and Math Skills

Do you find the ever-changing world of computer technology fascinating? With work available in every segment of society, information technology (IT) careers are among those most in demand. The IT career pathways include network systems, information and support services, programming and software development, and interactive media.

IT professionals must be able to make calculations and communicate with others using the language of math, so math skills are crucial to their success. Give examples of situations where an IT person would make calculations or use math skills.

Buying and Selling Bonds

Teaching Tip:
Point out to students that storing money or setting money aside does not build wealth; it just conserves the money they have already earned.

A bond may be kept by the original buyer until the maturity date, or it may be sold to another investor. The **bondholder** is the current owner of a bond. When a bond is sold to another bondholder, the amount for which the bond sells is simply the price agreed to by the buyer and seller. If a bond sells for more than the *par value,* the bond is said to be selling at a **premium.** If the bond sells for less than the par value, the bond is said to be selling at a **discount.**

The value of a bond is stated as a percentage of the face value. Any number under 100 indicates the bond is selling at a discount. Any number over 100 indicates the bond is selling at a premium. For example, a price quote of 95.125 means the bond is selling at 95.125% of *par value,* which is a discount. At that price, a $1,000 par value bond would sell for $951.25. A price quote of 101.000 means the bond is selling for 101% of par value, which is a premium. At that price, a $1,000 par value bond would sell for $1,010. Use the following formula to calculate the price of a bond:

$$\text{bond price} = \text{par value} \times \text{price quote}$$

Example 11-2B

See It

A school district bond with a par value of $1,000 has a price quote of 102.125. What is the price of the bond?

Strategy

Use the formula:

$$\text{bond price} = \text{par value} \times \text{price quote}$$

Solution

Step 1: Convert the price quote to a percentage by moving the decimal two places to the left.

102.125 → 1.02125%

Step 2: Determine the price of the bond. Multiply the par value by the price quote. Round to the nearest cent ($0.01) if necessary.

bond price = par value × price quote

bond price = $1,000 × 1.02125

bond price = $1,021.25

Check It

A corporate bond has a par value of $1,000 and a price quote of 97.150. Calculate the price of the bond.

Answer:
$971.50

Example 11-2C

See It

Jonathan is purchasing a corporate bond with a par value of $500 and a price quote of 103.450. What is the price of the bond?

Strategy

Use the formula:

bond price = par value × price quote

Solution

Step 1: Convert the price quote to a percentage by moving the decimal two places to the left.

$103.450 \rightarrow 1.0345\%$

Step 2: Determine the price of the bond. Multiply the par value by the price quote. Round to the nearest cent ($0.01) if necessary.

bond price = par value × price quote

bond price = $500 × 1.0345

bond price = $517.25

Check It

Hasita is purchasing a government bond with a par value of $200 and a price quote of 98.875. What is the price of the bond?

Answer:
$197.75

Interest payments provide income for a bondholder. The interest is based on the par value and is traditionally paid twice per year. To calculate the amount of interest payments on a bond, use the following formula:

interest payment = annual interest ÷ number of payments

Example 11-2D

See It

Christina purchased a corporate bond with a par value of $1,000 and a coupon rate of 6% that pays interest semiannually. What will be Christina's interest payments?

Strategy

Use the formula:

interest payment = annual interest ÷ number of payments

Solution

Step 1: Convert the coupon rate to a decimal by moving the decimal two places to the left.

6% → 0.06

Step 2: Determine the annual interest. Multiply the par value, coupon rate, and time (1 year).

annual interest = par value × coupon rate × time

annual interest = $1,000 × 0.06 × 1

annual interest = $60

Step 3: Determine the interest payment. Divide the annual interest by the number of payments per year.

interest payment = annual interest ÷ number of payments

interest payment = $60 ÷ 2

interest payment = $30

Check It

Malik purchased a county government bond with a par value of $2,000 and an annual interest rate of 5.5% that pays interest quarterly. What will be Malik's interest payments?

Answer:
$27.50

Bond yield is a way to measure the return on investment from a bond. If a bond is purchased for par value, bond yield is equal to the interest rate. But, when the price of the bond is above or below par, the yield changes. To calculate bond yield, use the following formula:

$$\text{bond yield} = \frac{\text{annual bond income}}{\text{bond price}}$$

Example 11-2E

See It

Clayton purchased a corporate bond with a coupon rate of 10% and a par value of $1,500. The value of the bond fell to $1,200. What is the bond yield?

Strategy

Use the formula:

$$\text{bond yield} = \frac{\text{annual bond income}}{\text{bond price}}$$

Solution

Step 1: Convert the coupon rate to a decimal by moving the decimal two places to the left.

10% → 0.10

Step 2: Determine the annual interest on the bond. Multiply the coupon rate by the par value.

annual interest = coupon rate × par value

annual interest = 0.10 × $1,500

annual interest = $150

Step 3: Determine the bond yield. Divide the annual interest (bond income) by the bond price.

$$\text{bond yield} = \frac{\text{annual income}}{\text{bond price}}$$

$$\text{bond yield} = \frac{\$150}{\$1,200}$$

bond yield = 0.125

Step 4: Convert the bond yield to a percentage by moving the decimal two places to the right.

0.125 → 12.5%

Check It

Madeline purchased a municipal bond with a coupon rate of 8% and a par value of $2,500. The value of the bond rose to $2,800. What is the bond yield?

Bond yield is a ratio. When the bond price falls, the yield increases because the denominator of the ratio is decreasing. When the bond price rises, the yield decreases because the denominator of the ratio is increasing. Hence, there is an inverse relationship between bond price and bond yield.

Answer:
7.14%

Savings Bonds

A *savings bond* is a way to loan money to the US government. Savings bonds, known as series EE bonds, are issued by the US Treasury Department. They are considered one of the safest ways to invest money because they are backed by the US government. Savings bonds are a good way to save for long-term goals.

In the past, savings bonds were represented by a paper document. The bond was purchased for half of its face value. At maturity, the bond was redeemable for the full face value of the bond. These paper bonds were popular as birthday gifts for children and for personal investment.

Paper savings bonds are no longer available. Instead, savings bonds are now sold electronically. The electronic savings bonds are sold at face value and the interest is paid electronically into a special account that belongs to the bondholder. An electronic savings bond must be held for at least five years to avoid a decrease in the principal.

Teaching Tip:
Explain to students that just like individuals, a government's level of creditworthiness determines how much interest it will have to pay on a loan.

Checkpoint 11.2

1. Manuel purchased a corporate bond with a face value of $2,500 at a coupon rate of 5.25% that will mature in four years. If Manuel keeps the bond for four years, how much total interest will he receive?

2. Shania is purchasing a government bond with a par value of $800 and a price quote of 101.625. What is the price of the bond?

3. Cheng is purchasing a municipal bond with a par value of $2,100 and a price quote of 98.875. What is the price of the bond?

4. Marjorie purchased a county government bond with a par value of $3,000 and coupon rate of 4.5% that pays interest quarterly. What will be Marjorie's interest payments?

5. Hakim purchased a corporate bond with a coupon rate of 8.5% and a par value of $2,000. The value of the bond rose to $2,500. What is the bond yield?

Answer:
1. $525
2. $813
3. $2,076.38
4. $33.75
5. 6.8%

Section 11.3 Stocks and Mutual Funds

Objectives

- **Describe how stock is bought and sold.**
- **Explain stock dividends.**
- **Calculate dividend yield.**
- **Identify the basic principles of a mutual fund.**

Terms

- *stockholder*
- *stock*
- *privately held company*
- *publicly held company*
- *initial public offering (IPO)*
- *broker*
- *stock exchange*
- *dividend*
- *preferred stock*
- *common stock*
- *dividend yield*
- *diversification*
- *mutual fund*
- *net asset value (NAV)*
- *load*
- *no-load fund*
- *prospectus*

Build Your Math Skills

Review these math skills to prepare for the lesson that follows.

1. Convert decimals to percentages by moving the decimal two places to the right. Example: $0.093 \rightarrow 9.3\%$

A. $0.714 \rightarrow$

B. $0.0714 \rightarrow$

C. $0.0569 \rightarrow$

D. $0.8409 \rightarrow$

2. Multiply and divide whole numbers. Round to the nearest cent ($0.01) if necessary. Example: $\$115 \times 40 = \$4{,}600$

A. $55 \times \$3 =$

B. $\$4 \times 70 =$

C. $\$450 \div 12 =$

D. $\$640 \div 52 =$

3. Multiply and divide decimals. Round to the nearest cent ($0.01) if necessary. Example: $\$15.50 \div 5 = \$3.10$

A. $\$250.50 \div 4 =$

B. $\$171.94 \times 3.5 =$

C. $12 \times \$65.04 =$

D. $\$874 \div 22 =$

4. Add and subtract decimals. Example: $\$165.78 + \$602.43 = \$768.21$

A. $\$109.07 + \$435.43 =$

B. $\$690.05 + \$83.81 =$

C. $\$1{,}084.06 - \$908.45 =$

D. $\$665.04 - \$78.85 =$

Answer:
1. A. 71.4%
   B. 7.14%
   C. 5.69%
   D. 84.09%
2. A. $165
   B. $280
   C. $37.50
   D. $12.31
3. A. $62.63
   B. $601.79
   C. $780.48
   D. $39.73
4. A. $544.50
   B. $773.86
   C. $175.61
   D. $586.19

Buying and Selling Stock

Companies have owners. Sometimes one individual may own an entire company, especially if the company is small. Often a company has multiple owners, sometimes hundreds or thousands of owners. Most companies with multiple owners organize as a legal entity called a *corporation.* **Stockholders,** or *shareholders* are the owners of company stock. **Stock** is the individual share of the company that the stockholder owns. That ownership is signified by a legal certificate called a *stock certificate.*

Companies can issue stock as a way to raise money. For example, if a company needs money to expand its operations internationally, the company may sell stock to raise money needed for the expansion. The individuals who buy the stock receive a share of company ownership in exchange for their money, which the company needs to expand.

Privately held companies are owned by a small group of individuals and the stock is not offered to the general public. *Publicly held companies* offer their stock to the general public and the shares of stock are openly traded between shareholders. Publicly held companies are also called *publicly traded* companies because the stock is traded on a public market.

When a company first sells shares of stock, the company receives the money from the sale of the stock. The first time the stock is sold, it is called an *initial public offering (IPO).* But once members of the public have purchased the stock, the stock is simply traded among investors. The price of a share of stock is determined by the market. In other words, the price is whatever someone is willing to pay.

Shares of stock are traded using *brokers,* who act as agents between the buyer and seller. A *stock exchange* is the site where the stock is traded. The most famous stock exchange is the New York Stock Exchange. Stocks are also traded electronically on exchanges such as the NASDAQ, which stands for National Association of Securities Dealers Automated Quotations.

When you purchase stock, you pay a commission to the broker. With the advancement in online trading, commissions have become less expensive due to automation and competition among online trading brokers. It is common to be able to make a stock trade online for less than $10. Brokers who offer more service to customers charge more and the commission may be based on a percentage of the sale. To determine the cost of a trade, use the following formula:

cost of trade = price of stock + commission

Most stock trading is actually done online. Figure 11-2 is similar to what you might find if you look up a stock on a site that reports stock trading activity. The *last trade price* is the current market price, because that is the price of the last trade. The *day's range* shows the lowest and highest trade for the day. The *52-week range* is the highest and lowest trade in the previous year.

Example 11-3A

See It

Rolando wants to purchase 20 shares of stock in Southland Airlines. The stock currently trades at $42.58 per share, and his online brokerage charges him an $8 commission per trade. What will the stock purchase cost Rolando?

Strategy

Use the formula:

cost of trade = price of stock + commission

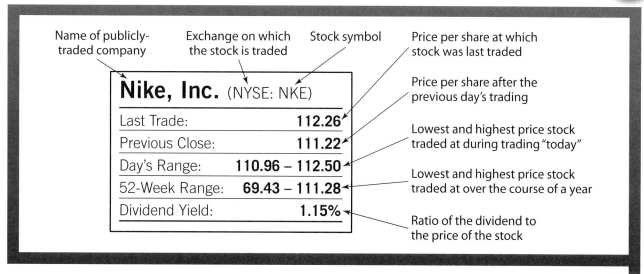

Name of publicly-traded company → **Nike, Inc.**

Exchange on which the stock is traded → (NYSE: NKE)

Stock symbol → NKE

Price per share at which stock was last traded → 112.26

Price per share after the previous day's trading → 111.22

Lowest and highest price stock traded at during trading "today" → 110.96 – 112.50

Lowest and highest price stock traded at over the course of a year → 69.43 – 111.28

Ratio of the dividend to the price of the stock → 1.15%

Nike, Inc. (NYSE: NKE)	
Last Trade:	112.26
Previous Close:	111.22
Day's Range:	110.96 – 112.50
52-Week Range:	69.43 – 111.28
Dividend Yield:	1.15%

Figure 11-2. Sample Stock Quote

Solution

Step 1: Determine the price of the stock. Multiply the price per share by the number of shares.

price of stock = price per share × number of shares

price of stock = $42.58 × 20

price of stock = $851.60

Step 2: Determine the cost of the trade. Add the price of the stock and the commission.

cost of trade = price of stock + commission

cost of trade = $851.60 + $8

cost of trade = $859.60

Check It

Abby has decided to purchase 45 shares of stock in Palm Tree Orchards. The stock currently trades at $31.45 per share, and her online brokerage charges a $4.50 commission per trade. What will the stock purchase cost Abby?

Answer:
$1,419.75

Stock Dividends

When you own shares of stock in a corporation, you actually own a piece of that company. While it may be a very small piece of the total corporation, you have a right to your share of the company's profits. The management of the corporation decides each year whether a portion of the profits is going to be distributed to the shareholders. A ***dividend*** is a distribution of profits to stockholders. To determine the total amount of money received from dividends, use the following formula:

dividend = number of shares × dividend per share

Teaching Tip:
Project or otherwise
display Figure 11-2, the
Nike stock quote. Remind
students that when
investing in stocks they
can actually lose money
if the price of the stock
falls below the price they
paid for it.

Many corporations have two classes of stock. *Preferred stock* is a class of stock that receives dividends first, sometimes receiving guaranteed dividends. *Common stock* is the non-preferred stock with no guaranteed dividend. Dividends are typically an amount per share.

Not every company pays dividends. More stable and established companies are more likely to pay dividends. Younger companies experiencing faster growth often choose to keep earnings in the company to fund their growth.

Example 11-3B

See It

Southland Airlines has decided to pay its shareholders a dividend of $3 per share. Rolando, who owns 20 shares of Southland Airlines stock, will receive a dividend on his stock. How much will Rolando receive in dividends from Southland Airlines?

Strategy

dividend = number of shares × dividend per share

Solution

Step 1: Determine the number of shares Rolando owns and the dividend per share.

number of shares = 20

dividend per share = $3

Step 2: Determine the amount of the dividend. Multiply the number of shares by the dividend per share.

dividend = number of shares × dividend per share

dividend = 20 × $3

dividend = $60

Check It

Palm Tree Orchards has decided to pay a dividend of $1.50 per share. Abby, who owns 45 shares of Palm Tree Orchards stock, will receive a dividend on her stock. How much will Abby receive in dividends from Palm Tree Orchards?

Answer:
$67.50

Calculating Dividend Yield

It is important to be able to measure and compare investments. When a stock pays a dividend, one way to measure the return on your investment is to calculate the *dividend yield,* which is a ratio of dividend to the price of the stock.

The formula for calculating dividend yield is as follows:

$$\text{dividend yield} = \frac{\text{annual dividend per share}}{\text{stock price per share}}$$

Example 11-3C

See It

Last year, Estacado Telecommunications paid an annual dividend of $4.80 per share, and the stock price at that time was $36 per share. Calculate the dividend yield for Estacado Telecommunications.

Strategy

Use the formula:

$$\text{dividend yield} = \frac{\text{annual dividend per share}}{\text{stock price per share}}$$

Solution

Step 1: Identify the annual dividend per share and stock price per share.

annual dividend per share = $4.80

stock price per share = $36

Step 2: Determine the dividend yield. Divide the annual dividend per share by the stock price per share.

$$\text{dividend yield} = \frac{\text{annual dividend per share}}{\text{stock price per share}}$$

$$\text{dividend yield} = \frac{\$4.80}{\$36}$$

dividend yield = 0.1333

Step 3: Convert the dividend yield to a percentage by moving the decimal two places to the right.

0.1333 → 13.33%

Check It

Community Bank and Trust paid an annual dividend of $2.75, and the stock price at the time was $22 per share. What was the dividend yield for Community Bank and Trust?

Answer:
12.5%

Teaching Tip:
Ask students what they think are the relative advantages and disadvantages of investing in mutual funds and individual stocks.

Mutual Funds

For people without large amounts of money to invest, buying individual shares of stock does not allow the investor to have a wide array of stock in their portfolio. For example, if you have $1,000 to invest in the stock market, you may only be able to buy shares from a few companies because the price per share could be high.

When investing, it is important that you spread your investments around so that your risk is less. **Diversification** is the process of spreading money around in multiple investments.

Mutual funds are a type of investment where the money from many investors is combined to buy a diversified group of stocks. You can buy shares in a mutual fund rather than buying shares in individual companies. Each share of a mutual fund is a share of a pool of money invested in many companies.

There are many types of mutual funds. Some mutual funds specialize in certain kinds of company stocks. For example, a technology fund will primarily own stock in technology companies. There are also funds that specialize in stock that pays dividends or in stock of companies expecting fast growth.

You have probably heard the saying *don't put all of your eggs in one basket.* In other words, diversify your investments. In order to build wealth, it is important to diversify. *Diversify* means to buy a variety of stocks, bonds, property, and other investments, rather than putting your money all in one place. Purchasing different types of investments protects you in the event that one does not do as well as you hoped. It is also important to start investing early. The earlier you start investing your money, the more valuable your wealth will become.

A mutual fund has a *fund manager* who decides what stock trades the fund should make. The fund manager is regularly making decisions to buy and sell stock held by the fund.

The price of a share in the mutual fund is determined by the value of the stock held by the fund. So, for example, if the total market value of the stock held by the mutual fund declines, the price of a share of the mutual fund will also decline. Mutual funds shares are priced based on net asset value. **Net asset value (NAV)** is the total assets of the fund minus any debts the fund may have, divided by the number of shares that are held by shareholders.

$$\text{net asset value} = \frac{\text{fund assets} - \text{fund liabilities}}{\text{number of outstanding shares}}$$

Example 11-3D

See It

Masterson Mutual Fund has combined assets of $85,000,000 and combined debts of $15,000,000. It has sold approximately 6,500,000 shares. Calculate the net asset value for Masterson Mutual Fund.

Strategy

Use the formula:

$$\text{net asset value} = \frac{\textbf{fund assets} - \textbf{fund liabilities}}{\textbf{number of outstanding shares}}$$

Solution

Step 1: Identify the fund assets, fund liabilities, and number of outstanding shares.

fund assets = $85,000,000

fund liabilities = $15,000,000

number of outstanding shares = 6,500,000

Step 2: Determine the net fund worth. Subtract the fund liabilities from the fund assets.

net fund worth = fund assets – fund liabilities

net fund worth = $85,000,000 – $15,000,000

net fund worth = $70,000,000

Step 3: Determine the net asset value. Divide the net fund worth by the number of outstanding shares. Round to the nearest cent ($0.01) if necessary.

$$\text{net asset value} = \frac{\text{fund assets} - \text{fund liabilities}}{\text{number of outstanding shares}}$$

$$\text{net asset value} = \frac{\$70,000,000}{6,500,000 \text{ shares}}$$

net asset value = $10.7693 per share

Check It

Harlass Mutual Fund has $70,000,000 in assets; $10,000,000 in debts; and has sold approximately 3,550,000 shares. Calculate the net asset value for Harlass Mutual Fund.

fyi

Typically, costs in dollars are rounded to the nearest cent. However, for some applications, such as net asset value (NAV), financial analysts report figures to a different precision, such as the nearest ten-thousandth of a dollar, or $0.0001. Using a precision other than the nearest cent is usually done when working with very large sums of money, such as you would find in a mutual fund.

Answer:
$16.9014

The company that manages the mutual fund makes its money through various fees and commissions. The commission charges on a mutual fund are called the *load.* A *no-load fund* is a mutual fund with no commission charges. No-load funds are sometimes more attractive to investors because they do not pay a commission charge. However, the mutual fund company still makes its money on fees from one source or another.

In a no-load mutual fund, a share trades at the net asset value. A loaded fund will have a price, called an *offer price,* which includes the commission charges.

To determine the total cost of investment, use the following formula:

investment cost = number of shares × price per share

Source: Shutterstock (EvrenKalinbacak)

The value of your assets is part of your net worth.

Example 11-3E

See It

Eastern Horizon Equity A is a no-load mutual fund with an NAV of $8.7547. Forrest wants to purchase 400 shares of the Eastern Horizon Equity A mutual fund. What will be his total investment cost?

Strategy

investment cost = number of shares × price per share

Solution

Step 1: Identify the number of shares and the price per share.

number of shares = 400

price per share = $8.7547

Step 2: Determine the cost of the investment transaction. Multiply the number of shares by the cost per share.

investment cost = number of shares × price per share

investment cost = 400 × $8.7547

investment cost = $3,501.88

Check It

North Creek Equity C is a no-load mutual fund with an NAV of $16.2706. Meena wants to purchase 350 shares of the North Creek Equity C mutual fund. What will be her total investment cost?

Answer:
$5,694.71

Example 11-3F

See It

Eastern Horizon Equity C is a loaded fund with an offer price of $9.4054. Tamara wants to purchase 300 shares of this fund. What will be her total investment cost?

Strategy

investment cost = number of shares × price per share

Solution

Step 1: Identify the number of shares and the price per share.

number of shares = 300

price per share = $9.4054

Step 2: Determine the cost of the investment transaction. Multiply the number of shares by the cost per share.

investment cost = number of shares × price per share

investment cost = 300 × $9.4054

investment cost = $2,821.62

Check It

North Creek Equity A is a loaded mutual fund with an offer price of $17.4638. Sergio wants to purchase 250 shares of the North Creek Equity A mutual fund. What will be his total investment cost?

Answer:
$4,635.95

When making investments, make sure you understand the fees associated with each investment. Mutual funds provide shareholders and potential shareholders with a document, called a ***prospectus,*** which provides the details of the risks and fees involved in the investment.

The idea behind an investment is that at some point, the investment will be sold, hopefully for more than the original cost of the investment. The return on the investment is the proceeds of the sale minus the original cost of the investment:

return on investment = number of shares × (sale price per share – purchase price per share)

Example 11-3G

See It

Alexis purchased 100 shares of Northern Lights Equity C mutual fund at an NAV of $7.5911. She later sold those shares at an NAV of $9.3573. Calculate Alexis' return on investment.

Strategy

Use the formula:

return on investment = number of shares × (sale price per share – purchase price per share)

Solution

Step 1: Determine the profit or loss per share. Subtract the purchase NAV from the sale NAV.

profit/loss = sale price per share – purchase price per share

profit/loss = $9.3573 – $7.5911

profit/loss = $1.7662

Step 2: Determine the return on the investment. Multiply the profit or loss by the number of shares.

return on investment = number of shares × profit or loss

return on investment = 100 × $1.7662

return on investment = $176.62

Check It

Elijah purchased 200 shares of Gulf Mutual Value Fund B mutual fund at an NAV of $12.8741. He later sold those shares at an NAV of $14.1383. Calculate Elijah's return on investment.

Answer:
$252.84

Checkpoint 11.3

Teaching Tip:
Checkpoint questions
offer opportunities for
formative assessment.

Use the information that follows to answer questions 1 and 2. At the beginning of the year, Ramona decided to purchase 75 shares of stock in Permian Basin Supply Company at $17.64 per share. Her online brokerage charges a $7.95 commission per trade. Permian Basin Supply Company pays a quarterly dividend of $0.55 per share each quarter of the year, and at the end of the year, the stock price was $18.50.

1. What did the stock purchase cost Ramona?

2. Calculate Ramona's quarterly dividend and her annual dividend yield.

3. Jackson is a fund manager for Eastern Seaboard Value Fund A. The fund has $92,000,000 in assets, $17,000,000 in debts, and currently has 4,600,000 shares. What is the NAV of the Eastern Seaboard Value Fund A?

4. Maia wants to purchase 220 shares of Appalachian Equity Fund C, which is a no-load fund with an NAV of $8.3178. What will be Maia's total investment cost?

5. Cody purchased 150 shares of Great Southern Value Fund B at an NAV of $13.0238. He later sold the shares at an NAV of $16.3852. What was the return on Cody's investment?

Answer:
1. $1,330.95
2. $41.25; 11.9%
3. $16.3043
4. $1,829.92
5. $504.21

Chapter Review

Build Your Vocabulary

As you progress through this course, develop a personal glossary of financial literacy terms and add it to your portfolio. This will help you build your financial literacy vocabulary. Write out a definition for each of the following terms, and add it to your personal glossary.

wealth	privately held company
financial plan	publicly held company
active income	initial public offering (IPO)
passive income	broker
net worth	stock exchange
bankrupt	dividend
bond	preferred stock
maturity date	common stock
face value	dividend yield
coupon rate	diversification
bondholder	mutual fund
premium	net asset value (NAV)
discount	load
bond yield	no-load fund
stockholder	prospectus
stock	

 ## Teamwork

Together with a partner, research how you can purchase and redeem different types of US savings bonds. Compare the rate of return you will receive on a savings bond versus what you would receive if you invested the same amount of money in a certificate of deposit or money market account. Prepare a matrix that shows the yields for each after 20 years. Which do you think is the best investment to help meet a long-term goal?

Review Your Math Skills

Practice and build on the math skills that you have learned.

1. Add and subtract integers. Example: −$650 + $1,250 = $600

A. −$746 − (−$61) =   B. $843 + (−$408) =

C. −$19 + $294 =   D. $157 − (−$817) =

2. Convert decimals to percentages by moving the decimal two places to the right. Example: 0.093 → 9.3%

A. 0.745 →

B. 0.0031 →

C. 0.017 →

D. 2.4816 →

3. Multiply and divide whole numbers. Round to the nearest cent ($0.01) if necessary. Example: $115 × 40 = $4,600

A. $316 × 13 =

B. $864 ÷ 108 =

C. $474 ÷ 6 =

D. $27 × 61 =

4. Add decimals. Example: $1,189.48 + $398.15 = $1,587.63

A. $450.19 + $5,802.67 =

B. $12,751.02 + $17,341.95 =

C. $8,052.99 + $649.12 =

D. $573.67 + $22,809.45 =

5. Multiply and divide decimals. Round to the nearest cent ($0.01) if necessary. Example: $81.60 ÷ 2 = $40.80

A. $517.10 ÷ 6 =

B. 79.12 × $15 =

C. $312 ÷ 7.5 =

D. 487 × $29.05 =

6. Add and subtract decimals. Example: $165.78 + $602.43 = $768.21

A. $318.27 − $246.94 =

B. $589.15 − $49.61 =

C. $601.51 + $176.46 =

D. $1,081.68 + $722.21 =

7. Subtract decimals. Example: $80,405.74 − $9,587.69 = $70,818.05

A. $98,437.32 − $5,849.15 =

B. $17,469.08 − $45,194.67 =

C. $9,056.48 − $816.05 =

D. $29,007.94 − $14,945.13 =

8. Convert percentages to decimals by moving the decimal two places to the left. Example: 4.5% → 0.045

A. 8.27% →

B. 74.08% →

C. 200.91% →

D. 23.14% →

9. Add and subtract decimals. Example: $714.62 + $86.43 = $801.05

A. $5,071.18 − $39.46 =

B. $316.27 + $781.52 =

C. $4,187.09 + $5,037.94 =

D. $8,834.11 − $607.89 =

10. Multiply decimals. Round to the nearest cent ($0.01) if necessary. Example: $115 × 0.06 = $6.90

A. $1,076 × 0.056 =

B. $8,723 × 0.005 =

C. $394 × 0.91 =

D. $7,094 × 0.12 =

2. A. 74.5%
   B. 0.31%
   C. 1.7%
   D. 248.16%
3. A. $4,108
   B. $8
   C. $79
   D. $1,647
4. A. $6,252.86
   B. $30,092.97
   C. $8,702.11
   D. $23,383.12
5. A. $86.18
   B. $1,186.80
   C. $41.60
   D. $14,147.35
6. A. $71.33
   B. $539.54
   C. $777.97
   D. $1,803.89
7. A. $92,588.17
   B. −$27,725.59
   C. $8,240.43
   D. $14,062.81
8. A. 0.0827
   B. 0.7408
   C. 2.0091
   D. 0.2314
9. A. $5,031.72
   B. $1,097.79
   C. $9,225.03
   D. $8,226.22
10. A. $60.26
    B. $43.62
    C. $358.54
    D. $851.28

Section 11.1 What Is Wealth?

Use the information in the table that follows to answer questions 11 and 12.

Mali Net Worth		
Category	Amount	Totals
Assets:		
Checking account	$ 1,431.04	
Savings account	11,876.43	
Retirement account	55,718.49	
Home	140,700.00	
Automobile	5,500.00	
Other assets	8,750.00	
Total Assets		
Liabilities:		
Mortgage	70,789.63	
Credit card debt	3,719.82	
Total Liabilities		
Net Worth		

11. Calculate Mali's net worth.

12. In the next year, Mali pays off her credit card debt and deposits $1,650 into her retirement account. What is Mali's new net worth?

Section 11.2 Bonds

13. Stephanie purchased a corporate bond with a face value of $3,500 at an annual interest rate of 4.75%. The bond will mature in four years and pays interest semiannually. Calculate both Stephanie's semiannual interest payment and the total amount of interest she will receive if she keeps the bond for four years.

14. Fernando bought two different municipal bonds. Sulphur Springs municipal bond has a par value of $1,200 and a price quote of 102.375. Muddy Waters municipal bond has a par value of $1,500 and a price quote of 98.750. What is the price of each bond?

15. Mena purchased a corporate bond with a coupon rate of 6.5% and a par value of $4,000. The value of the bond fell to $3,750. What is the bond yield?

Section 11.3 Stocks and Mutual Funds

16. Last year, Trans-Mississippi Energy paid an annual dividend of $4.35. The stock price at the time was $40.17 per share. What was the dividend yield for Trans-Mississippi Energy last year?

17. Brock wants to purchase 180 shares of Columbia Valley Equity Fund, which is a loaded mutual fund with an offer price of $9.0476. What will be Brock's total investment cost?

18. Janet purchased 240 shares of Rocky Mountain Value Fund B at an NAV of $14.7089 and then later sold the shares at an NAV of $19.5273. What was the return on Janet's investment?

Answer:
16. 10.8%
17. $1,628.57
18. $1,156.42

Reinforce Your Understanding

19. Alicia has a credit card with a 21.5% APR with a 30-day billing period. Her daily balances for one billing period are shown in the chart that follows. Determine Alicia's average daily balance.

Days 1–2	Days 4–7	Days 8–12	Days 13–20	Days 21–25	Days 26–30
$478.15	$607.14	$885.46	$504.13	$610.79	$680.09

20. Brad works as an independent contractor providing information technology services. He recently completed a contract for $8,850. Calculate Brad's self-employment taxes that he will pay on his earnings from this contract. Use the self-employment tax rate of 13.3%.

Answer:
19. $630.22
20. $1,177.05

Teaching Tip:
The Apply Your Technology Skills activities offer project-based authentic assessment opportunities.

Apply Your Technology Skills

Companion Website
www.g-wlearning.com

Access the G-W Learning companion website for this text at www.g-wlearning.com. Download each data file for this chapter. Follow the instructions to complete financial literacy activities to practice what you have learned in this chapter.

Data File 11-1—Researching Stock Quotes

Data File 11-2—Purchasing Shares of Common Stock

Data File 11-3—Calculating Earnings on Stock

Data File 11-4—Calculating Earnings on Bonds

12 Insurance

Materials:
Instructor's Resource CD
Student Workbook
G-W Learning companion website
EXAMVIEW® Assessment Suite
Microsoft Excel®–compatible software
Calculator with advanced-math functions

Everyone faces risks every day. Accidents, illnesses, and injuries are often accompanied by personal financial loss. Risks cannot always be avoided. However, you can avoid the financial toll they can take by purchasing insurance. The insurance company puts your money together with money from a group of others who also need to manage their risk. When one of the insured has a loss, the insurance company helps lessen the financial burden of that loss.

Section 12.1 Life Insurance

Section 12.2 Health and Disability Insurance

Section 12.3 Other Types of Insurance

College and Career Readiness

Reading Prep. What do you know about *risk?* How is the concept of risk related to insurance? As you read, consider how the authors connect these two ideas.

"Insurance is a great thing to have for any emergency that may suddenly occur." ~ Hannah V.

Money Matters
Insurance

- The first written insurance policy was found in Hammurabi's Code in 2100 B.C. It guaranteed the safe arrival of a merchant's goods by caravan.

- Lloyd's of London created the first insurance organization in 1688. Its insurance covered ships' cargo against pirates, shipwrecks, and other hazards of sailing.

- The first insurance company in the US started in 1732 in Charleston, South Carolina.

- In 1752, Benjamin Franklin helped form the Philadelphia Contributionship, a mutual insurance company that insured against loss resulting from building fires.

- The first automobile policy was issued in 1897 in Dayton, Ohio.

- In 2005, $41.1 billion in claims were paid for damage resulting from Hurricane Katrina.

- Most homeowners do not have insurance that covers flood damage.

- In 2010, the property and casualty insurance industry made charitable contributions of over $500 million.

Section 12.1 Life Insurance

Objectives

- **Explain term and permanent life insurance.**
- **Make an informed decision on how much life insurance you need.**
- **Describe cash value.**

Terms
- *life insurance*
- *insured*
- *policy*
- *beneficiary*
- *term life insurance*
- *permanent life insurance*
- *whole life insurance*
- *universal life insurance*
- *variable life insurance*
- *cash value*

Build Your Math Skills

Review these math skills to prepare for the lesson that follows.

1. Multiply whole numbers and decimals. Round to the nearest cent ($0.01) if necessary. Example: $55 × 180 = $9,900

A. $4.29 × 120 =

B. $301.15 × 240 =

C. $38.75 × 180 =

D. $3,140.45 × 12 =

2. Add decimals. Example: $4,189.27 + $14,171.04 = $18,360.31

A. $31,184.94 + $15,037.63 =

B. $40,019.44 + $13,809.30 =

C. $5,039.56 + $954.83 =

D. $4,918.33 + $998.36 =

Answer:
1. A. $514.80
   B. $72,276
   C. $6,975
   D. $37,685.40
2. A. $46,222.57
   B. $53,828.74
   C. $5,994.39
   D. $5,916.69

Life Insurance

One of the most common types of insurance, **life insurance,** pays a specified person money in the event of the death of an individual. You might be asking why anyone would want to buy insurance that pays when he or she dies. Life insurance eases the burden on the people left behind when someone dies. For example, if someone who makes the majority of the money for a household dies, life insurance can give the remaining family members enough money to pay off debts and a degree of financial security they would not otherwise have.

The **insured** is the person whose life is being insured by life insurance. An insurance **policy** is what is purchased when an individual buys insurance.

A life insurance policy is purchased for a specific dollar amount and is paid to a specific person. The **beneficiary** of a life insurance policy is the person who gets the money if the insured dies. For married couples, it is common for the spouse to be the beneficiary of a life insurance policy.

Even for people with no spouse or children, life insurance can provide money to cover burial expenses and settle any unfinished business the deceased person may have.

Term Life Insurance

The most basic kind of life insurance is term life insurance. **Term life insurance** is a simple policy that pays a certain amount to a beneficiary when the insured dies.

Term life insurance gets its name because the policy has a period of time, or *term,* that the insurance is active. For example, someone 40 years old might purchase a 20-year term life policy. The policy may guarantee the premiums will stay the same for 20 years. At the end of the term, when the insured is 60 years old, it will cost considerably more to get the same amount of insurance. This is because a 60-year-old person is more likely to die in the next 20 years than a 40-year-old person.

For example, suppose a 30-year-old male purchases a $500,000 term life insurance policy with a ten-year term. Because the person is a healthy nonsmoker, he pays only $21 per month for this policy. As long as he continues to pay his premiums each month, his beneficiary will receive $500,000 in the event the insured dies during that ten-year period.

To determine the cost of a term life policy, use the following formula:

$$\textbf{total cost = number of payments} \times \textbf{monthly premium}$$

Example 12-1A

See It

Benjamin is a 30-year-old man who purchased a $500,000 term life insurance policy with a ten-year term. He is in good health, so he pays $21 per month for this policy. What is the total cost of Benjamin's ten-year term life insurance policy?

Strategy

Use the formula:

$$\textbf{total cost = number of payments} \times \textbf{monthly premium}$$

Solution

Step 1: Determine the total number of payments. Multiply the length of the term of the insurance policy by 12 months.

number of payments = length of term × 12 months per year

number of payments = 10 years × 12 months per year

number of payments = 120

Step 2: Determine the total cost of the policy. Multiply the number of payments by the monthly premium.

total cost = number of payments × monthly premium

total cost = 120 × $21

total cost = $2,520

Check It

Araceli is a 30-year-old woman who is in good health. She wants to purchase a $500,000 term life insurance policy with a ten-year term. Her insurance agent told her that the policy will cost $57.66 per month. What is the total cost of Araceli's ten-year term life insurance policy?

If the policy owner pays only a few thousand dollars over a ten-year period, how can the insurance company afford to pay $500,000 in the event of the insured's death? Insurance companies study statistics and know the odds that a person of a particular age and health will die during the term of the policy. The company knows that for each person who dies during that term, hundreds, or even thousands will not. By collecting premiums from all of the insured, the company predicts that more than enough money will be collected to pay the $500,000 to the beneficiaries of the few that die.

Permanent Life Insurance

Permanent life insurance is a term used to describe any insurance policy that does not expire. Permanent life insurance is also known as *cash-value life insurance*. With this kind of insurance, the premium is higher than the equivalent term-life policy. Part of the premium goes toward death benefits, and part of the premium is invested. Over time, the cash value of the investment portion increases. The cash value of the policy grows, too. Some cash value policies are designed to reach a point where the amount of cash is large enough to pay the premiums for the rest of your life.

There are several types of permanent life insurance:

- whole life

- universal life

- variable life

Whole life insurance is a type of permanent life insurance that has unchanging premium and death-benefit amounts. The cash value builds slowly, but at a guaranteed rate.

With **universal life insurance,** the policyholder has flexibility to adjust the amount of the premiums as well as the amount of the death benefit.

As its name suggests, **variable life insurance** has a fixed premium payment and a death benefit that *varies*. A portion of the premium is invested in stock, bonds, or mutual funds. The death benefit amount depends on how well the investments are performing at the time the insured dies.

If you choose a permanent life insurance policy, you will need to research the details of each available option.

How Much Life Insurance Do You Need?

Teaching Tip: Engage students in a discussion about why people purchase insurance today.

How much life insurance a person needs depends on that person's stage in life. When you are young and do not yet have a mortgage, spouse, or family, you may only need minimal coverage. You might choose enough life insurance to pay for funeral expenses and possibly to pay off some debt that others may have to repay should you die. If you have a spouse or family, you will want to have enough life insurance to ease any financial burden that your death may create. For example, if your income is providing a major part of the family's income, you will want to ensure that your family does not fall into financial trouble without your contribution. If your family lives in a house with a mortgage, you probably want enough life insurance to pay off the mortgage.

Career Discovery
Health Science Careers and Math Skills

Health care is one of the fastest-growing industries in the US, so careers in this cluster are in high demand. The health science career pathways include therapeutic and diagnostic services, health information, support services, and biotechnology research and development. People who work in health sciences have a variety of responsibilities, from providing healthcare to managing data and providing support services. As a health-care professional, math skills are crucial and can impact patient care and the development of health science research.

Why do you think math skills are important to the health science industry? Explain why you think good math skills are important in this profession. In what situations would a health-care professional need to apply math skills?

Teaching Tip:
Point out to students that life insurance policies with certain high benefit levels require an examination of the insured by a doctor to certify that person's relative health.

A life insurance policy can pay off debts and leave behind enough cash to pay for college for the children and other family needs. Many people who are married choose to carry enough life insurance to leave a financial buffer for their family. Many financial professionals recommend that a person have enough life insurance to pay off their mortgage and provide 10 to 15 times the person's annual salary. The following formula can be used to determine the amount of life insurance needed:

life insurance needed = 10 × annual net pay + amount of mortgage

Example 12-1B

See It

Nina is married and has three children. She is the primary wage earner for the family and wants to purchase a term life insurance policy for herself. The mortgage on her home has a balance of $175,500. Nina has a monthly net pay of $6,183.27. She wants to purchase enough life insurance to pay off the mortgage and provide her family with ten full years of her net pay. How much life insurance will Nina need to purchase?

Strategy

Use the formula:

life insurance needed = 10 × annual net pay + amount of mortgage

Solution

Step 1: Determine Nina's annual net pay. Multiply her monthly net pay by 12 months.

annual net pay = monthly net pay × 12

annual net pay = $6,183.27 × 12

annual net pay = $74,199.24

Step 2: Determine ten times Nina's annual net pay. Multiply her annual net pay by 10.

10 × annual net pay = 10 × $74,199.24

10 × annual net pay = $741,992.40

Step 3: Determine the amount of insurance needed. Add Nina's annual net pay and the amount of the mortgage.

life insurance needed = ten years annual net pay + amount of mortgage

life insurance needed = $741,992.40 + $175,500

life insurance needed = $917,492.40

Check It

Niko is married with two children. He has a mortgage with a balance of $79,184.35. Niko estimates that his funeral expenses would be $6,750. His biweekly net pay is $1,846.15. He wants to purchase enough life insurance to pay off his mortgage and funeral expenses, as well as provide ten years of annual net pay. How much life insurance will Niko need to purchase?

Answer:
$565,933.35

Later in life, many people live in a house with no mortgage or rent a place to live. They may not need to carry as much life insurance as they did when they had a mortgage and young children to care for. Because life insurance gets more expensive as the insured gets older, it makes less sense to carry large life insurance policies.

Cash Value

Whole life and other permanent life insurance policies often build up a cash balance that you receive if you cancel the policy. The ***cash value*** is the money you get back when you cancel the policy. Cash value is sometimes referred to as *surrender value.* The cash value is not the same as the face value. The *face value* of a policy is the amount a beneficiary is paid if the insured dies. The cash value is usually less than the face value.

The policy may also allow you to borrow the cash value from the policy without cancelling. You must pay interest on the money borrowed from the policy, but the life insurance policy stays in effect. If you never pay back the loan, the loan would be repaid out of the life insurance benefit at the time of death.

Whole life insurance policies include a cash value table like the one shown in Figure 12-1. It shows what the cash value will be at particular points during the life of the policy.

Example 12-1C

See It

Ambika is 40 years old and has a whole life insurance policy. She purchased the policy five years ago. The cash value chart for a 35-year-old woman is shown in Figure 12-1. What is the difference between the total amount of annual premiums she has paid and the policy's cash value?

Strategy

Use Figure 12-1 and the formula:

difference between amount paid and cash value = total paid in premiums – cash value

Solution

Step 1: Identify Ambika's annual premium amount.

annual premium amount = $1,083

Step 2: Determine the total paid in premiums by multiplying the policy year by the annual premium amount.

total paid in premiums = (policy year × annual premium)

total paid in premiums = 5 × $1,083

total paid in premiums = $5,415

Step 3: Identify the cash value based on the policy year.

cash value = $3,439

Policy Year	Insured Age	Annual Premium	Cash Value	Death Benefit
1	35	$1,083	$ 0	$100,000
5	40	1,083	3,439	100,230
10	45	1,083	10,643	101,375
15	52	1,083	18,342	101,690
20	55	1,083	26,091	102,005
30	65	1,083	42,663	103,144
35	70	1,083	53,845	104,257

Figure 12-1. Cash Value Table

Step 4: Determine the difference between total paid in premiums and cash value.

difference between amount paid and cash value = total paid in premiums – cash value

difference between amount paid and cash value = $5,415 – $3,439

difference between amount paid and cash value = $1,976

Check It

Ming is 45 years old and has a whole life insurance policy. She purchased the policy ten years ago. The cash value chart for a 35-year-old woman is shown in Figure 12-1. What is the difference between the total amount of annual premiums Ming has paid and the policy's cash value?

Answer:
$187

Checkpoint 12.1

1. Bradley is 35 years old, male, and has a 20-year term life policy with a $750,000 death benefit. His monthly premiums are $43. What is the total cost of his term life policy?

2. Juanita is 25 years old, female, and has a 15-year term life policy that would pay $400,000. Her monthly premiums are $17.50. What is the total cost of her term life policy?

3. Gabrielle is 35 years old and earns $3,062 per month. She plans to retire when she is 65 years old. She wants to purchase enough life insurance to provide her family with all of the money she would earn before retirement. How much life insurance should Gabrielle purchase?

4. Sukhir is 27 years old and earns $5,019 per month. He and his family have a mortgage with a balance of $110,935.17. He wants to purchase enough life insurance to provide his family with money to pay off the mortgage and have ten years of net pay remaining. How much life insurance should Sukhir purchase?

5. Carlotta is 65 years old and has a whole life insurance policy. She purchased the policy 30 years ago. The cash value chart for a 35-year-old woman is shown in Figure 12-1. What is the difference between the total amount of annual premiums she has paid and the policy's cash value?

Teaching Tip:
Checkpoint questions offer opportunities for formative assessment.

Answer:
1. $10,320
2. $3,150
3. $1,102,320
4. $713,215.17
5. $10,173

Section 12.2 Health and Disability Insurance

Terms

- *health insurance*
- *group health insurance*
- *copayment*
- *coinsurance*
- *disability insurance*

Objectives

- **Describe health insurance.**
- **Calculate deductibles and coinsurance.**
- **Explain disability insurance.**

Build Your Math Skills

Review these math skills to prepare the lesson that follows.

1. Add decimals. Example: $278.56 + $718.46 = $997.02

A. $415.78 + $97.85 =

B. $77.74 + $189.37 =

C. $1,071.08 + $454.73 =

D. $976.74 + $820.04 =

2. Multiply decimals. Round to the nearest cent ($0.01) if necessary. Example: $247.15 \times 12 = $2,965.80

A. $817.41 \times 6 =

B. $674.15 \times 3 =

C. $347.18 \times 12 =

D. $718.41 \times 6 =

3. Divide decimals. Round to the nearest cent ($0.01) if necessary. Example: $185.74 \div 2 = $92.87

A. $850.25 \div 3 =

B. $452.96 \div 4 =

C. $9,478.56 \div 12 =

D. $8,714.43 \div 12 =

Health Insurance

Health insurance is a type of insurance that helps pay medical bills. Health insurance works like other types of insurance. A large number of people pay into a pool, and those people with medical expenses receive help with their medical bills.

While it is possible to purchase health insurance as an individual, most people receive health insurance through their job. Others may qualify to purchase health insurance through a group or organization. *Group health insurance* is health insurance provided by an employer or group. *Indemnity health insurance, health maintenance organization,* and *preferred provider organization* are types of health insurance. Figure 12-2 describes the features of each of these.

Like other types of insurance, health insurance involves paying premiums. The insured may pay all or none of the premiums, depending on the source of the insurance. Most health insurance policies also allow dependents to be added. To determine the annual cost of insurance, use the following formula:

annual cost = monthly cost × 12

fyi

Employers and organizations that offer group health insurance plans also frequently make dental and vision coverage available as well.

Teaching Tip:

Refer students to Figure 12-2. What type of person would each of these types of insurance fit best?

	What It Is	**How It Works**
Indemnity Health Insurance	Known as a fee-for-service plan. Lets the insured go to any doctor he or she chooses.	The insurance pays a portion of covered health-care costs.
Health Maintenance Organization (HMO)	An association of doctors, hospitals, and other health-care providers that provides comprehensive medical services.	The insurance pays part or all of the health-care costs only if the insured uses a doctor that is part of the HMO.
Preferred Provider Organization (PPO)	An association of providers that offers services at a lower cost to subscribers. Gives the insured more choice than an HMO.	The insurance pays part or all of the health-care costs only if the insured uses a doctor that is part of the PPO.

Figure 12-2. Types of Health Insurance

Example 12-2A

See It

Jacob has a job as a sheet metal worker. His employer pays half of the $454.46 monthly premium for health insurance. Jacob only has health insurance for himself. How much does Jacob pay each year for his health insurance?

Strategy

Use the formula:

annual cost = monthly cost × 12

Solution

Step 1: Determine the amount that Jacob pays each month for his health insurance premium. Divide the monthly premium by 2.

monthly cost = monthly premium ÷ 2

monthly cost = $454.46 ÷ 2

monthly cost = $227.23

Step 2: Determine Jacob's annual cost. Multiply the monthly cost by 12.

annual cost = monthly cost × 12

annual cost = $227.23 × 12

annual cost = $2,726.76

Check It

Ina works as a traffic technician. Her employer pays half of the $504.23 monthly premium for health insurance. Ina only has health insurance for herself. How much does Ina pay each year for her health insurance?

Answer:
$3,025.44

Example 12-2B

See It

Kathryn works as a food service manager, and her employer pays for all of her monthly individual health insurance premiums. To add her spouse to her health insurance coverage, Kathryn must pay $263.41 per month. What will be the total annual cost for Kathryn to provide health insurance for her spouse?

Strategy

Use the formula:

annual cost = monthly cost × 12

Solution

Step 1: Identify the monthly cost for spousal coverage.

monthly cost = $263.41

Step 2: Determine the annual cost. Multiply the monthly cost by 12.

annual cost = monthly cost × 12

annual cost = $263.41 × 12

annual cost = $3,160.92

Check It

Jermaine works as a tax accountant, and his employer pays the total monthly premium for his individual health insurance. To add his spouse to his health insurance coverage, Jermaine must pay $314.17. What will be the total annual cost for Jermaine to provide health insurance for his spouse?

Answer:
$3,770.04

Deductibles and Coinsurance

Health insurance involves a combination of premiums, deductibles, copayments, and coinsurance. Recall from chapter 9 that a deductible is the portion of the expense the insured is responsible for paying. The deductible is typically an annual amount that the insured pays before insurance begins to pay.

A ***copayment,*** or *copay,* is a specified amount the insured pays for a doctor visit. Many health insurance policies offer a $30 copayment for an office visit. If you have such a policy, when you visit the doctor for a routine medical need, you pay $30 to the doctor at the time of service. The insurance company will pay the remainder of the cost of the office visit itself.

However, some expenses you incur may not be covered by the doctor visit copay. For example, if you require a laboratory test or an X-ray, your insurance may not assist with payment for those expenses until your deductible has been met. The amount of the deductible will vary depending on the policy. For example, if a person has a $1,000 deductible, that person will pay $1,000 in medical bills before the insurance will begin to pay expenses other than doctor visits. Payments made from the insured in the form of deductibles or copays are called *out-of-pocket expenses*. To calculate total out-of-pocket expenses, use the following formula:

total out-of-pocket expenses = total cost of copayments + patient responsibility amount

Copayments do not apply toward satisfying your deductible. For example, if a patient has a $30 copayment for office visits and a $250 annual deductible. After making ten office visits, the patient will have paid $300 in copayments. However, none of the money spent on copays would apply to the deductible.

Teaching Tip:
Refer students to an online premium calculator to help them see what factors influence the cost of insurance premiums.

Example 12-2C

See It

Derrick has health insurance that includes a $20 office visit copayment for his primary care physician and a $500 annual deductible. Last year, Derrick visited his physician three times. One of the visits required an X-ray that cost Derrick $130 and was not covered with the copayment. How much did Derrick pay out of his pocket last year for medical care?

Strategy

Use the formula:

total out-of-pocket expenses = total cost of copayments + patient responsibility amount

Solution

Step 1: Determine the total cost of the copayments. Multiply the cost of a copayment by the number of copayments made.

total cost of copayments = cost of each copayment × number of copayments

total cost of copayments = $20 × 3

total cost of copayments = $60

Step 2: Determine the portion of the medical bills for which the patient is responsible.

patient responsibility amount = $130

Step 3: Determine whether the cost of medical expenses exceeded the deductible or not.

$130 < $500

The cost of the medical expenses did not exceed the deductible.

Step 4: Determine Derrick's total out-of-pocket medical expenses. Add the total cost of the copayments and the lesser of the deductible or the cost of medical expenses.

total out-of-pocket expenses = total cost of copayments + patient responsibility amount

total out-of-pocket expenses = $60 + $130

total out-of-pocket expenses = $190

Check It

Evona has a health insurance policy with a $25 copayment and a $750 deductible. Last year, she visited the doctor four times and had laboratory work done once that cost $225. How much did Evona pay out of her pocket last year for medical care?

Depending on the type of policy, the insured may be responsible for a percentage, often 10% to 30%, of the expenses after the deductible is fully paid. *Coinsurance* is the sharing of the expenses with the insurance company. There is usually a maximum amount the insured person will be responsible for. After that maximum amount is paid, the insurance company will pay 100%.

When a policy includes coinsurance, the insured person's responsibility can be determined using the following formula:

amount of coinsurance = (total expenses – deductible) × coinsurance percentage

fyi

The maximum amount the insured person is responsible to pay is often called the *maximum out-of-pocket expense.*

Example 12-2D

See It

Isabel has a hospital bill of $21,800. Her health insurance has a $500 deductible and will pay 90% of expenses after the deductible, with a maximum out-of-pocket expense of $2,500. Isabel has no medical care costs that have been applied to her deductible yet this year. Calculate Isabel's out-of-pocket expense for her hospital bill.

Strategy

Use the formula:

amount of coinsurance = (total expenses – deductible) × coinsurance percentage

Solution

Step 1: Determine the amount of the expenses subject to the coinsurance. Subtract the deductible from the total bill.

expenses eligible for coinsurance = total expenses – deductible

expenses eligible for coinsurance = $21,800 – $500

expenses eligible for coinsurance = $21,300

Step 2: Determine the coinsurance percentage. Subtract the percentage that the insurance policy will pay from 100%.

coinsurance percentage = 100% – insurance percentage

coinsurance percentage = 100% – 90%

coinsurance percentage = 10%

Step 3: Convert the coinsurance percentage to a decimal by moving the decimal two places to the left.

10% → 0.10

Step 4: Determine the amount of coinsurance. Multiply the expenses eligible for coinsurance by the coinsurance percentage.

amount of coinsurance = expenses eligible for coinsurance × coinsurance percentage

amount of coinsurance = $21,300 × 0.10

amount of coinsurance = $2,130

Step 5: Determine the total out-of-pocket expenses. Add the deductible and the amount of coinsurance.

total out-of-pocket expenses = deductible + amount of coinsurance

total out-of-pocket expenses = $500 + $2,130

total out-of-pocket expenses = $2,630

Step 6: Compare the total out-of-pocket expenses and the insurance policy's maximum out-of-pocket expenses. The patient will pay the lesser of the two.

total out-of-pocket expenses > or < maximum out-of-pocket expenses

$2,630 > or < $2,500

$2,630 > $2,500

Isabel will pay $2,500.

Check It

Garrett has a hospital bill of $11,540. His health insurance has a $500 deductible and will pay 80% of expenses after the deductible, with a maximum out-of-pocket expense of $2,500. Garrett has no medical care costs that have been applied to his deductible yet this year. Calculate Garrett's out-of-pocket expense for his hospital bill.

Teaching Tip:
Have students write a paragraph that describes the steps involved in the **See It** portion of **Example 12-2D.**

Until the value of each side of the inequality is determined, you will not know whether one value is greater than (>) or less than (<) the other value.

Answer:
$2,500

Example 12-2E

See It

Hina has a medical bill of $4,800. Her health insurance has a $1,000 deductible and will pay 80% of expenses after the deductible, with a maximum out-of-pocket expense of $2,000. Hina has no medical care costs that have been applied to her deductible yet this year. Calculate Hina's out-of-pocket expense for her medical bill.

Strategy

Use the formula:

amount of coinsurance = (total expenses – deductible) × coinsurance percentage

Solution

Step 1: Determine the amount of the expenses subject to the coinsurance. Subtract the deductible from the total bill.

expenses eligible for coinsurance = total expenses – deductible

expenses eligible for coinsurance = $4,800 – $1,000

expenses eligible for coinsurance = $3,800

Step 2: Determine the coinsurance percentage. Subtract the percentage that the insurance policy will pay from 100%.

coinsurance percentage = 100% – insurance percentage

coinsurance percentage = 100% – 80%

coinsurance percentage = 20%

Step 3: Convert the coinsurance percentage to a decimal by moving the decimal two places to the left.

$20\% \rightarrow 0.20$

Step 4: Determine the amount of coinsurance. Multiply the expenses eligible for coinsurance by the coinsurance percentage.

amount of coinsurance = expenses eligible for coinsurance × coinsurance percentage

amount of coinsurance = $3,800 × 0.20

amount of coinsurance = $760

Step 5: Determine the total out-of-pocket expenses. Add the deductible and the amount of coinsurance.

total out-of-pocket expenses = deductible + amount of coinsurance

total out-of-pocket expenses = $1,000 + $760

total out-of-pocket expenses = $1,760

Teaching Tip:
Point out to students that according to the Social Security Administration, 30% of men and 25% of women in the US will suffer a disabling illness or injury before they retire.

Step 6: Compare the total out-of-pocket expenses and the insurance policy's maximum out-of-pocket expenses. The patient will pay the lesser of the two.

total out-of-pocket expenses > or < maximum out-of-pocket expenses

$1,760 > or < $2,000

$1,760 > $2,000

Hina will pay $1,760.

Check It

Shaun has a hospital bill of $8,460. His health insurance has a $750 deductible and will pay 85% of expenses after the deductible, with a maximum out-of-pocket expense of $2,000. Shaun has no medical care costs that have been applied to his deductible yet this year. Calculate Shaun's out-of-pocket expense for his hospital bill.

Answer:
$1,906.50

Disability Insurance

fyi

The term *disability insurance* is used because the illness or injury has *disabled* the insured.

Disability insurance helps replace income when you cannot work due to illness or injury. Disability insurance comes in two basic types: short-term disability and long-term disability. *Short-term disability* is designed to protect your income during a relatively short period of disability. For example, if someone is in an automobile accident and recovering for two months, short-term disability would pay a portion of his or her normal income during the period he or she is recovering. Short-term disability begins paying fairly soon after the disability occurs, usually less than two weeks, or when you run out of sick days. The disability payment is typically 50% to 70% of normal salary and is usually paid for 10 to 26 weeks, or until the person returns to work. To calculate the disability insurance monthly benefit, use the following formula:

COBRA stands for the *Consolidated Omnibus Budget Reconciliation Act.* COBRA gives workers who lose their health benefits the right to continue group health benefits from their employers. This coverage is not free and must be paid for by the worker. The coverage can be expensive, but without COBRA, some workers who lose their jobs would not be able to purchase private health insurance on their own.

monthly benefit = monthly salary × benefit rate

Long-term disability is designed to protect your income during a long period of disability, or in the case of permanent disability. If a person is permanently disabled, some long-term disability policies will pay until he or she reaches age 65. Like short-term disability, long-term disability generally pays a percentage of what the insured made at the time of disability.

Teaching Tip:
Help students recall from chapter 2 that Social Security also makes disability payments to qualified recipients.

Example 12-2F

See It

Pauline works as an actuary for an insurance company with an annual salary of $98,620. She has short-term disability insurance that will pay 60% of her monthly salary after a two-week waiting period. What will be Pauline's monthly short-term disability benefit?

Strategy

Use the formula:

monthly benefit = monthly salary × benefit rate

Solution

Step 1: Determine Pauline's monthly salary. Divide her annual salary by 12.

monthly salary = annual salary ÷ 12

monthly salary = $98,620 ÷ 12

monthly salary = $8,218.33

Step 2: Convert the benefit percentage to a decimal by moving the decimal two places to the left.

60% → 0.60

Step 3: Determine the monthly short-term disability benefit. Multiply the monthly salary by the benefit rate.

monthly benefit = monthly salary × benefit rate

monthly benefit = $8,218.33 × 0.60

monthly benefit = $4,931

Check It

Fernando works as a computer systems administrator with an annual salary of $72,200. He has short-term disability insurance that will pay 55% of his monthly salary after a two-week waiting period. What will be Fernando's monthly short-term disability benefit?

Answer:
$3,309.17

Teaching Tip:
Checkpoint questions offer opportunities for formative assessment.

Checkpoint 12.2

1. Jenna's employer pays half of the $479.85 monthly premium for health insurance. Jenna only has health insurance for herself. How much does she pay each year for her health insurance?

2. Darnell works as a graphic designer, and his employer pays for his total individual health insurance monthly premiums. To add his spouse and children to his health insurance coverage, Darnell must pay $446.37. What will be the total annual cost for Darnell to provide health insurance for his spouse and children?

Answer:
1. $2,879.16
2. $5,356.44

3. Prema has health insurance with a $30 copayment and a $500 deductible. Last year, she visited the doctor four times. She also had laboratory work done that cost $195 and an X-ray that cost $115. How much did Prema pay out of her pocket last year for medical care?

4. Onani has a hospital bill of $14,150. His health insurance has a $750 deductible and will pay 80% of expenses after the deductible, with a maximum out-of-pocket expense of $2,000. Onani has no medical care costs that have been applied to his deductible yet this year. Calculate Onani's out-of-pocket expense for his hospital bill.

5. Delma works as a fashion designer with an annual salary of $74,440. She has short-term disability insurance that will pay 65% of her monthly salary after she has used all of her available sick leave. What will be Delma's monthly short-term disability benefit?

3. $430
4. $2,000
5. $4,032.16

Source: Shutterstock (Monkey Business Images)

Health insurance often helps pay the cost of medical care.

Section 12.3 Other Types of Insurance

Terms
- *umbrella policy*
- *professional liability insurance*
- *travel insurance*

Objectives
- **Describe liability insurance.**
- **Explain the purpose of business insurance.**
- **Calculate the cost of travel insurance.**
- **List other available types of insurance.**

Build Your Math Skills

Review these math skills to prepare for the lesson that follows.

1. Convert percentages to decimals by moving the decimal two places to the left. Example: 5.3% → 0.053

A. 4.5% →

B. 5% →

C. 5.75% →

D. 10.4% →

2. Multiply decimals. Round to the nearest cent ($0.01) if necessary. Example: $450 × 0.07 = $31.50

A. $395 × 0.06 =

B. $525 × 0.035 =

C. $3,019 × 0.055 =

D. $2,387 × 0.05 =

3. Divide decimals. Round to the nearest cent ($0.01) if necessary. Example: $1,250 ÷ 15.5 = $80.65

A. $678.41 ÷ 12 =

B. $1,198 ÷ 13.8 =

C. $1,516 ÷ 0.26 =

D. $987.50 ÷ 0.045 =

Answer:
1. A. 0.045
   B. 0.05
   C. 0.0575
   D. 0.104
2. A. $23.70
   B. $18.38
   C. $166.05
   D. $119.35
3. A. $56.53
   B. $86.81
   C. $5,830.77
   D. $21,944.44

Liability Insurance

In chapter 10, you learned about automobile liability insurance. Recall that automobile liability insurance pays for the expenses of a third party in the event of an accident. The liability insurance pays for damages caused, even if the accident is your fault.

A *liability* is another word for a debt you owe. So, for example, if you cause an automobile accident and another driver's car is damaged, the cost of repairing or replacing the other driver's car becomes a liability for you. Another way of stating this is to say that you are *liable* for the damages. Liability insurance protects you from debts for which you are liable.

There are other kinds of liability insurance as well. Homeowners insurance, which you learned about in chapter 9, generally includes liability insurance to protect the homeowner from liability if someone is injured or killed at their home.

An *umbrella policy* is an insurance policy that raises the total amount of liability insurance a person has. For example, if your automobile insurance has liability coverage up to $500,000 and your homeowners insurance has liability coverage up to $250,000, you might have an umbrella policy that brings both liability limits up to $1,000,000.

So what does it mean to have $1,000,000 in liability coverage? It means that the insurance company will pay your liabilities up to $1,000,000. The insurance company will do more than pay the bill; they will also defend you from the liability. For example, if you are in an automobile accident that is your fault, the insurance company will try to ensure that the person making the claim does not get more than they are entitled to receive.

fyi

Liability coverage can provide compensation to the injured party for any pain and suffering the accident may have caused.

Business Insurance

Almost any kind of business needs insurance. Because businesses need a variety of insurance products, insurance companies offer specially designed packages for businesses. Such packages include coverage in case business is disrupted through no fault of the owner as would be the case in a natural disaster.

For businesses that are strictly online, insurance needs will be different than for those businesses with a physical location. With a physical location, there will be a greater need for property protection in case the building is robbed or damaged. Liability coverage will also be important, just in case someone were to be injured on the business property.

Professional liability insurance is insurance that covers issues that may arise from a person's quality of work. Professionals, such as teachers, may choose to buy professional liability insurance to protect their financial assets in case of a law suit. Like other types of insurance, their employer may give them the opportunity to have the cost of the premium deducted from their paychecks. To determine the amount that will be deducted from each paycheck for professional liability insurance coverage, use the following formula:

Financial $marts

Identity theft occurs when someone uses another person's identity, usually to obtain credit or gain some other benefit. For example, by obtaining someone's name, Social Security number, and other personal information, an identity thief can apply for a credit card, make purchases using the card, and then skip out on making the payments.

Identity thieves can obtain a consumer's personal information in many ways. The smart consumer protects their personal information from identity theft by shredding important financial documents, immediately reporting missing credit or debit cards, and being careful when entering personal information into a website.

Increasingly, people have sought to protect themselves against the financial risk associated with identity theft. Some people purchase identity theft insurance, which helps offset the cost related to fixing any problems the theft caused. This kind of insurance does not, however, pay you back any money that may have been stolen.

amount per paycheck = annual cost ÷ number of annual paychecks

Teaching Tip:
Encourage students to explore careers in the insurance industry. What skills might be necessary for someone working in this field?

*Increasingly, pet owners are purchasing pet health
insurance to cover costs related to a pet's illness or injury.*

Example 12-3A

See It

Kristen is an architect. Because she designs buildings and approves the blueprints of others, she carries professional liability insurance in the event of damage to the building that results in death or injury. Through her professional association, she can purchase an annual professional liability insurance policy for $479.35 and pay the premiums through payroll deduction. Kristen is paid semimonthly. How much will Kristen have deducted from each paycheck to purchase the professional liability insurance policy?

Strategy

Use the formula:

amount per paycheck = annual cost ÷ number of annual paychecks

Solution

Step 1: Determine the number of annual paychecks. Since Kristen is paid semimonthly, multiply the number of paychecks per month by 12 months in a year.

number of annual paychecks = number of paychecks per month × 12

number of annual paychecks = 2 × 12

number of annual paychecks = 24

Step 2: Determine the amount per paycheck. Divide the annual cost by the number of annual paychecks.

amount per paycheck = annual cost ÷ number of annual paychecks

amount per paycheck = $479.35 ÷ 24

amount per paycheck = $19.97

Check It

Angelo is a nurse who carries professional liability insurance. His annual premiums are $121.18, and he has the premiums deducted from his paycheck. Angelo is paid once a month. How much does Angelo have deducted from each paycheck for his professional liability insurance?

Teaching Tip:
Explain to students that professional liability insurance for physicians and attorneys is called *malpractice insurance.*

Answer:
$10.10

Travel Insurance

Travel insurance is insurance that covers losses that result from issues related to travel. For example, suppose the airline cancels your flight or you have to cancel a hotel reservation due to illness or other reasons. Travel insurance will reimburse you for losses that result from these events. Travel insurance can also cover a flight delay that causes you to miss a critical travel connection. It could also cover expenses related to having to leave a trip unexpectedly due to illness or injury.

There are many kinds of travel insurance policies that cover a wide variety of potential expenses that could be incurred while traveling. Travel insurance is fairly affordable, especially when you consider how much you could lose if you had a problem. For example, a trip to a foreign country or even a cruise could cost thousands of dollars. If you have to cancel a trip at the last minute due to an unforeseen problem, you could lose your money if you don't have the right travel insurance.

To determine the cost of travel insurance, use the following formula:

cost of insurance = total cost of trip × insurance rate

Example 12-3B

See It

Kim and Cheng Nguyen booked tickets for a family cruise. They paid for five tickets at $799 each. Cheng decided to purchase travel insurance, which costs 4.5% of the total cost of the tickets. How much did the travel insurance cost?

Strategy

Use the formula:

cost of insurance = total cost of trip × insurance rate

Solution

Step 1: Determine the total cost of the cruise. Multiply the cost per ticket by the number of tickets purchased.

total cost of trip = number of tickets × cost per ticket

total cost of trip = 5 × $799

total cost of trip = $3,995

Step 2: Convert 4.5% to a decimal by moving the decimal two places to the left.

4.5% → 0.045

Step 3: Determine the cost of the insurance. Multiply the total cost of the trip by the insurance rate. Round to the nearest cent ($0.01) if necessary.

cost of insurance = total cost of trip × insurance rate

cost of insurance = $3,995 × 0.045

cost of insurance = $179.78

Check It

Angelique and Dennis Jackson booked a family vacation package to Costa Rica. The package includes airfare, hotel, and all local transportation and costs $1,499 per person. Angelique booked four tickets and wants to purchase travel insurance, which will cost 5% of the total cost of the vacation package. How much will the travel insurance cost?

Answer:

$299.80

Other Insurance

There is a type of insurance available to manage just about every kind of risk. There is a type of insurance to safeguard you against the risk of having to pay repair costs. When you purchase an *extended warranty* for an appliance or a car, you are purchasing a type of insurance that pays the cost of repairing or replacing the item during a certain period of time.

Those who have pets may want to purchase insurance that covers damage done to others or the property of others by their pet. They also have the option of purchasing pet health insurance, which covers the cost associated with treated illnesses or injuries.

In many locations around the country, flood insurance is a mandatory condition of securing a mortgage loan. The likelihood of floods in these areas is so great that private insurers do not offer coverage. Instead, the federal government, through the National Flood Insurance Program, provides such insurance to homeowners and renters.

Checkpoint 12.3

1. Indali is a mental health counselor who carries professional liability insurance. Her annual premiums are $510.75, and she has the premiums deducted from her paycheck. Indali is paid biweekly. How much does Indali have deducted from each paycheck for her professional liability insurance?

2. Marco is a photographer who carries professional liability insurance. His annual premiums are $1,075, and he has the premiums deducted from his paycheck. Marco is paid semimonthly. How much does Marco have deducted from each paycheck for his professional liability insurance?

3. Cheyenne is a soil engineer who carries professional liability insurance. Her annual premiums are $1,147.38, and she has the premiums deducted from her paycheck. Cheyenne is paid monthly. How much does Cheyenne have deducted from each paycheck for her professional liability insurance?

4. Anabel booked a holiday cruise for herself, her two brothers, and their mother and father. Each cruise ticket cost $695, and she chose to purchase travel insurance at 3% of the total cost of the tickets. How much did Anabel pay for travel insurance?

5. Fadil booked four airline tickets for himself and his family to take a Hawaiian vacation. Each ticket cost $545, and he chose to purchase travel insurance that costs 4% of the total cost of the tickets. How much did Fadil pay for travel insurance?

Answer:
1. $19.64
2. $44.79
3. $95.62
4. $104.25
5. $87.20

Chapter Review

Build Your Vocabulary

As you progress through this course, develop a personal glossary of financial literacy terms and add it to your portfolio. This will help you build your financial literacy vocabulary. Write out a definition for each of the following terms, and add it to your personal glossary.

life insurance

insured

policy

beneficiary

term life insurance

permanent life insurance

whole life insurance

universal life insurance

variable life insurance

cash value

health insurance

group health insurance

copayment

coinsurance

disability insurance

liability

umbrella policy

professional liability insurance

travel insurance

 ## Teamwork

In small groups, plan a one-week vacation with a budget of $900 per person. Use travel-planning sites to get information. Be sure to include all transportation and lodging costs. Choose at least one leisurely activity to take part in and determine its cost. Investigate the cost of travel insurance for this trip and what the travel insurance covers. Consider the variables that affect the cost of planning a vacation. Present the features of the trip you planned to the class.

Review Your Math Skills

Practice and build on the math skills that you have learned.

1. Subtract whole numbers. Example: 14,516 − 11,307 = 3,209

A. 38,719 − 36,796 =

B. 50,734 − 47,864 =

C. 908 − 176 =

D. 60,468 − 46,836 =

2. Multiply decimals. Round to the nearest cent ($0.01) if necessary. Example: 2,019 × $0.08 = $161.52

A. 1,198 × $0.065 =

B. 2,481 × $0.10 =

C. 4,489 × $0.11 =

D. 3,867 × $0.135 =

Answer:
1. A. 1,923
   B. 2,870
   C. 732
   D. 13,632
2. A. $77.87
   B. $248.10
   C. $493.79
   D. $522.05

3. Add decimals. Example: $241.19 + $40.89 = $282.08

A. $40.56 + $174.28 =   B. $107.08 + $99.46 =

C. $341.18 + $140.07 =   D. $662.34 + $78.19 =

4. Multiply whole numbers and decimals. Round to the nearest cent ($0.01) if necessary. Example: $55 × 1.8 = $99

A. $32.05 × 204 =   B. $1,840.95 × 13 =

C. $3,841 × 4.84 =   D. $142 × 1.23 =

5. Divide decimals. Round to the nearest cent ($0.01) if necessary. Example: $185.74 ÷ 2 = $92.87

A. $812.18 ÷ 3 =   B. $4,123.18 ÷ 4 =

C. $1,478.56 ÷ 24 =   D. $8,004.34 ÷ 12 =

6. Add decimals. Example: $4,189.27 + $14,171.04 = $18,360.31

A. $13,103.94 + $14,924.05 =   B. $40,519.14 + $26,914.61 =

C. $8,903.65 + $594.38 =   D. $998.61 + $94,128.35 =

7. Convert percentages to decimals by moving the decimal two places to the left. Example: 8.4% → 0.084

A. 58.24% →   B. 17% →

C. 6.57% →   D. 61.19% →

8. Multiply decimals. Round to the nearest cent ($0.01) if necessary. Example: $450 × 0.07 = $31.50

A. $7,389 × 0.05 =   B. $1,934 × 0.083 =

C. $6,813 × 0.09 =   D. $953 × 0.06 =

9. Divide decimals. Round to the nearest cent ($0.01) if necessary. Example: $1,250 ÷ 12 = $104.17

A. $745.76 ÷ 59 =   B. $8,727.51 ÷ 36 =

C. $198 ÷ 16 =   D. $1,135.38 ÷ 12 =

10. Convert percentages to decimals by moving the decimal two places to the left. Example: 564.39% → 5.6439

A. 948.465% →   B. 246.81% →

C. 4,167.28% →   D. 601.006% →

3. A. $214.84
B. $206.54
C. $481.25
D. $740.53
4. A. $6,538.20
B. $23,932.35
C. $18,590.44
D. $174.66
5. A. $270.73
B. $1,030.80
C. $61.61
D. $667.03
6. A. $28,027.99
B. $67,433.75
C. $9,498.03
D. $95,126.96
7. A. 0.5824
B. 0.17
C. 0.0657
D. 0.6119
8. A. $369.45
B. $160.52
C. $613.17
D. $57.18
9. A. $12.64
B. $424.43
C. $12.38
D. $94.62
10. A. 9.48465
B. 2.4681
C. 41.6728
D. 6.01006

Section 12.1 Life Insurance

11. Travis is 33 years old. He has a 20-year term life policy with a death benefit of $600,000. His monthly premiums are $35. What is the total cost of Travis' term life policy?

12. Zara is 41 years old and earns a net pay of $5,575 per month. She and her family have a mortgage with a balance of $149,307.85. She wants to purchase enough life insurance to provide her family with enough money to pay off the mortgage and have fifteen years of her net pay. How much insurance should Zara purchase?

Answer:
11. $8,400
12. $1,152,807.85

Section 12.2 Health and Disability Insurance

13. Muhammed works as an aerospace engineer, and his employer pays for half of his individual health insurance monthly premium, which is $425.18. To add his spouse and children to his health insurance coverage, Muhammed must pay $480.75. What will be the total annual cost for Muhammed to provide health insurance for himself, his spouse, and his children?

14. Cindy has health insurance with a $20 copayment and a $750 deductible. Last year, she visited the doctor three times. She also had laboratory work done once that cost $205 and an X-ray that cost $135. How much did Cindy pay out of her pocket last year for medical care?

15. Enrique has a medical bill of $4,130. His health insurance has a $750 deductible and will pay 90% of expenses after the deductible, with a maximum out-of-pocket expense of $3,000. Enrique has no medical care costs that have been applied to his deductible yet this year. Calculate Enrique's out-of-pocket expense for his medical bill.

Answer:
13. $8,320.08
14. $400
15. $1,088
16. $1,854.59

16. Tiya works as radio operator with an annual salary of $44,510. She has short-term disability insurance that will pay 50% of her monthly salary after she has used all of her available sick leave. What will be Tiya's monthly short-term disability benefit?

Section 12.3 Other Types of Insurance

17. Peter is a land surveyor who carries professional liability insurance. His annual premiums are $1,374.65, and he has the premiums deducted from his paycheck. Peter is paid semimonthly. How much does Peter have deducted from each paycheck for his professional liability insurance?

18. Margaret booked a cruise for her family. Each cruise ticket cost $550.45, and she bought six tickets. Margaret chose to purchase travel insurance at 3.5% of the total cost of the tickets. How much did Margaret pay for travel insurance?

Answer:
17. $57.28
18. $115.59

Reinforce Your Understanding

19. Sophia is the secretary for a folk dancing club. During one month, the club's statement showed cash inflows of $2,487.09 and cash outflows of $1,708.34. What was the folk dancing club's net cash flow for that month?

20. Candace and Jonathan Allen want to purchase a house that has a selling price of $215,450. Their bank requires a down payment of 20%. Calculate the Allens' down payment and the amount that they will finance through their mortgage.

Answer:
19. $778.75
20. down payment = $43,090
amount of mortgage = $172,360

Apply Your Technology Skills

Access the G-W Learning companion website for this text at www.g-wlearning.com. Download each data file for this chapter. Follow the instructions to complete financial literacy activities to practice what you have learned in this chapter.

Teaching Tip:
The Apply Your Technology Skills activities offer project-based authentic assessment opportunities.

Data File 12-1—Creating an Inventory of Your Assets

Data File 12-2—Completing an Application for Life Insurance

Data File 12-3—Researching Health Insurance

13 Financial Planning

Materials:
Instructor's Resource CD
Student Workbook
G-W Learning companion website
EXAMVIEW® Assessment Suite
Microsoft Excel®–compatible software
Calculator with advanced-math functions

Financial security does not come about by accident. Making and carrying out a financial plan will determine how well you get along financially in life. Once you make money, you have to make sure you protect it and make it grow. Planning will ensure that you have wealth throughout each stage of your life.

Section 13.1 Protecting Wealth

Section 13.2 Retirement Planning

Section 13.3 Other Investments

College and Career Readiness

Reading Prep. In preparation for reading the chapter, read a newspaper or magazine article on the Great Recession. As you read, keep in mind the author's main points and conclusions.

"I prefer to have tangible assets. I have learned from my parents and grandparents that land is a valuable asset." ~ Carson O.

Money Matters
Inflation

- The rate of inflation is constantly changing and has ranged from nearly zero to 23% in the US. The federal government tries to keep the rate of inflation between 2% and 3%.

- The highest paid US president was William Howard Taft. In 1909, his salary was $75,000. Adjusted for inflation, this is equal to a salary of more than $1.7 million today.

- A dollar from 1950 is worth only twelve cents today.

- The record for the most rapidly increasing inflation is held by Hungary. In July of 1946, the rate of inflation was 41,900,000,000,000,000%, which meant prices doubled every 13.5 hours.

- In 2010, the countries with the highest inflation were Venezuela (28.2%), Democratic Republic of the Congo (23.1%), and Argentina (22%).

- In 2010, the countries with the lowest inflation were Qatar (–2.4%), Republic of Seychelles (–2.4%), and Chad (–2%).

- For the past 25 years, college tuition in the US has increased at a rate 6% higher than the rate of inflation.

Section 13.1 Protecting Wealth

Objectives

- **Describe the effect of inflation on currency.**
- **Explain the purpose of a will.**
- **Identify the purpose of a trust.**

Build Your Math Skills

Review these math skills to prepare for the lesson that follows.

1. Convert decimals to percentages by moving the decimal two places to the right. Example: 0.038 → 3.8%

A. 0.0145 →

B. 0.624 →

C. 0.75 →

D. 0.076 →

2. Add and subtract decimals. Example: $471.80 − $263.90 = $207.90

A. $1,178.46 + $9,704.63 =

B. $2,078.95 − $708.06 =

C. $918.27 + $1,036.15 =

D. $7,819.69 − $3,800.99 =

3. Divide decimals. Round to the nearest thousandth (0.001). Example: 3.5 ÷ 214.1 = 0.016

A. 7.5 ÷ 145 =

B. 10.4 ÷ 263.7 =

C. 2.8 ÷ 98.1 =

D. 5.4 ÷ 378.1 =

Terms

- *will*
- *beneficiary*
- *probate*
- *executor*
- *trust*
- *trustee*
- *opportunity cost*

Answer:
1. A. 1.45%
   B. 62.4%
   C. 75%
   D. 7.6%
2. A. $10,883.09
   B. $1,370.89
   C. $1,954.42
   D. $4,018.70
3. A. 0.052
   B. 0.039
   C. 0.029
   D. 0.014

Inflation and Wealth

Recall from chapter 6 that inflation is the rise in the level of prices over a period of time. For example, the average price of a 12-ounce jar of peanut butter was $1.30 in the 1980s. Today, the average price increased to nearly $4 a jar. Over the years, the prices of food, housing, and most other items have increased.

We think of inflation in terms of rising prices. However, inflation is really the value of currency decreasing. In other words, a dollar can no longer buy as much as it used to. While the cost of goods and services generally increases due to inflation, average earnings also increase. The median household income in 1970 was a little less than $10,000. By 2012, the median household income was nearly $50,000. As prices rise, salaries generally rise as well.

As you might imagine, inflation can have a negative effect on building wealth. Historically, the value of currency has decreased over time. Therefore, in order to build wealth, the money you save and invest must grow at a rate greater than the rate of inflation. If it does not, your savings and investments actually lose value.

The rate of inflation is usually estimated using the Consumer Price Index (CPI), which measures the price of a variety of products and services that are

In 1971, President Richard Nixon instituted a 90-day freeze of both wages and prices as a way to combat inflation.

fyi

typically purchased by consumers. Each year has an index value, as shown in Figure 13-1. That value can be compared to estimate an inflation rate. To determine the rate of increase of CPI, use the following formula:

$$\text{rate of increase in CPI} = \frac{\text{increase in CPI}}{\text{CPI for a given year}}$$

Example 13-1A

Year	Average Annual CPI
2005	195.3
2006	201.6
2007	207.3
2008	215.3
2009	214.5
2010	218.1
2011	226.8

Source: The US Department of Labor Bureau of Labor Statistics

Figure 13-1. Consumer Price Indices

See It

Calculate the rate of inflation between 2005 and 2006.

Strategy

Use Figure 13-1 and the formula:

$$\text{rate of increase in CPI} = \frac{\text{increase in CPI}}{\text{CPI for a given year}}$$

Solution

Step 1: Determine the increase in the Consumer Price Index (CPI). Subtract the CPI for 2005 from the CPI for 2006.

increase in CPI = CPI for 2006 – CPI for 2005

increase in CPI = 201.6 – 195.3

increase in CPI = 6.3

Step 2: Determine the rate of increase in the CPI. Divide the increase in CPI by the starting CPI, or the CPI for 2005. Round to the nearest thousandth (0.001).

$$\text{rate of increase in CPI} = \frac{\text{increase in CPI}}{\text{CPI for a given year}}$$

$$\text{rate of increase in CPI} = \frac{6.3}{195.3}$$

$$\text{rate of increase in CPI} \approx 0.032$$

Step 3: Convert the rate of increase to a percentage by moving the decimal two places to the right.

$0.032 \rightarrow 3.2\%$

Check It

Calculate the rate of inflation between the years 2009 and 2010.

Answer:
1.7%

Wills and Trusts

An estate is comprised of all of a person's possessions, including all assets and liabilities. At the end of an individual's life, his or her estate must be settled. Any net assets will become the property of some other person or persons. The net assets could also become the property of a charity or some other organization. By planning your estate, you can make sure your wishes are met as to how your wealth will be handled after your death.

A *will* is a legal document that expresses a person's wishes for their estate after death. A will names one or more people to manage the estate. The *executor* is the person who will manage the estate. A will also names the beneficiaries of the estate. *Beneficiaries* are those who will receive the assets of the estate.

In recent years, various scandals have made ethics a topic of focus in financial management. Ethics are moral principles that guide behavior. Ethics are important anytime you are managing money that belongs to others and when you are reporting your own financial activity to others, including government agencies. It is important to maintain accurate financial records and to ensure that any reporting of finances is accurate. If you are appointed as an executor to a will, it is important to keep information secret that you are trusted to keep secret.

After a person dies, a legal process called *probate* settles any debts and claims against the estate. After debts and claims are settled, what remains is the estate's *net assets*. The net assets are then distributed according to the directions written in the will.

Intestate is a legal term that means to die without a valid will. If a person dies intestate, the state will determine who gets the remainder of the person's estate after all debts have been paid.

To determine the value of an estate, you can use the formula that follows:

net assets = total assets – total liabilities

Teaching Tip:
Explain to students that even if they have a professional financial planner help them with their finances, it is still their responsibility to understand and carry out the financial plan.

Example 13-1B

See It

Flora recently passed away. In her will, she designated her favorite charity as the sole inheritor of her net assets. Flora had a total of $718,950 in assets and $146,719 in liabilities. What is the value of the net assets that the charity will inherit from Flora?

Strategy

Use the formula:

net assets = total assets – total liabilities

Solution

Step 1: Identify the total assets and the total liabilities.

total assets = $718,950

total liabilities = $146,719

Step 2: Determine the difference between the total assets and the total liabilities. Subtract the total liabilities from the total assets.

net assets = total assets – total liabilities

net assets = $718,950 – $146,719

net assets = $572,231

Check It

Fernando's estate has a total of $850,610 in assets and $310,046 in liabilities. The net assets will be equally divided among his children. What is the value of the net assets that Fernando's estate contains?

Answer:
$540,564

A will might call for the establishment of a trust. A ***trust*** is a legal arrangement through which a trustee holds assets for the interest of a beneficiary. A ***trustee*** is a person or institution that safeguards a trust. Trusts are often established when beneficiaries are children under 18 years of age. For example, if a person's beneficiary is a child who is not yet of legal age, the estate may be placed into a trust. The trust will hold the property until the child has reached the age where the property can legally be transferred to the child.

Opportunity Cost

Time and money are always limited resources. Anytime you are working with limited resources, you must make choices regarding how you spend those resources. For example, if you have two hours of free time on a Saturday, you have to decide how to spend that limited amount of time. You choose one option at the expense of the other. ***Opportunity cost*** is what you give up by choosing one option over another. For example, you can choose to work or see a movie during that time. If you choose to work, you get paid, but you lose the opportunity to see the movie. If you choose to see the movie, you lose the opportunity to make money.

Opportunity cost also comes into play when investing. If you have $1,000 to invest, you have many options for how to invest that money. You have one option with promising returns, but high risk. You have another option with lower return, but much less risk. You decide on the less risky option. You earn a 2% return ($20) on your investment in the first year. The more-risky option that you passed up returned 8% ($80) in the first year. The opportunity cost for the investment you chose was the difference between what you could have earned and what you actually earned: $80 – $20, or $60. To calculate opportunity cost, use the following formula:

opportunity cost = value of option A – value of option B

Teaching Tip:
Ask students how they might use an opportunity-cost decision-making model to help them decide something in their own lives.

Example 13-1C

See It

Spencer has $3,000 to invest in a mutual fund. He decided to invest in Liberty Value Fund, a fund with little risk. This fund will generate a return of 3.5% for the year. Freedom Asset Fund, a more aggressive and more risky fund, would have generated a return of 6% for that same year. What is the opportunity cost of investing in Liberty Value Fund A?

Strategy

Use the formula:

opportunity cost = value of option A – value of option B

Solution

Step 1: Convert the rate of each return to a decimal by moving the decimal two places to the left for each fund.

Liberty Value Fund = 3.5% → 0.035

Freedom Asset Fund = 6% → 0.06

Step 2: Determine what the Liberty fund earned. Multiply the amount of the investment by the rate of return.

earnings = amount of investment × rate of return

earnings = $3,000 × 0.035

earnings = $105

Step 3: Determine what Spencer could have earned. Multiply the amount of the investment by the rate of return.

possible earnings = amount of investment × rate of return

possible earnings = $3,000 × 0.06

possible earnings = $180

Step 4: Calculate the opportunity cost. Subtract the actual earnings from the possible earnings.

opportunity cost = possible earnings – actual earnings

opportunity cost = $180 – $105

opportunity cost = $75

Stocks and bonds are not insured like savings accounts. So, it is possible to lose part or all of your investment.

Check It

Esme has $4,000 to invest in municipal bonds. She narrowed her choices to two bonds: Montgomery City Bonds and Westville County Bonds. Esme invests in Montgomery City Bonds, which had an annual yield of 4.1% and a lower rating. The Westville County Bonds had an annual yield of 6.2% for that same year. What was the opportunity cost of Esme's decision?

Answer:
$84

Checkpoint 13.1

1. Use the information in Figure 13-1 to calculate the rate of inflation between 2007 and 2008.

2. Jackson's estate has total assets worth $315,678 and total liabilities worth $95,167. Calculate the value of the net assets in Jackson's estate.

3. Dianne's grandmother's estate has total assets worth $485,617 and total liabilities worth $160,018. What is the value of the net assets in Dianne's grandmother's estate?

4. Hassan has $5,000 to invest in bond funds. He chose to invest in Bond Fund A, which had an annual yield of 3.8%. His other choice, Bond Fund B, had an annual yield of 6.3% for that same year. What was the opportunity cost of Hassan's decision?

5. Armen has $3,500 to invest in the stock market. He chose Western Telecommunication, which had an annual yield of 6.2%. His other choice, Eastern Financial Group, had an annual yield of 9.1% for that same year. What was the opportunity cost of Armen's decision?

Answer:
1. 3.9%
2. $220,511
3. $325,599
4. $125
5. $101.50

Section 13.2 Retirement Planning

Objectives

- **Describe individual retirement arrangements and 401(k) accounts.**
- **Explain Social Security and pensions.**
- **Determine the future value of an annuity.**
- **Calculate the present value of an annuity.**

Terms

- *individual retirement arrangment (IRA)*
- *401(k)*
- *pension*
- *annuity*

Build Your Math Skills

Review these math skills to prepare for the lesson that follows.

1. Convert percentages to decimals by moving the decimal two places to the left. Example: 3% → 0.03

A. 4.5% →

B. 10.1% →

C. 7.46% →

D. 8.2% →

2. Multiply decimals. Example: $25,450 × 0.03 = $763.50

A. $40,146 × 0.06 =

B. $38,973 × 0.08 =

C. $84,073 × 0.05 =

D. $36,716 × 0.04 =

3. Add decimals. Example: $1,419.18 + $978.95 = $2,398.13

A. $6,073.37 + $2,719.06 =

B. $941.85 + $1,765.84 =

C. $4,079.86 + $2,946.75 =

D. $6,718.21 + $915.07 =

4. Simplify exponents. Example: $1.05^3 \approx 1.1576$

A. $1.1^2 \approx$

B. $2.4^3 \approx$

C. $1.5^4 \approx$

D. $6.4^3 \approx$

Answer:
1. A. 0.045
   B. 0.101
   C. 0.0746
   D. 0.082
2. A. $2,408.76
   B. $3,117.84
   C. $4,203.65
   D. $1,468.64
3. A. $8,792.43
   B. $2,707.69
   C. $7,026.61
   D. $7,633.28
4. A. 1.21
   B. 13.824
   C. 5.0625
   D. 262.144

Teaching Tip:
Engage students in a discussion about what they would like to do when they retire.

IRAs and 401(k)s

When an investment, such as a stock or bond purchase, earns the investor additional money, the earnings are typically taxable as income. Because the government would like to encourage individuals to save and invest to prepare for retirement, there are special retirement accounts that allow invested money to grow tax free. Retirement accounts can be complicated because there are a lot of rules that govern how much can be saved and when the money can be withdrawn.

An *individual retirement arrangement (IRA)* is an account that allows individuals to save money for retirement. Individuals may contribute to an IRA from their earned income. The amount that can be contributed changes occasionally. In 2012, the contribution limit was $5,000 per year for people under 50 years of age.

An IRA is commonly thought to stand for an individual retirement *account*. In fact, an IRA is an individual retirement *arrangement,* that can be an account or annuity, in which individuals may place retirement contributions.

The money you contribute to the IRA is not taxed. So, for example, if you contribute $3,000 to an IRA, your taxable income for the year is reduced by $3,000. You can use the following formula to determine the tax savings:

tax savings = original tax amount – reduced tax amount

To determine tax savings, you will need to use an income tax table, like the one shown in Figure 13-2.

Example 13-2A

See It

Lee is single, and his taxable income for the year is $45,270. He deposited $3,000 into an IRA. What were Lee's tax savings?

Strategy

Use Figure 13-2 and the formula:

tax savings = original tax amount – reduced tax amount

Solution

Step 1: Determine Lee's original tax amount.

$45,270 lies between $45,250 and $45,300

original tax amount = $7,444

Step 2: Determine Lee's reduced taxable income. Subtract his retirement deposit from his original taxable income.

reduced taxable income = original taxable income – retirement deposit

reduced taxable income = $45,270 – $3,000

reduced taxable income = $42,270

Step 3: Determine Lee's reduced tax amount.

$42,270 lies between $42,250 and $43,300

reduced tax amount = $6,694

Step 4: Determine the tax savings. Subtract the reduced tax amount from the original tax amount.

tax savings = original tax amount – reduced tax amount

tax savings = $7,444 – $6,694

tax savings = $750

If line 43 (taxable income) is—		And you are—			
At least	But less than	Single	Married filing jointly *	Married filing separately	Head of a household
		Your tax is—			
41,000	41,050	6,381	5,304	6,381	5,546
41,050	41,100	6,394	5,311	6,394	5,554
41,100	41,150	6,406	5,319	6,406	5,561
41,150	41,200	6,419	5,326	6,419	5,569
...	...	...	...	...	...
42,200	42,250	6,681	5,484	6,681	5,726
42,250	42,300	6,694	5,491	6,694	5,734
42,300	42,350	6,706	5,499	6,706	5,741
42,350	42,400	6,719	5,506	6,719	5,749
...	...	...	...	...	...
45,200	45,250	7,431	5,934	7,431	6,176
45,250	45,300	7,444	5,941	7,444	6,184
45,300	45,350	7,456	5,949	7,456	6,191
45,350	45,400	7,469	5,956	7,469	6,199
...	...	...	...	...	...
79,600	79,650	16,031	12,156	16,330	14,674
79,650	79,700	16,044	12,169	16,344	14,686
79,700	79,750	16,056	12,181	16,358	14,699
79,750	79,800	16,069	12,194	16,372	14,711
...	...	...	...	...	...
89,600	89,650	18,712	14,656	19,130	17,174
89,650	89,700	18,726	14,669	19,144	17,186
89,700	89,750	18,740	14,681	19,158	17,199
89,750	89,800	18,754	14,694	19,172	17,211

Source: The Internal Revenue Service

Figure 13-2. Sample Income Tax Table

Check It

Omar and Juanita are married. They file their income taxes jointly. Their combined taxable income is $89,615. This year, they contributed a total of $10,000 to their individual 401(k) retirement accounts. What were Omar and Juanita's tax savings?

Answer:
$2,500

When the investor with the IRA reaches retirement age, he or she can begin withdrawing money from the IRA. The money will be taxed as it is withdrawn and will be treated as taxable income.

A **401(k),** pronounced *four-oh-one k,* is a retirement plan sponsored by an employer. A 401(k) is similar to an IRA. With a 401(k), employees can have money withheld from their paychecks and deposited into their retirement account. A 401(k) allows higher contributions than an IRA. Allowed contribution amounts can change from year to year based on governmental regulations. For example, in 2012 the contribution limit was $17,000 per year.

In many instances, the employer will match the contributions of employees up to a specified limit. For example, an employer may match the contributions of employees up to 3% of employee earnings. To determine your total contributions to an IRA, use the following formula:

total contributions = individual contributions + employer contributions

Example 13-2B

See It

Maribel works as a dental hygienist earning $67,530 per year. She contributes 5% of her annual salary to her 401(k) account, and her employer matches her savings up to 3%. How much per year will Maribel deposit into her 401(k) account, including her employer contributions?

Strategy

Use the formula:

total contributions = individual contributions + employer contributions

Solution

Step 1: Convert the percentages to decimals by moving the decimal two places to the left.

5% → 0.05

3% → 0.03

Step 2: Determine Maribel's individual contributions. Multiply her annual salary by her annual contribution rate.

individual contributions = annual salary × annual contribution rate

individual contributions = $67,530 × 0.05

individual contributions = $3,376.50

Step 3: Determine Maribel's employer contributions. Multiply her annual salary by her annual employer's matching rate.

employer contributions = annual salary × annual employer matching rate

employer contributions = $67,530 × 0.03

employer contributions = $2,025.90

Step 4: Determine Maribel's total contributions. Add the individual contributions and the employer contributions.

total contributions = individual contributions + employer contributions

total contributions = $3,376.50 + $2,025.90

total contributions = $5,402.40

Check It

Jeremiah is a hotel manager for a ski resort. He earns an annual salary of $54,570 and contributes 5% of his salary to his 401(k) account. His employer matches his contributions up to 2.5% of his salary. What was the total amount contributed to Jeremiah's 401(k) account last year?

Answer:
$4,092.75

Employee contributions to IRAs and 401(k)s are not always pretax dollars. Contributions to *Roth IRAs* and *Roth 401(k)s* are taxed as regular income. However, these accounts grow tax free. Because the money was taxed before it was contributed, the money is not taxed when withdrawn at retirement. The contribution limits are generally the same as with a traditional IRA or 401(k).

Teaching Tip:
Point out to students that the life expectancy since Social Security was established in 1935 has increased by nearly 20 years.

Social Security

Social Security taxes are paid by employees and their employers to fund the Social Security program. *Social Security* was originally a program to provide payments to those who were too old to work. Later, it was expanded to include disabled workers and surviving family members of deceased workers.

Most people can expect to receive some Social Security benefits when they retire. However, workers should not consider these benefits a main source of retirement income. Social Security benefits may change by the time you

Financial $marts

In 1935 when the Social Security Act was signed into law by President Franklin D. Roosevelt, most senior citizens had no retirement savings of any kind. Social Security was never designed to account for all of a person's financial needs during his or her retirement years. It should be thought of as only one source of retirement income. All financially smart people should prepare for their retirement through their own savings and investment.

retire. Therefore, you should consider the potential of collecting these funds as a supplement to your retirement.

Over the past 30 years, there has been an increase in the number of people approaching retirement age and an overall decrease in those entering the workforce. As a result, there is some question about whether Social Security is going to have enough funds in the future to pay benefits to all those who paid into it.

Pensions

A *pension* is a retirement plan set up by an employer through which an employee is provided income after he or she retires. Most pension plans are *defined-benefit plans.* This means the amount of benefit is based on a formula rather than being determined by the return on the investment of a fund.

The number of defined-benefit pensions is steadily declining in the United States. More employers are opting for 401(k) or similar retirement plans which are *defined-contribution plans.* This means the amount of benefit is based on a specific contribution amount determined by the return on the investment of a fund. Government employees, union members, and employees of large companies are more likely to have defined-benefit pensions.

Annuities

Annuities are a common way to save for retirement. An *annuity* is a type of insurance product used as an investment. Deposits are made in equal amounts and at specific intervals over a period of time. After a specified number of years, the owner of the annuity can begin withdrawing money from the account. Payments are generally received as equal installments.

If you make regular annuity payments into an account that earns interest, you can calculate the amount of money you will have in the future after a specified number of regular payments. The future value of an annuity is calculated using the following formula:

$$\textbf{future value} = \textbf{payment amount} \left(\frac{(1 + \textbf{interest rate})^{\textbf{number of payments}} - 1}{\textbf{interest rate}} \right)$$

In this formula, the interest rate must be expressed as a decimal. In addition, the time period for the interest rate must match the number of payments. For example, if the payments are made monthly, the interest rate must be a monthly interest rate.

fyi

The Social Security Administration has a Social Security retirement benefits calculator available on their website: www.ssa.gov.

Teaching Tip:
Explain to students that not every worker is eligible for Social Security. For example, in most states, teachers are not eligible because they do not pay into the fund.

Example 13-2C

See It

Jamal plans to start an annuity. He will deposit $100 per month for ten years. His annuity is guaranteed to have an annual interest rate of 5%. What will be the future value of Jamal's annuity at the end of the ten-year period?

Strategy

Use the formula:

$$\text{future value} = \text{payment amount} \left(\frac{(1 + \text{interest rate})^{\text{number of payments}} - 1}{\text{interest rate}} \right)$$

Solution

Step 1: Convert the annual interest rate to a decimal by moving the decimal two places to the left.

$5\% \rightarrow 0.05$

Step 2: Determine the number of payments. Multiply the number of years by 12 months per year.

number of payments = number of years × 12 months per year

number of payments = 10 years × 12 months per year

number of payments = 120

Step 3: Determine the monthly interest rate. Divide the annual interest rate by 12 months per year.

monthly interest rate = annual interest rate ÷ 12 months per year

monthly interest rate = 0.05 ÷ 12 months per year

monthly interest rate ≈ 0.004167

Step 4: Use the order of operations to work through the formula. First, simplify the numerator inside the large parentheses. Complete the innermost parentheses by adding 1 to the interest rate.

1 + interest rate = 1 + 0.004167 = 1.004167

Step 5: Next, perform the exponent. Raise the value (1 + interest rate) to a power equal to the number of payments. Round to the nearest ten-thousandth (0.0001).

$(1.004167)^{120} \approx 1.6471$

Step 6: Next, subtract 1.

1.6471 − 1 = 0.6471

Step 7: Simplify completely inside the large parentheses. Divide by the interest rate.

$$0.6471 \approx \frac{155.29}{0.004167}$$

Step 8: Multiply by the payment amount.

$100 × 155.29 = $15,529

Check It

Yvonne has decided to contribute to an annuity. She will contribute $150 per month for 15 years. Her investment advisor helped her find an annuity that will earn 5.5% annual interest. What will be the future value of Yvonne's annuity at the end of the 15-year period?

Answer:
$41,808.86

Annuities are used in ways other than as retirement plans. You could also be the *recipient* of an annuity. For example, suppose you have an aunt who wants to help you with a regular monthly payment for a car for the first five years following your high school graduation. Your aunt sets up an annuity to pay you a specific amount of money each month. Using a method called the *present value of an ordinary annuity*, you can calculate how much money must be set aside in order to fund the desired annuity. The formula for present value of an ordinary annuity is as follows:

Present value is the amount of money that must be invested today to get a desired sum in the future. It is also known as *present discounted value* or *discounting*.

$$\text{present value} = \text{payment amount} \left(\frac{1 - (1 + \text{interest rate})^{-\text{number of payments}}}{\text{interest rate}} \right)$$

This formula is similar to the future value formula, with a few differences. The interest rate must be expressed as a decimal, and the time period for the interest rate must match the time period for the number of payments. However, instead of subtracting 1, the exponential expression is subtracted from 1, and the exponent has a negative sign.

Teaching Tip:
Most graphing calculators, and many websites, have functions that will automatically calculate the future value if you enter values such as the payment amount, number of payments per year, and annual interest rate.

Example 13-2D

See It

Moselle wants to set up an annuity for her granddaughter's college fund. She wants her granddaughter to have monthly payments of $400 to help pay living expenses for four years. Moselle found an account with an annual interest rate of 3.5%. What is the amount of money Moselle must deposit into the account, or the present value of the annuity?

Strategy

Use the formula:

$$\text{present value} = \text{payment amount} \left(\frac{1 - (1 + \text{interest rate})^{-\text{number of payments}}}{\text{interest rate}} \right)$$

Solution

Step 1: Convert the annual interest rate to a decimal by moving the decimal two places to the left.

3.5% → 0.035

Step 2: Determine the number of payments. Multiply the number of years by 12 months per year.

number of payments = number of years × 12 months per year

number of payments = 4 years × 12 months per year

number of payments = 48

Step 3: Determine the monthly interest rate. Divide the annual interest rate by 12 months per year.

monthly interest rate = annual interest rate ÷ 12 months per year

monthly interest rate = 0.035 ÷ 12 months per year

monthly interest rate ≈ 0.002917

Step 4: Use the order of operations to work through the formula. First, simplify the numerator inside the large parentheses. Complete the innermost parentheses by adding 1 to the interest rate.

1 + interest rate = 1 + 0.002917 = 1.002917

Step 5: Next, perform the exponent. Raise the value (1 + interest rate) to a power equal to the opposite sign of number of payments. Round to the nearest ten-thousandth (0.0001).

$(1.002917)^{-48} \approx 0.8695$

Step 6: Next, subtract this value from 1.

1 − 0.8695 = 0.1305

Step 7: Simplify completely inside the large parentheses. Divide by the interest rate.

$$0.1305 \approx \frac{44.7377}{0.002917}$$

Step 8: Multiply by the payment amount.

$400 × 44.7377 = $17,895.08

Check It

Anthony knows that he will need $500 per month for a period of five years, so he wants to set up an annuity to provide the monthly payments. He found an ordinary annuity with an annual interest rate of 6.5%. Calculate the amount of money Anthony must deposit to fund the annuity, or the present value of the ordinary annuity.

fyi

With an ordinary annuity, payments are made at the end of each period.

Answer:
$25,558.45

Teaching Tip:
Checkpoint questions offer opportunities for formative assessment.

Checkpoint 13.2

Use the information in Figure 13-2 to answer questions 1 and 2.

1. Hope has a taxable income of $42,313 and files her federal income taxes as single. She has decided to make a $1,300 contribution to an IRA. What will be Hope's tax savings from the IRA contribution?

2. Alex and Julia Moreno are married and file their income taxes jointly. Their taxable income is $89,711. They decided to each contribute $5,000 to an IRA. What will be the Morenos' tax savings from the IRA contribution?

Answer:
1. $325
2. $2,500

3. Rosa began a new job as a chemical technician earning $44,200 per year and decided to contribute to a 401(k) retirement account. She will contribute 4%, and her employer will match up to 2.5% of her salary. What will be the combined annual contributions to her 401(k) account?

4. Clarissa has decided to contribute to an annuity. She will contribute $250 per month for 12 years. Her investment advisor helped her find an annuity that will earn 6% annual interest. What will be the future value of Clarissa's annuity at the end of the 12-year period?

5. Raj's aunt set up an annuity so that after he graduated high school he would receive $300 per month for a period of five years. The ordinary annuity has an annual interest rate of 4.75%. Calculate the amount of money Raj's aunt deposited to fund the annuity, or the present value of the ordinary annuity.

3. $2,873
4. $52,540
5. $15,992.94

There are many different ways to save for retirement.

Section 13.3 Other Investments

Terms

- *revenue-generating asset*
- *passive income*
- *royalty*

Objectives

- **Describe revenue-generating assets.**
- **Explain passive income.**

Build Your Math Skills

Review these math skills to prepare for the lesson that follows.

1. Convert percentages to decimals by moving the decimal two places to the left. Example: 5.45% → 0.0545

A. 3.5% →

B. 8.5% →

C. 5.4% →

D. 11.3% →

2. Multiply decimals. Round to the nearest cent ($0.01) if necessary. Example: $750 × 0.04 = $30

A. $950 × 0.05 =

B. $1,200 × 0.08 =

C. $1,250 × 0.055 =

D. $1,700 × 0.06125 =

3. Divide decimals. Round to the nearest thousandth (0.0001) if necessary. Example: 0.45 ÷ 4 = 0.1125

A. 0.055 ÷ 4 =

B. 0.07 ÷ 12 =

C. 0.065 ÷ 6 =

D. 0.08 ÷ 12 =

Answer:
1. A. 0.035
   B. 0.085
   C. 0.054
   D. 0.113
2. A. $47.50
   B. $96
   C. $68.75
   D. $104.13
3. A. 0.0138
   B. 0.0058
   C. 0.0108
   D. 0.0067

Revenue-Generating Assets

A ***revenue-generating asset,*** also called an *income-generating asset,* is anything in which you invest money that generates income. Stocks and bonds are examples of revenue-generating assets. However, there are many more revenue-generating assets in which you can invest. Often, wealth is best built with investments in assets other than stocks and bonds.

For example, purchasing a house for the purpose of renting it to others is an example of a revenue-generating asset. The rent payment that comes from the tenant becomes a source of income for the owner. A common investment strategy is to purchase one or more rental properties. These properties may have mortgages. The rent that the property owner collects will cover the mortgage payments and maintenance.

As time goes on, the owner's equity in the property increases. Eventually, the property owner no longer has mortgage payments, and the rent collected from tenants becomes a significant source of revenue for the investor. Not only does the asset generate revenue, but the asset has significant value itself and can be sold in the future if needed or desired.

In some cases, the revenue-generating asset does not require direct participation from the owner. ***Passive income*** is income from an activity or investment in which the owner does not actively participate. For example, if you invest in a business, but are not part of the operation of the business, the income from the investment would be passive income. Rent income is often considered passive income, as are earnings from online advertisements.

Teaching Tip:
Explain that passive income is considered *unearned* income for tax purposes.

To determine the net annual income from a revenue-generating asset, use the following formula:

net annual income = annual revenue − total annual expenses

Example 13-3A

See It

Sung owns a house that she uses for rental property income. She charges her tenant $1,050 per month in rent and pays $450 per month for the mortgage payment. She also pays $900 per year in insurance, $1,500 per year in property taxes, and $1,250 in annual maintenance. What is Sung's net annual income for the rental house?

Strategy

Use the formula:

net annual income = annual revenue − total annual expenses

Solution

Step 1: Determine the annual revenue generated. Multiply the monthly rent by 12 months per year.

annual revenue = monthly rent × 12

annual revenue = $1,050 × 12

annual revenue = $12,600

Step 2: Determine the annual expenses for the mortgage payment. Multiply the monthly mortgage payment by 12.

annual mortgage cost = monthly mortgage payment × 12

annual mortgage cost = $450 × 12

annual mortgage cost = $5,400

Step 3: Determine the total annual expenses. Add the annual mortgage cost, property insurance, property taxes, and annual maintenance.

total annual expenses = annual mortgage cost + property insurance + property taxes + maintenance

total annual expenses = $5,400 + $900 + $1,500 + $1,250

total annual expenses = $9,050

Step 4: Calculate the net annual income. Subtract the total annual expenses from the annual revenue.

net annual income = annual revenue – total annual expenses

net annual income = $12,600 – $9,050

net annual income = $3,550

Check It

Tanner owns a house that he uses for rental property income. He charges the tenant $1,200 per month in rent. He pays $650 per month for the mortgage payment. He also pays $1,100 per year in insurance, $1,800 per year in property taxes, and $1,450 in annual maintenance. What is Tanner's net annual income for the rental house?

Answer:
$2,250

Example 13-3B

See It

Calculate Sung's net annual income once the mortgage for her rental property is paid in full.

Strategy

Use the formula:

net annual income = annual revenue – total annual expenses

Solution

Step 1: Determine the total annual expenses. Add the property insurance, property taxes, and annual maintenance.

total annual expenses = property insurance + property taxes + maintenance

total annual expenses = $900 + $1,500 + $1,250

total annual expenses = $3,650

Step 2: Calculate the net annual income. Subtract the total annual expenses from the annual revenue.

net annual income = annual revenue – total annual expenses

net annual income = $12,600 – $3,650

net annual income = $8,950

Check It

Calculate Tanner's net annual income once the mortgage for the rental property is paid off.

Answer:
$10,050

Houses are not the only type of real estate investment. Property used for business is often owned by an investor and leased to a business. Farmers do not always own the land they farm. It is common for agricultural land to be leased to farmers. For example, an investor may purchase land in hopes that the land will be in demand in the future for a housing development. In order to generate revenue from the land while waiting for the development opportunity, the land could be leased to a farmer who is looking for land on which to raise a crop.

Teaching Tip:
Encourage students to explore the idea of an *encore career.*

Becoming an Entrepreneur

Many people go into business for themselves as a primary career, to supplement a regular job, or to make extra money for retirement. Creating your own business is known as becoming an *entrepreneur.* There are many ways you can become an entrepreneur.

Technology

If you are technology oriented, there may be many ways in which you can apply your talents to make money:

- create software programs you can license to users

- build a website or blog

- generate referral fees

If you have the skills necessary to write an application, or *app,* for a mobile device, this can be a source of income. Even an app that sells for $0.99 can generate a great deal of money if the app is purchased by thousands of users.

Building a website or blog site that attracts a substantial number of visitors can generate online advertising revenue. You could even create a company specifically to place ads on popular websites and blogs.

Career Discovery
Science, Technology, Engineering, & Mathematics Careers and Math Skills

Workers in this career cluster use math and the scientific processes in laboratory and testing services and also conduct research. Often their work leads to discoveries that have the potential to improve life. Careers in this cluster are available in two areas: science/mathematics and engineering/technology.

Individuals with careers in this field use math skills extensively to solve problems and conduct research. Give an example of a situation in which someone in this field might need to use math skills to solve a problem.

Many online retailers also pay referral fees when a customer comes to the retailers' website from a link on your website. For example, suppose you have a successful blog site about photography. If you recommend books and equipment on your blog and provide links directly to an online seller that pays referral fees, you could earn up to 15% of what the buyer who you referred spends with the online retailer.

These are just some ways to earn revenue by investing in technology. Technology changes quickly, and there are constantly new opportunities to make money using technology.

Business

You could start your own business from scratch, buy an existing business, or invest in someone else's business. For example, you could start a vending machine business. By investing money in the vending machines and placing them in various locations, you would collect the revenue that the machines generate.

Franchises are another way to create your own business. Many people invest in restaurants, service providers, and other familiar businesses through investing in a franchise.

You could also invest in someone else's business. Suppose a friend wanted to start a lawn mowing business and needed money to purchase equipment. You agree to fund the purchase of the equipment in return for a share of the profits.

Royalties

If you have other talents, such as writing, you could create an asset that generates ongoing royalties. **Royalties** are payments made to the owner of an asset for the use of that asset. For example, a recording artist often receives royalty payments based on how many copies of a song or album he or she sells. Book authors are usually paid a royalty based on the sales of the book. The asset is the creative work of the artist or author and the royalty is the income generated by the asset. Royalties are generally calculated using the formula:

$$\text{royalty} = \text{amount of sales} \times \text{royalty rate}$$

Example 13-3C

See It

Coral is the author of a novel. She receives an 8% royalty on all sales. For a six-month sales period, her book generated $16,992 in sales. How much will Coral receive in royalties for that period?

Strategy

Use the formula:

$$\text{royalty} = \text{amount of sales} \times \text{royalty rate}$$

Solution

Step 1: Convert the royalty rate to a decimal by moving the decimal two places to the left.

8% → 0.08

Step 2: Determine the amount of the royalty for the sales period. Multiply the amount of sales by the royalty rate.

royalty = amount of sales × royalty rate

royalty = $16,992 × 0.08

royalty = $1,359.36

Check It

Qadir is a recording artist who receives a royalty of $0.40 each time his song is downloaded from a music website. During one six-month period, his song was downloaded 1,457 times. Calculate the amount of royalties that Qadir will receive for this period.

Answer:
$582.80

Checkpoint 13.3

Use the information that follows to answer questions 1 and 2. Desmond owns a house that he uses for rental property income. He charges the tenant $1,400 per month in rent. He pays $845 per month for the mortgage payment. He also pays $1,250 per year in insurance, $2,050 per year in property taxes, and $1,500 in annual maintenance.

1. What is Desmond's net annual income for the rental house?

2. What will be Desmond's net annual income once the mortgage on the rental house is paid?

3. Neida wrote a book and receives a 5% royalty from all sales. During one quarter, her book generated $24,084 in sales. What will be Neida's royalty during this quarter?

4. Brent and Lee created a video game. Together they receive a 4.5% royalty on all sales. They split the royalties equally. If there were $14,000 in sales last year, what would be each partner's profit?

5. Gayle purchased an inflatable bounce house. She rents it to Trey, who sets it up at children's parties. Trey pays Gayle $35 for every party. Last year, Trey used Gayle's bounce house at 37 parties. What is Gayle's total passive income from this enterprise?

Answer:
1. $1,860
2. $12,000
3. $1,204.20
4. $315
5. $1,295

Chapter Review

Build Your Vocabulary

As you progress through this course, develop a personal glossary of financial literacy terms and add it to your portfolio. This will help you build your financial literacy vocabulary. Write out a definition for each of the following terms, and add it to your personal glossary.

will

beneficiary

probate

executor

trust

trustee

opportunity cost

individual retirement arrangement (IRA)

401(k)

pension

annuity

revenue-generating asset

passive income

royalty

 ## Teamwork

Working in teams, research the funding issues faced by the Social Security system. Brainstorm solutions to the issues that you discover. Develop a plan for these solutions and present it to the class.

Review Your Math Skills

Practice and build on the math skills that you have learned.

1. Convert decimals to percentages by moving the decimal two places to the right. Example: 0.038 → 3.8%

A. 0.415 →

B. 2.9142 →

C. 0.00123 →

D. 0.0745 →

2. Add and subtract decimals. Example: 471.8 − 263.9 = 207.9

A. $213.82 + $157.18 =

B. $1,864.99 − $657.19 =

C. $10,056.64 − $7,301.78 =

D. $2,820.16 + $3,911.61 =

3. Divide decimals. Round to the nearest thousandth (0.001) if necessary. Example: 3.5 ÷ 214.1 = 0.016

A. 9.2 ÷ 104.1 =

B. 1.5 ÷ 64.2 =

C. 25.6 ÷ 482.7 =

D. 10.9 ÷ 318.3 =

Answer:
1. A. 41.5%
   B. 291.42%
   C. 0.123%
   D. 7.45%
2. A. $371
   B. $1,207.80
   C. $2,754.86
   D. $6,731.77
3. A. 0.088
   B. 0.023
   C. 0.053
   D. 0.034

4. Convert percentages to decimals by moving the decimal two places to the left. Example: 3.2% → 0.032

A. 19.6% →   B. 5.42% →

C. 4.3% →   D. 8.01% →

5. Multiply decimals. Round to the nearest cent ($0.01) if necessary. Example: $25,450 × 0.03 = $763.50

A. $29,146 × 0.07 =   B. $51,846 × 0.01 =

C. $94,038 × 0.03 =   D. $40,067 × 0.09 =

6. Divide decimals. Round to the nearest ten-thousandth (0.0001) if necessary. Example: 0.45 ÷ 4 = 0.1125

A. 0.09 ÷ 16 =   B. 0.34 ÷ 5 =

C. 0.035 ÷ 7 =   D. 0.07 ÷ 4 =

7. Simplify exponents. Round to the nearest ten-thousandth (0.0001) if necessary. Example: $1.05^3 = 1.1576$

A. $6.2^2 =$ B. $0.9^6 =$

C. $1.3^4 =$ D. $3.7^4 =$

8. Convert percentages to decimals by moving the decimal two places to the left. Example: 5.45% → 0.0545

A. 9.61% →   B. 12.03% →

C. 615.7% →   D. 4.99% →

9. Add decimals. Example: $1,419.18 + $978.95 = $2,398.13

A. $3,182.94 + $164.02 =   B. $753.12 + $1,004.49 =

C. $4,976.08 + $689.27 =   D. $261.63 + $8,309.18 =

10. Multiply decimals. Round to the nearest cent ($0.01) if necessary. Example: $750 × 0.04 = $30

A. $834 × 0.09 =   B. $2,417 × 0.2 =

C. $1,702 × 0.19 =   D. $913 × 0.33 =

4. A. 0.196
   B. 0.0542
   C. 0.043
   D. 0.0801
5. A. $2,040.22
   B. $518.46
   C. $2,821.14
   D. $3,606.03
6. A. 0.0056
   B. 0.068
   C. 0.005
   D. 0.0175
7. A. 38.44
   B. 0.5314
   C. 2.8561
   D. 187.4161
8. A. 0.0961
   B. 0.1203
   C. 6.157
   D. 0.0499
9. A. $3,346.96
   B. $1,757.61
   C. $5,665.35
   D. $8,570.81
10. A. $75.06
    B. $483.40
    C. $323.38
    D. $301.29

Section 13.1 Protecting Wealth

11. The Consumer Price Index (CPI) for all urban consumers in the southern US in 2010 was 211.3. In 2009, this index was 207.8. Use these values to calculate the rate of inflation for urban consumers in the southern US between 2009 and 2010.

12. Daniel has $4,500 to invest in the stock market. He chose Gulf Coast Technologies, which had an annual yield of 4.6%. His other choice, Midwestern Agricultural, had an annual yield of 7.85% for that same year. What was the opportunity cost of Daniel's decision?

Answer:
11. 1.7%
12. $146.25

13. Five years ago, Toya invested $2,500 in a mutual fund that yielded a 2.15% return on her investment over that time. She chose not to invest in a stock fund that had a 2.5% return during the same period. What is the opportunity cost of Toya's investment decision?

13. $8.75

Section 13.2 Retirement Planning

14. Stephanie is single and has a taxable income of $33,298. She contributed $2,000 to an IRA. Use the following table to determine Stephanie's tax savings.

If line 43 (taxable income) is—		And you are—			
At least	But less than	Single	Married filing jointly *	Married filing separately	Head of a household
		Your tax is—			
31,200	31,250	4,259	3,834	4,259	4,076
31,250	31,300	4,266	3,841	4,266	4,084
31,300	31,350	4,274	3,849	4,274	4,091
31,350	31,400	4,281	3,856	4,281	4,099
...	...	...	...	...	...
33,200	33,250	4,559	4,134	4,559	4,376
33,250	33,300	4,566	4,141	4,566	4,384
33,300	33,350	4,574	4,149	4,574	4,391
33,350	33,400	4,581	4,156	4,581	4,399
...	...	...	...	...	...

Source: The Internal Revenue Service

15. Juan works as a technical writer and earns $66,240 per year. He contributed to a 401(k) retirement account. He will contribute 5%, and his employer will match up to 3.5% of his salary. What will be Juan's combined annual contributions to his 401(k) account?

16. Lakota has decided to contribute to an annuity. She will contribute $200 per month for eight years. Her investment advisor helped her find an annuity that will earn 5.5% annual interest. What will be the future value of Lakota's annuity at the end of the eight-year period?

Answer:
14. $300
15. $5,630.40
16. $24,049.74

Section 13.3 Other Investments

17. Colby owns a house that he uses for rental property income. He charges the tenant $1,250 per month in rent. He pays $680 per month for the mortgage payment. He also pays $975 per year in insurance, $1,350 per year in property taxes, and $1,100 in annual maintenance. What is Colby's net annual income for the rental house? What will be the net annual income after the mortgage is paid?

Answer:
17. net annual income = $3,415
    net annual income after the mortgage is paid = $11,575
18. $1,170.98

18. Kirstie wrote a book and receives a 6.5% royalty from all sales. During one quarter, her book generated $18,015 in sales. What will be Kirstie's royalty during this quarter?

Reinforce Your Understanding

19. Kenton is considering a payday loan for $315. The payday lender charges 22.5% for a brokerage fee, plus 0.39% in interest charges for a 14-day term loan. How much will Kenton pay back at the end of the 14 days?

20. Shayna works as an aerospace engineering technician and earns an annual salary of $59,990. Calculate the amount of her salary that she would receive if she were paid monthly, semimonthly, biweekly, or weekly. Round your answer to the nearest cent ($0.01) if necessary.

Apply Your Technology Skills

Access the G-W Learning companion website for this text at www.g-wlearning.com. Download each data file for this chapter. Follow the instructions to complete financial literacy activities to practice what you have learned in this chapter.

Data File 13-1—Calculating Income from an Annuity

Data File 13-2—Researching Inflation

Data File 13-3—Writing a Will

Data File 13-4—Investigating a Roth Account

Answer:
19. $387.10
20. monthly = $4,999.17
    semimonthly =
        $2,499.58
    biweekly = $2,307.31
    weekly = $1,153.65

Teaching Tip:
The Apply Your Technology Skills activities offer project-based authentic assessment opportunities.

Unit 4 Summative Assessment

On a separate sheet of paper or in a word processing document, apply what you have learned in this unit to answer the questions that follow.

Multiple Choice Questions

1. Last year, Miller Enterprises paid an annual dividend of $5.65 per share, and the stock price at that time was $42 per share. Calculate the dividend yield for Miller Enterprises.

   A. 16.14%   B. 21.65%

   C. 13.45%   D. 7.43%

2. _____ is money you earn from your work.

   A. Active income   B. Passive income

   C. An investment   D. A liability

3. Maria works as a veterinary technician earning $74,829 per year. She contributes 5% of her annual salary to her 401(k), and her employer matches savings up to 2%. How much per year will be deposited into Maria's 401(k) account?

   A. $3,741.45   B. $5,238.03

   C. $2,244.87   D. $3,816.28

4. Sebastian is married and has four children. He is the primary wage earner for his family and wants to purchase a term life insurance policy for himself. The mortgage on his home has a balance of $205,000. Sebastian has a monthly net pay of $6,718.87. He wants to purchase enough life insurance to pay off the mortgage and provide his family with ten years of his net pay. How much life insurance will Sebastian need to purchase?

   A. $2,011,718.87   B. $1,011,264.40

   C. $272,188.70   D. $423,437.74

5. _____ life insurance is permanent life insurance that has unchanging premium and death-benefit amounts.

   A. Variable   B. Universal

   C. Term   D. Whole

Answer:
1. C
2. A
3. B
4. B
5. D

Matching

Match the letter beside each equation to the situation to which it applies.

A. $\dfrac{\text{difference between amount}}{\text{paid and cash value}} = \dfrac{\text{total paid in premiums} -}{\text{cash value}}$

B. net asset value $= \dfrac{\text{fund assets} - \text{fund liabilities}}{\text{number of outstanding shares}}$

C. opportunity cost = value of option A − value of option B

D. future value = payment amount $\left(\dfrac{(1 + \text{interest rate})^{\text{number of payments}} - 1}{\text{interest rate}} \right)$

E. net worth = total assets − total liabilities

F. cost of trade = price of stock + commission

G. amount of coinsurance = (total expenses − deductible) × coinsurance percentage

H. bond yield $= \dfrac{\text{annual bond income}}{\text{bond price}}$

I. dividend yield $= \dfrac{\text{annual dividend per share}}{\text{stock price per share}}$

J. life insurance needed = 10 × annual net pay + amount of mortgage

6. Paul wants to determine the total cost of a stock trade.

7. Latoya wants to know how much money she will receive if she cancels her permanent life insurance policy.

8. Samir wants to know how much of his medical expenses he will have to pay after the deductible.

9. Sean makes regular annuity payments into an account that accrues interest. He wants to know how much money he will have after ten years.

10. Enrique wants to determine how much greater his assets are than his debts.

11. Cheyenne has the option to pick up a shift at work or do her homework.

12. Cheng wants to measure the return on his bond investment.

13. Marie needs to know how much life insurance to purchase.

14. Cindy wants to know the price of a mutual fund share.

15. Eduardo wants to calculate the return on his stock that pays a dividend.

Answer:
6. F
7. A
8. G
9. D
10. E
11. C
12. H
13. J
14. B
15. I

True/False Questions

16. *True or False?* If a person has a $1,000 deductible, the insurance company will only cover $1,000 in medical bills.

17. *True or False?* Inflation can have a negative effect on building wealth.

18. *True or False?* When you purchase a bond, you are taking out a loan from the company or government that issued the bond.

19. *True or False?* A life insurance policy *cannot* pay off debts of the insured after death.

20. *True or False?* Chapter 7 bankruptcy requires that the assets of the debtor are sold and the proceeds are used to pay as much debt as can be repaid.

Answer:
16. False
17. True
18. False
19. False
20. True

Mastery Questions

21. Daron works as a human resources manager for an energy company earning $108,600 annually. He owns 400 shares of stock in a communication company that pays a quarterly dividend of $0.65 per share. Daron also owns a municipal bond with a par value of $3,000 and an annual interest rate of 4.5% that pays interest semiannually. Calculate Daron's annual income.

22. Rina has decided to contribute to an annuity. She will contribute $300 per month for ten years. Her investment advisor helped her find an annuity that will earn 6% annual interest. How much interest will the annuity yield?

Answer:
21. $109,775
22. $13,164

23. Amy purchased a corporate bond from South Plains Airlines with a coupon rate of 7.5% and a par value of $2,000. She also purchased a corporate bond from Peach Country Communication with a coupon rate of 5.75% and a par value of $1,500. The value of the South Plains Airlines bond rose to $2,300, and the value of the Peach Country Communication bond fell to $1,300. Which bond had the higher bond yield?

24. Shannon has several investments. Among them, she owns two rental properties. For one property, she charges the tenant $850 per month in rent. She has a monthly mortgage payment of $450, annual property taxes of $1,155, annual insurance of $850, and annual maintenance costs of $1,175. For the second property, she charges the tenant $1,140 per month in rent. She has no mortgage payment, has annual property taxes of $1,857, has annual insurance of $1,200, and has annual maintenance costs of $1,300. What is Shannon's net annual revenue from her rental properties?

25. Christie wants to purchase life insurance. She can purchase a $750,000 term life insurance policy with a 20-year term for monthly premiums of $33.82. She could also purchase a $750,000 term life insurance policy with a 30-year term for monthly premiums of $51.54. What is the difference in total cost of the two insurance policies?

23. Peach Country
    Communication
24. $10,943
25. $10,437.60

Stages of Life Project

Stage 1 Student Years

Stage 2 Early Career Years

Stage 3 Earning Years

Stage 4 Retirement Years

Materials:
Instructor's Resource CD
Student Workbook
G-W Learning companion website
Microsoft Excel®–compatible software
Calculator with advanced-math functions

Life comes in stages. In this simulation, you will apply what you have learned in this text to four common stages of life. You will start as a senior in high school and make decisions for life after high school. After your education is complete, whether or not that includes education beyond high school, you begin a career. At this point in life, most people do not have a very impressive net worth, but it is the point where net worth can begin to grow. As your career progresses, your earnings and responsibilities will typically increase. After you retire, your financial responsibilities do not end. This simulation walks you through the *stages of life*, concluding with a summative exercise in which you complete a simulation for your own life.

In many of the exercises in this simulation, you will be asked to download data files from the G-W Learning companion website. The G-W Learning companion website is found at www.g-wlearning.com.

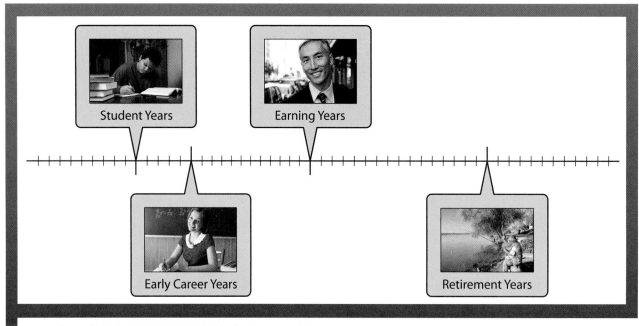

Sources: Shutterstock (Solaria, Petro Feketa, Tyler Olson, berna namoglu)

Stages of life for Financial Simulation

Stage 1 Student Years

Objectives

- Calculate gross earnings, Social Security tax, and Medicare tax.
- Determine an account balance after a payment is made.
- Calculate the amount needed for a student loan.
- Divide living expenses between roommates.
- Evaluate the impact of insurance premiums and deductibles on an insurance claim.
- Calculate savings in auto insurance premiums by changing insurance coverage.
- Create an annual budget.
- Create a cash flow statement.
- Calculate net worth.

Source: Shutterstock (Solaria)

Learning to manage money is an important life skill.

Working Part-Time

Teaching Tip:
Medicare is 1.45% and
Social Security is 6.2%.

Part-time work while in high school can be a good way to start learning financial responsibility. You will be earning money, which you will need to manage wisely. There are choices to make, such as how much to save and on what to spend your money. All of this starts with calculating how much money you will receive in your paycheck.

Exercise 1A

It is the holiday season and you are looking to earn some money. You get a part-time job at a home improvement store earning $7.35 per hour. The job pays time-and-a-half for hours over 40 in one week. Paychecks are issued every Friday. During the holiday break, you work 49.5 hours in one week. Your state has no income tax and you claim one withholding allowance on your federal taxes. Using the federal tax table in Figure 1, calculate your net pay for this week.

SINGLE Persons—**WEEKLY** Payroll Period

(For Wages Paid through December 20--)

And the wages are–		And the number of withholding allowances claimed is—										
At least	But less than	0	1	2	3	4	5	6	7	8	9	10
		The amount of income tax to be withheld is—										
$300	$310	$32	$21	$12	$5	$0	$0	$0	$0	$0	$0	$0
310	320	33	22	13	6	0	0	0	0	0	0	0
320	330	35	24	14	7	0	0	0	0	0	0	0
330	340	36	25	15	8	1	0	0	0	0	0	0
340	350	38	27	16	9	2	0	0	0	0	0	0
350	360	39	28	18	10	3	0	0	0	0	0	0
360	370	41	30	19	11	4	0	0	0	0	0	0
370	380	42	31	21	12	5	0	0	0	0	0	0
380	390	44	33	22	13	6	0	0	0	0	0	0
390	400	45	34	24	14	7	0	0	0	0	0	0
600	610	77	66	55	45	34	23	14	7	0	0	0
610	620	78	67	57	46	35	25	15	8	1	0	0
620	630	80	69	58	48	37	26	16	9	2	0	0
630	640	81	70	60	49	38	28	17	10	3	0	0
640	650	83	72	61	51	40	29	18	11	4	0	0
650	660	84	73	63	52	41	31	20	12	5	0	0
660	670	86	75	64	54	43	32	21	13	6	0	0
670	680	87	76	66	55	44	34	23	14	7	0	0
680	690	89	78	67	57	46	35	24	15	8	0	0
690	700	90	79	69	58	47	37	26	16	9	1	0
700	710	92	81	70	60	49	38	27	17	10	2	0
710	720	94	82	72	61	50	40	29	18	11	3	0
720	730	97	84	73	63	52	41	30	20	12	4	0
730	740	99	85	75	64	53	43	32	21	13	5	0
740	750	102	87	76	66	55	44	33	23	14	6	0
900	910	142	124	106	90	79	68	57	47	36	25	15
910	920	144	126	109	91	80	70	59	48	38	27	16
920	930	147	129	111	93	82	71	60	50	39	28	18
930	940	149	131	114	96	83	73	62	51	41	30	19
940	950	152	134	116	98	85	74	63	53	42	31	21
1,050	1,060	179	161	144	126	108	91	80	69	59	48	37
1,060	1,070	182	164	146	128	110	93	81	71	60	49	39
1,070	1,080	184	166	149	131	113	95	83	72	62	51	40
1,080	1,090	187	169	151	133	115	98	84	74	63	52	42
1,090	1,100	189	171	154	136	118	100	86	75	65	54	43

Source: Department of the Treasury, Internal Revenue Service

Figure 1. Single Persons Federal Withholding Table

Check It

Step 1: Calculate your gross earnings for the pay period.

Step 2: Use the table in Figure 1 to determine the amount of federal tax that will be withheld from your paycheck.

Step 3: Calculate the amount of Social Security and Medicare that will be withheld from your paycheck. Refer to chapter 3 for the applicable tax rates.

Step 4: Calculate your net pay for this paycheck.

Answer:
$334.24

Using a Bank Account

When you start earning money, you need some type of bank account to manage your money. Most people have at least a checking account. This type of account allows you to deposit money and write checks for payments. Additionally, many checking accounts offer a debit or ATM card as an option.

Exercise 1B

Your new job at the home improvement store offers direct deposit. However, since you are considered a seasonal employee, your paychecks are paper checks. In addition to your paycheck, you received a check from a friend for $11 to reimburse you for a movie ticket. Figure 2 shows a phone bill that must also be paid from your account.

Scamper Wireless
MONTHLY STATEMENT

John Doe
4222 Clinton Way
Los Angeles, CA 90201

Phone number: 323-555-5555
Account number: 0000-0000
Billing date: March 15, 20--

CALLING SUMMARY

	Included in plan	Used
Anytime minutes	300	315
Off-peak minutes	1000	720
In carrier minutes	Unlimited	100

CALLING CHARGES

Basic plan	$39.99
Overage fees	4.24
Taxes	9.68
Total Due	$53.91

Figure 2. Monthly Bill To Be Paid

Check It

Step 1: Download the data file Exercise 1B Deposit Slip.

Step 2: Fill out the deposit slip for the net pay you calculated in Exercise 1A and the check from your friend. What is the total deposit amount?

Step 3: Now, you write a check to pay the bill in Figure 2. What is the remaining balance in your account? Assume this is a new account you opened with your deposit.

Answer:
total deposit = $345.24
remaining balance =
$291.33

Many parents choose to save for their children's college education by investing in a 529 plan. These plans can be either prepaid tuition or college savings plans.

Paying for School

Pursuing education beyond high school can be expensive. You should look at all of your options for paying for continued education. These options can include applying for scholarships, grants, and student loans. You can also work part- or full-time to minimize the amount of money that you must take out in student loans.

Exercise 1C

As you plan for the next school year, you estimate your tuition, living expenses, and other school-related expenses at $18,500. Your search for scholarship money resulted in scholarships and grants totaling $6,500. You estimate that during the summer before the school year starts, you can earn $4,320 (after taxes) by working full-time. You also estimate that you can earn an average of $425 per month (after taxes) during the nine months of the school year.

Check It

Answer:
$3,855

What is the total you will need to borrow in the form of student loans to cover all of your expenses for the school year?

Sharing Living Expenses

Sharing living expenses is an easy way to lower your monthly expenses. Most students in college share a rental house or apartment with at least one roommate. Often, students have two or more roommates. The more roommates, the more the living expenses are reduced for each person.

Exercise 1D

Teaching Tip:
Remind students to work from left to right and apply PEMDAS to solve the equations.

You have graduated high school and are now in college. Currently, you are living alone in a student apartment. Your monthly rent is $400 and your utilities average $140 per month. You and a friend decide to be roommates and find an apartment for $825 per month. You expect the utilities to cost approximately $210 per month.

Check It

You and your friend will pay an equal share of the rent and utilities. What is the total amount you will save each month on rent and utilities?

Securing Renters Insurance

Once you move out of your parents' house, your belongings are no longer covered under their homeowners insurance. Whether you are renting or buying a house or condo, you should purchase insurance to cover your personal belongings. If you are buying a house or condo, you will be *required* by the mortgage lender to purchase homeowners insurance, which will cover your personal belongings.

Exercise 1E

You estimate your belongings to be worth over $10,000, so you purchase a $15,000 renters insurance policy. The policy has a $500 deductible and a premium of $21 per month. After paying premiums for nine months, your classic guitar valued at $3,400 is stolen. Because you have a replacement-cost policy, your insurance provider covers the entire $3,400 minus your deductible.

Check It

Step 1: Calculate the amount your insurance will pay after the deductible is applied.

Step 2: Considering the nine months of premiums already paid and the deductible, how much did purchasing the insurance save you compared to replacing the guitar without insurance?

Buying Auto Insurance

Most people purchase their first vehicle in their late teens or early twenties. Whether the reason for doing so is to commute to school or work or just to have the freedom offered by a vehicle, it is important to carry the proper auto insurance. Many states require at least liability insurance. If you finance the car, the lender will require collision coverage as well.

Exercise 1F

You decide your car is getting old, and you already have paid off the loan. To save money, you are going to renew your auto insurance without collision and comprehensive coverage. Figure 3 shows the annual premiums for the coverage types available for your vehicle. Your insurance provider allows you to pay the premiums in 12 equal monthly installments.

Coverage Type	Coverage Limits	Annual Premium ($)
Bodily injury liability	$250,000/person; $500,000/accident	$219.86
Property damage liability	$100,000/accident	271.40
Collision	$1,000 deductible	208.56
Uninsured motorist (bodily injury)	$100,000/person; $300,000/accident	53.66
Uninsured motorist (property damage)	$25,000/accident; $250 deductible	31.74
Comprehensive	$1,000 deductible	55.22

Figure 3. Insurance Coverages and Annual Premiums

Answer:

total annual premium = $576.66

monthly premium = $48.06

Check It

Step 1: Calculate your new total annual premium. Include all coverage types except collision and comprehensive.

Step 2: Calculate the monthly premium payment.

Creating Your Budget

No matter what your situation, it is very important to create and follow a budget. Good money management cannot be achieved unless you know how much money you have and what you are doing with it. That is where a budget comes into play. A budget is a plan for saving and spending your money. At every stage in your life, you must plan how you are going to use your money before you receive it.

Exercise 1G

Teaching Tip:
The data file and solution for Exercise 1G can be found on the Instructor's Resource CD.

As you finish your first year of college and prepare for the next, you decide to create a budget to live by, including the summer. Begin your budget by entering tuition and books for school and other known expenses. This is shown in Figure 4. Because your monthly income will vary depending on the time of year, and some of your income will come from scholarships and student loans, you decide to create your new budget as an annual budget rather than a monthly budget.

Check It

Download the data file Exercise 1G Budget Worksheet. This is the budget worksheet shown in Figure 4.

Step 1: Using the housing expenses you calculated in Exercise 1D, enter your annual budget for rent and utilities.

Step 2: Using the renters insurance premium given in Exercise 1E, calculate the annual expense and enter it in the budget.

Annual Budget		
Category	**Amount**	**Totals**
Income:		
Summer earnings		
Earnings during school		
Scholarships		
Student loan proceeds	_____	
Total Income		═════════
Expenses:		
Tuition	$6,150.00	
Books	850.00	
Rent		
Utilities		
Renters insurance		
Phone	900.00	
Gas and oil	576.66	
Auto insurance		
Food	2,756.00	
Clothing	360.00	
Entertainment	960.00	
Roth IRA		
Miscellaneous	_____	
Total Expenses		_____

Figure 4. Budget Worksheet

Step 4: Enter the annual auto insurance premium calculated in Exercise 1F.

Step 5: Refer to Exercise 1C to complete the income lines in the budget worksheet.

Step 6: You deposit 20% of your earnings from your summer and school-year jobs into a Roth IRA. This is a type of individual retirement account. Calculate this amount and enter it in the budget.

Step 7: Calculate your total income and expenses. Use the miscellaneous budget line to balance your budget. What is the annual budget for miscellaneous spending?

Answer:
$625.84

Creating a Cash Flow Statement

A budget is a plan for your money. A cash flow statement is a report of how much money actually came in and how much went out during a given period. A cash flow statement is a tool that can be used to determine if you are following your budget.

Exercise 1H

You were able to stay under budget on utilities by $100 for the year, and you were able to get your books for school for $794. You spent $200 more on food than you budgeted, but you spent only $280 on clothing for the year and your miscellaneous spending totaled $812. All other items in the budget were exactly as expected. Create a cash flow statement based on the budget you created in Exercise 1G. Divide the expenses into fixed and variable expenses.

Check It

Step 1: Download the data file Exercise 1H Cash Flow Statement.

Step 2: Complete the cash flow statement.

Step 3: What was your net cash flow for the year?

Calculating Your Net Worth

Assets are the things you own that have value. Liabilities are money that you owe others. Net worth is your total assets minus your total liabilities. Driving an expensive car, carrying around the newest smartphone, and living in an upscale house or condo are not measures of wealth. Net worth, on the other hand, is an important measure of wealth. It is a good idea to start tracking your net worth on an annual basis to see an accurate picture of how your wealth is building.

Exercise 1I

The cash flow statement you completed in Exercise 1H is the last one for the year. You have $1,467.84 in your checking account. You estimate your car is worth $3,300. You have no auto loan. Every month you pay the entire balance on your credit card. Your only liability is your student loan.

Check It

Calculate your net worth.

Stage 2 Early Career Years

Objectives

- Calculate tax withholdings from a paycheck.
- Differentiate between pretax and post-tax withholdings.
- Determine adjusted gross and taxable income.
- Calculate compounded interest.
- Determine total cost of a contract.
- Calculate credit card finance charges.
- Compute total financed amount for a loan.
- Evaluate the total cost of term life insurance.
- Calculate net worth.

Earning a Salary

After you graduate from school, you will need to find a job to start your career. Most people begin their careers in an entry-level position. This position

Source: Shutterstock (Petro Feketa)

With your first job will come increased responsibility and additional budget needs.

Teaching Tip:
Point out to students
that Social Security and
Medicare taxes are de-
ducted from paychecks.

allows them to learn the basics of their chosen career and to demonstrate their abilities. As opportunities present themselves, they can choose to move up in position and responsibility.

Exercise 2A

You have graduated from college. After several interviews at different companies, you have been offered a full-time, salaried position in your career field. The job pays $38,875 annually, and you are paid weekly. You are single and claim one withholding allowance.

Check It

Step 1: Calculate the amount of gross pay per pay period.

Step 2: Using the table in Figure 1, determine the amount of federal income tax that will be withheld from your paycheck assuming you are single and claiming one withholding allowance.

Answer:
gross pay = $747.60
federal income tax = $87
Social Security tax =
 $46.35
Medicare tax = $10.84
state income tax =
 $22.95
net pay = $580.46

Step 3: Calculate the amount of Social Security tax withheld from each paycheck. Refer to chapter 3 for the applicable tax rate.

Step 4: Calculate the amount of Medicare tax that will be withheld from each paycheck. Refer to chapter 3 for the applicable tax rate.

Step 5: Your state has a 3.07% flat state income tax. Calculate the amount of state income tax that will be withheld from each paycheck.

Step 6: Calculate your net pay for each paycheck.

Evaluating Benefits

Usually, full-time employment comes with benefits. As you progress in your career, new positions may offer more benefits. However, even for an entry-level position, you should consider the benefits offered by your employer. Many entry-level positions offer health insurance and some offer dental and vision insurance.

Exercise 2B

Your job provides health and vision insurance as part of your salary package. However, dental insurance is $34 per month. If you choose to enroll in the dental insurance, the premium will be deducted from each paycheck. The good news is that the premiums are withheld before taxes are applied. This will lower the amount of taxes taken from each paycheck.

Check It

Step 1: How much dental insurance premium is withheld from each paycheck?

Step 2: Recalculate the taxes withheld and the net pay of the paycheck from Exercise 2A.

Filing Your Tax Return

With few exceptions, everybody must file a federal income tax return each year. Many states also have an income tax and require a state income tax return to be filed each year. The amount of income tax withheld from each paycheck is an estimate of what you will owe at the end of the year. When you file an income tax return, you calculate the exact tax you owe and determine if you have to pay an additional amount or if you will receive a refund.

Exercise 2C

It is time to file your income tax return. You have been working for over a year in your entry-level position. Figure 5 shows your W-2 for the previous year. Your current position does not provide a 401(k) or other pension, so you made the maximum contribution of $5,000 to a traditional IRA, which is an adjustment to your gross income. Figure 6 shows a federal income tax table. You are filing as a single person and decide not to itemize your deductions.

22222	**a** Employee's social security number **123–45–6789**	OMB No. 1545-0008

b Employer identification number (EIN) **75-1234567**	**1** Wages, tips, other compensation **38,875.00**	**2** Federal income tax withheld **4,420.00**
c Employer's name, address, and ZIP code **Travis Nutrition & Fitness** **123 Broadway** **Chester, PA 19013**	**3** Social security wages **38,875.00**	**4** Social security tax withheld **2,384.72**
	5 Medicare wages and tips **38,875.00**	**6** Medicare tax withheld **557.96**
	7 Social security tips	**8** Allocated tips
d Control number **123456789**	**9** Advance EIC payment	**10** Dependent care benefits

e Employee's first name and initial   Last name   Suff.
Evan Rader
567 Locust Ave.
Chester, PA 19013

11 Nonqualified plans   **12a**
13 Statutory employee / Retirement plan / Third-party sick pay   **12b**
14 Other   **12c**
      12d

f Employee's address and ZIP code

15 State Employer's state ID number **PA** **123–45678**	**16** State wages, tips, etc. **38,875.00**	**17** State income tax **1,180.92**	**18** Local wages, tips, etc.	**19** Local income tax	**20** Locality name

Form **W-2**   Wage and Tax Statement   **20XX**   Department of the Treasury—Internal Revenue Service

Copy 1—For State, City, or Local Tax Department

Figure 5. W-2 Wage and Tax Statement

If taxable income is...		And you are...			
at least:	but less than:	single:	married filing jointly:	married filing separately:	head of household:
$5,000	$5,050	$503	$503	$503	$503
5,050	5,100	508	508	508	508
17,400	17,450	2,189	1,764	2,189	2,006
17,450	17,500	2,196	1,771	2,196	2,014
17,500	17,550	2,204	1,779	2,204	2,021
24,300	24,350	3,224	2,799	3,224	3,041
24,350	24,400	3,231	2,806	3,231	3,049
24,400	24,450	3,239	2,814	3,239	3,056
36,800	36,850	5,331	4,674	5,331	4,916
36,850	36,900	5,344	4,681	5,344	4,924
36,900	36,950	5,356	4,689	5,356	4,931
42,200	42,250	6,681	5,484	6,681	5,726
42,250	42,300	6,694	5,491	6,694	5,734
42,300	42,350	6,706	5,499	6,706	5,741
79,600	79,650	16,031	12,156	16,330	14,674
79,650	79,700	16,044	12,169	16,344	14,686
79,700	79,750	16,056	12,181	16,358	14,699
99,800	99,850	21,568	17,206	21,986	19,724
99,850	99,900	21,582	17,219	22,000	19,736
99,900	99,950	21,596	17,231	22,014	19,749
99,950	100,000	21,610	17,244	22,028	19,761

Figure 6. Tax Table

Check It

Step 1: Determine your adjusted gross income.

Step 2: Refer to chapter 3 to determine your standard deduction and personal exemption.

Step 3: Determine your taxable income.

Step 4: Use the table in Figure 6 to determine the tax due.

Step 5: Determine how much federal income tax was withheld during the year. Calculate whether additional federal income tax is due or if you will receive a refund, and the amount.

Answer:
adjusted gross income = $33,875
taxable income = $24,375
tax refund = $1,189

Saving for Emergencies

Having an emergency fund is always a good idea. It will allow you a reserve of money to pay for unexpected expenses such as car or house repairs or for times when you experience a temporary negative cash flow. While it is a good idea to start an emergency fund as soon as you have a part-time job, it is definitely a financially smart move to have an emergency fund once you are out of school and working full-time. A savings account can be used as an emergency fund.

Exercise 2D

With a full-time job, you are earning more than you ever have. You decide to begin building an emergency fund. After a few months, you have $700 in a savings account. The account yields 3% annual interest compounded monthly.

Check It

If you do not put any additional deposits into the account, what will be the balance of the account in two years?

Teaching Tip:
Explain to students that an exponent signals the number of times a number should be multiplied by itself.

Answer:
$742.63

Contracting for a Mobile Phone

While in college, many students have a mobile phone on their family's plan. However, there are many things that you have to assume responsibility for once you are out on your own. Basic living expenses become your responsibility. This includes finding a mobile phone contract of your own.

Exercise 2E

You find an offer for a smartphone contract than includes 1,000 minutes of talk time per month for a monthly fee of $46.99. For an additional $19.99 per month, you can get unlimited data and texting. There is a $35 activation fee. If the two-year contract is cancelled early, an early termination fee of $200 applies.

Check It

What is the total cost of the contract if you get the data and texting option and keep the plan for the full term?

Answer:
$1,642.52

Managing a Credit Card

Credit cards are widely used financial tools. If used wisely, they can be a good way to build a good credit rating. However, misused credit cards can also damage your credit rating. A good time to obtain a credit card is when you have a stable income that will allow you to wisely manage your use of the card.

Teaching Tip:
Explain to students that APR stands for *annual percentage rate*.

Exercise 2F

You have a credit card with a 12.9% APR with a 30-day billing period. Your balances over the current billing period are shown below.

Days 1–4	Days 5–7	Days 8–11	Days 12–20	Days 21–26	Days 27–30
$201.55	$304.81	$391.20	$410.28	$210.28	$349.39

Teaching Tip:
The solution spreadsheet for Exercise 2F can be found on the Instructor's Resource CD.

Check It

Step 1: Determine your average daily balance.

Step 2: Assuming your previous balance was $201.55 and you made a $200 payment on day 21, what is the new balance after finance charges are applied, based on the balances in the chart on the previous page? Use the unpaid balance method to compute the finance charge.

Financing a Car

Many students drive used cars that are inexpensive. Often, these cars have cosmetic or mechanical issues. While money may still be tight as you start your career, you might also take advantage of the steady income to purchase a new or newer car.

Exercise 2G

Since your current car has high mileage and is beginning to become unreliable, you decide to purchase a different car. You find a three-year-old pre-owned car that meets your needs and negotiate a price of $9,100. The dealer is also giving you a $900 trade-in allowance for your current car.

Check It

Step 1: What is the price of the car you are purchasing after the trade in?

Step 2: The sales tax of 6.5% applies only to the net price after trade in. Calculate the sales tax due.

Step 3: There is a license fee of $67 and a title transfer fee of $34. What is the total cost of the car?

Step 4: You have $2,500 for a down payment. What is the amount to be financed?

Step 5: You obtain financing for two years at 5.9%. How much is the interest portion of the first payment?

Buying Life Insurance

Life insurance eases the burden on the people left behind when someone dies. You might be asking, why would someone want to buy life insurance when they are young and just starting a career? One reason is premiums are lower for younger persons. Another reason is to provide a family financial benefit in the event that the insured person dies.

Exercise 2H

You decide to purchase some term life insurance. You are quoted $19.20 per month for a ten-year term policy. The policy has a $500,000 death benefit, and you name your brother and sister as beneficiaries.

Check It

How much will you pay in total premiums during the life of the policy?

Calculating Your Net Worth

Tracking net worth on an annual basis is an important measure of wealth. This allows you to see an accurate picture of how your wealth is building. A person's net worth may not seem very great while in school and during the first few years of a career. However, what is important is the year-to-year comparison. If the net worth is not increasing, then steps should be taken to identify ways to save more money or otherwise increase the net worth.

Exercise 2I

You began calculating your net worth when you were a student. Now that you have started a career and have been working for more than a year, it is a good time to calculate your net worth and compare it to your previous net worth. You have $3,767.55 in your checking account, $700 in your emergency savings account, and $3,500 in your IRA. The estimated value of your car is $8,750. You have not yet made a payment on the auto loan, so the balance on the loan is the amount originally financed. Your student loan balance is $9,446.33. You have other miscellaneous assets valued at $26,800.

Teaching Tip:
Remind students that loans are not the only way to finance an education. Others are discussed in section 8.4.

Check It

Step 1: Calculate your current net worth using the information above.

Step 2: Calculate the increase or decrease in net worth from your previously calculated net worth.

Stage 3 Earning Years

Objectives

- Evaluate financial differences between offers of employment.
- Calculate commission.
- Determine capital gains.
- Compute down payment and amount financed for a mortgage.
- Differentiate between the cost of mortgage terms and rates.
- Calculate a debt-to-income ratio.
- Determine total property tax.
- Compute interest earned for a specified time period.
- Create a monthly budget.
- Create a cash flow statement.
- Calculate net worth.

Source: Shutterstock (Tyler Olson)

A person's net worth should increase during his or her earning years.

Comparing Jobs

Most people will work in an entry-level position for a few years. After that, sometimes opportunities for advancement become available within the company. However, often people begin looking for better opportunities outside of the company. In any case, a comparison must be made between any job offers and your current position.

Exercise 3A

You have been working full-time in a salaried position for several years. Your current annual salary is $52,000 and you have benefits with an annual value of $5,780. You have been offered a different job with a base pay of $54,000 and these employee benefits:

- medical/dental/vision insurance valued at $3,450 annually

- cell phone allowance of $20 per month

- other benefits with a total annual value of $900

The job you have been offered is a few miles farther away than your current job. You estimate you will spend an additional $37 per month on fuel for your car.

Check It

Considering only the financial value of the job offer, should you accept the offer or stay in your current position?

Answer:
You should accept the offer because its value is $58,146, versus your current job value of $57,780

Earning Commission

There are various ways to be compensated for the work you do. Many professionals receive an annual salary, but others are paid an hourly wage. Some professionals receive an annual salary plus a bonus based on performance. The bonus may be a flat payment based on goals that are met. However, especially in sales positions, the bonus may be a commission paid based on the level of sales achieved.

Exercise 3B

Your company has restructured and now your compensation will be salary plus commission. You will earn a 2% commission on the first $100,000 in sales that you make each month and 4% on sales over $100,000 each month. Figure 7 shows your total sales for March, April, and May.

Check It

Step 1: Using Figure 7, identify your sales figures for each of the first three months after the company restructuring.

Step 2: Calculate your commission for each month.

Answer:
March commission = $1,740.68
April commission = $2,471.52
May commission = $6,100.88

Month	Total Sales for the Month
March	$87,034
April	$111,788
May	$202,522

Figure 7. Sales by Month

Calculating Capital Gains

Capital gains are profits that result from selling items for more than you paid for them. This is one of the ways money can be made with stocks and mutual funds. When the stock is sold, the difference between the sale price and the purchase price is the capital gain or loss.

Exercise 3C

A few years ago, you began purchasing shares in a mutual fund as part of a balanced approach to investing. You are considering buying a home soon and are thinking about selling the mutual fund shares to use as a down payment on the house. When you purchased the mutual fund shares, you invested $7,400. If you sell the shares today, you would receive $8,954.41 for them.

Check It

Step 1: What is the capital gain on the investment?

Step 2: If the capital gains tax rate is 15%, how much tax do you owe?

Buying a House

Purchasing a house or condo can be a good way to help build wealth. If you purchase wisely, you can increase your net worth. There are other advantages as well, such as being able to use the mortgage interest and property taxes as deductions on your annual income tax return. Many people choose to purchase their first house or condo after they have established a stable career.

Exercise 3D

You are ready to buy a house. You have found a house for $194,000 that you would like to purchase. Because you are a first-time home buyer, you qualify for a loan with a 3.5% down payment. The closing costs are $3,412.58, which are in addition to the down payment.

Check It

Step 1: How much will the required down payment be?

Step 2: What is the total of the required down payment plus closing costs?

Step 3: You will use all of the money from the sale of shares in your mutual fund in Exercise 3C, minus the capital gains tax. How much additional cash is required, or will you be able to have a larger-than-required down payment?

Step 4: How much will you finance through a mortgage?

Comparing Mortgage Terms

There are several options for the length of a mortgage. Most people obtain 15-, 20-, or 30-year mortgages. Often, a shorter-length mortgage offers a lower interest rate. However, the monthly payment will be more for a shorter-length mortgage because the loan amount is repaid over fewer payments.

Exercise 3E

In considering your options for mortgage length, you have decided that you can afford a loan payment of no more than $1,400 per month, not including escrow for taxes and insurance. Your interest rate would be 5% for a 15-year mortgage and 5.5% for a 20- or 30-year mortgage. Figure 8 shows the monthly payment required for various mortgage rates.

Check It

Step 1: What would be your monthly payment for 15-, 20-, and 30-year mortgages?

Step 2: Which is the shortest mortgage term that you can afford in your budget?

Step 3: What is the amount of the first month's interest payment for each mortgage?

Step 4: How much principal would be applied in the first month's payment for each mortgage?

Calculating Debt-to-Income Ratio

While net worth can show how your wealth is growing from year to year, your debt-to-income ratio shows how your debt load compares to your income. In a way, it shows you how well you are living within your means. Most financial experts recommend a debt-to-income ratio of 36% or less.

Monthly Payment per $1,000 of Loan Amortization			
Interest Rate	15 years	20 years	30 years
4%	$7.40	$6.06	$4.78
4.5%	7.65	6.34	5.08
5%	7.91	6.60	5.37
5.5%	8.18	6.88	5.68
6%	8.44	7.17	6.00
6.5%	8.72	7.46	6.32
7%	8.99	7.76	6.66
7.5%	9.28	8.06	7.00
8%	9.56	8.37	7.34
8.5%	9.85	8.68	7.69
9%	10.15	9.00	8.05
9.5%	10.45	9.33	8.41
10%	10.75	9.66	8.78
10.5%	11.06	9.99	9.15
11%	11.37	10.33	9.53
11.5%	11.69	10.67	9.91
12%	12.01	11.02	10.29

Figure 8. Monthly Payment per $1,000 of Loan Amortization

Exercise 3F

Including all sources of income, you now average $5,900 per month in income. You have a $412 monthly car payment and student loan payments of $214 per month. You pay your credit card balance in full each month, and each month you average a balance of $358. Your only other debt is your newly acquired mortgage from Exercise 3E. You selected the shortest mortgage term that you can afford in your budget.

Check It

What is your debt-to-income ratio, and is it less than what is recommended by financial experts?

Calculating Property Tax

Along with homeownership comes property tax. The total amount of property tax paid is usually a combination of taxes from several jurisdictions. For example, part of the total may be tax for the fire protection district in which the house is located. Part of the total may be tax for the local school district. A rate is used for each jurisdiction and the resulting dollar amounts are summed to calculate the total property tax.

Exercise 3G

Your property tax is collected as part of your monthly mortgage payment and held in escrow. However, you should keep track of the tax you are paying and compare this to the escrow statement from your mortgage lender. The table in Figure 9 shows the four tax jurisdictions that you are responsible for and the rates used to calculate the property tax for the current year.

Check It

Based on the table in Figure 9, what is the total property tax due for the year?

Answer:
$1,931.46

Investing

Investing is the key to building wealth for the future. While the earning years are when wealth is built for later in life, it is never too soon to start investing. There are many types of investments, and investments can be used for short- or long-term goals. It is important to invest wisely to grow your wealth and meet your financial goals.

Teaching Tip:
Explain to students that stock prices are calculated to many decimal places beyond to the hundredth place normally seen for money because stock is often purchased in huge blocks that make a fraction of a cent significant.

Exercise 3H

The past few months, you have earned more in commissions than your average. You decide to invest the extra money. To diversify the investments, you decide to invest in a corporate bond and a mutual fund. The bond you purchase for $3,000 is a five-year corporate bond at an annual interest rate of 6%. The mutual fund is a no-load mutual fund of small cap stocks with an NAV of $9.33452. You decide to purchase 250 shares of the mutual fund.

Check It

Step 1: How much interest will you receive on the bond over the five years?

Step 2: What is the total cost of the mutual fund investment?

Answer:
bond interest = $900
mutual fund investment = $2,333.63

Taxing Jurisdiction	Assessed Value	Tax Rate (%)
Lubbock County	$182,400	0.330343
Hospital District	182,400	0.120720
Shallowater ISD	182,400	0.600000
Hi Plains Water District	182,400	0.007850

Figure 9. Tax Jurisdictions for Property Taxes

Creating Your Budget

At every stage of life, you should create and follow a budget. Following a budget is a key to good money management. As most people progress through a career and life, they take on more expenses and earn more income. Planning how to use income before receiving it allows people to live within their means.

Exercise 3I

Since most of your expenses are monthly, you decide to create a monthly budget rather than an annual budget. This will require calculating the monthly cost of any annual expenses. Also, since your income is an annual figure plus a monthly commission, you will need to calculate your average monthly income.

Check It

Download the data file Exercise 3I Budget Worksheet. This budget worksheet is shown in Figure 10. Complete the budget worksheet using the information below.

Step 1: You accepted the job offer for a higher salary and are also earning commission. Using the average monthly income total from Exercise 3F, enter your monthly income.

Step 2: When you purchased your house, you budgeted an amount and decided to take the shortest loan term that was within that budget. Using the calculated payment from Exercise 3E, enter the monthly mortgage payment.

Step 3: Using the information from Exercise 3F, enter your monthly payments for car loan, student loans, and average monthly credit card balance that you pay in full.

Step 4: Your family averages $210 per week in groceries. Enter the monthly average into your budget.

Step 5: You are still under the phone contract from 2E. Using this information, enter your monthly phone payment, but be sure to deduct the benefit you receive from your job.

Step 6: Using the annual property tax calculated in 3G, calculate the monthly amount for property tax and enter it.

Step 7: Using the information on investments from 3H, round to the nearest one hundred dollars. Assume you will invest this amount every year. Enter your monthly investment into your budget.

Step 8: You max out your Roth IRA contribution each year, which is $5,000 until you reach age 55. You make monthly contributions. Enter your monthly Roth IRA contribution.

Step 9: You save $750 a month between CDs and a savings account. Enter this amount into your budget.

Step 10: Calculate your total income and expenses. Use the miscellaneous budget line to balance your budget. What is the monthly budget for miscellaneous spending?

Annual Budget		
Category	**Amount**	**Totals**
Income:		
Average monthly income		
Total Income		=====
Expenses:		
Mortgage		
Loans and credit cards		
Utilities	121.65	
Gas and oil	189.15	
Auto insurance	208.33	
Homeowners insurance	66.67	
Food		
Clothing	55.00	
Phone		
Entertainment	150.00	
Property tax		
Investments		
Roth IRA		
CDs/savings account		
Miscellaneous	─────	─────
Total Expenses		

Figure 10. Budget Worksheet

Creating a Cash Flow Statement

A cash flow statement can be used to see if you are following your budget. It shows your cash inflows and outflows over a specific time period. It is a good idea to complete a cash flow statement and compare it to your budget.

Exercise 3J

Create a cash flow statement for the current month based on the budget you created in Exercise 3I. Divide the expenses into fixed and variable expenses. You were thrifty this month and reduced your credit card bill by $247. Utilities were $5.07 more than average, and you spent $35 more on gas. This month, your family averaged $227 per week for food, and you spent $105.34 on clothing. You splurged on entertainment this month, spending $198. All other items in the budget were exactly as expected.

Teaching Tip:
The data file and solution for Exercise 3J can be found on the Instructor's Resource CD.

Check It

Step 1: Download the data file Exercise 3J Cash Flow Statement.

Step 2: Complete the cash flow statement.

Step 3: What was your net cash flow for the month?

Calculating Your Net Worth

A person's earning years are when wealth is built. Over these years is when a year-to-year comparison of net worth becomes critical. Net worth should increase each year. The next stage in life after the earning years is retirement. Building wealth by increasing net worth each year is important to a secure retirement.

Exercise 3K

You were financially smart and began calculating your net worth when you were a student. You continued calculating your net worth on an annual basis as you started and progressed through a career. You have been working in your career for 12 years. Your assets and liabilities are shown in Figure 11.

Check It

Step 1: Calculate your current net worth using the information shown in Figure 11.

Step 2: Calculate the increase or decrease in net worth from your previously calculated net worth.

Assets and Liabilities	Amount
Estimated house value	$205,375.00
Estimated car value	$14,350.00
Checking account balance	$4,061.49
CDs/savings account	$46,571.84
Roth IRA	$79,687.12
Car loan balance	$17,902.16
Student loan balance	$302.05
Mortgage balance	$169,957.48
Other miscellaneous assets	$56,845.00

Figure 11. Assets and Liabilities

Stage 4 Retirement Years

Objectives

- **Calculate a mortgage pay-off amount.**
- **Estimate annual income from rental property.**
- **Determine the effect of inflation on savings.**
- **Compute the total cost of a term life insurance policy.**
- **Calculate future value of an annuity.**
- **Evaluate opportunity cost.**
- **Calculate inheritance share and tax.**
- **Create a monthly budget.**
- **Create a cash flow statement.**
- **Calculate net worth.**

Paying Off the Mortgage

One path leading to a financially sound retirement is reducing or eliminating debt. A house is usually the largest debt a person will take on over his or her lifetime. Paying off a mortgage before retiring can be a big step toward financial security in retirement.

Source: Shutterstock (berna namoglu)

Insurance needs change as people age.

Exercise 4A

After many years of hard work, you have decided to retire. You are close to paying off your mortgage, but you still have about a year left on the loan. Figure 12 shows the remaining payments on your mortgage amortization schedule. To eliminate this debt, you decide to pay off the mortgage early.

Check It

Step 1: You decide to pay off the mortgage in August.

Step 2: Based on the information in the amortization table in Figure 12, what is the final payment to pay off the mortgage?

Answer:
$6,299.06

Purchasing Revenue-Generating Real Estate

While reducing or eliminating debt is important, generating revenue during retirement is another way to ensure a financially successful retirement. One way to generate revenue is to purchase real estate and rent it out. There are, of course, downsides to owning rental property. But, for some people, owning rental property can help offset some debts in retirement that cannot be eliminated.

Exercise 4B

With the mortgage on your house now paid off, you decide to invest in a house as rental property to generate some income. The house you select has a mortgage payment of $930 per month and annual insurance cost of $1,866, property taxes of $2,180, and an estimated $1,700 in maintenance. You estimate that the house will rent for $1,725 per month.

Check It

Answer:
$3,794

How much annual income can you expect from the real estate investment?

Month	Payment	Principal	Interest	Balance
July	$1,288	$ 1,247.82	$40.18	$ 7,518.15
August	1,288	1,253.54	34.46	6,264.60
September	1,288	1,259.29	28.71	5,005.32
October	1,288	1,265.06	22.94	3,740.26
November	1,288	1,270.86	17.14	2,469.40
December	1,288	1,276.68	11.32	1,192.72
January	1,288	1,282.53	5.47	0.00

Figure 12. Partial Mortgage Amortization Schedule

Determining the Effect of Inflation on Savings

Inflation is an ever-present concern. One dollar today will buy more than one dollar will in ten years. Thinking of this in terms of retirement savings, one million dollars in the bank today is a lot of money, but in fifty years it may not be enough to live on in retirement. Fifty years ago, somebody who had $100,000 saved was probably considered a very wealthy individual. Today, it is not uncommon for household income to be greater than $100,000.

Teaching Tip:
Help students to recall from chapters 6 and 13 that inflation is the rise in the level of prices and wages over a period of time.

Exercise 4C

In the last 12 months, the value of your retirement account grew by 8.45%. The rate of inflation during those same 12 months was 2.91%.

Check It

What was the net percentage growth of the value of your retirement account during the period after inflation?

Answer:
5.54%

Adjusting Insurance Needs

As a person progresses through life, insurance premiums change. For example, older drivers typically have lower auto insurance premiums than younger drivers. Premiums for health care and life insurance increase as a person gets older. On the other hand, insurance needs also change. For example, when children are no longer dependent on parents for financial stability, the life insurance needs of the parents may be lower.

Exercise 4D

You decide that a $250,000 life insurance policy is enough for your needs at this stage of life. Because you do not know what might happen with your health over the coming years, you decide to secure a 20-year term life policy with level monthly premiums. The monthly premium you are quoted is $172.30 per month.

Teaching Tip:
Explain to students that insurance is a common way of managing risk.

Check It

What is the total cost of the 20-year term life insurance policy?

Answer:
$41,352

Saving for Grandchildren's College

The cost of attending college continues to increase. Many parents find they cannot afford the entire cost of college, even with scholarships and grants, and must take out student loans. Some grandparents are taking on part of the responsibility of paying for college costs. This helps reduce or eliminate the amount of money that must be made up with student loans.

Exercise 4E

You decide to start saving for your grandchildren's college expenses by starting an annuity. You decide to deposit $250 per month for 15 years. This is when your first grandchild will enter college. The annuity is guaranteed to have an annual interest rate of 4.5%.

Check It

What is the future value of the annuity at the end of the 15-year period?

Evaluating Opportunity Cost

When building and maintaining wealth, there are always opportunity costs. Choices must be made between investments considering risk versus return. Choices must also be made between keeping money in an investment such as stocks, bonds, or CDs and redeeming the investment for cash. To make financially wise decisions, the opportunity cost of the choices must be evaluated.

Exercise 4F

You have $3,000 to invest. You have narrowed your choices to two bonds: Springfield City bonds and Arlington City bonds. The Springfield City bonds have an annual yield of 5.1%. The Arlington City bonds have an annual yield of 6.3% for that same year. You choose to invest in Springfield City bonds because you believe it is a safer option.

Check It

What was the opportunity cost of your decision?

Receiving Inheritance

Many people receive inheritances throughout their lives. In some cases, the amount of money received may not be great, only several hundred or a few thousand dollars. In other cases, the inheritance may involve a transfer of significant wealth. The person receiving the inheritance may have to pay a tax on the amount of the inheritance. Inheritance tax varies from state to state.

Exercise 4G

Your aunt passed away and left you one-third of her estate. She had a total of $434,788 in assets and $182,904 in liabilities. You must pay a 14.3% inheritance tax.

Check It

Step 1: What is your share of the net estate?

Step 2: What is the amount of inheritance tax that you must pay?

Creating Your Budget

Even after retiring from work, a budget should be used. In fact, many people feel that a budget is even more important in retirement than when working. This is because most people must live on a fixed or limited income in retirement. So, any missteps in money management may mean running out of money.

Exercise 4H

Most of your expenses are still monthly, and you receive monthly Social Security payments and withdrawals from your Roth IRA. You decide to stick with a monthly budget. A portion of your income and expenses is shown in Figure 13.

Check It

Step 1: Download the data file Exercise 4H Budget Worksheet. Complete the budget worksheet using the information below.

Step 2: Enter your monthly Social Security benefit into your budget.

Step 3: Calculate the annual withdrawal from your Roth IRA, then determine how much you will withdraw each month and enter that amount into your budget.

Step 4: Calculate the monthly income from the rental house in Exercise 4B and enter that amount into your budget.

Income and Expenses	Amount
Social Security benefit	$1,967 per month
Roth IRA withdrawal	4% annual withdrawal taken monthly; current value $967,718.23
Medicare supplemental insurance	$144.46 per month
Auto insurance	$875.04 per year
Food	$65 per week
Long-term care insurance	$3,547.56 per year

Figure 13. Partial Income and Expenses

Step 5: Enter the monthly expenses for the rental house into your budget. Include mortgage, homeowners insurance, property taxes, and maintenance costs.

Step 6: Enter the monthly premium for Medicare supplemental insurance into your budget.

Step 7: Calculate the monthly premium for long-term care insurance and enter that amount into your budget.

Step 8: Calculate the monthly premium for auto insurance and enter that amount into your budget.

Step 9: Calculate the monthly cost of food and enter that into your budget.

Step 10: Enter the monthly payment for the annuity you took out for your grandchildren's college tuition.

Step 11: Adjust the withdrawal from your Roth IRA to balance the budget. What withdrawal amount is needed to balance the budget?

Creating a Cash Flow Statement

A cash flow statement should always be used to see if you are following your budget. However, it becomes even more important in retirement when you need to make your savings last for the rest of your life.

Exercise 4I

Create a cash flow statement for the current month based on the budget you created in Exercise 4H. Divide the expenses into fixed and variable expenses. This is the month you receive the inheritance from your aunt, so include the post-tax inheritance in the cash flow statement as a variable income. Your credit card bill was $142.58 less than average. Utilities were $12.73 more than average, and you spent $17 more on gas. This month, your family averaged $98.47 per week for food, and you spent $32.98 on clothing. You spent $108.75 on entertainment this month. All other items in the budget were exactly as expected.

Check It

Step 1: Download the data file Exercise 4I Cash Flow Statement.

Step 2: Complete the cash flow statement.

Step 3: What was your net cash flow for the month? How do you explain the result?

Calculating Your Net Worth

During retirement years, most people see a decline in net worth from year to year. This happens because income is limited and most people begin drawing from their retirement savings. However, some people see their net worth increase during their retirement years.

Exercise 4J

You retired four years ago. You were financially smart during your career, and you continue to be so in retirement. Your assets and liabilities are shown in Figure 14.

Check It

Step 1: Calculate your current net worth using the information shown in Figure 14.

Step 2: Calculate the increase or decrease in net worth from your previously calculated net worth.

Answer:
net worth =
    $1,661,122.33
change in net worth =
    $1,442,939.57

Assets and Liabilities	Amount
Estimated house value, home	$273,125.00
Estimated house value, rental	$135,100.00
Estimated car value	$5,350.00
Checking account balance	$2,127.06
CDs/savings account	$78,527.68
Roth IRA	$1,224,998.90
Mortgage balance, rental	$132,854.27
Annuity	$13,120.96
Other miscellaneous assets	$61,627.00

Figure 14. Assets and Liabilities

Summative Exercise

In this summative exercise, you will work through the financial aspects of four stages of life. You will need to come up with your own realistic values for wages, expenses, investments, and living costs. Be prepared to defend your decisions.

Download the profile worksheet data file Summative Exercise Life Stage Profile. For each section in the summative exercise, you must complete a life-stage profile worksheet and submit it to your instructor for approval. Once your instructor has approved your profile, you may complete the corresponding section. Once you have finished a section, complete a profile worksheet for the next section.

Student Years

In this life stage, you must consider working part-time, using a bank account, paying for school, sharing living expenses, securing renters insurance, buying auto insurance, creating your budget, creating a cash flow statement, and calculating your net worth. Download the data files Summative Exercise Budget Worksheet, Summative Exercise Cash Flow Statement, and Summative Exercise Net Worth Worksheet. Complete the budget, cash flow statement, and net worth calculation.

Early Career Years

In this life stage, you must consider earning a salary, evaluating benefits, filing your tax return, saving for emergencies, contracting for a mobile phone, managing a credit card, financing a car, buying life insurance, and calculating your net worth. Download the data files Summative Exercise Budget Worksheet, Summative Exercise Cash Flow Statement, and Summative Exercise Net Worth Worksheet. Complete the budget, cash flow statement, and net worth calculation.

Earning Years

In this life stage, you must consider comparing jobs, earning commission, calculating capital gains, buying a house, comparing mortgage terms, calculating debt-to-income ratio, calculating property tax, investing, creating your budget, creating a cash flow statement, and calculating your net worth. Download the data files Summative Exercise Budget Worksheet, Summative Exercise Cash Flow Statement, and Summative Exercise Net Worth Worksheet. Complete the budget, cash flow statement, and net worth calculation.

Answer:
Student answers will vary; evaluate individually.

Retirement Years

In this life stage, you must consider paying off a mortgage, purchasing revenue-generating real estate, determining the effect of inflation on savings, adjusting insurance needs, saving for grandchildren's college, evaluating opportunity cost, receiving inheritance, creating your budget, creating a cash flow statement, and calculating your net worth. Download the data files Summative Exercise Budget Worksheet, Summative Exercise Cash Flow Statement, and Summative Exercise Net Worth Worksheet. Complete the budget, cash flow statement, and net worth calculation.

Answer:
Student answers will vary; evaluate individually.

Selected Answers

Chapter 1 Ways to Earn Money

Section 1.1, pages 35–40

Check It

Example 1-1A: $123.25; **Example 1-1B:** $10.30; **Example 1-1C:** 35 hours; **Example 1-1D:** $1,177.40

Checkpoint

1. $291.50; **3.** 35 hours; **5.** $975

Section 1.2, pages 41–45

Check It

Example 1-2A: $63,315; **Example 1-2B:** monthly = $5,216.67/semimonthly = $2,608.33/biweekly = $2,407.69/weekly = $1,203.85

Checkpoint

1. $70,132.70; **3.** monthly = $4,430/semimonthly = $2,215/biweekly =$2,044.62/weekly =$1,022.31; **5.** Continental Lumber

Section 1.3, pages 46–53

Check It

Example 1-3A: $13,230; **Example 1-3B:** $58,000; **Example 1-3C:** $6,068; **Example 1-3D:** $15,600; **Example 1-3E:** $20,740

Checkpoint

1. $81,600; **3.** $65,500; **5.** $14,445

Chapter Review and Assessment, pages 54–57

11. 34 hours; **13.** $68,490; **15.** Monthly = $5,414.17/ semimonthly = $2,707.08/biweekly = $2,498.85/ weekly = $1,249.42; **17.** $3,700; **19.** Kelvin worked 15.2 hours, which is about the same as what he normally works.

Chapter 2 Understanding Your Paycheck

Section 2.1, pages 59–70

Check It

Example 2-1A: $69; **Example 2-1B:** $62.38; **Example 2-1C:** $31.45; **Example 2-1D:** $34.56; **Example 2-1E:** $959.20; **Example 2-1F:** $533.52

Checkpoint

1. federal tax withholdings = $81/Social Security tax = $44/Medicare tax = $10.29; **3.** federal tax withholdings = $93/Social Security tax = $68.12/ Medicare tax = $15.93; **5.** $522.57

Section 2.2, pages 71–77

Check It

Example 2-2A: $99.11; **Example 2-2B:** $54,480; **Example 2-2C:** $60,938.20

Checkpoint

1. $71.79; **3.** $40,480; **5.** $59,654

Section 2.3, pages 78–85

Check It

Example 2-3A: Alicetown; **Example 2-3B:** $24.80; **Example 2-3C:** $36.28

Checkpoint

1. Alexander's job, with a net annual value of $10,390.20; **3.** $57.04; **5.** $46.45

Chapter Review and Assessment, pages 86–89

11. federal withholding = $30/Social Security tax = $22.51/Medicare tax = $5.26/state income tax = not applicable; **13.** federal withholding = $32/Social Security tax = $38.22/Medicare tax =

$8.94/state income tax = $26.81; **15.** $47.13; **17.** Bianca's current job has a greater net annual value of $85,220.84; **19.** weekly gross pay = $785.60/ monthly gross pay = $3,404.27/annual gross pay = $40,851.20

Chapter 3   Income Taxes

Section 3.1, pages 91–98

Check It

Example 3-1A: $56,070.66; **Example 3-1B:** $480.78; **Example 3-1C:** Tonya and Nicholas owe additional taxes of $383.

Checkpoint

1. $54,604.63; **3.** $35,193; **5.** Ethan and Isadora owe additional taxes of $1,056.

Section 3.2, pages 99–104

Check It

Example 3-2A: $3,145.25; **Example 3-2B:** $3,225; **Example 3-2C:** $34,225; **Example 3-2D:** −$9,011;

Checkpoint

1. $2,000; **3.** $3,217.50; **5.** −$653

Section 3.3, pages 105–109

Check It

Example 3-3A: $407.75; **Example 3-3B:** $2,250

Checkpoint

1. $1,530; **3.** $535.50 **5.** $3,170

Chapter Review and Assessment, pages 110–117

11. $48,814.67; **13.** They will receive a refund of $1,408; **15.** $6,906; **17.** $635.19; **19.** weekly pay = $925.77/biweekly pay = $1,851.54/semimonthly pay = $2,005.83/monthly pay = $4,011.67

Chapter 4   Banking Basics

Section 4.1, pages 121–124

Check It

Example 4-1A: $406.40

Checkpoint

1. $242.92; **3.** $3,417.11 **5.** $3,154.34

Section 4.2, pages 125–137

Check It

Example 4-2A: $381.91; **Example 4-2B:** $474.23; **Example 4-2C:** The account reconciles with an adjusted balance of $405.26; **Example 4-2D:** $944.20

Checkpoint

1. $266.42; **3.** $395.34; **5.** $950.71

Section 4.3, pages 138–149

Check It

Example 4-3A: savings balance = $1,667.71/ checking balance = $764.29; **Example 4-3B:** $10.50; **Example 4-3C:** $801.53; **Example 4-3D:** $6,771.38; **Example 4-3E:** $6,830.78; **Example 4-3F:** 22 years

Checkpoint

1. new savings account balance = $1,613.21/new checking account balance = $962.66; **3.** $27; **5.** 17 years

Chapter Review and Assessment, pages 150–153

11. $2,813.87; **13.** $421.81; **15.** $724.73; **17.** $1,350.90; **19.** Plan A. In 10 years, Viola will have $2,501.73. If she invested in Plan B, she would only have $2,484.57.

Chapter 5 Making Purchases

Section 5.1, pages 155–163

Check It

Example 5-1A: $32.40; **Example 5-1B:** $28.30;
Example 5-1C: $19.40; **Example 5-1D:** $48.72;
Example 5-1E: $549.78; **Example 5-1F:** $53.66

Checkpoint

1. $314.45; **3.** $40.73; **5.** $69.62

Section 5.2, pages 164–170

Check It

Example 5-2A: $7.54; **Example 5-2B:** $297.66;
Example 5-2C: layaway fee = $30/weekly
payment = $94.49

Checkpoint

1. $17.81; **3.** $1,671.16; **5.** down payment = $21.09/
weekly payment = $8.94

Section 5.3, pages 171–177

Check It

Example 5-3A: $0.67 per cloth diaper;
Example 5-3B: $627.82; **Example 5-3C:** $189.71;
Example 5-3D: $50.22

Checkpoint

1. $0.06 per fluid ounce; **3.** $389.76; **5.** $96.33

Chapter Review and Assessment, pages 178–181

11. $237.91; **13.** $20.83; **15.** layaway fee = $11.00/
down payment = $32.99/weekly payment =
$32.99; **17.** $659.76; **19.** $37,160.68

Chapter 6 Budgeting

Section 6.1, pages 183–194

Check It

Example 6-1A: $254.91; **Example 6-1B:** $26;
Example 6-1C: Kaley will save $40 per month and
Amanda will save $50 per month.

Checkpoint

1. $139; **3.** $18.50; **5.** Mason saves $57.50 per
month, and Esteban saves $62.50.

Section 6.2, pages 195–205

Check It

Example 6-2A: $166.75; **Example 6-2B:** −$778.73;
Example 6-2C: total inflow = $47,145/total fixed
expenses = $24,808/total variable expenses =
$17,910/total outflow = $42,718/net cash flow =
$4,427

Checkpoint

1. $302.78; **3.** −$437.62; **5.** total inflow = $55,825/
total fixed expenses = $36,214/total variable
expenses = $17,253/total outflow = $53,467/net
cash flow = $2,358

Section 6.3, pages 206–212

Check It

Example 6-3A: Sunna will need to save $850 per
month for 11 months to meet her goal.
Example 6-3B: new clothing budget = $23.50/
new miscellaneous budget = $48.50
Example 6-3C: overall inflation rate = 311.11%/
average annual inflation rate = 10.04% per year

Checkpoint

1. 20 months; **3.** $126; **5.** overall inflation rate =
27.9%/average annual inflation rate = 9.3% per year

Chapter Review and Assessment, pages 213–223

11. $165.01; **13.** −$100.49; **15.** −$573.40; **17.** new
entertainment budget = $60/new clothing
budget = $15; **19.** $1,378.20

Chapter 7 Credit Cards

Section 7.1, pages 227–234

Check It

Example 7-1A: $357.40; **Example 7-1B:** $1,454.33; **Example 7-1C:** $6.18

Checkpoint

1. $41.37; **3.** $639.57; **5.** $4,500

Section 7.2, pages 235–249

Check It

Example 7-2A: $283.04; **Example 7-2B:** 1.9333%; **Example 7-2C:** $34.59; **Example 7-2D:** $2,354.65; **Example 7-2E:** $803; **Example 7-2F:** $45.29; **Example 7-2G:** $26.25; **Example 7-2H:** $105.09; **Example 7-2I:** $51.25

Checkpoint

1. 1.8917%; **3.** $1,219.62; **5.** $13.46

Section 7.3, pages 250–257

Check It

Example 7-3A: 19.71%; **Example 7-3B:** 39.5%; **Example 7-3C:** $261.49

Checkpoint

1. 19.3%; **3.** 41.7%; **5.** $765.39

Chapter Review and Assessment, pages 258–261

11. $574.20; **13.** 2.0583%; **15.** $22; **17.** 24.72%; **19.** $31.62

Chapter 8 Loans

Section 8.1, pages 263–273

Check It

Example 8-1A: $118.75; **Example 8-1B:** $176.55; **Example 8-1C:** $35.42; **Example 8-1D:** $2,296.53;

Example 8-1E: $29.33; **Example 8-1F:** $36.63; **Example 8-1G:** 8%

Checkpoint

1. $296.99; **3.** $2,933.43; **5.** 6%

Section 8.2, pages 274–280

Check It

Example 8-2A: interest payment = $12.49/ principal payment = $337.31; **Example 8-2B:** down payment = $48,700/amount financed = $194,800; **Example 8-2C:** $785.72

Checkpoint

1. interest payment = $72.19/principal payment = $309.67; **3.** down payment = $3,534/amount financed = $25,916; **5.** $2,531.56

Section 8.3, pages 281–287

Check It

Example 8-3A: $282.15; **Example 8-3B:** $868; **Example 8-3C:** $104.72

Checkpoint

1. $410.19; **3.** $915.08; **5.** $143.92

Section 8.4, pages 288–295

Check It

Example 8-4A: $2,922.60; **Example 8-4B:** $2,228.60; **Example 8-4C:** $2,770

Checkpoint

1. $1,459.25; **3.** $4,099.60; **5.** $25,744

Chapter Review and Assessment, pages 296–299

11. $202.21; **13.** interest payment = $40.08/ principal payment = $121.95; **15.** $306.08; **17.** $3,756; **19.** 29 months

Chapter 9 Housing

Section 9.1, pages 301–307

Check It

Example 9-1A: $432.50; **Example 9-1B:** $1,525; **Example 9-1C:** $34.67; **Example 9-1D:** $475

Checkpoint

1. $478.33; **3.** $2,230; **5.** $445

Section 9.2, pages 308–321

Check It

Example 9-2A: down payment = $34,650/ mortgage amount = $80,850; **Example 9-2B:** $3,789.53; **Example 9-2C:** $367.48; **Example 9-2D:** $662.98; **Example 9-2E:** $759.78; **Example 9-2F:** 3,469 kilowatt hours; **Example 9-2G:** $208.42; **Example 9-2H:** $541.36

Checkpoint

1. down payment = $29,841.30/amount of mortgage = $135,943.70; **3.** $3,463.08; **5.** $100.49

Section 9.3, pages 322–329

Check It

Example 9-3A: $688.34; **Example 9-3B:** interest payment = $507.45/principal payment = $180.89/ new loan balance = $135,138.90; **Example 9-3C:** $171,498.13; **Example 9-3D:** $761.16

Checkpoint

1. $842.01; **3.** monthly payment = $483.30/ interest payment = $375.03/principal payment = $108.27/new loan balance = $89,891.73; **5.** $684.54

Chapter Review and Assessment, pages 330–333

11. $461.67; **13.** down payment = $34,102.25/ amount of mortgage = $160,767.75; **15.** City of Dogwood = $1,098.24/Dogwood Park District = $33/Newtown Public Schools = $1,431.80/ Newtown County = $666.50/State of Georgia = $23.50; **17.** monthly payment = $908.82/interest payment = $445.50/principal payment = $463.32/ new loan balance = $363.68; **19.** 21.34%

Chapter 10 Automobiles

Section 10.1, pages 335–346

Check It

Example 10-1A: $21,850; **Example 10-1B:** $18,100; **Example 10-1C:** $12,286.25; **Example 10-1D:** $672.12; **Example 10-1E:** $1,508.33; **Example 10-1F:** 17.4%; **Example 10-1G:** The lease plan is $1,810 less expensive than the purchase plan.

Checkpoint

1. $20,400; **3.** $707.40; **5.** The purchase plan is $1,981 less expensive than the lease plan.

Section 10.2, pages 347–353

Check It

Example 10-2A: $2,000; **Example 10-2B:** $2,143.55; **Example 10-2C:** $187.80

Checkpoint

1. $1,607.40; **3.** $2,939.10; **5.** $71.83

Chapter Review and Assessment, pages 354–357

11. final price = $25,900/total cost = $28,027.50; **13.** average annual depreciation = $3,831.67 per year/depreciation rate = 13.6%; **15.** $2,037; **17.** $104.15; **19.** $437.08

Chapter 11 Building Wealth

Section 11.1, pages 365–371

Check It

Example 11-1A: $95,102.37; **Example 11-1B:** $129,383.73

Checkpoint

1. $158,605.40; **3.** $165,105.40; **5.** $272,918.91

Section 11.2, pages 372–378

Check It

Example 11-2A: $1,050; **Example 11-2B:** $971.50; **Example 11-2C:** $197.75; **Example 11-2D:** $27.50; **Example 11-2E:** 7.14%

Checkpoint

1. $525; **3.** $2,076.38; **5.** 6.8%

Section 11.3, pages 379–389

Check It

Example 11-3A: $1,419.75; **Example 11-3B:** $67.50; **Example 11-3C:** 12.5%; **Example 11-3D:** $16.9014; **Example 11-3E:** $5,694.71; **Example 11-3F:** $4,635.95; **Example 11-3G:** $252.84

Checkpoint

1. $1,330.95; **3.** $16.3043; **5.** $504.21

Chapter Review and Assessment, pages 390–393

11. $149,466.51; **13.** semiannual interest payment = $83.13/total interest = $665; **15.** 6.93%; **17.** $1,628.57; **19.** $630.22

Chapter 12 Insurance

Section 12.1, pages 395–401

Check It

Example 12-1A: $6,919.20; **Example 12-1B:** $565,933.35; **Example 12-1C:** $187

Checkpoint

1. $10,320; **3.** $1,102,320; **5.** $10,173

Section 12.2, pages 402–411

Check It

Example 12-2A: $3,025.44; **Example 12-2B:** $3,770.04; **Example 12-2C:** $325; **Example 12-2D:** $2,500; **Example 12-2E:** $1,906.50; **Example 12-2F:** $3,309.17

Checkpoint

1. $2,879.16; **3.** $430; **5.** $4,032.16

Section 12.3, pages 412–417

Check It

Example 12-3A: $10.10; **Example 12-3B:** $299.80

Checkpoint

1. $19.64; **3.** $95.62; **5.** $87.20

Chapter Review and Assessment, pages 418–421

11. $8,400; **13.** $8,320.08; **15.** $1,088; **17.** $57.28; **19.** $778.75

Chapter 13 Financial Planning

Section 13.1, pages 423–428

Check It

Example 13-1A: 1.7%; **Example 13-1B:** $540,564; **Example 13-1C:** $84

Checkpoint

1. 3.9%; **3.** $325,599; **5.** $101.50

Section 13.2, pages 429–437

Check It

Example 13-2A: $2,500; **Example 13-2B:** $4,092.75; **Example 13-2C:** $41,808.86; **Example 13-2D:** $25,558.45

Checkpoint

1. $325; **3.** $2,873; **5.** $15,992.94

Section 13.3, pages 438–443

Check It

Example 13-3A: $2,250; **Example 13-3B:** $10,050; **Example 13-3C:** $582.80

Checkpoint

1. $1,860; **3.** $1,204.20; **5.** $1,295

Chapter Review and Assessment, pages 444–447

11. 1.7%; **13.** $8.75; **15.** $5,630.40; **17.** net annual income = $3,415/net annual income after the mortgage is paid = $11,575; **19.** $387.10

Stages of Life Project

Stage 1 Student Years, pages 453–460

Check It

Exercise 1A: $334.24; **Exercise 1B:** total deposit = $345.24/remaining balance = $291.33; **Exercise 1C:** $3,855; **Exercise 1D:** $22.50; **Exercise 1E:** amount covered by insurance = $2,900/amount saved by insurance = $2,711; **Exercise 1F:** total annual premium = $576.66/ monthly premium = $48.06; **Exercise 1G:** $625.84; **Exercise 1H**: –$150.16; **Exercise 1I:** $762.68

Stage 2 Early Career Years, pages 461–467

Check It

Exercise 2A: gross pay = $747.60/federal income tax = $87/Social Security tax = $46.35/Medicare tax = $10.84/state income tax = $22.95/net pay = $580.46; **Exercise 2B:** premium per paycheck = $7.85/new net pay = $575.45/change in federal tax = $2/change in net pay = –$5.01; **Exercise 2C:** adjusted gross income = $33,875/taxable income = $24,375/tax refund = $1,189;

Exercise 2D: $742.63; **Exercise 2E:** $1,642.52; **Exercise 2F:** average daily balance = $321.24/ finance charge = $3.76; **Exercise 2G:** price after trade in = $8,200/sales tax = $533/total cost of car = $8,834/amount financed = $6,334/interest portion of first payment = $31.04; **Exercise 2H:** $2,304; **Exercise 2I:** net worth = $27,737.22/ change in net worth = $26,974.54

Stage 3 Earning Years, pages 468–476

Check It

Exercise 3A: You should accept the offer because its value is $58,146, versus your current job value of $57,780. **Exercise 3B:** March commission = $1,740.68/ April commission = $2,471.52/May commission = $6,100.88; **Exercise 3C:** capital gain = $1,554.41/capital gains tax = $233.16; **Exercise 3D:** required down payment = $6,790/ required down payment and closing costs = $10,202.58/additional cash required = $1,481.33/ amount financed = $187,210; **Exercise 3E:** monthly payment : 15-year = $1,480.83; 20-year = $1,288; 30-year = $1,063.35/shortest affordable term is the 20-year mortgage/first month's interest: 15-year = $780.04; 20-year = $858.05; 30-year = $858.05/first month's principal: 15-year = $700.79; 20-year = $429.95; 30-year = $205.30; **Exercise 3F:** Your debt-to-income ratio of 38.5% is greater than the recommended maximum debt-to-income ratio. **Exercise 3G:** $1,931.46; **Exercise 3H:** bond interest = $900/mutual fund investment = $2,333.63; **Exercise 3I:** $355.93; **Exercise 3J:** –$77.56; **Exercise 3K:** net worth = $218,728.76/change in net worth = $190,991.54

Stage 4 Retirement Years, pages 477–483

Check It

Exercise 4A: $6,299.06; **Exercise 4B:** $3,794; **Exercise 4C:** 5.54%; **Exercise 4D:** $41,352; **Exercise 4E:** $64,106.68; **Exercise 4F:** $36; **Exercise 4G:** share of inheritance = $83,961.33/ inheritance tax = $12,006.47; **Exercise 4H:** $983.40; **Exercise 4I:** $72,242.91 due to the inflow from $71, 954.86 for the inheritance; **Exercise 4J:** net worth = $1,661,122.33; change in net worth = $1,442,939.57

Glossary

401(k). Retirement plan sponsored by an employer, similar to an individual retirement account. (13)

529 plan. College savings plan that requires payments be made over time for use in the future. (8)

A

actual cash value policy. Insurance that pays what the property was worth at the time it was damaged or stolen. (9)

adjusted gross income (AGI). Gross income minus selected government-approved deductions. (3)

advertising. Public promotion of a product, service, business, or event. (5)

amortization. Process of paying down a loan by making regular payments of interest and principal. (9)

amortization table. Schedule that shows the amount of interest and principal for each payment so a loan can be repaid within a specific period of time. (8)

amount financed. Cost that will be covered by a loan after a down payment is made. (8)

annual fee. Fee charged by many credit cards for the privilege of having the card. (7)

annual percentage rate (APR). Rate of return on an investment, or interest on a loan, for a one-year period. (4, 7)

annuity. Insurance product used as an investment. (13)

appraisal. Professional assessment of the value of a home. (9)

assessed value. What a property is worth as determined by a tax assessor. (9)

asset. Anything owned that is of value. (3)

automated teller machine (ATM). Computerized machine that allows a person to do basic banking functions without going to a bank. (4)

automobile dealer. Individual or company whose business is selling cars. (10)

automobile insurance. Insurance that protects a person and his or her vehicle in accidents involving the vehicle. (10)

available credit. Amount of money that can be used for purchases with the credit card. (7)

average daily balance method. Method of calculating finance charges using an average balance for the period as a basis for the finance charge. (7)

B

balance. Amount of money in an account at a given point. (4)

balloon payment. Large final payment on a loan. (9)

bank statement. List of all account activity for the reporting period. (4)

bankrupt. When a person or entity is unable to pay debts as the payments are due. (8, 11)

bankruptcy. Court order that excuses the debtor from having to repay some or all of his or her debts. (8)

bartering. Trading items other than money. (1)

base pay. Pay the employee receives for the work performed. (1)

beneficiary. In insurance terms, the person who will receive the value of a life insurance policy in the event the insured dies. (12) In probate terms, the person who will receive the assets of an estate as stated in a will. (13)

biweekly pay period. Pay structure in which employees are paid every two weeks, often on a Friday. (1)

bond yield. Way to measure the return on investment from a bond. (11)

bondholder. Current owner of a bond. (11)

broker. Person who acts as an agent between the buyer and seller of stock. (11)

budget. Plan for saving and spending money. (6)

C

capital asset. Anything of value that is owned. (3)

capital gain. Profit that results from selling something for more than the buyer paid. (3)

capital loss. Amount lost when a capital asset is sold for less than the buyer paid. (3)

cash advance. Loan against the available credit on a credit card. (7)

cash flow. Movement of cash. (6)

cash flow statement. Report of how much money actually came in and how much went out during a given period. (6)

cash inflow. Any money that comes in. (6)

cash outflow. Anything that takes cash away. (6)

cash value. Money a policyholder gets back when a qualifying life insurance policy is cancelled. (12)

certificate of deposit (CD). Type of savings vehicle that earns a higher interest rate than a regular savings account. (4)

charge account. Arrangement in which a customer receives a good or service in exchange for the promise to pay at a later date. (5)

checking account. Bank account that allows a customer to deposit money and write checks from the account. (4)

claim. Detailed report of losses that is filed with the insurance company when a person experiences a loss. (9)

cleared. When a check is processed and the money is transferred out of the checking account. (4)

coinsurance. Sharing of expenses with the insurance company. (12)

collateral. Any asset that is pledged as security for a loan. (7, 8)

collision coverage. Insurance that covers damage to a person's own vehicle. (10)

commission. Percentage of the amount of a business transaction paid to a sales agent or broker. (1)

common stock. Non-preferred stock with no guaranteed dividend. (11)

comparison shopping. Finding the price of an item at two or more stores. (5)

compound interest. Interest calculated on the principal and accumulated interest. (4)

comprehensive coverage. Insurance that protects a person's car from a wide range of other hazards, such as theft, storm and hail damage, vandalism, and broken windows; also called *full coverage*. (10)

consumer price index (CPI). Measure of the change in the price of goods and services purchased by households. (6)

contract. Formal agreement between two or more entities, such as people or organizations. (1, 5)

convenience check. Paper check that will be charged against a person's credit card account. (7)

copay. See *copayment*.

copayment. Specified amount the insured pays for a doctor visit, also called a *copay*. (12)

coupon. Certificate that grants a discount or even a free good or service to its holder. (5)

coupon rate. Interest rate of a bond. (11)

credit. Term that describes the contractual agreement between a borrower and a lender in which the borrower agrees to pay back the lender for money that the borrower receives, usually with interest. (7)

credit card. Plastic card that allows a person to borrow money from the bank or financial institution that issued it. (7)

credit card statement. Report that shows the purchases made with a credit card, the current balance, and the amount of money that is owed by the due date. (7)

credit limit. Maximum amount of money available on a line of credit. (7)

credit report. Summary of all the companies that have extended credit to a person. (7)

credit score. Number that shows how well a person handles credit. (7)

current balance. Total amount of money owed to a lender. (7)

D

debit card. Plastic card linked to a checking account that gives the account holder access to the money in that account. (4)

debt-to-income ratio. Amount of money required each month to pay debts divided by the debtor's (or borrower's) monthly gross income. (7)

deductible. Portion of an insurance claim for which the policyholder is responsible. (9)

deduction. Adjustment to income that comes after the adjusted gross income is determined. (2, 3)

dependent. Child or other person whom an individual is supporting financially. (2)

depreciation. When an asset loses value. (10)

digital cash. Form of currency that can be used online. (5)

direct deposit. Automatic deposit of a person's paycheck into his or her checking account. (1)

disability insurance. Type of insurance that helps replace income when a person cannot work due to illness or injury. (12)

disclosure statement. Document that details finance charges, annual percentage rate, and cardholder rights. (7)

discount. Term used to describe a bond that sells for less than the par value. (11)

diversification. Spreading money around in multiple investments. (11)

dividend. Portion of a company's profits that is distributed to its stockholders by its management. (11)

dividend yield. Ratio of dividend to the price of the stock. (11)

down payment. Amount a borrower pays up front. (8)

E

early repayment. Borrower pays off the installment loan sooner than the original term. (8)

earned income. Pay that comes from a person's work. (1)

effective annual rate (EAR). Nominal rate compounded. (7)

electronic funds transfer (EFT). Transfer of money from one person or entity to another without any cash or checks involved. (4)

employee benefits. Anything of value that is offered or provided to employees in addition to wages; also called *fringe benefits*. (2)

employer. Person or company who hires a person and pays him or her for work done. (1)

entrepreneur. Person who starts a business venture and assumes the risk of its success or failure. (1)

equity. Amount of an asset's value that exceeds what is owed. (9)

escrow account. Account that adds an amount of money to a mortgage payment to cover taxes and insurance. (9)

estate. All of a person's possessions, including assets and debts. (3)

estate tax. Tax that is paid out of the value of an estate before the estate is transferred to the heirs. (3)

exact interest method. Method by which interest is calculated that uses the exact length of the term divided by 365 to get an exact fraction of the year. (8)

executor. Person who is appointed by a will to manage an estate. (13)

exemption. Amount that a person can claim on a tax form for each other person who depends on his or her income. (3)

extended warranty. Optional additional warranty offered by manufacturers and third-party companies that can be purchased by the consumer. (5, 10)

F

face value. Amount borrowed; also called the *par value*. (11)

federal income tax return. Form used to file income tax with the Internal Revenue Service that is due by April 15 each year; also called a *tax return*. (3)

FICA tax. Percentage of the employee's gross pay that is withheld from each paycheck. (2)

FICO score. Most common credit score, named for the Fair Isaac Corporation, which provides the calculation for the score. (7)

finance charge. Fee associated with credit. (7)

financial goal. Measurable objective related to acquiring or spending money. (6)

fixed expense. Expense that stays the same each month. (6)

fixed income. Income that stays the same each month. (6)

flat-rate tax. Same rate of taxation paid by all taxpayers, regardless of income level; also called *flat tax*. (2)

flat tax. See *flat-rate tax*.

foreclosure. When the ownership interest in a piece of real estate is transferred to the lender. (8)

Free Application for Federal Student Aid (FAFSA). Form issued by the federal government that is used by postsecondary schools to determine a student's need for financial aid. (8)

fringe benefits. See *employee benefits*.

full coverage. See *comprehensive coverage*.

fund manager. Person who decides what stock trades should be made on behalf of a mutual fund. (11)

G

gift card. Type of payment card that is preloaded with funds that can be spent electronically. (5)

gift tax. Law that limits the amount of money a person can give away as a gift without potentially costing their estate additional taxes. (3)

good. Physical product. (5)

grace period. Time during which you can pay off the balance of your card and not incur finance charges. (7)

grant. Funding that does not have to be repaid. (8)

gratuity. See *tip*.

gross income. Sum of earned and unearned income within a specific period of time. (3)

gross pay. Employee's total pay before deductions. (1)

group health insurance. Health insurance provided by an employer or group. (12)

H

health insurance. Type of insurance that helps pay medical bills. (12)

heir. Recipient of an inheritance. (3)

home equity loan. Loan in which the homeowner borrows money using the equity as collateral. (9)

home warranty. Service contract that covers the repair and replacement costs of appliances and systems that commonly need repair. (9)

homeowners insurance. Insurance that includes coverage for the structure of the house as well as its contents. (9)

hourly wage. Amount of money paid for each hour worked. (1)

I

income. Money received by a person or company. (1)

income-generating asset. See *revenue generating asset*. (13)

independent contractor. Person who provides a service to the public or to a company for money. (1)

individual retirement arrangement (IRA). Retirement account that allows individuals to save money for retirement. (3, 13)

inflation. General rise in prices and wages. (6)

inheritance. Individual's portion of an estate. (3)

inheritance tax. Tax imposed by some states on a person receiving an inheritance. (3)

initial public offering (IPO). First time the stock in a company is sold. (11)

installment loan. Loan for which payments are made at predetermined intervals. (8)

installment plan. Agreement where the total amount owed is made in payments over time. (5)

insurance policy. Name of the product purchased when an individual buys insurance. (12)

insured. Person whose life is being insured by life insurance. (12)

interest. Fee charged for borrowing money. (4)

J

job expense. Any costs an employee has to pay because of the job he or she was hired to do. (2)

L

late fee. Fee charged if a person fails to make at least a minimum payment before the due date. (7)

layaway plan. Type of installment plan where the store sets the item aside while the customer makes payments toward the purchase price. (5)

lease agreement. Contract used to lease property for a predetermined period of time. (9)

lessee. Person renting the property under the lease. (9)

lessor. Owner of the property that is being leased. (9)

level payment plan. Repayment plan designed to have the same payment amount in each installment. (8)

liability coverage. Insurance that pays for bodily injury or property damage that a person or his or her automobile causes. (10)

lien. Legal agreement giving the lender the right to claim assets of a borrower if it is necessary to repay a loan. (8)

life insurance. Insurance policy that pays a specified person money in the event of the death of an individual. (12)

line of credit. Maximum amount of money a person may borrow with a credit card. (7)

load. Commission charges on a mutual fund. (11)

long-term capital gain. Any profit from the sale of an asset that was held more than a year. (3)

M

manufacturer's suggested retail price (MSRP). Price of an item set by its manufacturer. (10)

manufacturer's warranty. Guarantee from a manufacturer that the item purchased will perform to a certain standard or be free of defects for a specified period of time. (10)

market. Any arrangement that allows buyers and sellers to meet with the purpose of exchanging goods, services, or information. (5)

market size. Number of buyers for a product or service. (5)

maturity date. Date on which a bond must be repaid by the entity that issued it. (11)

Medicare. Federal health insurance program for people over 65 years of age. (2)

merit-based scholarship. Scholarship that a student earns based on ability or performance. (8)

minimum wage. Lowest hourly wage employers are legally required to pay employees. (1)

monetary value. Amount something is worth in money alone. (2)

money. Tool that makes it easier to trade one thing of value for another. (1)

money market account. An interest-bearing bank account that often requires a minimum balance and limits the number of transactions per month. (4)

monthly pay period. Pay structure in which salaried employees receive 1/12 of their annual salary on the last day of each month. (1)

mortgage. Contract between a home buyer and a lender where the property being purchased is held as collateral. (9)

mutual fund. Type of investment in which the money from many investors is combined to buy a diversified group of stocks. (11)

N

need. Thing required to survive. (6)

net asset value (NAV). Total assets of a mutual fund minus any debts the fund may have, divided by the number of shares held by shareholders. (11)

net cash flow. Balance remaining after cash outflows are deducted from cash inflows. (6)

net pay. Final calculated amount of a paycheck after federal taxes, FICA taxes, and state taxes are withheld; also called *take-home pay*. (2)

net worth. Person's total assets minus his or her total liabilities. (11)

nominal APR. Simple interest rate for the year. (7)

O

offer price. Price of a mutual fund including the commission charges. (11)

online bill pay. Service that allows a person to direct payment from his or her bank account to companies and individuals. (5)

opportunity cost. What a person gives up by choosing one option over another. (13)

oral contract. Agreement that has been acknowledged only through spoken words. (1)

ordinary income. Income earned from sources other than capital gains, such as wages. (3)

ordinary interest method. Method for calculating interest that assumes each month has 30 days, for a total of 360 days in the year. (8)

outstanding check. Check that has not yet been presented to the bank for payment or deducted from a person's account. (4)

overdraft fee. Fee charged by a bank for an overdrawn account. (4)

overdraft protection. Service offered for a fee that covers overdrawn checks within certain limits. (4)

overdrawn. When a person spends more money than is available in his or her account. (4)

overtime. See *overtime pay*.

overtime pay. Wages that are earned when an employee works more than 40 hours in a week; also known as *overtime*. (1)

P

par value. See *face value*.

passive income. Income from an activity or investment in which the owner does not actively participate. (11, 13)

pawnshop. Business that offers loans requiring personal property as collateral. (8)

pay period. Repeating time frame that an employer uses to calculate and pay salaries and wages. (1)

payday loan. Short-term loan designed to be repaid when the borrower gets his or her next paycheck. (8)

payment card. Any card that is presented as payment for a purchase. (5)

pay-per-click advertising. Advertising that charges the advertiser each time a viewer clicks the link in the advertisement. (5)

payroll. List of employees a company pays. (1)

pension. Retirement plan that is provided by employers for their employees to be used as income after they retire. (13)

periodic rate. Annual percentage rate divided by the number of periods in the year that finance charges will be applied. (7)

permanent life insurance. Life insurance policy that does not expire. (12)

preferred stock. Class of stock that receives dividends first, sometimes receiving guaranteed dividends. (11)

premium. In investment terms, a term used to describe a bond that is selling for more than the par value. (11) In insurance terms, amount paid to purchase insurance. (9)

pre-tax deduction. Payment employees make for the cost of benefits. (2)

previous balance. Balance on a credit card the last time finance charges were calculated, typically the last time a statement was issued. (7)

principal. Initial amount of a deposit or loan. (4, 8)

privately-held company. Organization that is owned by a small group of individuals; its stock is not offered to the general public. (11)

probate. Legal process that settles any debts and claims against a person's estate after he or she has died. (13)

professional liability insurance. Type of insurance that covers issues that may arise from a person's quality of work. (12)

progressive tax. The more a person makes, the higher the rate of taxation. (2)

promissory note. Written promise, or contract, to pay back a loan. (8)

property tax. Tax levied against the value of real estate. (9)

prospectus. Document that shareholders and potential shareholders are provided with that has the details of the risks and fees involved in the investment. (11)

publicly-held company. Organization that offers its stock to the general public; the shares of stock are openly traded between shareholders on a public market; also called *publicly-traded company*. (11)

publicly-traded company. See *publicly-held company*. (11)

R

raise. Increase in pay. (2)

rebate. Offer to pay back a portion of the money a customer spent on an item. (5)

reconcile. Process by which a person can confirm each transaction on a statement against his or her own records, mark the records to show which items have cleared the bank, and verify that the account holder and the bank agree on the balance. (4)

recordkeeping. Keeping track of money. (6)

recursion. Application of the same set of operations to the answer of the previous step. (7)

refinancing. Replacing a mortgage with a high interest rate with another mortgage at a lower rate. (9)

register. List of transactions and a running total of the balance after each transaction. (4)

renters insurance. Type of insurance purchased by a tenant that provides financial protection should that person's personal property be damaged or stolen. (9)

replacement cost policy. Insurance that will pay what it actually costs to replace the item damaged or stolen. (9)

revenue-generating asset. Anything in which a person invests money that generates income; also called an *income-generating asset*. (13)

revolving line of credit. Line of credit with a balance that is constantly changing. (7)

royalty. Payment made to the owner of an asset for the use of that asset. (13)

rule of 72. Method of estimating how long it will take to double an amount of money. (4)

S

salary. Fixed payment for a person's work, usually paid monthly or twice per month. (1)

sales tax. Flat rate applied to the sales price of a good or service. (5)

savings account. Bank account that pays interest to the account holder but limits the number of withdrawals per month. (4)

scholarship. Amount of money awarded to a student that must be used toward payment for college. (8)

security deposit. Payment held by the lessor to cover the costs of potential damage to the property during the term of the lease. (9)

self-employed. Someone who creates his or her own job and works for him- or herself. (3)

self-employment tax. FICA taxes that must be paid by a self-employed person. (3)

semimonthly pay period. Pay structure that divides the month into two pay periods; payday is often at the middle and the end of the month. (1)

service. Activity of value. (5)

service charge. Fee charged by a bank for having an account. (4)

shareholder. See *stockholder*.

short-term capital gain. Any profit from the sale of an asset that was held less than a year. (4)

simple interest. Interest paid only on an original sum of money, or principal. (4)

single-payment loan. Loan that is repaid in one payment with interest. (8)

Social Security tax. Contributes to retirement and disability benefits. (2)

standard deduction. Fixed amount that can be claimed instead of listing individual deductions. (3)

sticker price. Suggested price of a car being sold at an automobile dealer. (10)

stipend. Payment for taking on additional work duties or for completing work-related classes. (2)

stock. Certificate that signifies legal ownership. (11)

stock exchange. Place where stock is traded. (11)

stockholders. Owners of company stock; also called *shareholders*. (11)

straight commission. When the only compensation received by an employee is commission. (1)

straight-line method. Most commonly used approach for determining depreciation, the rate of which can be found by dividing average annual depreciation by the original purchase price of an item. (10)

T

take-home pay. See *net pay*.

tax deductible. Expense that qualifies as a deduction from adjusted gross income. (3)

tax preparer. See *tax return preparer*.

tax return preparer. Any person who completes tax returns for others; also called a *tax preparer.* (3)

tax, title, and license (TT & L). Sales tax, title transfer fee, registration or license fee, and other costs that must be paid at the time a car is purchased. (10)

taxable income. Portion of earnings taxed when a person files his or her tax return. (2)

tenant. Occupant of the property being rented. (9)

term. Length of time money will be borrowed. (8)

term life insurance. Simple insurance policy that pays a certain amount to a beneficiary when the insured dies. (12)

tip. Extra payment voluntarily made to a worker; also called a *gratuity.* (5)

title. Document that legally establishes ownership of property, such as an automobile or real estate. (8)

title insurance. Insurance that protects the lender in case any questions arise regarding who has title, or ownership, of a piece of real estate. (9)

title loan. Loan in which the lender takes possession of the title of a person's car as collateral until a short-term loan is repaid. (8)

totaled. When the damage to a vehicle reaches or exceeds its value. (10)

trade-in allowance. Discount in the price of a car that is a result of the trade-in of another car. (10)

travel insurance. Type of insurance that covers losses that result from issues related to travel. (12)

trust. Legal arrangement through which a trustee holds assets for the interest of a beneficiary. (13)

trustee. Person or institution that safeguards a trust. (13)

U

umbrella policy. Insurance policy that raises the total amount of liability insurance a person has. (12)

unearned income. Income that is not derived from a person's work. (1)

uninsured motorist coverage. Insurance that covers damage and bodily injury in cases where a driver without insurance is at fault. (10)

unit pricing. Price per unit for a product. (5)

universal life insurance. Life insurance policy that gives the policyholder flexibility to adjust the amount of the premiums as well as the amount of the death benefit. (12)

unpaid balance method. Method of calculating finance charges based on the portion of the previous balance that is unpaid at the time of the calculation. (7)

utilities. Basic services such as telephone service, cable and Internet services, electricity, natural gas, and water for a residence or business. (9)

V

variable life insurance. Life insurance policy with a fixed premium payment and a death benefit that varies. (12)

W

W-2 form. Form that summarizes an employee's earnings and the amounts withheld from the employee's paychecks for the year. (3)

want. Thing that a person desires but that is not essential to survival. (6)

warranty. Guarantee that the item purchased will perform to a certain standard or be free of defects for a specified period of time. (5)

wealth. Abundance of resources or possessions that you own. (11)

weekly pay period. Pay structure in which employees are paid each week. (1)

whole life insurance. Type of permanent life insurance that has unchanging premium and death-benefit amounts. (12)

will. Legal document that expresses a person's wishes for their estate at death. (13)

withholding allowance. Number of dependents a person claims on his or her W-4 form. (2)

Index